WmBate

SOCIAL BEHAVIOR
Its Elementary Forms

Revised Edition

GEORGE CASPAR HOMANS
HARVARD UNIVERSITY

Under the General Editorship of
Robert K. Merton, Columbia University

Harcourt Brace Jovanovich, Inc.

NEW YORK   CHICAGO   SAN FRANCISCO   ATLANTA

To the memory of
Bernard DeVoto
Charles Pelham Curtis

Friends and Teachers

ISBN: 0-15-581417-6

Library of Congress Catalog Card Number: 73-11539

Printed in the United States of America

PREFACE TO THE REVISED EDITION

In calling this the Revised Edition of *Social Behavior: Its Elementary Forms*, first published in 1961, I mean just what I say: the book has been thoroughly revised, with very few chapters or even pages unchanged. It is not that I have much altered the substance of the underlying argument; rather, I have tried, in the light of criticism and my own further thinking, to tighten up the argument and to make it more lucid and logical. In the original edition, for instance, the discussion of *power* certainly appeared (pp. 55–56 and 64–68), but I did not mention the word itself; nor did I use, as I do now, payoff matrices of the sort developed by Thibaut and Kelley to illustrate how power works. I have used a version of balance theory to explain the effects on the relationship between two persons of the addition of a new kind of exchange to a previously existing kind. And I have tried to make the discussion of *status* more lucid, orderly, and comprehensive. Readers familiar with the original edition will recognize other examples.

Some things have been omitted. Gone is the old Chapter 2 on the behavioral psychology of the pigeon. I concluded that the argument would be just as effective and more economical if it started right out with the behavioral psychology of humans. I have also substituted descriptions of newer empirical researches for several studies described in the original edition. But, as before, I have not attempted to review all the reported research that bears on the main argument. That task is even more impossible now than it was then. I have thus left out much research by men and women whose work I admire and respect.

I am grateful to Mrs. Elizabeth E. Burnham, who typed the final manuscript of the present edition, to my wife, Nancy Parshall Homans, who drew the figures for the original edition, and, once more, for permission to reprint excerpts from Peter M. Blau's book *The Dynamics of Bureaucracy*.

GEORGE CASPAR HOMANS

CONTENTS

PREFACE   v

1 Introduction   1

The Elementary Forms of Social Behavior   2
Small Groups   3
The Intellectual Organization of the Field   6
Explanation   8
The General Propositions   11
The Plan of the Book   13

2 The General Propositions   15

The Success Proposition   15
The Measurement of Behavior   18
Alternative Actions and Rewards   21
The Stimulus Proposition   22
Imitation and Vicarious Reward   24
The Value Proposition: Reward and Punishment   25
The Deprivation-Satiation Proposition   28
Cost and Profit   30
The Value Proposition as a Tautology   33
The Aggression-Approval Proposition   37
The Propositions as a System of Propositions   40
The Historicity Implied by the Propositions   40
The Rationality Proposition   43
Conclusion   47

3 Interpersonal Relationships: Balance   51

The Payoff Matrix   51
Social Exchange   53
The Results of Exchange   57
The Effect of Multiple Exchanges: Balance   59
Interaction, Liking, and Similarity   64
The Impersonal and the Personal   65
The Position of Economics   67
Summary   68

4   Power and Authority   70

Effect of the Scarcity of Reward   70
The Principle of Least Interest   73
The Bases of Power   74
The Tendency toward the Equalization of Power   75
The Definitions of Power   76
Coercive Power   78
A General Definition of Power   82
Fate and Behavior Control: A Digression   83
Bargaining   87
Authority   89
Persuasion   90
The Relations between Power and Authority   91
Summary   93

5   Cooperation, Conformity, Competition   94

Groups   94
Norms in Exchange within a Pair   96
Group Norms and Collective Goods   98
Types of Conformers and Nonconformers   100
Pressures to Conform   102
The Power of the Group   105
The Holdouts   106
A Summary Quotation   108
Differentiation in the Group   108
Cooperation and Individual Work   110
Competition   111
Horizontal and Vertical Divisions   112
Summary   113

6   Experimental Research   115

Experimental and Field Research   115
Approval and Compliance   117
Cost and Profit   119
Alternative Sources of Reward   124
Similarity as a Source of Reward   127
When Influence Fails   130
Cooperation and Competition between Individuals   133
Summary   137

7   Field Research   139

Tendencies toward Balance: The Acquaintance Process   139
Proximity and Friendship   143
Cohesiveness and Conformity: A Housing Study   147
Explanation and Causal Chains: A Digression   152
Cohesiveness and Conformity: An Industrial Study   153
The Distribution of Power and Esteem   157
Summary   165

8   Structures of Sentiment and Interaction   167

Matrices of Interpersonal Relationships   167
Rivalry and Hostility in the Upper Class   171
Solidarity of the Lower Class   171
Given Conditions and Structure   174
Interaction and Approval   175
Interaction and Rivalry between Groups   178
Interaction, Esteem, and Power   179
The Matrix of Interaction   182
The Origination of Interaction   187
Interaction with Equals   188
Summary   191

9   Status   193

Power and Status   193
Consensus on Status   196
The Accretion of Status Dimensions   199
Status Congruence   200
Congruence, Similarity, and Productivity   202
Congruence, Liking, and Effectiveness   208
Congruence and Job Assignment   209
Status Symbols   210
Back Effects of Status on Exchange: Noblesse Oblige   215
Back Effects of Status: The Maintenance of Equality   217
Doing Favors   221
Back Effects: Deference   222
Summary   223

10   Satisfaction   225

What Satisfaction Is Not   226
The Determinants of Satisfaction   227

The Determinants at Work: Examples   229
Satisfaction and the Level of Aspiration   233
Productivity and Satisfaction   235
Summary   239

11 Distributive Justice   241

An Example   242
Analysis of the Example   245
The Rule of Distributive Justice   248
Justice, Satisfaction, and the Choice of Comparisons   252
Injustice and Intergroup Hostility   257
Injustice and Power   262
Responses of the Beneficiaries of Injustice   264
Summary   268

12 Leadership   269

Who Becomes a Leader?   269
Status and Leadership: Empirical Research   271
Channels of Communication and Command   275
Participation in Decision-Making   276
Obedience to Orders   277
The Maintenance of Justice   280
Leadership as Risk-Taking   282
Command and Liking   282
Command and Liking: Empirical Research   285
The Degree of Ambivalence toward Authority   290
Familiarity Breeds Contempt   293
Summary   297

13 Stratification   299

Equality and Similarity   299
Equality and Escape   302
A Resultant of Superiority and Equality   304
Stratification in Society at Large   307
Social Climbing and the Like   310
The Initiation of "Social" Interaction   313
Links between Alternate Statuses   315
Summary   317

14 Status, Conformity, and Innovation 319

Status and Conformity: Experimental Research 319
Upper Status and Originality: Experimental Research 323
Nonconformity in the Lower Status 326
Vying for Acceptance 329
Conformity and Nonconformity in the Upper Status 331
Roles 334
Conformity in the Middle Status 336
Status and Conformity in Society at Large 337
Summary 338

15 A Summary Group 340

A Federal Agency: Consultation among Colleagues 341
Rewards and Costs of Consultation 343
"Social" Interaction 346
Esteem and Authority 350
Nonconformity and Isolation 352

16 The Institutional and the Subinstitutional 356

The Group as a Microcosm 356
The Small Group in History 358
From Group to Society 359
The Pattern of Social Behavior in the Emerging Society 363
The Precariousness of Civilization 365
The Persistence of Elementary Social Behavior 366
The Conflict between the Institutional and the
   Subinstitutional 367

REFERENCES 374

INDEX 381

For o thyng, sires, saufly dar I seye,
That freendes everych oother moot obeye,
If they wol longe holden compaignye.
Love wol nat been constreyned by maistrye.
When maistrie comth, the God of Love anon
Beteth his wynges, and farewel, he is gon!

GEOFFREY CHAUCER
The Franklin's Tale

1 Introduction

OUR SUBJECT IS A FAMILIAR CHAOS. NOTHING IS MORE FAMILiar to men than social behavior—their own behavior toward others with whom they are in immediate contact and the behavior of others toward them. Should a social scientist try to offer any generalization about it, he runs the risk that with the first word he utters his readers will find that they know better and will cut him off without a hearing. They have been at home with the evidence since earliest childhood and have every right to an opinion.

The social scientist's only justification is that the subject, perhaps just because it is so familiar, remains intellectually a chaos. Every man and woman has thought about it, and mankind through the centuries has embodied the more satisfactory of their insights in proverbs and maxims about social behavior, what it is and what it ought to be. Every man has his price. Nothing succeeds like success. You can't eat your cake and have it too. Birds of a feather flock together. You scratch my back and I'll scratch yours. Do as you would be done by. To each his own. Fair exchange is no robbery. No cross, no crown. *Noblesse oblige.* Whosover hath, to him shall be given. . . . And so forth. What makes the subject of everyday social behavior an intellectual chaos is that each of these maxims and proverbs, while telling something of the truth, can never tell much of it at a time, and what is more, nobody tries to put them together. Has *noblesse oblige,* for instance, anything to do with fair exchange? What is the relation between them? In the same way every man sets up his own generalizations about his own social experience, but applies them *ad hoc* within the range of situations to which each seems fitted, dropping them as soon as their immediate relevance is at an end and seldom asking how they mask or modify one another. Everyone has, of course, every excuse for this shortcoming, if it be one: social experience is apt to come at us all too fast to leave us time to grasp it as a whole. Nevertheless the purpose of this book is to bring out of the familiar chaos some intellectual order.

The Elementary Forms of Social Behavior

Our subject, we declare, is not just social behavior but its "elementary forms." In using these words we do not mean in the least to imply that we can draw any clear line between behavior that is elementary and behavior that is not. The distinctions between the two—there is more than one—are of a different kind. Unlike many social scientists, we shall not be concerned with the characteristics of communities, like the city of Cambridge, or organizations, like the Standard Oil Company of New Jersey, or societies, like the United States of America. Each of these social units consists of networks of social behavior, and all of the findings that we shall describe and explain come from research carried out within such social units. Yet it will be the behavior—not the units—which will interest us, especially the general features of the behavior.

In all of these units, for instance, norms—statements about how their members ought to behave—are put forward, and persons conform to the norms more or less well. Indeed without some degree of conformity to some norms the units would not last long enough to let us recognize their identities. What the particular norms may be in a particular social unit has been determined by a long historical process which is still going on. We shall not be interested in their content, though we shall be interested in the reasons why persons come to state any norms at all. What we shall be most interested in is the process of conformity itself, the process by which in any group some members are brought to abide by its norms—and some, perhaps, are never brought to do so.

Again, in all large-scale units of the kinds mentioned, some persons give orders or their equivalent and some others obey or disobey them. The chains of command or other sorts of influence that connect members of the units together are often long and complicated, but at every link in the chain there is a person faced with the question whether he will give an order and another faced with the question whether he will obey it. Even if the persons in question hold offices or occupy positions in the unit, it is still never just the office or the position that gives the order and is or is not obeyed. In spite of all the efforts to make organizational behavior impersonal, it is still an individual that does so. We shall not be interested in why the chains of command have come to be what they are or what the content of the orders may be. But we shall be much interested in the general characteristics of power, authority, and influence—the processes by which some people are able to change the behavior of others. In short, one thing we mean by the "elementary forms" of social behavior is its fundamental processes, regardless of the various and complicated ways in which these processes combine to establish and maintain, at least for a time, particular social units.

The forms of social behavior we shall be concerned with are elementary in another sense. Once more, we can best make the point by illustration. In setting up a formal organization a man or body of men can often deliberately design a status system—a system of positions arrayed in ranks from highest to lowest—and can then appoint individuals to fill these positions. But a status system can also arise out of the interactions of a number of persons and can maintain itself spontaneously, as it were, without any deliberate or conscious design whatever on the part of the persons concerned. Under favorable conditions, such status systems are emerging all the time, and it is doubtful whether the deliberately designed systems would have taken the forms they do, if many of their features had not first arisen naturally and spontaneously and had not, moreover, shown themselves to be effective in producing concerted action. Accordingly, another meaning of elementary social behavior is behavior that will appear as if of its own accord among men whether or not they have consciously tried to organize it.

Small Groups

There is still a third sense in which the social behavior we shall be concerned with is elementary. Although we are not going to study the characteristics of large-scale, formally organized social units as such, this does not mean that we are not going to study any social units at all. But we are going to confine ourselves to small units, either those which occur naturally and, as we are pleased to say, in real life and which are studied through fieldwork or those which social scientists create experimentally and study in the psychological laboratory. Indeed the field covered by this book is sometimes called the field of small-group research. The behavior we shall study is then elementary in the sense that the units observed, small groups, are the elements of which larger social units are made up. If indeed, as the anthropologists now believe, mankind possessed for many millennia no continuing organization larger than the band of hunters and gatherers, the small group is the unit in which mankind learned social behavior; it is the unit from which all the organizations and societies of larger scale have historically evolved.

We are not going to name a specific number of persons below which the membership of a group must remain if it is to be considered small. More important is the nature of the network that links members to one another. Consider two sorts of social network. In one, Tom is in contact with Dick, and Dick with Harry, but Harry has no contact with Tom. This has been called an *open* network, and many of the chains of influence between men are of this sort. In another, Tom is still in contact with Dick, and Dick with Harry, but the circle is now closed by Harry's being in contact with Tom, and so a network of this sort has been called *closed* (Bott, 1957: 58–59). We shall speak of a small group when a number of persons, defined as its members, participate in a closed network, when during a given period of time—for many groups do not remain in continuous session—each of its members is in contact with each of the others more often than he is with outsiders, or at least is able to be thus in contact.

The decision to study behavior in small groups follows from an interest in the other elementary features of the behavior. Suppose we are interested in the fundamentals of a process like conformity. We can perhaps establish the statistics of conformity to a rule applying to a large number of persons, and then determine the overall results of that degree of conformity by carrying out rather coarse observations, perhaps by questionnaire, of a sample of individuals drawn from the larger number. But if we are really to understand why particular individuals comply with influences coming from other particular individuals in particular circumstances, we need more detailed observations of the individuals concerned. We need the particulars of a few situations, if only to provide a basis for explaining why other and coarser studies show that some categories of persons conform to a norm while others do not. We need the particulars to establish generalizations about how influence really works. Moreover the cost of detailed observation of social behavior is prohibitive unless only a small number of persons is studied at a time, especially persons who are already together, or can be brought together, in one place. Accordingly, research with this purpose must often, as a practical matter, be research on small groups. From this point of view, small groups are not so much what we study as where we study it.

If the features of social behavior we are interested in are those that, given half a chance, men create naturally and without deliberate design, we must study them in the places where the deliberate design of social relationships is least in evidence or does least to interfere with their appearance. We must study social behavior where it is least institutionalized, where it is least determined by the rules established by some formal organization or body politic, and this again points to the small and, as it is sometimes called, the *informal* group. It is not that institutionalized behavior is marked by processes essentially different from those of other social behavior. Bureaucratic behavior, for instance, is still social behavior. But in large institutions the processes are often more segregated from one another, combined in more complicated ways, or more roundabout, as it were, in operation. For example, compare a group of men establishing their own norms, recognizing violations of them for themselves, and punishing the violations informally, with a body politic that has over the generations developed a legislature, a judiciary, and a police. The same sorts of activities are being carried out in both units; but the organization is more complex in the latter to match the greatly increased scale of the unit.

An institution, whether it is a set of customary rules for the practice of medicine or a system of government, has a long and special history behind it, and in their institutions societies often differ greatly. But within institutions, in the face-to-face relations between individuals, at the grass roots of social interaction, characteristics of behavior are always reappearing in which mankind betrays its underlying social unity. The latter is what we are concerned with in this book, and, as we have said, the institutions themselves have emerged historically out of this undifferentiated matrix. At the level of the elementary forms of social behavior there is neither Jew nor Gentile, Greek nor barbarian, but only man. As Claude Lévi-Strauss put it, in his description of a tribe he studied in the Brazilian jungle: "I was looking for a place where society was reduced to its simplest expression. Among the Nambikwara it was so far reduced that I found only men there" (Lévi-Strauss, 1955: 339).

It is lucky for us that, even in the largest and most highly organized societies, there are still plenty of places where the elementary features of social behavior may be studied and that many of them can be reproducd in the laboratory. Quite a few of these features will only appear in networks that are in some degree closed (that is, in small groups). It is doubtful, for instance, whether status systems will spontaneously appear in open networks. Still, there are plenty of small, informal groups available for study. In order to observe primitive social behavior in the United States, you need not go to Indian country; any working group in a factory, even a group of factory executives, would do as well. True, the framework of the behavior may be institutionalized by higher management—the division of work, the physical layout, and so forth—but within these limits the behavior that emerges always goes beyond and sometimes defeats management's design. The characteristics of a street gang are even less fully determined by the actions of any formal organization. Naturally the rewards produced and distributed in a street gang are not quite those of a hunting band. Yet in the way whatever rewards may be available are exchanged among the members and in the way differences in status emerge from the exchanges, the two groups may be more alike than one might guess from the differences in their physical surroundings.

We cannot demonstrate that the elementary forms of social behavior are universal among mankind; we must take it on faith. Most of the experimental and field research bearing on the subject has in fact been carried out in Western societies, particularly in the United States of America, and so grounds for a sufficient comparison with other societies are lacking. There is no inherent reason why anthropologists working in nonliterate societies should not have studied the more informal features of their behavior, and some of them, including some of the greatest, have done so. (For example, see Malinowski, 1959.) Nothing they have discovered and described is inconsistent with our faith, and we shall cite some of their evidence later. But naturally many anthropologists have been more concerned with recording the institutions, the formal organization and norms, of the societies they have studied, especially when the institutions are on the verge of disappearing forever. Accordingly, the actual research we shall describe in this book is almost wholly American.

The Intellectual Organization of the Field

Now that we have roughly outlined the subject matter of this book, we can begin to say how we propose to deal with it. Perhaps a good way of beginning will be to consider the relation between this book and my book, *The Human Group* (Homans, 1950). Though that book dealt with groups, some of them were not really very small, one being the whole population of a New England town. The groups that this book deals with will be, on the whole, much smaller. But the difference that deserves emphasis now goes deeper than the size of groups. It is a difference in intellectual aims: *The Human Group* did not try to explain much of anything, while we shall at least try to explain and, by explaining, provide the field with a better intellectual organization than any it possesses now. The subject of social behavior is not an intellectual chaos just for the amateurs, which we all are; it is still largely a chaos for the professional students of the field.

Let me go back some distance. To say that *The Human Group* did not try to explain much of anything is not to say that what it did try to do was negligible. In that book I tried to do two things. I chose from the literature five detailed field studies of human groups, ranging from a small body of industrial workers to an entire town. Of these studies I first asked what classes the observations made by the investigators might reasonably be divided into. The question was not what classes of observations the investigators, according to somebody else's theoretical views, ought to have made, but what they really did make. I tried to show that the observations made by the various investigators might be divided into the same four classes: sentiments, activities, interactions, and norms. In the present book these terms will reappear, though with some differences in emphasis.

The second question I asked of the five studies was what propositions about the relationships among the four classes of observation they gave support to. I was not interested in any old statement but in propositions about the relationships between variables, propositions of the general form "x varies as y." Again the question was not what propositions ought to have been tested against the data, or how they ought to have been tested, but what propositions did empirically and approximately hold good, whether or not they had any theoretical right to do so. I tried to show that several such propositions did hold good in more than one of the studies; for example: "The higher the rank (or status) of a person within a group, the more nearly his activities conform to the norms of the group" (Homans, 1950: 141). *Rank* was defined as a measure of the favorable sentiments expressed toward a man by other members of his group.

Some sociologists, and particularly those who set themselves up as "general theorists," are apt to refer patronizingly to such propositions as "mere empirical generalizations," but for me they are our most enduring possessions. Give me a man's actual findings, so long as he has taken some pains about his methods of reaching them, and I care not what obviously silly theory he may have incorporated them into. As Mr. Justice Holmes used to say, "Men's systems are forgotten, their *aperçus* are remembered" (Holmes, 1953: I, 277). Science has been built by some of the damnedest methods, but the strategy I have followed starts with my scanning the literature within a particular field in search of its sheer empirical propositions and trying to state them in some single set of terms.

This was practically as far as *The Human Group* went. It provided a method of analyzing group behavior into its constituent classes of observations, and it stated in a single language the propositions that appeared to hold good of the relations between the classes. It thus provided some degree of intellectual organization, but where it stopped is no place to stop forever. The inevitable next step is to ask why the empirical propositions should take the form they do. It is to ask for explanations and in finding them to provide a higher order of organization for the subject.

The Human Group was concerned with only five pieces of field research. There is, of course, an immense amount of other research on the elementary forms of social behavior. Especially notable is the work of the social psychologists using both experimental and survey methods. The rate at which investigations are carried out appears to be accelerating, and no one can now pretend to have reviewed them all. With such a mass of research results available, some means of organizing it intellectually and digesting it might seem to be badly needed. At the very least the student who is new to the field needs it, so that he will not have to waste his time learning a long series of unrelated findings but can subsume them from the first under general principles. Yet if one looks at the various textbooks and surveys of social psychology, one wonders how much intellectual organization exists in this field. In even the best of them, such as Roger Brown's *Social Psychology* (1965), though there is some degree of organization of particular topics, some effort to show how the findings follow from general principles, the topics themselves are only loosely strung together without much intellectual relationship between them. As for the worst of the textbooks, they consist of little more than long strings of summaries of research results, cataloged under various topical headings. A catalog is often useful for practical purposes; but it does not provide any intellectual organization.

The purpose of the present book is to provide an intellectual organization for empirical propositions about social behavior, such as those stated in *The Human Group* and those discovered in much other experimental and survey research, by providing a single procedure for explaining the propositions.

Explanation

Both ordinary men and philosophers use the word *explanation* in a number of different ways, and they are perfectly at liberty to do so provided they do not change their minds in mid-sentence. But I shall use the word in only one way—the way, I believe, it is used by several philosophers, notably Braithwaite (1953), Nagel (1961), and Hempel (1965). My own views on explanation in social science have been stated elsewhere at greater length than I shall state them now (see Homans, 1967).

What is to be explained, the *explicandum,* is always a proposition stating a relationship between at least two properties of nature. If the properties are variables, the proposition takes the general form "x varies as y." Rather than being variables, some properties may be either present or absent, and in this case the proposition takes the general form "if x, then y"; that is, the two are positively and perfectly associated. In either case, if a proposition is to serve as a proper *explicandum,* it is not enough for it merely to assert that there is *some* relationship between x and y. It must go further and begin to assert something about the nature of the relationship; for instance, that x increases as y increases, that x, as the mathematicians would say, is not just some function of y but a monotonically increasing one.

An explanation consists of the *explicandum* and a number of other propositions, each of which must meet the same requirements for being a valid proposition as the *explicandum* itself. Some of these propositions must be what are called *contingent:* propositions to whose acceptance or rejection fact, data, observations, evidence—whatever one wishes to call them—are relevant. Others may be *noncontingent,* representing assumptions adopted *a priori* or derived from them, such as the propositions of mathematics.

To count as an explanation the whole set of propositions must form a deductive system in the sense that the *explicandum* follows in logic from, can be logically deduced from, the others in the set. When the *explicandum* is so deduced, it is said to be explained. The requirement of logical deduction means that the number of propositions in the set must be at least three, the number in the classic syllogism.

According to the present definition of explanation, though not in some others, to point out the cause or causes of a phenomenon is not sufficient to explain it. Thus, to take a very ancient example, pointing out that the passage of the moon across the local meridian causes the succeeding high tide does not explain the tide. The reason is that what is to be explained is always a relationship between properties of nature, in this case the relationship between the passage of the moon and the rising of the tide—that is, the relationship of cause and effect itself. Not until this relationship is shown to follow in logic from Newton's laws under specific given conditions is it explained.

In the set of propositions forming the deductive system, at least one of the propositions must be more general than the others, in the sense that it cannot itself be deduced from them (if it could be, the argument would become circular). Thus, in Aristotle's illustration, the proposition "All men are mortal" (the major premise) is more general than either "Socrates is a man" or "Socrates is mortal," for from the latter two propositions the former cannot in logic be derived. From this requirement comes the practice of referring to the present view of explanation as the "covering-law" view.

Yet to say that at least one of the propositions in the deductive system must be more general than the others does not mean that it must be in some sense absolutely general. Some explanatory principles that at one time looked very general indeed have turned out later to be derivable from, to be the *explicanda* of, deductive systems containing propositions still more general. Apparently this was the fate of Newton's laws at the hands of Einstein.

Other propositions state the given conditions to which the general propositions must be applied if they are to explain the empirical relationships in question. Thus scientists explain the relationship between the movement of the moon and that of the tides by showing how it follows from Newton's laws under the given conditions that the earth is largely covered with water, that it rotates on its axis once a day, that the moon moves in orbit around it, and so forth. Sometimes the given conditions can in turn be explained; sometimes they cannot; sometimes they could be explained, but the person who is doing the explaining does not bother to explain them because it would take too much time or space. In any case, it is not necessary, if given conditions are to serve in explanation, that they themselves should be either explained or explainable: all they need to be is *known*.

The above account of explanation is enough for us to go ahead with for the moment. Some of the subtler issues, including some of the special difficulties encountered by explanation in the social sciences, we shall take up as it becomes necessary in dealing with particular problems. But let there be no suspicion that we believe the process of explanation to be essentially different in the social sciences from what it is in the natural sciences. The actual propositions to be explained and to be used in explaining will of course differ in content; they will differ also in precision. The rigor of the logic by which deductions are made will often be greater in the latter than in the former. But the same "covering-law" view of explanation holds good in both.

We have said that explanation organizes intellectually the phenomena explained. It should now be obvious why it does so. It allows a large number of propositions of low generality, in the sense that they only hold good in special circumstances, propositions of the sort often called empirical, to be derived under a variety of given conditions from a much smaller number of general propositions. In so doing, explanation makes possible a great economy of thought. The student need not remember a whole collection of isolated findings. If he has mastered the general propositions and the method of applying them to a range of given conditions, he can, if necessary, reconstruct the individual findings for himself and indeed predict new ones. When Newton showed that, under suitably chosen given conditions, propositions describing such seemingly unrelated phenomena as the rolling of balls down inclined planes, the path of projectiles, the movement of the tides, and the orbits of the planets could all be derived from a few general propositions (his laws), he created an intellectual organization of the field of mechanics—the first thoroughly successful feat of this sort in the history of science.

A cluster of deductive systems, each explaining a particular empirical relationship and employing one or more of the general propositions in the same set, is sometimes called a theory of a particular subject. Thus Newton produced a theory of mechanics. But in the social sciences the word *theory* has been used so pretentiously and with so many other meanings that we hesitate to call what we propose to produce by that name. Called by that name it is damned at its very christening. Much modern sociological theory seems to us to possess every virtue except that of explaining anything. Part of the trouble is that much of it consists of systems of categories, or pigeonholes, into which the theorist fits different aspects of social behavior. No science can proceed without its system of categories, or conceptual scheme, but the scheme in itself is not enough to give it explanatory power. If a theory of a phenomenon is an explanation of it, a conceptual scheme is not a theory. The science also needs a set of general propositions about the relationships among the categories, for without such propositions explanation is impossible. No explanation without propositions! But much modern sociological theory seems quite satisfied with itself when it has set up its conceptual scheme. The theorist shoves various aspects of behavior into his pigeonholes, cries "Ah-ha!" and leaves it at that. Like magicians in all times and places, the theorist thinks he controls phenomena if he is able to give them names, particularly names of his own invention. In fact he has written the dictionary of a language that has no sentences. He would have done better to start with the sentences.

We propose to show how a number of the better established empirical propositions about social behavior may be derived from, and thus explained by, a relatively small number of general propositions applied to a variety of commonly occurring given conditions. In so doing, we shall be trying to provide a more adequate intellectual organization of the field than any, we believe, that exists at present. Yet let no one say we are would-be Newtons. The general propositions we shall use can only at present be stated with far less mathematical precision than Newton's, and the process by which we shall derive the empirical propositions from them will have far less logical rigor. Certainly many steps will be left out because they are obvious; most readers would take them for granted and would be bored by their inclusion. We shall produce what have been called "explanation sketches" rather than logically watertight explanations. Or rather, to use a still less pretentious term, we shall at the very least try to produce arguments suggesting how the empirical findings might follow from the general propositions under conditions we can take as given.

The General Propositions

Our book will differ from Newton's *Principia* in still another way. Newton was faced with the problem of discovering or inventing his own general propositions and had the genius to do so. We can take the easier way out and borrow our propositions from the work of others. They come from the research of a series of behavioral psychologists, the most notable recent member of which is B. F. Skinner. (See especially Skinner, 1938 and 1953.) There are a number of schools of behavioral psychology, but they seem to say much the same things in somewhat different words. We tend to favor the way in which Skinner states the propositions, since he seems to make the fewest unnecessary assumptions. Yet after we have stated the propositions with Skinnerian austerity at least once, we shall be inclined to lapse into more everyday forms of speech. Skinnerian language tends to become cumbersome because it refuses to use certain words like "purpose" and can replace them only with circumlocutions, which may be intellectually pure but which also becomes tedious. Ordinary language is perfectly satisfactory so long as we first understand the mechanisms to which words like "purpose" refer.

There is a good reason *prima facie* for choosing the propositions of behavioral psychology as the ones to be used in explaining human social behavior: they are supported by a very large amount of experimental research, wholly independent of the findings we shall use them to explain. True, this research has largely been given over to the behavior of higher animals other than man, but its critics are quite mistaken when they imply that only pigeons and rats support the findings of behavioral psychology. For obvious moral and other reasons it is more difficult to experiment on men than on animals; yet man is also a higher animal and research on man's behavior supports the findings too. (For a good example, see Bandura, 1969.) The same general propositions hold good of the behavior of all the higher animals, though they have more complicated implications for the behavior of man than they do for that of the others, by reason of his exceptional intelligence and his use of language.

In the next chapter we shall state the propositions, but now we must take note of one of their fundamental characteristics. They all refer to the behavior of an individual organism, in our case, an individual human being; they all have to do with the fact that his or her behavior is a function of its payoffs, of its outcomes, whether rewarding or punishing, and they hold good whether or not the payoffs are provided by the nonhuman environment or by other human beings. That is, we shall use propositions that hold good of the nonsocial behavior of single individuals to explain the social behavior of several individuals in contact with one another. We assume now, and we shall see the assumption borne out later, that though much emerges in social behavior, and is emerging all the time, which goes beyond anything we can observe in the behavior of isolated individuals, yet nothing emerges that cannot be explained by propositions about the individuals as individuals, together with the given condition that they happen to be interacting. The characteristics of social groups and societies are the resultants, no doubt the complicated resultants but still the resultants, of the interaction between individuals over time—and they are no more than that. In making this assumption we run counter to an intellectual tradition going back in sociology at least to Emile Durkheim's *The Rules of Sociological Method* (1927). Durkheim believed that groups and societies were indeed more than the resultants of the interactions between individuals. He believed that their characteristics could not be wholly accounted for by the combined actions of the persons who belong to them now or belonged to them in the past. Whereas Durkheim argued (1927, p. 125) that sociology was not a corollary of psychology, that its propositions could not be derived from those of psychology, we take here what is in effect the opposite position and confess ourselves to be what has been called—and it is a horrid phrase—a psychological reductionist.

This statement may lead to misunderstanding which only utter clarity may hope to forestall. The general propositions we shall use in explanation are psychological in two senses: they refer to the actions of individuals and they have for the most part been formulated and tested by persons who have called themselves psychologists. Yet we remain stubbornly sociological in our interests, and it is social phenomena that we shall call upon the propositions to explain. Indeed we shall be especially interested in explaining just those processes of social behavior which are most apt to create and maintain relatively enduring structures of relationships between men in groups and societies—*relatively* enduring, for no social structure lasts forever. We shall be especially concerned with situations in which, though it sounds paradoxical, processes of change produce stability. After change has done its worst, a structure survives which is, for that very reason, unlikely for the time being to change further. It is in just such structures that sociologists are most interested, and it is our view that the chief intellectual task of sociologists at the moment is to show how individual human choices can produce and maintain social organizations. When this task is well done, the arbitrary lines we draw between the psychological and the social will disappear.

The Plan of the Book

The plan of the book will follow the usual procedures of explanation. We shall begin, in the next chapter, by stating the general propositions we propose to use and attempting to deal with any issues that may arise concerning their status and meaning. In succeeding chapters we shall apply the propositions to increasingly complicated—or what we believe to be increasingly complicated—sets of given conditions: first to a single type of social exchange between two persons, next to multiple exchanges between them, then to multiple exchanges among more than two persons, and so on. We shall try to show what empirical findings may, under these increasingly complex conditions, be derived from the general propositions and thus explained. We hope that some of the propositions we shall have explained in earlier chapters will prove to be of use in explaining the more complex findings we shall consider in later ones.

The book will not consist wholly of explanatory (or, if you prefer, theoretical) arguments. From time to time, and at increasingly briefer intervals, we shall consider the research data that support the empirical truth of the relationships we shall try to explain and that often support the type of argument we use to explain them. In *The Human Group* (Homans, 1950) the research we examined consisted only of field studies. In the present book we shall consider both field studies and investigations carried out by experimental and survey methods. But no attempt will be made to "survey the literature." In this book, as in *The Human Group,* we shall prefer to look closely at a few good studies rather than superficially at many, especially since some of the good studies furnish evidence for a number of different findings and not one or two at a time.

And just as we do not pretend to survey all the literature, so let no one say we pretend to explain everything about social behavior. No single book, no single person, no single group is ever going to be able to do that.

It is, moreover, much easier to explain some of the main processes of social behavior, such as conformity, than to explain in detail just how they combine to produce the specific structures of concrete groups. The reason is that, though the general relationships may hold good of all groups, the given circumstances within which they apply differ from group to group, and a small difference in the given conditions may produce a surprisingly large difference in the resultant group structures. Only the most accurate kinds of quantitative formulations and measurements, together with the use of a computer, can hope to deal satisfactorily with this kind of problem—the problem of synthesis rather than analysis—and we shall not attempt to deal with it here. Nevertheless we shall try to take a few small first steps in this direction, and in the next to last chapter we shall try to illustrate some of the processes we have considered earlier and at least suggest how they combine to form the structure of one particular group for which we possess especially rich field data.

One cryptic last word from one of our favorite men of general wisdom, Mr. Justice Holmes. Speaking of the words Jesus spoke on the Cross, "Father, forgive them, for they know not what they do," Holmes said: "That seems to have in it the recognition of the inevitables, of the mechanical nature of what seems the spontaneity of man. . . ." (Holmes, 1964: 186). We are concerned in this book with the mechanical nature of what often seems the spontaneity of man's social behavior.

2 The General Propositions

Now we shall state the general propositions that we shall use later to explain some of the empirical findings about human social behavior. We shall also discuss some of the issues concerning their meaning and status to which the propositions give rise. We shall state the propositions as if they applied only to the behavior of men and women. In fact, though, they apply to the behavior of all the higher animals.

We have said that a proposition states a relationship between properties of nature. The propositions we shall use will avoid each of two extremes. On the one hand, they will not take the form of saying merely that there is *some* relationship between the properties, that x is *some* function of y, for logic is unable to draw any definite conclusions from propositions of this sort. Nor, on the other hand, will they take the form of saying that x is a definite function of y, such as $x = \log y$, for the data rarely justify any such precision. Instead they will take the form of saying that, for instance, as x increases in value, so does y (or in the case of some of the propositions decreases), without saying how much y increases. Propositions of this form do say something, though obviously they say it pretty crudely. They are only approximate truths, but an approximate truth is far more valuable than no truth at all. If even our general propositions take this form, the conclusions in logic we are entitled to draw from them cannot be of a higher degree of precision. Luckily the propositions to be explained are as crude as the general ones. Though certainly a science, social science is certainly not an exact science.

The Success Proposition

"In the beginning was the act," said Goethe. In this book we shall be much more interested in men's actions than in their attitudes, especially if attitudes do not lead to action. We are sick of a social science in which men are always "orienting" or indeed "orientating" themselves to action, but never acting. Yet we shall not be concerned with all the actions of men. Our propositions will not refer to reflex action, such as the familiar knee jerk, but will refer to what Skinner (1938) calls *operants* and we might call voluntary actions to distinguish them from reflexes, which are clearly involuntary. Our first proposition relates a man's (or woman's) action to its success in getting a favorable result. In classical psychology it is called "the law of effect." Because we believe another name will make its meaning more obvious, we shall call it the *success proposition.*

We may state it as follows:

I. *For all actions taken by persons, the more often a particular action of a person is rewarded, the more likely the person is to perform that action.*

The proposition in itself says nothing about the reasons why the person performed the action in the first place. In the case of an experimental animal like a pigeon, its repertory of innate behavior seems to include a tendency to explore or investigate its environment by pecking at the objects within it. The psychologist may have so arranged its cage that the motion of a metal key will release a grain of corn to the pigeon. If, in the course of exploring its cage, the pigeon happens to peck at the key and thus gets the corn to eat, the probability that the pigeon will peck the target again will increase. Not until then will the psychologist be able to use the pigeon's tendency to repeat its action for the purposes ·of further experimentation. The same sort of behavior is characteristic of men. What the success proposition says is that, whatever be the reason why a person performs an action, once he has in fact performed it and the action has proved successful—the result has for the person what we shall later call positive value—then the person is apt to repeat the action.

The result of an action is what follows it. The success proposition holds good even if success was not, in the eyes of some informed observer, caused by the action but was rather a matter of chance. Much of the magic men have performed has been maintained by fortuitous success, especially when success is much desired and alternative means of producing it are not known. After all, rain usually does follow the magic of rainmaking—sooner or later.

The proposition may sound as if it said that an action were caused by its result, which is absurd to those of us who do not believe in teleology. But it does not say that. What we observe is a sequence of at least three events: (1) a person's action, which is followed by (2) a rewarding result, and then by (3) a repetition of the original action or, as we shall see, by an action in some respects similar to the original. It is the combination of events (1) and (2) that causes event (3), and since the former two precede the latter in time, we are saved from teleology. It is natural to call the original sequence of three events a learning process, and therefore the general propositions we shall use are often called the propositions of "learning theory." We believe this to be a mistake, since the propositions continue to hold good long after the behavior has in every ordinary sense of the word been learned.

The fact that a person's action has been rewarded on one occasion makes it more probable that he will repeat it on the next occasion. If there are many such occasions, the probability that he will perform the action will vary directly with the frequency with which it has been rewarded, and we have deliberately cast the proposition so that it takes this form. Remember that we are particularly concerned in this book with the process by which social behavior gives rise to relatively enduring social structures. Without repeated social actions there are no enduring social structures.

The proposition implies that an increasing frequency of reward leads to an increasing frequency of action, but it is obvious that such an increase cannot go on indefinitely. It has built-in limits, as we shall see later when we consider satiation. The proposition also implies that the less often an action is rewarded, the less often it is apt to be repeated. At the extreme, if an action once rewarded is never rewarded thereafter, a person tends in time never to perform it at all. In the technical language of behavioral psychology, it eventually becomes *extinguished*. But the time required for extinction may be very long indeed, and a single occasion on which the action is rewarded may be enough to *reinstate* it at full strength.

Let us now consider some qualifications of the success proposition. The shorter the interval of time between the action and the reward, the more likely the person is to repeat it—the more likely, to use the language of everyday life, he is to "see" the connection between his action and its reward. If we wish a person to learn, we shall do well to reward his correct responses promptly. This is the principle on which "teaching machines" are based. The reason why we do not use ordinary language but a proposition which merely sums up the facts is that everyday language is apt to embody assumptions about human behavior that are not always justified. Thus prompt reward is apt to make action more probable even if the person does not "see" the connection between his action and its reward in any conscious sense. The greater, moreover, is the value of the reward, the more likely is the person to make the connection, but we shall have much more to say about value later.

The frequency with which the person performs the action depends also on the pattern in which the reward comes. (On this matter see especially Ferster and Skinner, 1957.) For a given total number of rewards within a given period of time, it looks as if a man, like an experimental animal such as a pigeon, will repeat an action less often if it is rewarded regularly—for instance, if it is rewarded every time it is performed—than he will if it is rewarded at irregular intervals of time or at irregular ratios between the number of times he performs the action and the number of times it is rewarded. Furthermore an action once regularly rewarded will, when the reward ceases, become extinguished sooner than one rewarded irregularly. One reason why people are willing to work so hard at gambling, fishing, or hunting, even when they have little success, is that such actions are characteristically rewarded irregularly. Indeed the tendency to repeat an action more often if its reward comes irregularly may have arisen in animals, including the ancestors of men, because of its survival value. If one depends for one's food on activities such as fishing and hunting, one had better not give up too easily if one is unsuccessful, but persist. The tendency implies that animals will do just that.

Though we take note of these relationships subsidiary to the success proposition, we shall have little more to say about them. They do not render invalid the success proposition itself. Even in its crude form, the latter holds good over a wide range of behavior. In gross and in a first approximation it will serve us well in explanation.

The Measurement of Behavior

The success proposition raises the question how the variables that enter into it are to be measured. It relates two frequencies: the frequency with which a person performs a certain kind of action and the frequency with which the action is rewarded. To apply the proposition we must first be able to distinguish one kind of action from another and then be able to divide the action into separate events, for a frequency is the number of times a particular kind of event occurs within a given period of time. In the present case, this amounts to asking what constitutes a unit of action and a unit of reward. Like the pigeon's pecks, many kinds of human actions come in easily discriminable and countable units. An example is the number of units of a particular object a factory worker produces in a day. At a grosser level we could distinguish fishing from other kinds of activity and count the number of times a man went fishing in a year. Yet for other human actions it may not be so easy to discriminate between units and thus to estimate frequencies. It is, for instance, difficult to say what natural units verbal behavior should be divided into, and it is sometimes difficult to say whether a laugh should not really count as a sneer. The same sorts of difficulty arise over units of reward, but since, in the case of social behavior, one man's unit of reward is another man's unit of action—since what one man gives the other gets and therefore both sorts of unit are units of action—we shall not dwell further on this side of the problem.

Even in the difficult cases, experience shows that observers can be trained to score human behavior to obtain reliable results. That is, two observers scoring the same behavior will come up with results that are not intolerably dissimilar by the standards of precision aimed at in the research. Since much of the activity that enters into social behavior is verbal, let us examine some of the ways in which investigators have measured the frequency of verbal action. The most rigorous method is probably that of E. D. Chapple (1940, 1953), but we shall use as our first example the method of R. F. Bales, because we shall want to examine later some of his research results. Bales studies the behavior of groups of some half-dozen students who are assembled in a special experimental room to discuss a problem. (See especially Bales, 1950.) From behind a one-way mirror, unobserved by the students, a research assistant scores on a moving roll of paper what each of them says. For him, the unit of action is any item of symbolic behavior that has a discriminable meaning, even if it is only a laugh or a shrug of the shoulders. He scores each such unit as being performed by a particular member of the group and as being directed to a particular other member or to the group as a whole. He further scores it as falling within a certain class of actions, in a scheme of classification Bales devised. "Gives suggestion," "gives approval," and "shows tension release" (for example, jokes) are some of the classes of action in his scheme. The observer's score will, for example, yield counts of the number of such units of action directed by each member to every other member or to the group as a whole in the course of an experimental session. It will also yield counts of the number of such units falling within a particular class of actions in the course of a session or any part of it. The difficulty with the method lies in training different observers so that they will score in the same way, especially so that they will treat as units the same items of behavior.

The Bales method can only be used in special circumstances that are not easily realized: the group must be small and the observer must be able to hear what each of the members says. Should we wish to study groups under natural conditions—what some of us are pleased to call "real-life" groups—we may have to put up with cruder methods than Bales'. Suppose a man is to study social behavior on an office floor where some fifty men and women are working. (See Homans, 1954.) The best he may be able to do is get himself a seat at the back and watch what is happening. There may be a good deal of moving about and several conversations going on at once. Unless they go on directly in front of him, he will not be able to score their content. That is, he will not be able to score the particular kind of action that is taking place. But he may, for instance, be able to count the number of times in the course of a day he sees one person talking to another, even if he cannot tell who started the conversations or what was said in them. And he can do the same for other pairs of conversationalists. After a time he will have scores of the number of times each person in the office talked to every other, and from these crude data he can develop various subsidiary scores, for instance, the total number of conversations a particular person took part in or the number of different persons he talked to. And all this, though crude, may still tell him much about the web of relationships in the group.

Should all else fail, the investigator may be reduced to asking people whom they talked to and how often they talked to each other. This method is liable to all the distortions that can creep into a man's perception of his own behavior, but it is not utterly unreliable, and sometimes the investigator can turn the distortions themselves to account. Suppose one man says he had lunch with another, but the other fails to mention it. They cannot both be correct, yet the very discrepancy may tell us something about the relation between the two. (See Blau, 1955: 123–136.)

Most of the actions (like talking) that we shall be interested in come only in successive units (like words) so that we are able to measure their quantity as a frequency: the number of units performed within a given period of time. In other cases it is obviously relevant to measure the quantity of action in a different way. Suppose that a man gives another five apples all at once and gets all at once a certain number of cents in return. It obviously makes a difference whether the man gives five apples for the same number of cents or only one. In these cases, and economics is not the only social science interested in them, we do not measure the quantity of action by frequencies. We measure it by the number of physical objects handed over or the number of monetary units paid out. We shall assume that for our purposes such measures are very like frequencies.

In this book the one thing we shall never be is methodological snobs. We shall never assume that "crude" is necessarily a synonym for "unreliable." No piece of research that is interesting for other reasons shall we reject just because someone has said that its methods are unsophisticated. The choice of methods is an economic problem like any other. The methods of social science are dear in time and money and getting dearer every day. Sometimes they cost more than the data they bring in are worth in enlightenment. For some purposes it may be enough to know that a man spent more time with a second man than he did with a third, and superfluous to know just how much time he spent with each. There are cases in science in which the question whether a proposition holds good depends on how the variables are measured. We have stated the success proposition crudely enough so that it will hold good for a variety of measures of its variables, provided that a particular measure is used consistently within a given study. It will hold good of gross units of action, which we shall call *activities* ("fishing" is an example), and for the finer units of which the gross units are composed, which we shall simply call *acts* or *actions* ("baiting a hook" is an example). This same sort of methodological democracy will hold good of the other propositions we shall put forward later.

Alternative Actions and Rewards

We stated the success proposition as if it applied to a single kind of act and a single kind of reward at a time: the higher the absolute frequency of the reward, the higher the absolute frequency of the action. It is both true and convenient to state the proposition in this way. But men, like other organisms, are not usually so constrained that they can perform one kind of action and one only. Alternative kinds of action, which get men alternative rewards, are open to them. In this case we may be less interested in the absolute frequencies with which they perform actions and receive awards than in the relative frequencies, or how they distribute their actions among alternatives. The success proposition implies that the relative frequencies with which a man performs alternative actions should equal the relative frequencies with which the actions are rewarded.

This proposition, though plausible, has not been experimentally demonstrated for men. But Herrnstein (1971) has demonstrated it experimentally for pigeons, and it may be worthwhile to enter into a short digression on his work in order to understand what the finding means.

A pigeon is living in its experimental cage, and in the cage are two keys, a left-hand key and a right-hand one. The pigeon has learned that pecking either key will on occasion get him a standard unit of food. The experimenter has arranged to provide the food and thus to reward the pecks on either key (or, to use the technical language of the behavioral psychologists to *reinforce* them) on a variable-interval schedule, but otherwise the schedules are different in that the number of reinforcements within a given period of time (the rate or frequency of reinforcement) is greater for pecks at one of the keys than for pecks at the other. How will the pigeon distribute his pecks between the keys?

If the schedules on which he is reinforced provide the pigeon with food so infrequently that he remains constantly hungry—and this is not difficult to arrange—and if he is given plenty of time—and it takes a long time—for his behavior to settle down, the evidence is that "the absolute rate of responding to each key is directly proportional to the absolute rate of reinforcement," or:

$$P = kR \qquad (1)$$

where P is the rate of pecking and R, the rate at which reward in standard units of food is delivered. This is our success proposition. We shall ask later what meaning should be assigned to the constant of proportionality, k. The fact is that it does not always remain constant, and in the present research it should be looked on as saying simply that for the moment "other things are equal."

As for the frequency of pecks on the left key (P_L) relative to pecks on the right (P_R), it follows at once from the first equation that:

$$P_L = \frac{kR_L}{R_L + R_R} \tag{2a}$$

$$P_R = \frac{kR_R}{R_L + R_R} \tag{2b}$$

or:

$$\frac{P_L}{P_R} = \frac{R_L}{R_R} \tag{3}$$

That is, the ratio of the frequencies at which the actions are performed equals the ratio of the frequencies at which they are rewarded.

Herrnstein says that the general case, for a situation containing n alternative sources of reinforcement, is:

$$P_1 = \frac{kR_1}{\sum\limits_{i=1}^{n} R_i} \tag{4}$$

That is, the number of times any one action out of a number of alternative actions is performed is proportional to the number of times that action is rewarded, out of the total number of rewards received by all the alternative actions within a given period.

We shall not pursue this digression further, but we must try to keep the findings in mind, for we shall be returning later to the problem of alternative actions and rewards.

The Stimulus Proposition

We turn now to the second of our general propositions—but remember that they are "our" propositions only in the sense that we use them and not that we discovered them. This proposition concerns the effect on action of the circumstances attending it. Since in many accounts of operant or voluntary behavior these attendant circumstances are called *stimuli,* we call this the *stimulus proposition.*

We may state it as follows:

II. *If in the past the occurrence of a particular stimulus, or set of stimuli, has been the occasion on which a person's action has been rewarded, then*

*the more similar the present stimuli are to the past ones, the more likely
the person is to perform the action, or some similar action, now.*

In formulating their theories some psychologists include the reward of
the action itself among the stimuli, referring to it as a *reinforcing stimulus.* We believe it is confusing to do so. It is true that the sight of some
object that we have coveted and obtained earlier is a stimulus to our
efforts to obtain it again; but it is the sight of the object, not the success
in obtaining it, that is the stimulus. If we confuse the two, proposition
(II) would seem to say the same thing as proposition (I), whereas they
really say something different.

Proposition (II) says that the reappearance of the circumstances attending successful action make more probable the repetition of the
action. Thus a fisherman who has cast his line into a dark pool and has
caught a fish becomes more apt to fish in dark pools again. The connection between the stimuli and the action is subject to both *generalization*
and *discrimination*. If our fisherman has been successful in a dark pool,
he may come to fish more often in any pool that is to some degree shady.
Indeed his action itself may generalize. If he has been successful at one
kind of fishing, he may become prepared to try other kinds and even
other related sports, such as hunting. On the other hand, he may learn
to fish only under very specific conditions of water, light, and shade,
provided he has been successful under these but not under other conditions. In this case, the stimuli that govern his behavior have become
highly discriminated. Should the conditions under which success is alone
possible become complicated, they may not establish themselves at all
as stimuli for his action. He is, as we say, unable to recognize them. As
in the case of reward, the temporal relationship between stimulus and
action makes a difference: if the crucial stimulus precedes the action by
too long a time, the actor may not make the connection. The greater the
value of the reward, the more sensitive to stimuli the person may become
—so much so that if the value to him of a potential reward is very high,
he may become oversensitive and, until corrected by failure, respond to
irrelevant stimuli. Finally, alertness to stimuli or attentiveness to stimuli
is itself an action which, like any other kind of action, a person may
perform more often if it has brought him reward. All of these relationships should be looked on as subsidiary to the main stimulus proposition.

In social behavior persons and their attributes become crucial stimuli.
Did this person, rather than another, reward a man's action? If he did,
his identity was one of the circumstances attending successful action, and
his presence on some new occasion is a stimulus making it more likely
that the man will once more direct similar action toward him. Does this
person display the cold blue eyes that a man's father did when the father
punished him long ago? Then the grown man may show some slight
tendency to avoid such a person. In human social behavior, what com-

plicates the stimuli even more is the fact that they are largely verbal. The use of language sets the behavior of men further apart from that of animals than does anything else. The same general propositions apply to the behavior of both, but within these propositions the complexity of the stimuli available to men in their interaction with each other make possible a higher order of complexity in their behavior.

The crucial variable in the stimulus proposition is obviously the degree of similarity between present stimuli and those under which an action was rewarded in the past. Yet similarity may not vary along a single dimension but along many, and indeed it may depend on a complicated pattern of measures. The ways in which persons discriminate among, or generalize across, combinations of stimuli is the subject of the field of psychology called *perception* or *cognition*. So various and so many are the findings in this field that in this book we shall only state the stimulus proposition, though we shall feel free to use more specific findings *ad hoc* to explain particular cases. The real intellectual danger is not that the findings are complex but that some social scientists should believe perception and cognition to be essentially different from other behavior and thus require a different type of explanation. They are not essentially different. The ways in which men perceive and think are just as much determined by the results they achieve as are other kinds of behavior.

Imitation and Vicarious Reward

Yet we do not wish to appear so rigidly behaviorist as to deny reality to some processes in which perception plays a large part and which are of great importance in social behavior. Our view of these processes has been greatly influenced by the work of Bandura (1969).

Men, like many animals, often imitate the behavior of others of their kind. Imitation of others naturally requires some degree of observation of their behavior. We believe that a tendency to imitate others is genetically inherited and not initially learned through operant conditioning. Yet, whatever its origin, a man will not persist in performing an action he has imitated unless that action eventually brings him reward. If it is successful in bringing him reward, he will not only be apt to repeat it but also to adopt imitation as a generalized form of behavior. Then his practical success will support the genetic tendency; and the persons he has imitated will become stimuli in whose presence he will be especially likely to carry out imitative actions again.

Evidence is also accumulating that men can learn to act in a certain way even when, at first, the reward they get from the act is only vicarious. Suppose that a child sees another child put a box against a wall and use it to climb successfully out of his yard. At the moment, the first child has no occasion for climbing a wall himself, but if he does have such occasion later, the evidence suggests that he is much more likely to look for a box than he would have been if he had not observed the other child, even though he has as yet received no reward himself. Naturally he will not go on repeating the action unless sooner or later he is personally rewarded for performing it, but the initial stimulus to the action is the observed success of the other child, not his own. This kind of learning has been called *model learning*. The success of any one action originally modeled on the action of another may lead to a generalization of modeling behavior. As Bandura and Walters put it (1963:5): "Most children develop a generalized habit of matching the responses of successful models." They cannot help developing at the same time a generalized habit of observing those who are successful, or indeed of observing others to discover whether they are successful. The matching presupposes the observation.

If we did not accept the reality of model learning, we should be hard put to it to account, as we shall try to do later, for the effect of a man's behavior not only on the others with whom he is in immediate contact but also on members of an audience, who take no part in the social behavior themselves but only watch it.

The Value Proposition: Reward and Punishment

In proposition (I) we stated the effect of the success of an action in obtaining a reward on the probability that a person will repeat it. In speaking of the reward, we assumed that the value to the person of the result of his action was greater than zero—that is, he was not indifferent to it nor did he find it actually punishing. But the proposition had nothing to say about *how* rewarding the person found it. This variable, the degree of reward, we shall now bring in and call it *value*. The value in question is always that of a given unit of the reward, no matter how that unit be defined, since, as we shall see, the values of successive units may change. The gross effect of this variable upon behavior may be expressed by the *value proposition:*

III. *The more valuable to a person is the result of his action, the more likely he is to perform the action.*

The variable, *value*, may take either positive or negative values (now used in the mathematical sense of the term). The results of a person's actions that have positive values for him we call rewards; the results that have negative ones, punishments. The zero point on the scale is where the person is indifferent to the result of his action. The proposition implies that just as an increase in the positive value of the reward makes it more likely that the person will perform a particular act, so an increase in the negative value of the punishment makes it less likely that he will do so. And by an obvious extension of the stimulus proposition, if the occurrence of a particular stimulus was the occasion on which an action was punished, the recurrence of the stimulus on a new occasion makes it less likely that the person will perform the action. All of this is obvious enough.

Any action that has the result of allowing a person to avoid or escape punishment is rewarded by that result, and the person becomes more likely to perform the action. Thus there are two classes of reward: intrinsic reward and the avoidance of punishment. Similarly, there are two classes of punishment: intrinsic punishment and the withholding of reward.

The use of punishment is an inefficient means of getting another person to change his behavior: it may work but it seldom works well. On the other hand, it may give great emotional satisfaction to the man who does the punishing, and that is something not altogether to be despised. Punishment may be enough when all that is required is that the person stop doing something. Even then, if his action has otherwise brought him valuable reward, it will soon reinstate itself unless the punishment is often repeated and severe. Much more efficient as a means of eliminating an undesirable activity is simply to let it go unrewarded and thus eventually become extinguished, but applying this method sometimes takes strong nerves. Suppose we wish to stop a child's crying, when we suspect he cries only because it gets him attention. The best thing for us to do would be to ignore him when he cried. But a mother often finds it heart-rending to carry out a policy like this. What if there really were something wrong with him?

Punishment or its threat it still less efficient when it is used not just to stop a person from doing something but to get him to perform a particular action. Then we punish him if he does *not* perform the action. The difficulty here is that punishment makes rewarding *any* action that allows him to avoid or escape the punishment and not just the one we have in mind. Accordingly, we must also be prepared to punish or otherwise block off all avenues of escape except that one. Doing so is apt to prove a costly business, especially if we add the cost of surveillance to determine whether he is really doing what we wish him to do. Punishment, moreover, is apt to produce hostile emotional behavior in the person punished, and we must be prepared to cope with it. We shall have more to say about such emotions in later chapters. To get a man to perform an action by rewarding him if he does it, rather than by punishing him if he does not do it, avoids these costs—but then the positive rewards may not be available. We must face the fact that positive rewards are always in short supply. Accordingly, while recognizing its disadvantages, there are times when we shall use punishment, for lack of anything better, as a means of controlling behavior.

The things that men find rewarding—their values—are infinitely varied. Some of them are innate—that is, genetically determined and therefore shared by many men, such as the value set on food and shelter. Even some social values may be innate. It now looks as if men had evolved from apes that hunted in packs in open country. As a result, we seem today to be more "social" in our behavior than our cousins, the present anthropoid apes, just as wolves, who hunt in packs, are more "social" than their cousins, the jackals. Men could hardly have maintained pack behavior if they did not find social life as such innately rewarding. But this is speculation, and in any event, the capacity to find reward in social interaction must be highly generalized, not tied down to specific kinds of social reward.

What makes values infinitely varied is that, besides being born in men and animals, they can also be learned. A value is learned by being linked with an action that is successful in obtaining a more primordial value. (See especially Staats and Staats, 1963: 48–54.) Suppose a mother often hugs her child—and getting hugged is probably an innate value—in circumstances in which the child has behaved differently from other children and, as the mother says, "better." Then "behaving better" than others is a means to a rewarding end and is apt to become, as we say, "rewarding in itself." In other words, it is an *acquired* value. The reward may generalize, and the child may be well on the way to setting a high value on status of all kinds. By such processes of linking, men may learn and maintain long chains of behavior leading to some ultimate reward. Indeed apart from obvious anatomical differences and the use of language, the chief difference between the behavior of men and that of other animals may lie in the capacity of men to maintain longer chains relating, as we say, means to ends. For the animals the ultimate reward cannot long be postponed, if the sequence of behavior is not to fall to pieces. And even for men the ultimate reward must come sooner or later. Note that the process by which values are acquired and linked to one another is the same for men as for other animals, but the number of links that can be put together in a chain is greater for the former than for the latter. As usual, the differences are not differences in kind but in degree.

Since different individuals may encounter different circumstances in the course of their upbringing and thus acquire different values, men are apt to be more unlike one another in their acquired than in their innate values. Yet there are some values that men in particular kinds of society would have difficulty in *not* acquiring. These are the so-called *generalized values,* good examples of which are money and social approval. The act of fishing can be made more probable only by its success in getting a rather specific reward, that is, by the catching of fish—though some men seem to use fishing only as an excuse for daydreaming or admiring the scenery. But money and social approval can serve as rewards for a wide variety of actions and not just for some single kind. It is for this reason that they are called generalized values. In this book we shall be especially interested in social approval as a generalized value.

So numerous are the values men can acquire, and so varied are the circumstances in which they acquire them, that it is idle to make any general statement about which ones they will hold. But if the particular values held by particular individuals in particular circumstances are known or can be reasonably inferred from the attendant circumstances (if the values in question can be taken as given—and they often can be) then this variable can certainly be used in accordance with our propositions to predict or account for other aspects of behavior. But let no one talk about human values in abstraction from the past history and present circumstances of particular men.

In spite of all this talk about rewards, the reader should never assume that our theory is a hedonistic one, concerned only with materialistic values. The values a man acquires may perfectly well be altruistic. All our theory asks is that the values in question be a man's own values, not those that somebody else thinks he ought to have. A man's success in obtaining altruistic values has just the same effect on his behavior as his success in obtaining egotistical ones: he becomes more likely to perform the actions that have proved successful, whatever they may be. My sisters and I once knew a woman who set a high value on doing good to others, including ourselves. People sometimes say that virtue like hers is its own reward, that no external reward, no change in the behavior of others, is needed to maintain it. We soon discovered that this was not true in her case. Her high-minded behavior did require an external reward, and it was nothing less than our willingness to allow her to do good to us. Strangely enough, we were sometimes unwilling, and then she got as angry as the most materialistic of women deprived of the most material of goods. The language she used was more likely to disguise her anger, but we soon became aware that it was anger just the same. We suspect that the same sort of thing may be true of other persons who hold altruistic values, which does not in the least mean that we must be cynical about them or admire them less. They are out to help others, and why should the fact that in so doing they also reward themselves be held against them?

The Deprivation-Satiation Proposition

It is something to know what a man finds rewarding or punishing, what his values, positive or negative, *are*. But the value proposition (III) is not really concerned with what a person's values *are*. It is concerned rather with *how valuable* they are, how valuable a person finds a particular reward in comparison with other rewards. This question in turn must be divided into two separate ones. First: Is the same kind of reward more valuable on one occasion than on a different occasion? Does a person find catching fish more rewarding, for instance, this morning than he will this afternoon? Second: Is one kind of reward more valuable than a different kind on the same occasion? Does, for instance, a person this afternoon find catching fish more rewarding than the results of working in his garden?

What we shall call the *deprivation-satiation proposition* deals only with the first question. We may state it as follows:

IV. *The more often in the recent past a person has received a particular reward, the less valuable any further unit of that reward becomes for him.*

If a man has received the reward often, he is beginning, as we say, to be satiated with it. Its value for him decreases, and by the value proposition (III), he becomes less apt to perform an action that is followed by this reward. The proposition emphasizes the "recent past" because there are many rewards with which a man can only temporarily be satiated. Food is the best example. If, on the other hand, a man has learned to value a particular kind of reward but has received it only rarely in the recent past, we say he is deprived of it. For him, its value increases and by the value proposition he becomes more apt to perform an action that is followed by this reward.

Obviously the deprivation-satiation proposition is not very precise and states only a very general tendency. What constitutes the recent past within which deprivation or satiation takes place must be different for different kinds of rewards. Food can satiate men quickly, but it soon recovers its value. Most persons are not so easily satiated with money or status, if indeed they ever can be wholly satiated. The reason is that these are *generalized rewards,* which can be used to obtain a large number of more specific ones. Unless a person is satiated with all the things that money can buy, he will not be satiated with money itself.

As for the second question—whether one kind of reward is more valuable than a different kind on the same occasion—we can state no general proposition that will help us to answer it. We can only try to deal with particular cases. The number of possible comparisons is infinite, and in each case we must rely as best we can on the accumulated experience and knowledge that men have of other men and even at times of our own knowledge of particular persons. We know, for instance, that a man caught out in a chill rain without a coat is likely for the moment to set a relatively high value on shelter compared to other rewards, but that even then he would stay out in the rain if seeking shelter meant losing his life. Again, we know that a man who is new to his job is likely to set a relatively high value on getting good advice on how to do it. At the other extreme, there are preferences, differences in value, which are far from obvious. Thus we are told that the Chinese, faced with a choice of drinks, do not like milk and far prefer tea. It is easy to say that they have been taught to like tea and not milk, but that is not really an answer to the question. Why should they have been taught the preference? The ultimate answer may lie in differences between the traditional agriculture of China and that of the West. Yet if we have some confidence that we know what the values of a man or of a group of men *are*, even if we do not know why they hold these values—if we can take their values as given in given circumstances—we can, with the help of our general propositions, make some good bets on what their other behavior is apt to be.

We have begun by separating the two kinds of questions about relative values. In the end we may have to bring them together again, so that we do not leave the different values of the same reward at different times wholly unrelated to the different values of different rewards at the same time. In general, a man's satiation with a particular reward renders all his other rewards relatively more valuable to him. Moreover, it may turn out that the values can be placed in some kind of rank order, or hierarchy, of values, such that unless a man is first satiated with a particular kind of reward, the next higher kind in the hierarchy will have little value for him. Or rather, to bring in the success proposition (I), the man, if not actually satiated, must be pretty sure of getting enough of the first kind before he can set much store by the next. (See Maslow, 1954.) Thus unless a man knows where his next meal is coming from, he is unlikely to set a high value on some other reward such as status: he can forgo status more easily than he can food. Americans are said to set a high value on democratic processes. Would they do so if democracy got in the way of their getting enough to eat? One may guess that democracy would be the loser, but fortunately most Americans have not had to make the choice. There are some intangible and ideal rewards on which men will set a very high value—but only if other "lower" needs are being met. We can only raise the question here. We know too little about the ways in which men rank values in a hierarchy of this sort.

Cost and Profit

One reward is an alternative to another when it is not a perfect substitute for the other in the sense in which two nickels are usually a perfect substitute for a dime. Now that we have brought up the question of alternative rewards, we are in a position to go back to the value proposition (III) and restate it in a different, and sometimes more useful, form. Indeed there may be more than one such form. Some actions that get a man reward necessarily incur him punishment at the same time. Thus if a fisherman is to get a successful day's fishing, he may have to scramble through thickets or wade into a pool and get soaked to the skin. We may go even further and argue that, since the withdrawal of a reward is itself a punishment, most actions must incur punishment. For when a man chooses to perform one of two alternative actions followed by two alternative rewards, he necessarily withdraws from himself or, as we shall now say, forgoes the reward to be gotten from the action he did not perform. Thus the fisherman who scrambles through thickets to cast his fly in a secluded pool forgoes the reward he would have received from any alternative action that would have gotten him out of being scratched.

Following the economists, we shall say that the *cost* of any action performed is the forgone reward of an alternative action not performed. There may, of course, be several alternatives, though never an infinite number of them. We have in mind the best alternative, the one that would have brought the most valuable reward. And we shall call the excess of the reward a person gets from an action over the cost he incurs his *profit* or net reward from the action. (For those who are interested in such niceties we point out that *cost* thus defined is identical to what Thibaut and Kelley (1959: 100–125) call the *comparison level for alternatives.*)

Since reward tends to increase the frequency with which a man performs an action and cost, being a punishment, tends to decrease it, we are now in a position to reformulate the value proposition by saying: the greater the profit a person receives as a result of his action, the more likely he is to perform the action. The reformulation does not bring in anything essentially new, it merely makes explicit the effect of alternative rewards forgone and incidentally, we believe, conforms to the intuitive notions men have concerning what determines their actions.

A still better formulation may be one which puts the matter in terms of the relative frequency at which men perform alternative actions. At the risk of gross oversimplification, let us suppose that a man can perform two alternative actions, 1 and 2. The frequency with which he performs one let us call A_1 and the frequency with which he performs the other, A_2. Similarly, the value of a unit of reward that he receives from one is V_1 and the value of such a unit that he receives from the other is V_2. Then according to the value proposition (III), if the frequencies with which the actions are rewarded are equal:

$$\frac{A_1}{A_2} = \frac{V_1}{V_2} \tag{5}$$

Profit has been defined as $V_1 - V_2$ in the case of action 1, that is, as its reward less its cost, the forgone value of the alternative reward, and as

$V_2 - V_1$ for action 2. As V_1 and V_2 tend toward equality, the profit of either action tends toward zero, which now must be looked on as the profit of either action *relative* to that of the other. Under this condition, equation (5) does not imply that the man will cease to perform either action but only that he will perform one just as often as the other; in this sense, he is indifferent between the two.

If a particular kind of action is repeated in successive units, each with its associated units of reward and cost, and if the value of the reward of successive units decreases (as is usual in satiation) while their cost increases (as, for instance, in fatigue), then the science of economics would say that a man would maximize his total reward from this kind of action if he stopped repeating it when the value of the reward from its latest unit just equaled the cost associated with that unit. Or, marginal cost should equal marginal return. But this statement helps little in explaining or predicting human behavior in the cases, not often studied by economics, in which action does not meet these conditions and men cannot assess the value of successive units of reward and cost in money but only by far grosser processes. In this book we need not assume that men try to maximize their rewards. For us they need not be maximizers but only meliorizers. They do try to make their rewards greater. Whether they ever really try to make them the greatest possible is another question, and one which it would be exceedingly difficult to answer.

The value proposition, in the present way of putting it, implies that the probability of a man's performing one action rather than another depends only on their relative values, on the excess of reward over cost, and not at all on the absolute values of either. It implies that if the profit is the same, the probability remains the same whether the costs and rewards are absolutely high or low. At extreme values this does not remain true. If the value of the reward of an action is very high, but the cost is very high too, especially if both the reward and the cost are uncertain, then a man may be overcome by anxiety and "freeze up"—he may be unable to perform any action at all. An example of extreme values would be a great prize that can only be obtained at the risk of great danger. Nevertheless the value proposition, as stated now in terms of the relation between reward and cost, holds good in its crude way over a wide range of values, and if we do not press it beyond its limits it will serve us well.

For an action to incur cost, an alternative and rewarding activity must be on hand to be forgone. Unless a real alternative is open to a man, so that he is able to forgo it, his action costs him nothing, and he is apt to perform it even if the absolute value of its reward is low. Great captains try to arrange, if they can, that their soldiers shall have no alternative to fighting the enemy, as Cortez did when, before his advance into Mexico, he burnt his ships behind him. Nor should we overlook here a special and weighty kind of cost. If a man has chosen a certain course of action, and it is one that will take time to accomplish—if he has, as we say, committed himself to this course—one of the costs he incurs, one of the values he forgoes, is that of availing himself of other opportunities, which might turn out later to be even more attractive, but which are incompatible with his chosen course. As Marshal Foch, the generalissimo of the Allied armies at the end of World War I, put it: "One should not sell one's freedom of action except for a high price."

The value proposition, some scholars argue, must, if it is valid, imply that a man can rank all his values on a single scale. In fact, efforts to get a man to do just that by means of a questionnaire of some sort often result in inconsistencies: the man will rank value A higher than value B, and B higher than C, but then rank C higher than A. Whatever may happen in the abstract and in answer to a questionnaire, the issue is not one of great importance in real life. Again, for example, once the fisherman has gone off to fish and left the camp far behind, once he has committed himself to fishing, he cannot easily go back to the camp and play bridge, especially if others, his possible partners in bridge, have made the same choice he has made. It is idle then for him to compare the rewards of fishing with those of playing bridge. The only choice now open to him may be between fishing in one pool and fishing in another. The fact that a man never has to choose among all his values but only between those open for him to gain at a particular point in time makes it easier for others, including social scientists like ourselves, to predict his behavior. For many purposes, indeed, we only need to know which of two or three rewards has the greatest value for him. We need not know, if indeed we could possibly find out, just how much greater it is. This characteristic of human behavior may, on the other hand, make trouble for the man who is doing the choosing. Once a man has committed himself at a series of choice points to particular courses of action, he may find himself in the end, even if he chose the better alternative at every point, in a position he would not have intended or preferred if he could have foreseen the whole sequence from the beginning. Nothing in the human condition leads to greater tragedies than this.

The Value Proposition as a Tautology

A common criticism of the value proposition in any of its forms is that it is "only a tautology." Let us try to understand what this means by comparing the success proposition (I) with the value proposition (III). The success proposition relates the frequency with which an action is performed to the frequency with which it is rewarded. A method could be devised for measuring the value of each of these variables independently of that of the other, and accordingly each is said to be operationally defined. But is this true of the value proposition, which relates the frequency with which an action is performed to the value, positive or negative, of the reward? The former variable could be measured, as we have already noted, but how about the variable *value?* To be sure, one could often ask a person which of two rewards he found the more valuable, or whether he found a particular reward more valuable on one occasion than on another. Then one would have an independent measure of value. Yet what men say about their values does not always bear a close relation to what others, for one reason or another, believe their values really are. If we rule out questionnaires or the like as methods of measuring value, what are we left with? The answer given by those who lay the charge of tautology is that we are left with nothing. Or rather, they say that the only measure of value is the other variable in the proposition, the frequency with which the action is performed, and that it is just this fact which makes the proposition tautological.

We shall try to deal with this criticism indirectly. It is not as if the value proposition were the only proposition in science against which the charge of tautology has been laid. Far more famous propositions have suffered the same indictment. One of them is the proposition which we owe to Sir Isaac Newton in the science of mechanics and which states that the force exerted by a body is equal to its mass times its acceleration, or:

$$f = ma \tag{6}$$

The charge that this proposition is only a tautology rests on the fact that there is no measure of force independent of the other two variables, mass and acceleration. This is just the sort of criticism made of the value proposition.

The only way of meeting this kind of criticism is by asking ourselves not to look at the proposition in isolation but at the way it is used in a set of propositions—indeed in a number of such sets—forming a deductive system for purposes of explanation or prediction. Suppose, for instance, that one wishes to use equation (6) as part of a deductive system from which one can draw conclusions about the gravitational attraction of two bodies for one another, such as the gravitational attraction of the earth for a nearby body like the moon. One uses Newton's gravitational law: two bodies attract one another with a force proportional to the product of their masses and inversely proportional to the square of the distance between them. Or:

$$f_1 = \frac{Mm}{d^2} \tag{7}$$

where M is the mass of the bigger and weightier body, such as the earth, and m, the mass of the smaller. From equations (6) and (7) it follows that the acceleration of the smaller body in the direction of the larger can be stated as follows:

$$ma = \frac{Mm}{d^2} \tag{8}$$

Since the m terms cancel out, it follows that the acceleration of the smaller body depends only on the mass of the larger one and on the square of the distance between the two.

We shall not pursue this deductive system any further, since we perhaps have done enough to illustrate the point we wish to make. Note that by the time we reach equation (8), the term force, f, which had no operational definition, has been eliminated. And though, since force is not operationally defined, we cannot test the empirical truth of equation (6) directly; we can perfectly well test the conclusion of a deductive system in which it appears. The variables in the conclusion, the *explicandum*, can be independently measured, if not all those in the premise. To put the matter crudely, a tautology can take part in the deductive system whose conclusion is not a tautology.

The nature of the charge against propositions like the value proposition or the law of force then changes somewhat. If terms like force tend to be eliminated in the course of the deductions in which they appear, why bother to introduce them at all? Why not, in order to solve particular sorts of problems, work directly with a variety of empirical equations such as (8)? A number of philosophical reasons might be offered for retaining equations like the law of force, but we here, who are not philosophers, will offer only the reason that they are convenient for purposes of teaching. Thus there are a number of things besides what we call gravitation that produce a similar sort of effect, an effect of force, as we say. These can be expressed in a variety of equations called *force functions*. The gravitational law (7) is one of them, but there are many others. One, for instance, is Hooke's Law of the force exerted by a spring:

$$f_2 = -kx \tag{9}$$

where k is a constant depending on the material the spring is made of, etc., and x is the distance the spring is stretched. It is convenient, if only for the purpose of teaching students, to retain general formulas like equation (6), to which, according to the particular problem to be solved, one or another of the specific force functions such as (7) or (9) may be applied in order to explain or predict empirical findings. The pedagogical convenience created by their generality is the justification we offer for such propositions.

Though we may not otherwise put the value proposition in the same class as force equals mass times acceleration, we consider its position to be the same from a logical point of view. Suppose that we set up a fairly trivial deductive system such as:

1. The more valuable to a person is the result of his action, the more likely he is to perform the action. (The value proposition.)
2a. To a Chinese tea is more valuable than milk.
3a. Therefore a Chinese is more likely to take action that results in his getting tea than in action that results in his getting milk.

Or consider another example:

1. The more valuable to a person is the result of his action, the more likely he is to perform the action.
2b. A man inexperienced in his job is likely to find some amount of advice about how to do the job more valuable than the result of just doing the job without advice.
3b. Therefore an inexperienced man is more likely to try to get some advice than to do his job without it.

Just as the force term got eliminated in the deductive systems we took as examples from the science of mechanics, so the value term gets eliminated in these examples from behavioral science. Just as was the case in the former, the major premise in the latter, the value proposition, cannot be directly tested, but the conclusions of the deductive systems, propositions (3a) and (3b), can be so tested. And, as before, the question arises why we should retain the value proposition instead of working directly with propositions like (3a) or (3b)? The answer we offer here is that propositions taking the latter form are infinite in number; they cannot be enumerated; new ones are being discovered all the time. For the sake of formulating an intellectually organized science and above all for convenience in teaching such a science to students, why not state a single proposition in which *value* stands for all those circumstances, *other than* sheer success, as it appears in the success proposition, and attendant circumstances (stimuli), as they appear in the stimulus proposition, which affect the likelihood that a man will perform an action? In effect, this is the definition of the word *value*. This general proposition may then be applied to given conditions such as propositions (2a) and (2b) in the examples above in order to reach empirical conclusions.

Here we justify terms like *value* and the propositions in which such terms appear by their usefulness in teaching only. In fact they raise far more general philosophical issues. They are what are called *theoretical concepts,* defined implicitly by the propositions in which they appear rather than by explicit operations. Since this book is not a treatise on the philosophy of science, and since it would take us too long to discuss the status of such terms in scientific explanation and the problems inherent in their use, we shall do no more here than refer the reader to Braithwaite's book *Scientific Explanation* (1953: 50–87), in which their status is admirably discussed, though at great length, and the problems resolved.

The Aggression-Approval Proposition

So far we have had nothing to say about the emotional behavior of men, and thus have left out much that makes them human. A fuller psychology than ours pretends to be would include several propositions about emotional behavior, among the most important of which would be statements about the causes and effects of anxiety. But in this book, in order to keep the treatment as simple as possible, we shall introduce only one proposition about emotional behavior, the only one we shall badly need in order to explain the findings about social behavior considered in later chapters. This proposition we call the *aggression-approval proposition* and we can perhaps state it most conveniently by dividing it into two parts, one concerned with aggression and the other with approval.

The first part is usually called the *frustration-aggression* hypothesis (Miller and Dollard, 1941):

Va. *When a person's action does not receive the reward he expected, or receives punishment he did not expect, he will be angry; he becomes more likely to perform aggressive behavior, and the results of such behavior become more valuable to him.*

Let us now comment on each clause of this complicated proposition.

When a person does not get what he expected, he is said to be frustrated. A purist in behaviorism would not refer to the expectation at all, because the word seems to refer, like other words such as "purpose," to a state of mind. Yet if we did not use it we could only replace it by a long circumlocution, without any offsetting gain in rigor. Nor need the word refer only to an internal state; it can refer to wholly external events, observable in principle not just by the person himself but by outsiders. What a man expects to get by way of reward or punishment under a given set of circumstances (stimuli) is what he has in fact received, observed, or was told others received, under similar circumstances in the past; and none of these things are private events confined within the individual's head. This is what we shall mean by the word *expectation*. In later chapters we shall be especially interested in a kind of experience many men have shared, which gives rise to a very generalized expectation Aristotle (1967) called a rule of distributive justice. Since what a man expects depends in the long run on what has actually happened to him, his failure to receive an expected reward, if repeated often enough, finally results in a change in what he expects. What was once unexpected now becomes the expected thing, and his anger fades, but it may take a long time to do so.

When a man is frustrated, he is apt to feel some degree of the emotion we call anger. Again, a purist in behaviorism might not refer to anger in his version of the proposition but only to the aggressive behavior; we keep the anger in so that we may not do too great violence to the common sense of men. Men show that the experience of anger has much the same meaning for all of them through the ease with which they can communicate to others the fact that they are angry. No doubt the more valuable to a person is the reward he expected or the more painful the punishment he did not expect, the greater is his frustration and hence his anger.

When a man is frustrated, he is apt to perform aggressive actions. These are actions that attack, break, hurt, or threaten the source of the frustration, whether the real source or what the man perceives it to be. If for any reason the real source cannot be attacked, almost any target will do in a pinch. The target may of course be an inanimate object. We do not kick a stuck door just because a kick will help to open it, for it usually will not. We kick the door in order to hurt it. But in this book we are naturally much more interested in human sources of frustration and targets of aggression. In anger, moreover, the successful results of aggressive action reward a man as they would never have done without the anger. When we are furious at someone and hit him, the sight of his wincing under our blow becomes intensely rewarding.

In our first four propositions we were dealing with voluntary or, as the behaviorists call it, operant behavior. Operant behavior and emotional behavior such as aggression differ in the initial conditions that make their appearance more probable. No previous stimulus can automatically get a man to perform an operant the first time. He must just happen to perform it, even as a matter of chance, and be rewarded by it before he will perform it again. Only after he had been rewarded will the attendant stimuli begin to get some control over his action. Aggressive behavior can, on the contrary, be automatically produced the first time by a stimulus—the failure of an action to get the expected reward. In this respect, its initial release by a stimulus, aggression resembles a reflex like the familiar knee jerk.

Yet in another and more important respect aggression differs from a reflex. A reflex cannot be learned—one cannot learn to do a convincing knee jerk—but aggression can be learned. That is, an aggressive action, originally purely emotional, can become voluntary. Whatever the conditions of frustration that led a man to perform an aggressive action in the first place, if in fact his aggression is followed by a reward, wholly apart from the satisfaction of his anger, he becomes more likely to perform it again, just as if it were an ordinary operant. As we all know to our cost, aggression may pay, and if it does will be repeated. Many men and groups use aggression simply as an instrument for attaining practical results. In their case, the aggression may create the anger, not the anger, the aggression. But by the same token, a man may come to perform aggressive actions less often if they have not been successful or have actually resulted in punishment. He may learn to get his outward aggression, if not his inward anger, under control. Or he may still attack but may learn to displace his attacks from targets that respond with punishing reprisals to less dangerous ones. In this book aggression and the like will be treated as if they were, at one and the same time, both emotional and voluntary activities.

Let us now turn to the second part of the aggression-approval proposition. We have long believed that the special emphasis psychologists have placed on the first part, that is, the frustration-aggression hypothesis, has tended to give a one-sided view of the emotional behavior of men since it has pointed only to their negative emotions. But if they can be frustrated and hate, they can also be fortunate and love. Let us therefore propose with some diffidence the following as the second part of the aggression-approval proposition:

Vb: *When a person's action receives reward he expected, especially a greater reward than he expected, or does not receive punishment he expected, he will be pleased; he becomes more likely to perform approving behavior, and the results of such behavior become more valuable to him.*

If the reader is not altogether happy with the words *pleased* and *approving* which we have used in the proposition—and we confess we are not altogether happy ourselves—let him find his own opposites to *angry* and *aggressive.*

Many of the comments that we made about the first part of the proposition we may repeat, *mutatis mutandis,* for the second part. Two points are of particular importance. First, though men often give what we call their spontaneous admiration to others who have provided them with unusual reward, they obviously can also learn to give approval to others simply as an instrument for getting further reward from them, apart from the expression of the admiration itself. Approval can become such an instrument because many men find the approval they receive from others rewarding, just as they find aggression punishing. In short, approval like aggression may become a voluntary as well as an emotional action. In later chapters we shall have a great deal to say about approval as one of the most important rewards of social behavior. Second, if what was once an unexpected and unusual reward becomes by repetition an expected and usual one, the person's original emotional reaction will tend to decline in strength, which need not mean that he will cease to use approval instrumentally. Following *The Human Group* (Homans, 1950) we shall refer to variables like anger and approval, whether spontaneously or instrumentally expressed, as *sentiments*.

The Propositions as a System of Propositions

Now that we have stated the general propositions we shall later use in explaining social behavior, we must make one or two comments on the set of propositions as a whole. We have stated each proposition baldly, without qualifications, without adding the escape clause that each holds good only under the condition that "other things are equal." The reason we have done so is that what these "other things" are and where they are "equal" are determined for each proposition by the other propositions in the set. The effects that would be predicted by any one of the propositions may, in concrete cases, be masked or modified by the effects of other propositions in the set. That is, the set must be taken as a whole system of propositions.

Let us offer just one crude illustration. The success proposition (I) says that the more often an action is rewarded, the more often a man will perform it. But this relationship certainly does not always hold good in real life. For if the reward comes often enough, the value the man sets on a further unit of it will, by the satiation proposition (IV), decline, perhaps even to the extent that he is indifferent to it for the time being. But as the value of the reward decreases, then the man, according to the value proposition (III), becomes less likely to perform it and not more likely. What follows from the three propositions taken together is that a man will perform an action at the fastest rate when the action is rewarded only just often enough to keep him slightly deprived of it. If he were wholly deprived, it would mean that his action was utterly unsuccessful in getting the reward; and complete lack of success leads to inaction just as much as satiation does.

The Historicity Implied by the Propositions

The propositions imply, if we did not know it already, that the past history of men makes a big difference to their present behavior, and not just the recent past but often the past of long ago. A man's past history of success, of stimulation, of the acquisition of values all affect the way he behaves now. The choices he made in the past may still be limiting the opportunities available to him today, or he may perceive them as limiting; hence the great weight attached to a man's early experience by all schools of modern psychology. The ill effects of some early experiences may of course be overcome, but it may be difficult to do so—there is something to *be* overcome.

The effect of past experience extends beyond the history of individuals to the history of societies. Since children learn much of their behavior and values from parents and other members of the older generation, the past culture of a society tends to perpetuate itself. We need not believe that a society maintains itself by teaching its members just those actions it is prepared to reward, just those values it is prepared to satisfy. If a child acquires at his mother's knee a value like independence, he may, when he grows up, try to change his society radically instead of preserving it. Indeed we know that old values and actions whose success in attaining these values were learned long ago may, in new circumstances, lead to radical, unforeseen, and quite unintended social change. For instance, it was old values and old types of action that finally, in new circumstances, created the Industrial Revolution. Yet there is always some tendency for past behavior to maintain itself, at least in the sense that every new generation has to start from something that already exists; it can never make a wholly fresh start. Indeed the men of the past may, in pursuit of the values of their time and by its methods, have created institutions to which their descendants are committed, at least to the extent that they cannot change all their institutions at once. Past institutional commitments have the same effect on the history of societies that past choices often have on the history of individuals.

It is this historicity that makes it difficult to explain human behavior and human institutions. Other sciences do not suffer from it nearly as much. It makes little difference in explaining the mechanical action of a lever what sort of past history the material it is made of may have had. All it needs to be is strong enough, and there is an infinite number of paths by which it could have become strong. Were there only a single path by which a lever could meet the requirement, we might be called upon to explain why a particular lever took just that path and not some other. But there are cases, such as that of magnetic hysteresis—the tendency of a piece of iron to acquire a magnetic field in particular circumstances, which it then tends to preserve in new circumstances—in which historicity does make a difference even in physical science, and then the science has as much trouble in dealing with it as social science does.

Historicity makes least trouble when the forces acting on men or societies are convergent, when, that is, strong forces are tending to make men or societies more like one another, whatever their initial differences. In explanation we can then afford to neglect the details of the paths by which they reached this similarity. The real difficulty comes when we deal with divergent phenomena, such as the one we cite in the proverb: For want of a nail the shoe was lost; for want of a shoe the horse was lost; and so on. Then a force weak in itself but just tipping the scales in a balance of stronger forces may have great and widening effects over time.

If the present precipitates of a man's past history—the acts in which he has been successful, the stimuli that have accompanied them, the values he has acquired—can be taken as known and given, we can then apply our general propositions to these given conditions in order to explain or predict his behavior. But we seldom know enough about these conditions to predict or explain accurately. In practice, we cope with the problem as best we can by predicting or explaining the behavior of a number of men at a time, so that if we go wrong in some instances the general tenor of our results may still hold good. We cope with it also by assuming that, the more similar are the known "backgrounds" of men, the more similar their past histories must have been, and so the more similar their behavior in present circumstances is likely to be. We assume, for instance, that sophomores in American universities are apt to have shared some kinds of past experience. In this respect they resemble one another more than they do, say, their French contemporaries. If we know from acquaintance with American sophomores what these similarities are, if we can take them as known and given, we can often predict with the help of our general propositions what some other features of their behavior are likely to be; but we shall never be able to do so perfectly. Through some accident in his upbringing a particular sophomore may, for instance, have acquired values altogether unlike those of men who appear on the surface to share the same background, and so may not respond in the same way to our questionnaires or experimental manipulations. For this reason our findings, our correlations, can at best be only statistically significant and never perfect.

In any event, this book cannot include a treatise on what is called developmental psychology, the study of the process by which a newborn child becomes morally and intellectually an adult. In studying social behavior we shall simply assume that we are dealing with persons who have experienced some of the same gross features of psychological development.

This may be a useful point at which to enter a warning. Although the general propositions we shall use are often called the propositions of "learning theory," we are far from believing that men are equally likely to learn anything in the way of behavior, provided only that they encounter in the social and physical environment the appropriate stimuli and rewards. They do not, so to speak, start life as blank sheets of paper on which the environment can readily write whatever occurs to it to write in the way of learning. Not only their experience but their genetic endowment—not only nurture but nature, to use the neat antithesis—determines what they learn.

It is not a question of which is the more important, nurture or nature, though that was the question psychologists asked themselves for several decades. The real question is how the experience of men interacts with their genetic inheritance. To take an obvious example, a big, strong man is more likely than a small, puny one to find that certain kinds of action, such as physical aggression, get him reward in his contacts with other men. Accordingly big, strong men are more likely than small, puny ones to learn and to perform physically aggressive actions. Size and strength, apart from differences in nutrition, are genetically inherited characteristics. Yet they do not affect the behavior of men directly; they affect it only because they alter the contingencies in which learning takes place. Less obviously, an intelligent person may be able to learn, under appropriate conditions of stimulation and reward, types of behavior that a less intelligent person cannot learn, or cannot learn so quickly. Yet intelligence, if it is the sort of thing measured by intelligence tests, is certainly in some degree genetically inherited. Mankind itself, as we have already suggested, has probably inherited and not just learned a generalized capacity to find social contact with other human beings rewarding, and if it had not inherited this value, it would probably not be able to learn and maintain some of the forms of social behavior it does in fact learn and maintain. It may also turn out that individuals inherit different degrees of this general value, and that these differences, interacting with their experiences of the social environment, produce further differences in learning.

The Rationality Proposition

We have less need to bring in past history in explaining some kinds of behavior than others. In order to understand this point let us begin by looking at a proposition that in effect sums up the first three of our propositions, those concerned with success, stimuli, and value. (As for the last two propositions, the *deprivation-satiation* proposition (IV) states one of the causes for a change in the value of a reward and the *aggression-approval* proposition (V) states the conditions under which the results of certain kinds of actions become valuable.) The proposition has been called the principle of rational choice or the *rationality proposition*. (See, for instance, Harsanyi, 1967.) It may be stated as follows:

In choosing between alternative actions, a person will choose that one for which, as perceived by him at the time, the value, V, of the result, multiplied by the probability, p, of getting the result, is the greater.

In so acting, a person is said to maximize his expected utility (Ofshe and Ofshe, 1970: 3). In the case of repeated actions, the rationality proposition implies that, if the rate at which a man performs an action is designated by A, then

$$A = pV \tag{10}$$

Suppose, for example, that a man faces a choice between two actions. The first, if successful, will bring him a result worth, let us say, three units of value to him, but he estimates the chance that his action will be successful as only one out of four. The second will bring a result worth only two units, but he estimates its chance of success as one out of two. Since $3 \times \frac{1}{4}$ is less than $2 \times \frac{1}{2}$, the rationality proposition predicts that the man will take the second action.

The proposition becomes simplified if each of the alternative actions is certain of success, so that $p = 1$. Then the man's choice depends only on the relative value of the results. This condition is, of course, sometimes satisfied in real life. For instance, in the kind of market which classical economics for its purposes of analysis assumed to exist and which some real markets in fact resembled, a willing buyer could always find a willing seller. His success in the act of buying was certain, and so his decision to buy depended only on whether he was ready to pay the price—whether the value of the goods bought was greater to him than that of the forgone alternative of keeping his money to spend on something else. Much economics uses the rationality proposition in this stripped-down form as its single general proposition, often without actually stating it.

Now let us consider in what sense the rationality proposition embodies, or corresponds to, our first three propositions. It states that one of the two factors determining whether a man will perform an action is its probability of success as he perceives it. But the proposition says nothing about what in turn determines his perception. In the case of actions repeated over time, one of the determinants of his perception will be the actual frequency with which the past action has been followed by the reward. Then this aspect of the rationality proposition is stated by the success proposition (I): the more often the action is in fact rewarded, the more often it is performed. Let us write this in the form of Herrnstein's equation (1, p. 21), substituting for his variable P, the rate at which a pigeon pecks, the more general variable A, the rate at which a man performs any given action.

$$A = kR \tag{11}$$

Here R, the actual frequency with which an action has been rewarded replaces the variable p, the perceived probability of success, in the rationality proposition.

The rationality proposition also embodies our stimulus proposition

(II), in that a man's perception of the probability that his present action will be successful is further determined by the similarity of the circumstances attending the action at present to those under which the action was successful in the past.

Now let us look at the constant of proportionality, k, in Herrnstein's equation. It is a constant there because the actions of his pigeons were identical in form (pecks) and in reward (grain). They differed only in the rates, R, at which pecks at two different keys were rewarded. But most alternative actions differ in form and in the kind of reward they receive. When they differ in form, they generally also differ in cost; and when they differ in reward, they generally also differ in the value of the reward. That is, they differ in the net value of the reward they receive. In a more general formulation the constant in Herrnstein's equation must be replaced by the variable, V, and then the equation takes the form

$$A = RV \qquad\qquad (12)$$

We should now be able to recognize how each variable in this formulation corresponds to a variable in the rationality proposition, remembering that "corresponds to" does not have the same meaning as "is identical with."

Just as the rationality proposition has nothing to say about why a man perceives his chances of success as high or low, so it has nothing to say about why he has acquired certain values and not others, why he sets a higher value on one reward than he does on another, or why he values a particular reward more highly on one occasion than he does on another. A more fully developed psychology, and one that deals with the effects of a man's past history on his present behavior, is needed to account for these things.

Yet we must always remember that, besides what a man perceives to be his chances of success in various actions, there are always the actual chances of success as given by the outside world independent of his perceptions, including at the extreme the certainty that some kinds of actions will be successful. Suppose we have reason to believe that a man's perceptions of the outside world are accurate, that the outside world and his map of it coincide. Suppose we can assume further that his values are common values, values that most persons share, or that are common to a class of men to which he is known to belong. Then, in explaining his behavior, we can neglect the details of his past history. For example, if we know a man is a skilled carpenter, then we explain what he does in building a house, though not necessarily in other activities of life, by the laws of physics, so to speak, and not by reference to his individual past. Nor do we have to account for his particular values. We confidently assume that, simply because he is a carpenter, he will set some value on building a house that will stand up. Apart from professional pride, he will set some value on it if only because he will not earn his living very long as a carpenter if his houses will not stand up. If a man's chances of success in his actions are given by the outside world, and if his values are those known to be held by the class of men to which he belongs—if, that is, his values and his perceived chances of success can simply be taken as given—then the rationality principle alone, without the use of a broader set of propositions, will explain and predict his behavior pretty well. Of course, our carpenter may make mistakes, but in the long run his behavior will approximate to what the rationality proposition predicts. Much human behavior, of course, meets these conditions and can be explained in this way.

But much behavior cannot be explained by the rationality proposition. If a man's values are somewhat queer, not as easily taken for granted as those of a skilled carpenter in the exercise of his trade, and if his chances of success are not given by the outside world, or at least not accurately known by him, then the rationality proposition by itself may not help us much. Our favorite example, among the enormous number that could be cited, is the decision by William the Conqueror (then simply the Bastard), Duke of Normandy, to invade England in 1066. That he set a high value on the result of successful conquest, becoming king of England, those of us who have some knowledge of other feudal lords will find no difficulty in accepting. But what about the other term in the rationality proposition, his chance of success as perceived by him? He could not know what his chances were. As the economists would say, his condition was one of uncertainty and not of risk. In risk the odds on success are accurately known; in uncertainty they are not known. Even if he were fairly sure he could get an army and a fleet together, there remained for him the dangers of a sea voyage, of landing on a hostile shore, and of battle with an English army under the experienced and hitherto successful command of Harold Godwinsson. Defeat in battle would almost certainly mean death. William's contemporaries might well have judged his chance of success to be small. On the record, we have no reason whatever to believe that he was a foolish man. Why then did he go ahead with the enterprise? In trying to answer this question it is surely relevant to point to the almost unbroken series of his military victories over the preceding twenty years. It is not the rationality proposition but the success proposition that will account for the effect of these victories on his decision. Past success in military action made his future military action more probable. Or, as we say in ordinary language, past success had given him confidence.

Certainly, if we keep the rationality proposition firmly in mind, we shall never forget that human action is determined by two kinds of factor, not one. Many persons, including many social scientists, talk as if what determines a man's action was his "motivation" alone—in our terms, the value he sets on the result of his action. But a man may be highly motivated in this sense and still not take action, if his similar actions in the past have been uniformly unsuccessful. Again, some social scientists talk as if the reason why some lower-class groups, like blacks in the United States, remain unassimilated to the larger society in which they live is that their values are different from those of other groups in the society. Their values may be just the same as those of the rest of society, but if their actions have been, for whatever reason, unsuccessful in obtaining those values, they will turn to alternative actions. If these alternative actions are successful in obtaining a different kind of reward, their actions may keep them as effectively cut off from the rest of society as if their values had been different all along. The rationality proposition serves to remind us that action is determined by success and value jointly.

Conclusion

We must recognize that not one of the propositions we have put forward is new. It is not just that they are not original with us but have been put forward, if not in the same words at least with the same substance, by many psychologists. They were not new even to the psychologists. Undoubtedly in one crude form or another they have been known to men for ages. They hardly come as a surprise to any of us, though some of their further implications, in psychopathology for instance, may indeed be surprising. Accordingly, the propositions may appear to be obvious, but they are not to be rejected just for that reason. It is also obvious that the obvious need not be untrue, and what we seek is the truth. Perhaps there are general propositions in social science that remain to be discovered, but those that have long been known are not made trivial by that fact.

Let not a reader reject our argument out of hand because he does not care for its horrid profit-seeking implications. Let him ask himself whether he and mankind have ever been able to advance any general explanation why men change or fail to change their behavior other than that, in their circumstances, they would, as they see it, be better off doing something else or that they are doing well enough already. On reflection, the reader will find that neither he nor mankind has ever been able to offer another explanation; it is a truism. He may ease his conscience by remembering that if hedonists believe men take profits only in materialistic values, we are not hedonists here. If men's values are altruistic, they can take a profit in altruism too. In fact, some of the greatest profiteers we know are altruists.

Though we have called the last proposition the rationality proposition, we should be aware of the different meanings men have given to the word *rationality*. The first is rationality from the point of view of some omniscient outside observer who views behavior as irrational if he knows its reward is harmful to a man. A person is irrational if he pursues rewards that he ought not to find valuable. In this sense a man who takes certain kinds of drugs, including tobacco, behaves irrationally. So is a masochist, a man who finds punishment rewarding, though here the criterion of "goodness" or "health" is not so clear. But since in this book we are not interested in how men ought to behave but only in how they do in fact behave, we care not here—though surely we do care elsewhere—whether a man's values are rational or not. What we are interested in is what he does with them once he has somehow picked them up. Suppose a man is a masochist. Is it still true that, if he has taken a lot of punishment recently, he will find further punishment for the moment somewhat less valuable? Will the first kick in the teeth give him more of a kick than the last? Will the satiation proposition apply to him too? These are the types of question we are interested in.

Even if, in the eyes of the omniscient observer, a man's values are rational, his actions may still be irrational if they are not well designed to obtain these values. A man may be ill-informed or misperceive the situation that faces him or fail to realize that a different action might be more successful or successful at a lower cost. If the standard of rationality is set by the omniscient outside observer, the man's behavior is then irrational. All we can say is that the rationality assumed by the rationality proposition is not of that sort. Whatever a man's information, perceptions, and designs might conceivably be, if he does not in fact possess the best possible ones but acts in accordance with those he does possess, though they may be wrong or inadequate, he is acting rationally.

The second meaning of rationality is closely related to the first. Whatever a man's values may be, his behavior is irrational if it is not consciously calculated to get him the largest supply of these values in the long run. Here the emphasis is not on the kind of value being pursued—it may be capital gains or eternal salvation—but on the way it is being pursued: the emphasis is on calculation and the long run, the longer the better. By this standard, an irrational man is one who is either unwilling to forgo some immediate reward in order to invest in some greater future or unwilling to acquire the knowledge and make the calculations that would show him how to reach that future. A large part of many sciences, from divinity to the Theory of Games (Von Neumann and Morgenstern, 1944), is devoted to providing him with this knowledge and enabling him to make the calculations. The Theory of Games should, for instance, make him better able to choose a strategy among alternative courses of action, when the risks and returns of each are matters of probability, not certainty.

Although calculation for the long run plays its part in human affairs, we make no special allowance for it in our propositions. Above all we assume that the propositions hold good whether the behavior in question is conscious or unconscious. In the fields of human endeavor we shall be interested in, conscious and unconscious behavior very often come out at the same place. One man may offer another a greater reward in social approval in return for a more valuable kind of help; his behavior may be utterly economic, without his being any more conscious of what he is doing than a pigeon is—but then we do not know how conscious a pigeon can be.

We neither rule out nor rule in conscious calculation. Our first justification is that we shall not often need it in order to explain the research results considered in this book. And our second lies in plain sight: calculation for the long run is the exception and not the rule. The Theory of Games may be good advice for human behavior but a poor description of it.

The fact is that the question whether behavior is rational or not by any of the definitions proposed is irrelevant to our purposes. All the good advice, from ethics to economics, that wise men give their fellows is meant to change behavior and not to explain it; but our business is with explanation. The advice tries to answer the question: Given that you value the attainment of certain ends, how could you have acted so as to attain them more effectively? But what men or pigeons could have done is what they did do, and much social science has gone to show some of the surprising reasons why they could not do in fact what some wise-acre says they could. This does not mean that all the advice goes for nothing. So far as men will take it, so far as they will learn from it, it may change the way they behave the next time. But behavior observed is behavior past, and for the purposes of explaining how men have indeed behaved, it is seldom enough to ask if they were rational from the point of view of an omniscient observer. The relevant question is what in fact determined their behavior—though of course the advice they have listened to may be among the determinants.

The persons who will appear in this book are, if you like, no less rational than pigeons. If it be rational of pigeons to learn and take the shorter of two paths to a reward, so it is of our men. They choose among a few alternatives immediately open to them; they choose with little regard for the really long-term results of their choice, which sometimes surprise them. But the short-term results they do know, and they often know them less as matters of probability than of certainty. Within these limits, our men do not choose foolishly—that is, at random—but only in the way our propositions say they do. All that we impute to them in the way of rationality is that they know enough to come in out of the rain unless they enjoy getting soaked. To be sure, such rationality as we have now left them may not amount to much, for rational behavior in our sense, and not in that of the omniscient observer, is only behavior that is determined.

Let us make sure we are not snobs about the common pigeon or the common man. When the future is not easily foreseen and science is weak, the pursuit of immediate reward is by no means irrational even by the austere standards of the Theory of Games. "A bird in the hand is worth two in the bush" is by no means always an unintelligent policy. And so far as the pursuit of rationality entails study, forethought, and calculation, and such things hurt, as they often do, the pursuit of rationality is itself irrational unless these costs are reckoned in the balance. The costs of rationality may make rationality itself irrational.

3 Interpersonal Relationships: Balance

IN CHAPTER 2 WE STATED THE GENERAL PROPOSITIONS WE
shall use in trying to explain some of the principal features of social behavior. We stated the propositions as if it made no difference where the
reward of a person's action came from, whether from the physical environment or from another person. We are, indeed, convinced that the
form of the propositions need not change when behavior becomes social,
that is, when a person's action is rewarded by the action of another person rather than by, for instance, catching a fish. Naturally, since the
behavior of each of at least *two* persons in contact with one another
is now governed by the propositions, new phenomena will emerge in
the social situation that were not present when a man was alone with the
physical environment. But we need no new propositions to explain the
new phenomena; we need only apply the old propositions to the new
given conditions, to the fact that the behavior of each man is now social.
The notion that, if a phenomenon emerges, it requires by that fact alone
new propositions to explain it is a common error among sociologists. Indeed it is *the* error in much that passes for sociological theory (see
Homans, 1967: 61–64). With this introduction, we turn once and for all
to our main task, the explanation of social phenomena, especially to the
repeated exchanges of rewards between men which we shall refer to as
interpersonal relationships.

The Payoff Matrix

For some purposes a useful tool in thinking about social behavior is
the so-called payoff matrix (see especially Thibaut and Kelley, 1959:
100–125). To illustrate it, let us first suppose that two men, whom we
shall call Person and Other, are each, without the knowledge of the
other, sick of living in a crowded city and are considering whether or

not to seek solitude by going to the mountains. Each person may take one out of two possible actions and get the reward associated with it: to remain in the city and gain what pleasure he can out of doing so or to seek solitude in the mountains. We assume that for each person the value of the latter alternative is greater than that of the former. Let us now set up Payoff Matrix 1.

Payoff Matrix 1   Unintended Conflict of Interest

OTHER'S ACTIONS

		o_1 Home	o_2 Mountains
	p_1 Home	1 / 1	1 / 2
PERSON'S ACTIONS	p_2 Mountains	2 / 1	0 / 0

The matrix is divided into four boxes, or cells, representing four contingencies. Box o_1p_1 represents the contingency in which both persons stay at home in the city; o_2p_1, the contingency in which Person stays home while Other goes to the mountains; o_1p_2, the contingency in which Other stays home while Person goes to the mountains; and finally o_2p_2, the contingency in which both go to the mountains.

Each box is divided by a diagonal into two halves. The number in the northeast or upper right-hand half represents the payoff, the value of the reward, to Other in the contingency in question, and the number in the southwest or lower left-hand half represents the payoff to Person. Do not take the absolute numbers too seriously. The figure 2 for each man simply means that solitude in the mountains is more valuable to him than staying in the city. The cost of going to the mountains is the forgone value of the alternative action 1, for we assume that staying in the city is rewarding in some degree, so that each will get a net reward of $2 - 1 = 1$ from going to the mountains—provided that the other stays at home.

Since neither is aware of the other's action, since neither is a stimulus for the other, we predict by the value proposition that both will go to the mountains. That is, contingency o_2p_2 will occur. But if both go to the mountains, we shall assume for the purposes of our argument that they are bound to run into one another there. By definition, therefore, the mountains will no longer provide them with solitude, and both will find themselves worse off than they would have been had they stayed at home. For this reason we have entered two zeros in the o_2p_2 cell. Of course, once they have recognized that they are denying solitude to one another, there is nothing, we presume, to prevent their negotiating a deal whereby on the next occasion they will go to the mountains at different times. But that would be a new situation.

What are the characteristics of the behavior described here? Each of two or more persons acts in ignorance of the behavior of the others; each acts without communicating with the others; the potential rewards and costs of each are equal to those of each of the others, and their interests conflict. We might be justified in not calling this kind of situation social at all. Though each affects the others' rewards, none of them immediately influences the others' behavior, and as a result all suffer. Human affairs, especially economic affairs, are full of situations like this. If, for example, many men, fearing a rise in prices, start buying and hoarding goods and commodities, they are helping collectively to bring about the very condition they individually wish to avoid. Obviously this is not the sort of situation that, in itself, leads to what we shall be especially interested in: enduring relations between men. If, of course, the two did manage later to negotiate an arrangement by which they divided the time spent on the mountains between them, that would be another matter, which would need a different matrix to represent it. And the same would be true if the collective and unintended result were rewarding to both, instead of being, as we have assumed here, valueless.

Social Exchange

Now that we are familiar with one example of a payoff matrix, let us turn to a different kind of situation, one which, more than all others, does lead to enduring relations between men. This situation differs from the former in that each of the two persons acts in the presence and under the stimulus of the other; each can and does communicate with the other; and the collective result is rewarding to both. The only respect in which the two situations are similar is that we assume the rewards and costs of each person to be equal to those of the other. We shall later remove even this condition.

Let us visualize a characteristic situation that meets the conditions we have just set up. We have taken the situation from research carried out by Blau (1955: 99–179). Suppose that two men are both doing paper work in an office—preparing reports or something of that sort. According to the rules laid down by the administration, each man should do his job on his own or, if he needs help or advice on how to do it, should consult the supervisor. One of the men, whom we shall again call Person, is new to the work and unskilled at it. He could get it done better and faster if he received some help from time to time. But in spite of the rules he is reluctant to seek help from the supervisor, because he believes that by doing so he would, in effect, confess his incompetence and thus damage his chances for promotion. The other man, whom we shall indeed call Other, presents to Person the sort of stimuli under which in the past he has found that requests for help were apt to be rewarded. That is, Other has worked in the office for some years, he seems to be experienced in the job and he has time to spare. Person also has reason to suppose that the supervisor will not go out of his way to look for a breach of the rules; and therefore Person seeks out Other and asks him for advice about a problem he has run into in his work. Other does give him help, and in return Person gives Other approval in the form of heartfelt thanks.

At the risk of unduly complicating the obvious—but so long as we have been careful and systematic at least once we shall be able to take shortcuts later—let us try to represent the situation by Payoff Matrix 2.

Payoff Matrix 2   Exchange of Advice for Approval

OTHER'S ACTIONS

		o_1 Own work	o_2 Advice
PERSON'S ACTIONS	p_1 Own work	1 \ 1	0 \ 1
	p_2 Approval	1 \ 0	2 \ 2

Each person, we assume, has two alternatives open to him. Other can either continue to do his own work or stop and give Person advice; Person can either do his own work or listen to the advice and give Other approval. In the matrix, cell $o_1 p_1$ represents the contingency in which each man continues to do his own work; $o_2 p_1$, the contingency in which Person does nothing but his own work while Other, apparently spontaneously, gives him advice; $o_1 p_2$, the contingency in which Other does nothing but his own work, while Person, apparently for no reason at all, gives him approval; and finally o_2p_2 represents the contingency in which Other gives Person advice and Person gives Other approval.

The figures for the values of the rewards are arranged to show that Person values getting advice more than he does doing his own work. He does so, of course, because he is unskilled at his own work. But this does not mean that the completion of his own work has no value to him— after all, that is what he is supposed and paid to do. The forgone value of this reward is the cost to him of getting advice—and there are other kinds of cost that we shall speak of later. Thus Person's net reward for giving approval is $2 - 1 = 1$.

In the same way we assume that Other sets a higher value on getting approval than he does on the rewards of doing his own work. Giving up the latter is the cost to him of getting approval. But if he is so experienced that he can easily do his own work and have time to spare, this cost will not for the moment be very great. For him too the net reward for giving advice is $2 - 1 = 1$.

In contrast to the first matrix we looked at, the present one includes two highly unlikely contingencies: o_1p_2, when Other only does his own work but Person still gives him approval, and o_2p_1, when Person only does his own work but Other still gives him advice. The reason why these contingencies are unlikely to occur is, of course, that the full interchange consists of three actions and not two, one for each man, as in the first matrix. The exchange of advice for approval is preceded by Person's request for advice, without which Other is unlikely to proffer advice spontaneously; and unless he gets advice, Person is unlikely to give Other approval in return.

If the actors in our drama rule out these two contingencies, they are left with only o_1p_1 and o_2p_2. Since the latter produces a reward of greater value for each man, each is, by the value proposition, likely to perform the action that gets this reward. But the value proposition is not the only one necessary to explain what happens: other propositions are implicitly required. For Other, as for most persons in our society or perhaps in any society, a verbal stimulus in the form of a request is apt to have been the occasion on which the action of acceding to the request has been followed by social approval. Thus the stimulus proposition has also been at work. As for Person, he gives approval in part because he has learned that, if he does not do so, Other will be less apt to honor a request for advice on the next occasion. That is, Person has learned that approval rewards other men and that men are unlikely to repeat actions that have not been rewarded. Like most men, Person has learned how to make the success proposition work for him. Facts like these are the basis for our claim that men have commanded for ages a working knowledge of the principles of behavioral psychology. Person's expression of approval is thus in part an instrumental action.

We assume that both parties to the transaction have rewarded one another on good terms, without punishment or frustration. Person has not made himself a nuisance in asking Other for his time and has apparently been sincere in his thanks. Other has not played hard-to-get or exacted humiliating self-abasement from Person. In the language of everyday life, they have made a fair exchange. We shall have much more to say about fair exchange later, but we must note here that, by the aggression-approval proposition, *both* Person and Other, as parties to a fair exchange, will tend, over and above Person's instrumental use of approval, to display toward one another some degree of the emotional reaction we shall in this connection call liking.

In this example, quite unlike the first we looked at, the action of each person has been a stimulus to the action of the other; the action of each has been a response to the action of the other. Accordingly, we may speak of the two as interacting and measure the frequency of their *interaction,* that is, how often within a given period of time have they directed action to one another and responded to that action.

The action of each has, moreover, rewarded the action of the other, so that it becomes natural for us to speak, as we have begun to do, of their interaction as an exchange of rewards, specifically an exchange of advice for approval (see Homans, 1958; 1964). True, Person will ultimately find Other's advice rewarding only if it turns out to be good advice, if it actually helps Person in doing his work. Should it not prove to be good advice, that fact will surely affect Person's future behavior toward Other. But we have assumed that the advice is indeed good, and we already know that a result which is a means to a further reward may become a reward in its own right. The two men might also, of course, have exchanged punishments. For instance, Other might have refused to give Person advice, and Person, frustrated and angry, might have proceeded to insult him. Since much social behavior may thus be looked on as an exchange, some social scientists have tended to call the type of explanation we put forward "exchange theory." We believe that this practice should be given up. It implies that exchange theory is somehow a distinct and independent theory, whereas in our view it consists simply of behavioral psychology applied to the interaction of men.

In any case we do not imply here that all social behavior—behavior in which the action of one man is a stimulus to, or reward for, the action of another—can be envisaged as a direct exchange between the two. We only believe that a study of exchanges of the sort we have illustrated is a good place at which to begin the study of social behavior.

In our example, we have spoken of the alternative actions available to each man, but we have not mentioned another and very important kind of alternative: alternative persons by whom these actions could be rewarded. We have assumed, in effect, that Person and Other are alone in the office, except for the supervisor. If there were alternative persons from whom Person could get advice or Other, approval, we should have to explain why each sought out the other rather than alternative persons. By the value proposition we should expect each to approach that one of the other persons who is likely to reward the approach most highly in relation to its cost; and we must recognize one common kind of cost that affects the choice between alternative persons. It is easier (less costly) for a man to approach someone near him than someone far away. Indeed it may be impossible at any particular time for him to get in touch with distant others. Even if there were—which would naturally be unlikely—someone outside the office who could give Person as good advice about his job as Other can, Person would still be apt to approach Other. Physical proximity is one of the factors reducing the costs of human interaction. It is, of course, not the only factor; in particular circumstances others may override it. But it is a very general factor.

The Results of Exchange

We have gone into one example of exchange in excruciating and obvious detail for two reasons: so that no one may accuse us later of disregarding the details and so that we may be able to take them for granted in the discussion of other cases unless there is some special reason for emphasizing one or more of them. In fact we are less interested in the exchange itself than in what follows from it. In their well-known book, *The Social Psychology of Groups* (1959: 18–19), Thibaut and Kelley say that they propose to disregard what they call *sequential effects*—that is, the effects of repeated exchanges—in entering figures in their payoff matrices. This may be reasonable as far as single matrices are concerned, but if our purpose is to explain social behavior, nothing could be more mistaken as a general principle. Repeated interactions between particular persons are the very guts and marrow of social life, and we cannot understand repeated interactions unless we consider the sequence of actions—that is, the effect of past actions on present ones.

In their exchange of advice for approval Person and Other have each rewarded the action of the other. Accordingly, by the success and the stimulus propositions, each man has become more apt to repeat his action on the next similar occasion, and to repeat his action toward the same other person. Note that an increased propensity to interact with a specific other person may imply a lowered propensity to interact with some third party. By stimulus generalization, moreover, each person may become for the other the kind of person from whom reward in general may be expected and not just the specific rewards of advice or approval. Other experiences may override these tendencies, but the tendencies will, so to speak, be there to be overridden.

If Person and Other repeat their original exchange of advice for approval, the value to each of successive units of his reward is apt, by the deprivation-satiation proposition, to decrease and the cost to increase, at least in the short run. Other begins to get satiated with approval; and since giving advice takes more and more time from his doing his own work, the value of the latter increases. Person, too, may be getting as much advice as he can use for the time being. Moreover, each time that he asks for help, he confesses more clearly his own inferiority in skill to Other. Since confessing his inferiority may be punishing to him, and since doing his own work unaided enables him to escape this punishment, the value of his alternative action may be increasing for him just as it is for Other. We shall postpone until later the consideration of this kind of cost. At any rate, as the two men repeat their exchanges of advice for approval, each may reach a point where he is ready to break off the exchange for a while and stick to his own job. But note that the two may not reach this point at the same time. Person may still need a little advice at a time when Other is quite ready to turn back to his own work. We shall have more to say about this condition when we come to the discussion of the relative power of the two men. In any event, their readiness to break off the exchange need not last: when they come into the office the next morning they may be quite prepared to enter into exchange again. That is, the effects of deprivation and satiation may wear off in the long run.

In the still longer run, effects of a different sort may make themselves felt. Person, the unskilled worker, may become skilled, both through his own increasing experience with his job and through the advice he has received from Other. Advice will then become less valuable to him, and therefore he will become less apt to interact with Other, at least for the purpose of getting advice. But by that time he may well have found new reasons for interacting with Other. To these we shall turn shortly.

Repeated interaction also makes a difference to future behavior because it changes expectations. Suppose that Other has been giving Person advice whenever he has asked for it, and then suddenly, for whatever reason, refuses to do so. Then, since Person has come to expect the advice, he is apt, by the aggression-approval proposition, to get angry. It seems hard that our failure to reward another, which would not arouse his resentment if we had never rewarded him before, will do so if we have—but such is the way of the world. We are trapped by even our best deeds.

Since in anger the results of hostile actions, actions that hurt the source of frustration, become rewarding, Person may then try to hurt Other. And since the withholding of an expected reward is a punishment, he may refuse to enter into any further exchanges with Other, even when he still needs advice and Other is ready to give it. He thus denies Other the approval he had given him in the past. He is cutting off his nose to spite his face, but in anger the result may be worth the cost. Insofar as Other values his exchanges with Person, he may learn to avoid the punishment by living up to Person's expectations. He is the more likely to do so the more the punishment would hurt him, which may mean that there is no alternative person from whom he can get the kind of reward—social approval—that Person would deny him. To sum up: repeated interactions are apt to form expectations, and expectations are apt to produce aggressive reactions if they are not met, thus bringing in a new kind of reward, precisely that of avoiding the aggression, which may help to maintain the relationship between the two persons. We shall now go into this matter in further detail.

The Effect of Multiple Exchanges: Balance

Suppose that a pair like Person and Other have repeatedly entered into a particular kind of exchange, such as that of advice for approval. It is almost inevitable that they will begin to enter into other kinds of exchange as well, if only because the first exchange reduces the costs in spatial movement of the second exchange. Since each has rewarded and been rewarded by the other on favorable terms, each is ready to express liking for the other. And since one kind of action by each has already been rewarded by the other, each may expect by stimulus generalization that the other will also reward new kinds of action.

Let us suppose, for instance, that the two persons start to exchange opinions on the issues of the day, all the way from baseball to politics. The expression of an opinion is an action that is rewarded by agreement with it and punished by disagreement. Accordingly, an exchange of opinions is likely to be repeated if each person agrees with the other's views. Stated baldly, of course, this is not quite true. If a person does nothing but agree with us, if he is nothing but a yes-man, we are apt to find him insipid. We need a little disagreement to give us something to keep on talking about. But the matters on which we are ready to tolerate much disagreement are not apt to be matters by which we set much store. If someone expresses disagreement with opinions we hold strongly, he hurts us and makes us angry.

Let us suppose that Person and Other, who have rewarded one another in one kind of exchange and who like one another as a result, start exchanging opinions about any subject, X, of some importance to them. And let us also for the sake of generality consider the case in which they dislike one another—each has hurt the other in some way—but still manage to exchange opinions. Under these circumstances, any one of four situations can arise: (1) they like one another and agree about subject X; (2) they dislike one another and disagree; (3) they like one another and disagree; and (4) they dislike one another and agree. These four situations may be diagramed as shown in Figure 1, in which plus or minus signs beside the line $O - P$ indicate whether Other and Person like or dislike one another respectively, and plus or minus signs beside the lines $P - X$ and $O - X$ indicate whether the person concerned takes a favorable or unfavorable attitude toward X: if the signs are the same, the two persons agree about X; if they are different, they disagree. We have left out as redundant the case in which the two agree in taking an unfavorable attitude to X, and have shown only favorable agreement.

This method of analysis was invented by Heider (1958: 174–217), who called situations like (1) and (2) *balanced* and situations like (3) and (4) *unbalanced,* presumably because balance implies stability and balanced situations do indeed tend, as we shall see, to be stable. The psychologists who have carried this kind of analysis further tend to speak of it as "balance theory." We believe that it is just as misleading to speak of "balance theory" as it is to speak of "exchange theory." Neither is a separate theory with its own general propositions. In particular, balance theory, especially as we shall present it here, is simply the application of general psychological principles to explain the effect on a relationship between two persons of the addition of a second kind of exchange to an original exchange. Let us see how this works.

In situation (1) the two men like one another, which implies that

Figure 1

Balanced Relationships

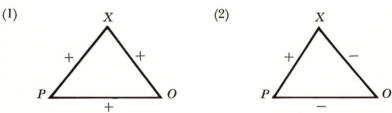

Unbalanced Relationships

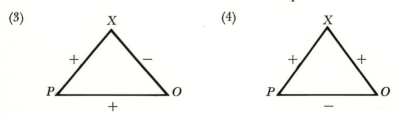

they have rewarded one another in earlier exchanges. They now find that they also agree with one another about subject X and so further reward one another. Under these circumstances the effect of the new exchange is to reinforce the old one. The interaction between Person and Other will continue and may even increase in frequency. Likewise in situation (2) the new exchange tends to reinforce the effects of the old, though in a different direction. Here the two persons begin by disliking one another; by also disagreeing with one another they again punish one another. Thus they increase their mutual dislike still further and make it even less likely that they will interact with one another in the future. These situations are balanced because they tend to perpetuate the existing relationships between Person and Other.

The unbalanced situations imply no such stability. Consider first situation (3). Here Person and Other like one another, which must mean that they have rewarded one another in earlier exchanges. At odds with their liking is the fact that they have now punished one another by disagreement. What is likely to happen? Conceivably nothing will happen. There certainly are persons who are able to maintain an ambiguous or ambivalent relationship in which they both reward and punish one another; and, as we shall see later, certain kinds of relationships, such as those of authority, are almost bound to be ambivalent. But the betting is that, in a number of pairs placed in this unbalanced situation, quite a few persons will act so as to change the relationship.

There are two possibilities. First, one of the two persons, if he fails to persuade the other to change his opinion about subject X, may break off the original exchange. The disagreement has left him frustrated and angry, especially as the original exchange led him to expect nothing but good from the other. Accordingly, by the aggression-approval proposition, he is apt to take action that will hurt the other. Let us suppose that Person is the one that feels more hurt. He can get back at Other by denying Other the reward he has been giving him in the original exchange. To be sure, this will entail denying himself reward too, but if he is angry enough, the aggression may be worth the sacrifice. The sacrifice may not even be very great if there is some third party from whom he can get the same original reward—but we have not brought in third parties yet. If Person does take this action he will make Other dislike him, and thus the unbalanced situation (3) will turn into the balanced situation (2), in which the two men both dislike one another and disagree.

Second, one of the persons may change his opinion to make it agree with that of the other. Let us suppose it is Other that does so. We assume that men are able to acquire at least a working, if not always a conscious, knowledge of the principles of behavioral psychology. In particular they are able to learn that a man one has punished is a man who may take aggressive action against one. Moreover any action allowing one to avoid the aggression is by that fact rewarded. Accordingly, Other may have learned that, by changing his opinion, he can forestall the danger that Person will break off the original exchange, a danger the reasons for which we have given in the preceding paragraph. If Other does change his expressed opinion about subject X, he may come in time, by the principle of the reduction of cognitive dissonance (Festinger, 1957), to believe sincerely that he was mistaken in his original opinion. By his action he turns the unbalanced situation (3) into the balanced situation (1), in which the two men both like one another and agree. Many treatments of "balance theory" tend simply to assume that unbalanced relationships must turn into balanced ones. In considering the two possible reactions to situation (3), we have suggested actual mechanisms by which the changes toward balance might take place.

Under what circumstances are the persons concerned apt to choose one of the two possibilities rather than the other? Again, there are two questions. First, how does the relative value of the rewards from the two different exchanges affect the persons' choice? Second, which of the two persons is the more likely to change his behavior? Let us take the questions up in order.

It should be obvious that a person who sets a higher value on getting agreement from the other than he does from the reward of the original exchange is likely to adopt the first possibility and break off the original exchange, for he is more hurt by disagreement than he is by ending the original exchange, and so is more likely to indulge his anger. By the same argument, a person for whom the original exchange outweighs in value the cost of giving up his expressed opinion is likely to adopt the second possibility and change his opinion toward agreement with the other.

As for the second question, remember that taking the first possibility will lead to decreased interaction, decreased exchange between the two men, while taking the second possibility will lead to an increase. Accordingly we may guess that the person who sets the lesser overall value on exchange with the other is more likely to adopt the first possibility; the person who sets the greater value on exchange with the other is more likely to adopt the second possibility. Note that a person who adopts the second possibility increases the other's overall reward; the latter now gets both agreement and the reward from the original exchange. Accordingly, we may suggest that the person who sets a higher value on exchange with the other than the other does on exchange with him is the one more likely to change his behavior so as to increase the reward of the other. As we shall see in the next chapter, this is the person with less power. We may also suggest that another condition under which the first possibility is likely to be adopted is that both men set a higher value on maintaining their own opinions than on keeping up the original exchange and that each sets the same value on overall exchange with the other.

Let us turn finally to situation (4), in which the two persons dislike one another but find that they agree about subject X. This situation is less apt to occur than the other unbalanced one (3) because the dislike implies that, in some original exchange, neither has rewarded the other. Accordingly, interaction between them is apt to be infrequent, and the opportunity for exchanging opinions may never arise for them at all. If it does, it creates two possibilities, analogous to the possibilities in situation (3). One of the persons may change his opinion toward disagreement with the other. He may do so in order to get back at the other for hurting him in the original exchange. As one of us might put it: "How can a man like *that* possibly hold a correct opinion? His opinion must be wrong, and so I must be mistaken in agreeing with him." If this person does change his opinion, he turns the unbalanced situation (4) into the balanced situation (2), in which the two persons both dislike and disagree with one another.

On the other hand, the fact that the two men have now rewarded one another with agreement may lead them to revise the original exchange so as to make it more rewarding to them both. The stimulus each presents to the other has become to some degree more favorable. Accordingly each may begin to direct new actions toward the other on the presumption that these will be rewarded too. And if they are indeed rewarded, the two men will have replaced an originally punishing exchange with a new rewarding one. As one of us might put it: "Since that fellow agrees with me, he cannot be all bad. I'll try him again." A change of this sort turns unbalanced situation (4) into balanced situation (1), in which the two persons both like and agree with one another.

A warning is needed here. Though there is some tendency for men, upon repeated interactions, to develop balanced relationships with one another—relationships in which one kind of exchange is consistent with and reinforces the other kinds—not all men succumb to the tendency. Some men are able to tolerate a higher degree of ambiguity in their relationships than can others. Indeed the ability to tolerate ambiguity may be the mark of a superior and civilized moral education. It is all too easy for us to assume that a person who disagrees with us on one issue is not just that, but rather a moral leper across the board. This is the tendency that allows political conflict to degenerate so often into mere savagery; although it must also be said that the tendency can mobilize energy for political action when energy is needed. It is easier to fight a man if you have persuaded yourself that he is altogether without redeeming features. Unfortunately if he knows you think him depraved beyond redemption, he is apt to respond in kind and thus mobilize his own fighting spirit too. In emphasizing the tendency toward balance, we do not mean that we always approve of it or claim that all men succumb to it or ought to do so. All we argue is that even the best of men will find something here for them to overcome.

Interaction, Liking, and Similarity

Balance theory, as we have developed it, is concerned with the mutual influence of two or more different kinds of exchange on the relationships between persons. Balanced relationships tend to persist and unbalanced relationships tend to turn into balanced ones. Accordingly, among a group of persons in contact with one another the total number of balanced relationships between pairs tends to increase over time. A change from an unbalanced relationship to a balanced one tends *either* to increase the degree to which two persons reward one another, like one another, and interact with one another *or* to decrease jointly the values of these variables. If interaction and liking either increase together or decrease together, then it follows from both processes that at any given time in any given group of men considered as a set of pairs, the frequency of interaction between any two of them varies with their degree of liking for one another (see Homans, 1950: 111). But perhaps we had better say the same thing in a cruder way: if the liking between any two men is greater than the liking between any other two chosen for comparison, then the frequency of interaction in the first pair is apt to be greater than the frequency of interaction in the second.

As a practical generalization, this proposition stands up very well for many groups of men. If you see persons interacting often, it is a good bet that you will find them ready to express liking for one another, and, on the other hand, if they express liking for one another, you will be apt to find them interacting frequently. But like all propositions that are not general propositions but only derivations from them, this proposition does not hold good in all circumstances. One important case in which it does not hold good is the one in which the two men are not, as we say, "free" to decrease interaction with one another even though they dislike one another. For example, two men may be working for the same company and required by the company to collaborate with one another, yet they know that they are rivals for promotion. Since if either one gets promoted, he by that fact denies reward to the other, each is, by the aggression-approval proposition, apt to inspire some degree of hostility in the other. In this case, their frequent required interaction is not likely to increase their liking for one another but rather the reverse. They are not "free" to cut off interaction because, as we shall assume, each is independently rewarded by employment in the company and so is unwilling to leave it, even though each hurts the other. In cases of this sort we should not expect the empirical generalization that associates interaction with liking to hold good.

We believe that the argument we have presented holds good of cases in which a new exchange has come in either to reinforce or to undermine an original one. But we must point out that we have chosen a particular kind of exchange, an exchange of opinion, as our example of the new exchange. To speak very crudely, exchanges can take two main forms: the exchange of dissimilar, or complementary, rewards and the exchange of similar ones. Our original exchange between Person and Other of advice for approval is an example of a dissimilar exchange. An exchange of opinions, when the opinions agree, is an example of a similar exchange. Both kinds of exchange play their part in social life, but they differ in one important respect which we have not yet considered. When two men are exchanging similar actions, neither is able to rank his action as somehow superior to that of the other. This need not be the case when they are exchanging dissimilar actions. How important this distinction between the two kinds of exchange may become will appear when we take up the phenomena of status.

There is one further consequence of the tendency for unbalanced relationships to change, upon repeated interactions, toward balanced ones. If balanced relationships are those in which the persons concerned either interact frequently with one another and resemble one another in some aspect of behavior such as expressed opinion or interact infrequently and differ, then it follows that for a number of persons in these circumstances, considered as a set of pairs, the more frequent is the interaction between any two of them, the more likely they are to be similar in some respect. We base this generalization not only on the tendency for the two to become more similar if interaction is maintained between them—here the interaction causes the similarity—but also on the tendency for them to reward one another and thus to increase their interaction if they are initially similar—here the similarity causes the interaction. It is a good, practical, working generalization that persons who interact frequently are apt to be similar in some respect. We believe it is likely to hold good of other kinds of similarity besides similarity of opinions—similarity of dress, manners, and speech, for example. Like the association between interaction and liking, no doubt it has its exceptions.

The Impersonal and the Personal

If a person enters into a single exchange with another person for some particular single kind of reward, and there are many persons easily accessible to him from whom he can get this reward, so that if one refuses it he can easily get it from another, we shall say that the relationship between the two persons is relatively *impersonal*. That is, the man behaves in much the same way toward any one of a large number of other men, and the same is true of their behavior toward him. His behavior is governed by the nature of the reward and not by the identity of the particular person he gets it from. But if—and this is the case we have been considering—the number of persons from whom he can get a particular reward is very limited, so that the man tends to interact repeatedly with one particular other person and, in so doing, begins to enter into more than one kind of exchange with him, then we shall say that the relationship becomes more *personal*. The man's behavior gets to be governed by his whole past history of exchanges with that person rather than by the nature of any single reward he gets from him. Indeed as highly personal relationships develop, some of the many exchanges may hurt the man rather than reward him, though no doubt the tendency toward balance will produce some degree of consistency in behavior. Then it is the total or overall value of the relationship between them that governs the man's behavior toward the other. The total value may be positive while the relationship still remains ambivalent in that it includes punishing exchanges as well as rewarding ones.

Relationships between persons obviously vary greatly along the dimension from the impersonal to the personal. The persons with whom a man is initially most likely to develop highly personal relationships are members of his family. The members of his family, even if his family is what the anthropologists call an extended one, are relatively few in number, so that the child does not face many alternative sources of reward. He encounters these sources early in life, so their behavior toward him makes a relatively large difference to his later behavior; and there is plenty of time for him to build up a variety of different kinds of exchange with his mother, father, and other members of the household. Though there is some tendency toward consistency in the exchanges, some of them, if only because they are numerous, are apt to hurt the child as well as reward him, so that his relationships may become somewhat ambiguous or ambivalent.

In primitive societies, where institutions other than those of kinship are not well developed, and where the circumstances faced by any single family much resemble those faced by any other, these kin relationships tend to build up in much the same fashion in one family after another. Then people begin to recognize that the way, for instance, one boy behaves toward his mother, father, mother's brother, and so forth, much resembles the way any other boy behaves toward his corresponding kinsmen; and that the way one father behaves toward his son much resembles the way any other father does; and so forth. Then the characteristic relationships get described and enshrined in social norms. What most persons in fact do becomes what all ought to do, and the stray individual, whose experiences and present circumstances may happen to be different from those of the rest, and who does not conform to the norms, may get punished for it. But note that unless the behavior comes naturally, so to speak, to many persons it is not likely to get embodied in a norm.

Even in modern formal bureaucracies—where in theory interaction takes place not between individuals but between occupants of positions or offices, where the interaction is supposed to be limited to official acts, to particular types of exchange, where, that is, relationships are designed to be impersonal—the personal aspects of relationships will keep breaking in. The persons who occupy the positions, however temporarily, are in fact men; and they will develop with other men with whom they interact repeatedly other kinds of exchanges besides those called for by the rules of the formal organization. This process in bureaucracies has been called the development of informal organization or the elaboration of social behavior (Homans, 1950: 108–110). Some of its results may further the efficiency and effectiveness of the organization as a whole and some may not.

We mention these things—kin relationships and the development of informal organization—not because we propose to pursue them further here, but to suggest how these subjects might fit into a fuller explanation of the characteristics of human societies than we can possibly offer in this book. Other effects of the development of personal relationships we shall consider later.

The Position of Economics

We believe that the propositions of behavioral psychology are the general explanatory propositions of all the social sciences. Accordingly, they are the general propositions of economics, so far as economics tries to account for how persons do behave rather than to advise them how they ought to behave. But even if sciences share the same general propositions, they may apply them to somewhat different given conditions. Economics is surely more advanced than the other social sciences. One reason is that its field of study is provided with built-in variables whose values can be easily measured: the quantities of largely material goods which are bought and sold, together with their prices. Another reason is that the values of men as economics considers them are largely material. It is not the fact that they are material which is crucial but rather that material values are those shared by many men. Economics can take material values as given: it does not have to account for persons holding values that are somehow queer. Since the pursuit of these values affects the behavior of many men, economics is able to make statements about the overall results of the economic behavior of large populations, their results for an economy as a whole. It can account for the gross effects, such as inflation, produced by the pursuit of these widely-held values by many individuals and firms—effects to which the actions of individuals pursuing more idiosyncratic goals are irrelevant, or in which they tend to cancel one another out.

Another difference between at least classical economics and other social sciences lies in the nature of the situation in which the behavior it seeks to explain occurs. This is often a market of some sort. In the market as it is assumed to exist in classical economics, the success of action is not problematic. A willing buyer can always find a willing seller: the only question is the price at which the transaction takes place. But from our present point of view, the most interesting characteristic of classical economics is that it limits itself to studying one kind of impersonal behavior. Under the conditions assumed to exist in a market, a large number of traders are readily available to one another, all offering much the same kind of rewards in goods or money. In these circumstances no one trader will have any reason to trade regularly with any particular other one. No doubt some persons do in fact trade regularly with others—the personal will keep breaking in—but economics can afford to disregard its effects. That is, classical economics does not concern itself with the permanent or semi-permanent relationships, the repeated exchanges, between particular individuals or groups that make up so much of the subject matter of the other social sciences, including sociology. Economics can explain many features of behavior provided that it takes certain things called institutions—the market itself, for instance—as simply given. Yet these institutions, however difficult it often is to account for all their detailed characteristics, are at least the product of the very things economics disregards—the relatively permanent relationships between individuals or between groups, which form social structures. The general propositions of our present subject are not, we believe, different from those of economics, but we use them to try to explain just those features of social behavior which classical economics takes for granted.

Summary

In the present chapter we began to apply the general propositions of behavioral psychology to explain some of the principal features of social behavior, that is, the features that emerge when each of at least two persons rewards (or punishes) the actions of the other. We introduced the device of the payoff matrix as a means of illustrating the contingencies that may occur in the social situation, using as our first example one in which the persons concerned, without previously communicating with one another, may unintentionally act so as to hurt one another. We then turned to an example of true social exchange, in which, after some communication, however brief, two persons reward one another by exchanging advice for approval. The persons concerned tend to repeat a mutually rewarding exchange and in so doing tend to add new types of exchange to the original one. The example we used of such a new type was the exchange of opinions on a given subject. We used a version of what is called "balance theory" to explain the effects of the two types of exchange upon one another. Under many circumstances, though not all, the result is that persons will either increase their interaction with, their liking for, and their similarity to one another or decrease the values of all these variables; both processes tend to produce a positive correlation between them. We ended by trying to show that economics, though undoubtedly employing some of the same general propositions as sociology, applied them to different given conditions. Unlike economics, sociology applies the propositions to explain the features of frequently repeated exchanges, relatively enduring relationships between particular persons. Such relationships are the stuff of which social structures are made.

4   Power and Authority

IN CONSIDERING OUR EXAMPLE OF SOCIAL EXCHANGE, THE EX-
change between Person and Other of advice for approval, we saw that
each party changed his behavior under the influence of the other. But
we did not consider how *much* each changed his behavior. Now we take
up the case in which there is some asymmetrical change, in which the
behavior of one of the parties changes in some sense more than the behavior of the other. In ordinary language, one person influences or controls the behavior of one or more persons. If the basis of his ability to
control the other lies within the exchange between the two, we shall
speak of his *power*. If it lies without, we shall speak of his *authority*.

Effect of the Scarcity of Reward

Let us begin by considering a new matrix, similar in all respects but
one to the matrix in Chapter 3 (Payoff Matrix 2, p. 54) which represented the payoffs of Person and Other in their exchange of advice for
approval. In accordance with the argument made there, we leave out
the payoffs for the contingencies p_1o_2 and o_1p_2, which are highly unlikely to occur (see Payoff Matrix 3).

The only difference between this matrix and the original one lies
in the payoff figures. In the original matrix we had each party to
the exchange making an equal profit from the exchange: by exchanging
advice for approval each gained one unit of value over his next best
alternative, doing his own work. In matrix 3, Person still gains one unit,
but the value to Other of doing his own work has increased compared
to what it was in matrix 2, and since $2 - 2 = 0$, he now makes no
gain at all by exchanging advice for approval with Person. That is, he
is indifferent in deciding whether to help Person or to do his own work.

To put the matter in relative terms, Other now gets less out of the

Payoff Matrix 3   The Condition of Least Interest

OTHER'S ACTIONS

PERSON'S ACTIONS	o_1 Own work	o_2 Advice
p_1 Own work	1 　　　　2	
p_2 Approval		2 　　　　2

exchange than Person does. This is the general condition that establishes interpersonal power. There are many reasons why this condition might exist. We shall emphasize only one of them here—one that is particularly important for the development of stable social structures.

In the situation represented by the original matrix, we assumed the presence of only two parties to a potential exchange, Person and Other. Let us now relax this assumption and suppose that there is another man present, whom we shall indeed call the Third Man, and that he resembles Person and not Other. That is, he is inexperienced like Person; he too needs advice; he too is ready to ask Other for advice and willing to give him approval in return. Two men are now asking for advice where only one did before.

Should Other now provide advice for both of the men, he will take more time from his own work than he did before. Accordingly, by the deprivation-satiation proposition, the value of doing his own work will increase for him. Since he will also be getting more approval than he did before, the value of further approval will decrease for him. For both reasons, the value of doing his own work will increase relative to the value of the approval he receives for giving advice. Accordingly, the new matrix, unlike the old, shows that, faced with two alternatives, it is a matter of indifference to him whether he chooses to give advice or to do his own work.

Let us turn now to the behavior of Person and the Third Man. Under the new circumstances Person, like the Third Man, is in danger of not getting any further advice. To deal with this problem, we assume that he is able to learn to offer Other a warmer grade of approval, one that Other will find more valuable, and thus, by the value proposition, render Other more likely to keep on giving advice. That is, we assume once more that men have a working knowledge of behavioral psychology and thus are able to take action that, in accordance with the propositions, is apt to get from others results rewarding to the men themselves. Payoff Matrix 4 represents the new situation, in which p_3, the warmer grade of approval, replaces the p_2 of both the earlier matrices.

Payoff Matrix 4   The Equalization of Power

OTHER'S ACTIONS

	o_1 Own work	o_2 Advice
p_1 Own work	1 2	
p_3 Warmer approval		2 3

PERSON'S ACTIONS

Let us offer one aside here, before we get down to the main issue. In our earlier discussion and in our earlier matrices, we assumed that a man could perform alternative actions and receive alternative rewards and that both the actions and the rewards were sharply different in kind. For instance, doing one's own work and giving advice are actions different in kind. We did so because we thought it made the argument simpler and clearer. But now, when we have had Person offer a warmer grade of approval, we have introduced an action that does not vary in kind but in degree from an earlier one, and there may obviously be a continuous series of such alternatives. The fundamental argument does not change in dealing with these circumstances, but continuous variations could lend themselves to the sort of treatment the economists use in similar cases—to the use, for instance, of indifference curves and marginal analysis. Yet we shall not develop this kind of treatment here. In theory it should apply, and it leads to the drawing of elegant diagrams. But it is difficult to show for a wide range of human behaviors that indifference curves correspond to anything real. No doubt they do; yet it is difficult to show that they do. Accordingly, we shall stick to a kind of analysis that, though it may be cruder than indifference curves and marginality, is closer to what might actually be demonstrated.

Let us now get back to our main concern. In response to the new situation, in which two persons want advice where only one did before, in which, therefore, advice has become a relatively scarce good, Person has changed his behavior from what it was in the original exchange: he is now giving Other a better grade of approval. And no doubt the Third Man will do the same if he expects to get any advice. But Other, for his part, has not changed at all: he is, we assume, giving Person the same old advice. In short, Other now is getting more for his advice than he did before; he is getting approval on better terms. A difference between men in their capacity to change the behavior of others and to change it in their own favor is what we mean by a difference in power. Note that Other need not have intended the change; he need not have asked Person for more approval; indeed he may have been quite unconscious of what was happening; yet he gets more approval nevertheless. We suspect that men often exert power unintentionally. But then some of us would not consider unintended power to be really power at all.

The Principle of Least Interest

Look again at Payoff Matrix 3 (page 71), which represents the situation before Person has changed his behavior. Here Other stands to make a smaller net gain from the exchange than Person does. Indeed we have set up the figures so as to show that he will get no more from the exchange than from doing his own work. But Person will gain $2 - 1 = 1$ unit of value for giving approval in return for advice. This is the general condition for establishing differences of power: the party to the exchange who gets the lesser reward from it is less likely to change his behavior in favor of the other than is the party who gets the greater. He is less dependent for reward on the other than the other is on him (see Emerson, 1962). Though we have used approval as an illustration, approval is naturally not the only reward from which the more powerful person in an exchange can increase his income. If in one set of circumstances he may increase the amount of love he gets, in another he may increase the amount of money. This rule, like most generalizations applying to human behavior, has often been recognized. It has been called "the principle of least interest": "That person is able to dictate the conditions of association whose interest in the continuation of the affair is least" (Thibaut and Kelley, 1959: 103n, quoting Waller and Hill, 1951: 191). Note that this way of putting the matter refers not just to exchanges of a single kind of reward for another kind but also to the multiple exchanges we spoke of in the last chapter: the person who has the greater power in a relationship with another person is the one who gets least out of the exchanges taken as a whole. And note, above all, that the principle of least interest follows directly from the value proposition, for the proposition implies that if one person sets a lower net value on the reward he gets than another does on the reward the other gets, then the latter is more likely to take action that gets him the reward than is the former. Since the latter is the less powerful party to an exchange, he is more likely to change his behavior to insure his getting the reward than is the former.

Yet we are still not being realistic enough. We have talked as if Other had power over Person because he set a lower value on approval than Person set on advice. This manner of putting things may seem to violate a cardinal principle of social science, a principle stating that there can be no comparison of "subjective" values. For example, one man may know very well that another person is getting the same amount of pay that he is getting himself, but he cannot tell whether that amount "means more" (that is, is subjectively more valuable) to the other than to himself. But the violation is really no violation at all. In real social behavior, no comparison of values, as such, need in fact be made. When Person responds to Other's superior power by increasing the approval he gives to Other, he has not directly compared his own subjective values with Other's. Instead he has responded to the perfectly overt—"objective," if you like—stimuli that Other has presented. Person, for instance, may be able to see that Other has had many demands made on him for advice and that he has already taken much time from his own work. And Person is highly likely to have learned that a man presenting stimuli of this sort is going to require extra inducements if he is to remain a party to an exchange. That is, what Person compares are not his values with Other's but rather the stimuli he himself presents with the stimuli Other does. In some circumstances, this fact puts a premium on the presentation of misleading stimuli. We shall turn later to this phenomenon. But even then the principle of least interest still holds: the person who is perceived by the other as the less interested, the more indifferent, to the exchange is apt to have the greater power.

The Bases of Power

The principle according to which power is actually exercised, and produces a change in the less powerful person's behavior, is the principle of least interest: one person has a greater capacity to reward another in an exchange than the other has to reward him. But the reasons why a person possesses this capacity may, according to the circumstances, be many and varied. These reasons we shall call the *bases* of power. Some are acquired by special experience or practice and make for differences in power only in special situations. Thus in our example, Other's superiority over Person in power depends on the fact that Other has acquired expert knowledge of office procedures, which Person has not yet had time to acquire and the benefit of which he badly needs. Some of the bases make for differences in power in a wide range of circumstances—such as superiority in money, physical strength, or intellectual ability. And sometimes—perhaps often—a man may acquire one kind of power base as a result of having acquired another kind earlier. If a ruler's guards will obey him for love or money, he may be able to get ordinary subjects to obey him out of fear. Power has a tendency to generalize.

Remember once more, what we emphasized in our concrete example, that a high capacity to perform a particular kind of action is not a basis for power unless other people find that action rewarding. Thus a high capacity to perform, let us say, as a concert whistler is not a basis for power, not a means, for instance, of getting money out of others, unless there are people—and they appear to be few—who enjoy listening to concert whistling. To use the language of economics, there must be some demand for the reward. Moreover, the supply of the reward must be low in relation to the demand. In our hypothetical situation, Other's power rests on the fact that he is the only man who can provide what two other men want. If there were many who could supply what Other does, he would not be able to get nearly so much approval out of Person and the Third Man. This principle applies at every level of society. It is the state's monopoly of force, through the army and the police, that gives it its power in those affairs in which force makes a difference. If, finally, the exercise of power is rewarding, and if it rests on a monopoly, then any action that helps maintain the monopoly is rewarding too.

The Tendency toward the Equalization of Power

Observe next that, after Person has changed his behavior in order to give Other more approval, the power of the two men is shown in Payoff Matrix 4 to have become equal once more, in the sense that each is again getting equal net reward out of the exchange, reward in relation to alternatives. Other's $3 - 2$ equals Person's $2 - 1$. Both men now have an equal interest in the exchange instead of Other's having less. We have deliberately set up the figures so as to show the net rewards equal, in order to indicate that in repeated exchanges between persons, provided that there is no other change in the circumstances, differences in power tend to disappear, and neither party will unilaterally change his behavior any further. Person, for instance, will not make his approval any more fulsome than it is now.

We say that differences in power *tend* to disappear, but they certainly do not always disappear in fact. Other, for instance, may not have brought to bear all the power of which he is capable. He might have been able to get even more approval out of Person if he had asked for it. And in any case the exchange may not be repeated or the surrounding conditions remain the same. Thus when Person has fully learned his job, Other will lose the power over him that came from Other's superior knowledge.

Still, there is a tendency in repeated exchanges between men for their power to equalize, so that neither will change his behavior toward the other any further. This point is very often misunderstood. It does not mean that Other will lose whatever advantages his superior power may have given him in the past. It implies, on the contrary, that the changes that have already occurred will be maintained. But neither party will be able to get any *more* out of the other. Neither will be better off if he increases the value to the other of the reward he gives him, but neither, on the other hand, will be better off if he decreases it. It is this process, more than any tendency to follow habit or custom, that maintains such stability as there is in the relations between men. That is, the condition of equal power is a condition of social equilibrium. Sociologists have often talked as if social control, the maintenance of the relationships between men, were a process external to the relationships themselves. And of course it sometimes is, as in the case in which laws have been promulgated stating what the relationships ought to be and they are enforced by outsiders such as judges and police. Of course, too, there are often in casual groups the informal equivalents of judges and police. But the great bulk of controls over social behavior are not external but built into the relationships themselves, in the sense that either party is worse off if he changes his behavior toward the other. This is what Malinowski (1959: 122–123) had in mind when he wrote down one of the most perspicacious statements ever made about society: "Law and order arise out of the very processes which they govern."

Let us not be misunderstood. We posit here no universal tendency toward equilibrium in human affairs. There is some tendency in this direction when exchanges are repeated and the circumstances surrounding them remain unchanged. But these conditions are not easily met. Human history, particularly recent human history, hardly underlines any general tendency toward social stability. Above all, we shall not employ any notion of equilibrium to explain other features of social behavior. Social equilibrium, when it exists, is something that must itself be explained.

The Definitions of Power

So far we have only considered the case of power in which the parties exchange positive rewards. We must soon turn to the case of power exercised through the threat of punishment, through coercion. We shall see that the same general rule applies to coercive power as applies to the other kind. But we shall lead up to the discussion by considering some of the definitions that have been given to the word *power*. Though few words have been more often used, few have meant so many different things. Yet the commonest definitions of *power* refer to coercive power.

One meaning given to the word *power* is illustrated by Herbert Simon's statement (1957: 5): "For the assertion '*A* has power over *B*' we can substitute the assertion that '*A*'s behavior causes *B*'s behavior.'" One difficulty with this definition is that it makes power identical with all social behavior, for social behavior is simply behavior in which the action of one man causes the action of another. And if we already have one expression, "social behavior," we do not need another whose meaning is identical with it.

The definition runs into another difficulty. If *A* can cause *B*'s behavior, *B* can also cause *A*'s. The definition makes no reference to power as an asymmetrical relationship between two persons. Yet some form of asymmetry lies at the heart of all our everyday notions of what power is. An asymmetry can be reintroduced if we agree to say, for instance, that *A* has more power than *B* if *A* can "cause" *B*'s behavior more often than *B* can cause *A*'s, or if *A* can cause the behavior of more other persons than *B* can. Even when revised in this way, this class of definition makes no reference to the psychological mechanisms through which power is exercised. After all, one man can cause another's behavior by accidentally kicking a stone under his feet so that he stumbles. This is certainly not what we intuitively mean by power. We shall call this class of definition the class of *bare causality*.

What some have called power, others have called by other names. Another common definition of power is illustrated by Barnard's definition of authority (Barnard, 1938: 163): "Authority is the character of a communication (order) in a formal organization by virtue of which it is accepted by a contributor to or 'member' of the organization as governing the action he contributes; that is, as governing or determining what he does or does not do so far as the organization is concerned." This class of definition is a little more specific than the first in that it makes a particular sort of stimulus the cause of *A*'s power over *B*. The stimulus is something called an *order,* usually a matter of words but not necessarily so; and *A* has power over *B* to the extent that *A* issues an order and *B*'s actual behavior matches it to some degree. That Barnard limits his definition to formal organizations makes little odds. He himself is wholly aware that the equivalent of obedience to orders also occurs in thoroughly informal groups.

A more interesting difficulty with this class of definitions is that much of what we recognize as power can be exercised without any stimulus remotely resembling an order. In our example, Person changed his behavior so as to make it more favorable to Other without Other's having issued an order of any kind, though no doubt he might have done so. We are far from implying that orders are unimportant. All we imply is that a definition of power limited to the nature of the stimulus is an insufficiently general one. Moreover it resembles the definitions of the first class in that it points to no psychological mechanism by which the stimulus, the order, acquires its power or why the person to whom the order is addressed obeys it. We shall call this class of definition the class of *bare causality: nature of the stimulus.*

The next class of definitions of power differs from the first two in that it begins to refer to psychological mechanisms, at least to the extent of speaking of the motivations of the persons concerned. Let us begin with Max Weber's celebrated definition of *macht*, which is usually translated as *power* (Weber, 1947: 152): "Power is the probability that one actor within a social relationship will be in a position to carry out his own will despite resistance, regardless of the basis on which this probability rests." Here the powerful man has at least a "will" and the less powerful one "resists" it, but the definition still does not let us know why the powerful man is able to carry out his own will.

Blau's definition finally begins to tell us why. His definition of *power* is the following (Blau, 1964: 117): ". . . It is the ability of persons or groups to impose their will on others despite resistance through deterrence either in the form of withholding regularly supplied rewards or in the form of punishment, inasmuch as the former as well as the latter constitute, in effect, a negative sanction." This definition finally escapes from bare causality, since it certainly suggests a psychological mechanism by which the powerful person is able to impose his will on the other. He does so by his ability to punish the other. We shall call this class of definitions the class of *coercive power.*

Coercive Power

Now that we have led ourselves up to coercive power let us examine a concrete example of it. Let us assume that a bandit has caught Person unprotected, has drawn a gun on him, and said to him, "Your money or your life!" Since anything that allows a man to avoid or escape punishment is rewarded by that fact, Person will be tempted to seek avenues of escape from his predicament other than turning his money over to the bandit. Let us assume that, with the help of his gun, the bandit has effectively closed these other avenues. We can then set up a payoff matrix to represent the situation. Each party has two alternative actions open to him: Person can either pay or not pay; the bandit can either shoot or not shoot. This situation is shown in Payoff Matrix 5.

Payoff Matrix 5   "Your Money or Your Life!"

BANDIT'S ACTIONS

	b_1 Shoot	b_2 Not shoot
p_1 Not pay	−15 / −100	−10 / +10
p_2 Pay	−5 / −100	+10 / −10

PERSON'S ACTIONS

Let us first consider the cells off the major diagonal; $b_2 p_1$ represents the contingency in which Person refuses to pay and the bandit, in spite of his threat, does not shoot, either because he is bluffing and his gun is not loaded or because he thinks better of the whole affair at the last moment and decides he does not want to have a murder on his hands. We can suggest very roughly the relative payoffs to the two men in this contingency. Person has the benefit, which we have set at +10, of still having his money. But the bandit (−10) is worse off than he was at the beginning because he has gained no money but still has gotten himself recognized as a potential criminal.

The other cell off the major diagonal, $b_1 p_2$, represents the contingency in which Person hands over his money but the bandit shoots him anyway, perhaps on the theory that dead men tell no tales. We have arbitrarily set Person's expected loss of life, which we assume is infinitely punishing to him, at −100. The bandit (−5) may also have something to lose in this contingency. Though dead men tell no tales, murderers have still been apprehended, and the bandit might now conceivably face a rap for murder as well as armed robbery.

In any event, these two contingencies, as in the original Matrix 3 representing the exchange of advice for approval, are probably ruled out by the very first step in the coercive exchange, the implied bargain expressed in the words, "Your money or your life!" Person may well believe that the bandit will not stand by the bargain, but Person might as well act as if he would, because if he refuses he will be dead anyhow. We should incidentally note here that the figures for the payoffs of the two parties in the various contingencies should each really represent not just the value to the individual of the result in question but the value multiplied, in accordance with our discussion in Chapter 2, by the individual's perception of the probability that the contingency will in fact occur. Person's assessment of the probability that the bandit will in fact carry out the bargain and spare him if he hands over his money is an obvious example. And the reason we have left blank two theoretically possible contingencies in the exchange of advice for approval is that both parties would unquestionably judge that they are extremely unlikely to occur.

There remain the two other contingencies: b_1p_1, in which Person refuses to pay and is shot, and b_2p_2, in which he turns his money over to the bandit and the latter keeps the bargain and spares him. Compared to their alternatives, the latter is the best contingency for both men, and therefore in accordance with the value proposition we assume that this is the contingency both will adopt. Person's net gain is the loss of his money minus the *avoidance* of the loss of his life, or $-10 -(-100) = 90$. In coercive exchange Person does not forgo a positive reward, as he does in the other kind of exchange, but avoids a punishment. The bandit's net gain is the value to him of Person's money minus the *avoidance* of the need to shoot Person, which, were he caught, might lead to his being tried for murder. His net gain is $10 -(-5) = 15$.

Now let us compare this example of coercive power with our earlier example of the noncoercive kind. One feature they certainly have in common, and it is a feature that defines the word *power* in general. We shall note that in the last example Person makes a net gain of 90 from the exchange, while the bandit only gains 15 points by our system of scoring. Person gains his life, while the bandit only gains some money. In short, the person who stands to gain least from the exchange is the one who has the greater power to change the other's behavior, and the principle of least interest applies to this case just as much as it does to the earlier one. It may seem paradoxical to argue that Person has the greater interest in the exchange, since after it is all over he winds up by losing his money while the bandit gains it. Yet in the immediate circumstances of the exchange itself he has more to gain and so, by the value proposition, is more apt to give in.

Moreover the bandit owes his power in this case, as Other did in the earlier exchange, to his monopoly of a scarce capacity to reward, in this case the monopoly of the power of life and death. Again, it may seem paradoxical to call the capacity to kill a capacity to reward. But if the withdrawal of a punishment is a reward, as indeed it is, and if the capacity to kill is also the capacity to spare, then the capacity to kill is also the capacity to reward.

In other respects, of course, the two cases differ sharply. For one thing, the order of events is different. In the noncoercive case, the less powerful person originates the interaction by asking for advice; the next action in the sequence is that of the more powerful person, who gives advice; the final action is that of the less powerful person, who gives approval. In the coercive case, the distribution of events in the sequence is exactly reversed. The more powerful person originates the interaction by demanding money; the less powerful one then complies; the final action is that of the more powerful person, who withdraws his threat. In general, we expect the less powerful person to originate the interaction in noncoercive exchanges, and the more powerful to do so in coercive ones. But we can easily think of exceptions—for instance, those who try to forestall the wrath of a tyrant by propitiating him in advance.

More important, the two cases differ in their effects on future behavior. Since the final result for Person after the exchange is over is punishing, he is unlikely to enter into such an exchange again if he can help it. This does not mean in the least that persons never remain continuously under the coercive control of others. We know all too many cases of tyranny. But they do so only if they cannot escape, and often the tyrant takes good care that they cannot do so. The two cases also differ in the degree of Person's satisfaction with the result. In the latter case, unlike the former, Person is thoroughly dissatisfied. Given the way we use words, it is very easy to confuse reward with satisfaction, but as we shall see in more detail in a later chapter, the two must be kept intellectually separate. Person receives a net reward from the exchange itself, even if it only amounts to getting the lesser of two evils, and so he acts to gain the reward; but, though rewarded, he is of course dissatisfied. This amounts to saying that the emotional results of the two types of exchange are different. In the latter case Person, robbed of his money, is frustrated and angry. Accordingly, by the aggression-approval proposition, Person is apt to take action in the future that will hurt the author of his frustration, if he meets him and thinks he can get away with it. There are those of us who have learned to turn the other cheek, but they are few. The need to guard against this response of the coerced, the need to guard against their anger, is one of the great costs incurred by those who do the coercing. It is especially great when the coercers plan to remain continuously in power. We doubt that our bandit will be able to rob Person more than once.

Suppose a person has tried to get another to comply with his will by threatening him with punishment if he does not comply, and the other indeed refuses to comply. Unless the man's threat is a bluff, he will then actually have to punish the other. According to our present definition, his power has failed and not succeeded. It may seem paradoxical to say so, since he has certainly demonstrated his physical ability to coerce the other. But what he has really demonstrated is only what we have called his power base. A power base does not become power unless persons respond to it by actually changing their behavior, and in the present case the other man has not changed his behavior. It is true enough that a person who tries to control others by the threat of punishment may wish from time to time actually to punish someone. Such a display of his power base renews the credibility of his threat in the eyes of the others, renders his threat a more effective stimulus to compliance. But he will wish to do so sparingly. It may cost him more to punish than to threaten effectively, if only because the emotional reaction of those coerced may be greater to actual punishment than simply to threat, and so he may have to guard himself in the future against a greater resentment. In general, the outward sign of effective control by coercion is the absence of actual punishment, not its presence.

Let us mention here a variety of coercive power of which Schelling (1960: 6) has reminded us. It does not play a large part in human affairs, but when it does play a part it leaves us feeling peculiarly helpless. In the case of the bandit, we have assumed that he would not run any extravagant risk if he carried out his threat and shot his victim. Now consider the case in which the threatener would, if he carried out his threat, inevitably and severely hurt himself. Let us suppose that a child declares to us, his parents, "If you don't let me have such-and-such, I'll jump out of the window!" and we know that jumping out of the window would hurt him badly and probably kill him. We do not think that what he asks for would be at all good for him, but since we presumably love the wretched brat, we should suffer greatly if he actually carried out the threat. True, he would suffer far more, but he does not seem to know it. Since he is immature and does not adequately imagine what breaking a limb or getting himself killed would really mean to him, he might indeed jump out of the window. We, the parents, may say to ourselves, "My God! he might actually do it!" and we give in. He has the greater power because he cares less about the threat to himself than we do. But he ought not do so, and would not do so if he were a normal adult. Since not to know what's good for you and not to act on that knowledge is, from one point of view, irrational, we speak of this variety of power as irrational power, and we find it used most often by persons who are not fully adult, such as children and neurotics. But it is a queer kind of irrationality that succeeds in getting the child what it wants. A similar kind of threat may be credible and effective if it comes from a man who is out of his senses with rage. He is so furious at his enemy that he will get his own blows in, even if the other can crush him in return.

A General Definition of Power

We may now be in a position to draw up a definition of the word *power* that embraces both the noncoercive and coercive types. In the case of coercion, the bandit has certainly exerted power as defined by

Max Weber: the bandit has a "will" and has carried it out despite the resistance of Person—Person's emotional resistance, that is, for in actual behavior he has not resisted but complied. And the bandit has certainly issued an "order." Yet in the noncoercive case, the exchange of advice for approval, Other, the more powerful person, has issued no order, nor has he made any threat. There is of course an implied threat that, if Person does not increase the amount of approval he gives to Other, Other may confine himself for a time to his own work. But Other has not made this threat and may not be conscious of it at all. It is simply inherent in the situation as perceived by Person. Nor has Other expressed any "will" to receive more approval. As we have suggested, if anyone has a will here it is not the more powerful person but the less powerful one: he badly wants advice. And who is showing resistance here? The resistance, if any, comes from the more powerful person. Yet who shall say that Other has not exerted power over Person? Who shall say that a man who offers others good pay to do his bidding, and they jump at the chance, has not exerted power over them? The trouble is that in the everyday thinking of many of us we do not consider power to be really power unless it is accompanied by orders, threats, the imposition of wills, and resistance. We believe power to be inherently evil, though sometimes necessary. Yet none of these things is essential to power as we shall define it. Indeed if we could count up all the examples of the exertion of power, we suspect that we should find the noncoercive form to be far more common than the coercive.

The one essential characteristic of power, essential to both types, is given by the principle of least interest. Accordingly, let us define power as follows:

When A's net reward—compared, that is, with his alternatives—in taking action that will reward B is less, at least as perceived by B, than B's net reward in taking action that will reward A, and B as a result changes his behavior in a way favorable to A, then A has exerted power over B.

Remember that this is *our* definition of power. Obviously others have defined it in other ways.

Fate and Behavior Control: A Digression

Let us digress here from the main argument to consider a discussion of power that, while not incorrect if read closely, may and indeed has led to misunderstanding. In their book, *The Social Psychology of Groups*

(1959: 102–103), Thibaut and Kelley present two different payoff matrices. The first looks like Payoff Matrix 6.

Payoff Matrix 6   Fate Control

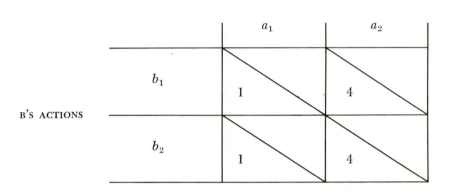

A'S ACTIONS

B'S ACTIONS

Thibaut and Kelley say that, in a situation represented by this matrix, person *A* has *fate control* over person *B*: "If, by varying his behavior, *A* can affect *B*'s outcomes *regardless of what B does, A* has *fate control* over *B*." This is strong language. What it means is this: the matrix shows that, no matter which of his alternative actions, b_1 or b_2, *B* performs, it is wholly up to *A* whether *B* gets a payoff of 1 or 4. In analyzing this assertion, note first that, though *A* "can" thus affect *B*'s outcomes, there is still no way of telling whether or not he "will" do so. To answer that question we need to know the outcomes for *A* as well as those for *B*, and the matrix does not show them. Suppose we fill in *A*'s outcome values as shown in Payoff Matrix 7.

Payoff Matrix 7   Fate Control Revised

A'S ACTIONS

Even if we admit that under these circumstances A "can" perform a_1, it is highly unlikely that he will in fact do so, and it is not what people can do but what they will do that determines their social interactions. A is in fact highly likely to perform a_2, since that gets him his best outcome; and then B is also sure of getting his best possible outcome, regardless of which of the two actions open to him he chooses to perform. Is it reasonable then to say that A has control over B?

Let us go back to the original Matrix 6, which does not include our entries for A's payoffs. The problem may simply be one of the use of words like *control*. If we give this word its ordinary meaning, we must recognize that while A "can" control B's fate, he has no control "over" B at all—that is, he has no control over B's behavior. For it is a matter of perfect indifference to B which of his alternative actions he performs. By performing either one of the two he will do equally well or equally ill. But to have control over another's behavior one must not make the other's choice of action a matter of indifference to him. By this standard A has no control over B at all.

To understand *power,* as we have used the word, it is necessary to know the payoffs for both parties, not just for one of them. From this point of view let us return to Matrix 7 with A's hypothetical payoffs included. Here A will wish B to perform b_2. Suppose he tries to threaten B by saying, "If you don't perform b_2, I shall perform a_1, causing you a loss of 3 $(4 - 1)$ from your best payoff." B is then in a position to make a counterthreat: "If you perform a_1, I shall perform b_2, causing you a loss of 5 $(6 - 1)$ from your best payoff. I can cause you greater loss than you can cause me." We suggest that, in these conditions, regardless of A's having "fate control over" B, he has, by the principle of least interest, less real power than B, and would be well advised, if he wants B to perform b_2, to find some *new action* that could provide a greater inducement for B to perform b_2 than a_2 does now. That is, A is more likely to change his behavior than B is. Our analysis of power is based on considerations like these. We are sure that Thibaut and Kelley understand them too, but they obscure the issues by using the words "control" and "control over" in situations in which the payoffs of only one of the parties are considered.

Thibaut and Kelley then speak of another kind of control, which they call *behavior control;* it is illustrated by Payoff Matrix 8. They say of this matrix: "If, by varying his behavior, A can make it desirable for B to vary his behavior too, then A has *behavior control* over B." Again the question is: A can do so, but will he? If we assume that A has no values himself, it is true that, in the situation represented by this matrix, he can, by changing his own action from a_1 to a_2, make it likely that B will change his action from b_2 to b_1. But people are not in fact without values. As before, let us assume a certain set of payoffs for A in the various contingencies and construct Payoff Matrix 9.

Payoff Matrix 8   Behavior Control

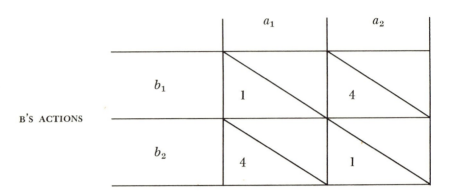

A'S ACTIONS

		a_1	a_2
	b_1	1	4
B'S ACTIONS	b_2	4	1

Payoff Matrix 9   Behavior Control Revised

A'S ACTIONS

		a_1		a_2	
	b_1	1	2	4	3
B'S ACTIONS	b_2	4	1	1	6

Once again, regardless of what A "can" do, it is highly likely that he will in fact in these circumstances perform a_2, in which case B can get his maximum payoff by performing b_1. Of course A could do still better if B performed b_2 instead of b_1. But what inducement has B to do so? Suppose again that the matter came to negotiation, and A said, "If you do not perform b_2, I shall perform a_1." B will be in a position to counter him by saying, "If you do so, I shall perform b_2 and still get my best payoff, while yours will be your lowest (1)." B is in effect still indifferent between b_1 and b_2 in the present matrix as he was in the fate control matrix (see page 84). Who has the greater power? A is supposed to have behavior control over B, but he will not use it because he himself will suffer from doing so, and suffer more than B. He will do well to continue to perform a_2, which at least gets him his second-best payoff (3). Or, if he really wants to get B to perform b_2, he must find some new action, a_3, which will reward B more than either a_1 or a_2 does now. It will, in short, be he and not B who is under pressure to change his behavior, in spite of the claim that he has behavior control over B.

Power is always a matter of negotiation, implicit or explicit. The analysis of power always begins with the examination of a situation that may be represented by a payoff matrix, and the matrix must in effect have the value of the rewards to both parties in the different contingencies filled in. If, in this matrix, there is a cell in which the payoffs are best for both parties, they are both apt to perform the actions that get these payoffs. If such a cell does not exist—if, for instance, one of the two persons is indifferent in deciding between his two best payoffs, then the party with the most interest in a particular action of the other is likely to be the first to change his behavior so as to create some new contingency more rewarding, relative to alternatives, to both parties than the old ones.

Bargaining

Since we have quite properly spoken of bargaining power, let us consider briefly the relation between what we have been discussing and economic bargaining. In the exchange between Person and Other of advice for approval, it was not apparent that what the one party gained in bargaining the other lost. In the economic bargaining situation, there is an apparent conflict of interests, if only because the things being exchanged are money, on the one hand, and something that can be measured in money, that is, in some common standard of value, on the other. After all, if you are haggling with a dealer to buy an antique, and he manages to get you to pay more for it than you originally meant to pay, he winds up with more money and you with less than you would have liked. Accordingly, such explicit bargaining may arouse hostility between the two parties and is unlikely by itself to lead to repeated interactions. Bargaining is thus relatively impersonal; it is not often a part of enduring personal relationships. The fact that some skilled bargainers, for the very purpose of improving their bargaining positions, try to create the impression of having formed personal relationships with their adversaries is only the exception that proves the rule.

Yet bargaining has analogies with the exchange between Person and Other of advice for approval. In the latter case, each party incurs costs and for each the costs may become too high for him to be willing to enter into the exchange: costs to Other in time taken from his own work, costs to Person in acknowledging his inferiority in skill. Similarly, in classical bargaining there are terms that either one party or the other is unwilling to accept because, if he did, he would make no net gain from the exchange. Between these extremes, there is an area in which both parties will make a net gain.

The question always is at what point within this area the bargain will be struck. The bargaining tends, of course, to move in a direction favorable to the more powerful person and to stop at the point where the relative power of the two becomes equal, so that neither can get the other to agree to change his behavior further. Or rather, in accordance with our earlier argument, it tends toward the point at which at least one of the parties perceives their powers to be equal. Accordingly, each party may have an interest in leading the other to believe that his power is greater than the other's, whatever it may be in reality. Since the person with the greater power is the one with the least interest in making a deal at any particular point, the basic strategy of bargaining is, and has been for ages, for each person to try to persuade the other that he is indifferent about meeting the other's terms. To speak more precisely, each party will try to present stimuli to the other to which the other, on the basis of his past experience, will respond in a certain way. The presentation of stimuli of a particular kind is itself an action that, just like other actions, may be rendered more probable if it is followed by success in getting a reward, and the more valuable the reward the higher the probability. That is, this special kind of action conforms to the propositions governing all human actions. But note that the form the stimuli take—the display of indifference—depends upon the underlying rule about power, the principle of least interest, and accordingly we shall speak of such actions—and they are not limited to bargaining—as *secondary actions*. Men would never perform them unless they had first learned more fundamental relationships.

The person who can put on the most convincing appearance of being indifferent is, strangely enough, the one who is in fact indifferent. If he is not, his ability to put on a convincing act depends on whether he is able to control the information (stimuli) that reaches the other. If the situation itself offers information independent of either party, if, for instance, it indicates that one of them is in desperate straits to strike a bargain, he has little to gain by pretending to be indifferent. For this reason a bargainer often tries to get control of information that reveals his true condition, in order to hide it from his adversary. This too is one of the reasons why explicit bargaining can hardly be a part of a personal, as distinguished from an impersonal, relationship between men. Not only is the pretense of indifference in order to gain a person's own advantage a hostile action toward the other party and thus incompatible with an enduring tie with him, but personal relationships, with their multiple exchanges, are also apt to reveal so much of his real situation that he could not keep up the pretense. If, moreover, there are many persons demanding or supplying the same kind of rewards, as in the classical market, no particular pair of bargainers can remain far apart for very long in the terms they offer: it is too easy for either party to shift to others who will offer better terms, if these terms are to be had at all. Finally, bargaining is unlikely to occur if the cost of bargaining itself, for instance, in time taken from other activities, is high relative to the value of what is bargained for. This is the reason why we do not bargain for toothpaste—the shops rule it out by the one-price system because it gets in the way of a high volume of sales—but do often bargain for cars and even more for turboelectric generators that may cost a million dollars each.

Authority

Let us now turn to the principal method other than power by which one man may be able to change the behavior of another. It too has often been called power, but since it depends on a somewhat different psychological mechanism from power as we have defined it, we prefer to call it by a different name. We might call the former *power A* and the latter *power B,* but that would be clumsy. Instead we shall continue to call the former plain *power* and quite arbitrarily call the latter *authority,* recognizing that this word, like *power* itself, has been used in a number of different ways, and our usage might easily be questioned.

How does authority, as we shall use the word, differ from power? In cases of power, one man has the capacity to change the behavior of another because he himself can take action that will alter the other's payoffs. True, he may not be able to do so directly but only because third parties will also obey his orders. Thus the emperor may have power over a subject not because he can whip the subject himself but because his guards will obey his orders to do so. Still, it is his word that makes the difference. In these cases the process of control is *internal to the exchange* between the two men. In cases of authority it is *external to the exchange.*

Let us first take a simple example. Suppose Person tells Other that if he goes to a certain place he will find that the fishing is good there. Person has given Other an order, though it is not often looked on as such: he has sent a message to Other telling him to do something. If for any reason—he enjoys good fishing and has heard of no better place to fish—Other does fish in that place and discovers that the fishing is indeed good, then by the stimulus proposition, Other becomes more likely to take Person's advice on a new occasion and even, by generalization, to take his advice on matters other than fishing. Person has thus acquired some capacity to change the behavior of Other. In this book we call his capacity authority and not power because Person has no means of providing Other's reward himself: he is quite unable to arrange personally that the fishing shall be good at the place he has suggested. Other's reward must come, if it comes at all, from the external environment, but if in fact it does come, Person has begun to acquire authority over Other, for the basis of his control is external to the exchange between the two.

In this example we have made the tacit assumption that Person himself is perfectly indifferent whether or not Other fishes at the place he suggests. In other cases Person may wish very much for Other to take a particular action; he may himself be rewarded if Other takes the action, but if he cannot personally affect Other's reward, he has, in our language, authority rather than power.

Persuasion

In introducing the notion of authority we have begun with the simple example of fishing, in which a man's reward comes from the physical environment. But naturally we are far from believing that authority depends only on rewards of this sort. In general, a person acquires what we call authority over another if, for any reason, the other acts in accordance with the person's advice, instructions, or orders—call them what you will—and finds the results of doing so in fact rewarding, under the condition that the person who gives the advice is himself unable to provide the reward, when the reward comes from some source other than the advisor.

This more general authority Parsons (1963a: 44) calls *persuasion*. He writes: "Persuasion is ego's attempt to get compliance by offering reasons why it would, from alter's own point of view, independent of situational advantages, 'be a good thing' for him to act as ego wished." Ego and alter are Parsons' equivalents of our Person and Other. Since Parsons makes it clear that he means by "situational advantages" those that ego himself can manipulate, and that persuasion is independent of them, his definition of persuasion is a definition of authority.

Yet we must always remember that, if his authority is to be established, it is not essential for Person to "wish" Other to act in any particular way or to provide arguments why it would be to Other's advantage so to act. The bare essentials are that Other should at least once and for whatever reason do as Person suggests; that he should find the result rewarding compared with some alternative, when the reward is not within Person's power to provide; and that Other's propensity to follow Person's suggestion on some new occasion be strengthened accordingly. If my taking a man's advice has led to results unpleasant for me, the chances that I shall take his advice the next time have decreased, no matter how logical in themselves are the arguments he uses. Success, not reason, is the final persuader.

Included finally among those who exercise authority is the man who has the capacity, wherever it comes from, to make the moral obligations of others govern their actions. Such is the man who says, and makes it stick, "Do this, because to do this is to fulfill your moral obligations to your party, your home, your country, your God." The capacity to activate the moral commitments of others may be rare, but when it exists, it is one of the most powerful forms of authority. But how does it fit under our definition of authority as the capacity to change the behavior of another when the control is external to the exchange between them? Let us sketch out an argument. Many men have learned to set a high value on the degree to which their acts correspond to obligations they have undertaken, the degree to which they have lived up to what has been called their self-concept (see Bandura, 1969: 32–38). Now suppose that a person follows the advice, suggestion, order of another and discovers that he has, as a result, lived up to his ideal for himself; then the likelihood that he will take the advice of the other on some new occasion has increased. The other has acquired authority over him, even if the reward is not good fishing but something far more intangible. By our definition it is still authority and not power that the other has acquired, since the other himself has not been able to provide the reward. The reward may be internal to the person but it is external to the exchange. Some of the most powerful of men have been those whose orders others have taken and as a result have felt morally worthy.

It is clear that authority, as we have now defined it, can display the various kinds of asymmetry that we attribute to power. Person may have authority over Other, but not Other over Person. Person's authority may be effective over a wider range of activities than Other's is. Or Person may have authority over a larger number of individuals than Other does. We shall return to these matters later, in Chapter 12 on leadership.

The Relations between Power and Authority

We can separate power and authority in our minds or, as we sometimes say pompously, analytically. But concretely the two are apt to go together. An authoritative person is apt also to be powerful and vice versa. Let us ask why this should be the case.

Suppose, for instance, that one man has established to another's satisfaction that his advice is apt to be good, that action in conformity with his advice will be rewarded. The man has thus begun to acquire some authority over the other. But in so doing he has begun to acquire power too, for advice that is a means to a reward is itself rewarding; and the man may then, without necessarily intending it, use the implicit threat of with-holding advice from the other as a means of getting the other to take action favorable to him. Indeed in the example of the exchange between Person and Other in the office, we assumed in effect that this stage had already been reached and that Other's advice was established as being good advice. Here Other's authority leads to his power.

The reverse may also be true: a man may not be able to acquire authority without first acquiring power. A man cannot even begin to win authority over another unless the other takes his advice at least once, for if the other never takes his advice, the other can never find that the result rewards him. The difficulty is always to get him to obey the first time, and for that purpose power over him may be necessary. If he can be induced or compelled to obey once, he may obey spontaneously thereafter.

This is in effect what happens in the case of successful military leaders. When an officer is new to a unit and bears no reputation other than his insignia of rank, he may get his men initially to obey his orders through the implication, inherent in his rank, that they ought to obey him and that he can get them punished if they do not obey. But once they have obeyed his orders and have found that obedience leads to victory over the enemy without their suffering unnnecessary casualties—once, that is, obedience has led to their gaining reward at least in comparison with possible alternatives—then the officer will have begun to acquire authority over them as well as power. If he is successful enough in this respect, they will come in time to follow him, as we say, blindly. In this case he will never have to use his power. If, on the other hand, obedience to his orders does not result in success, his official power may not be enough to save him. His soldiers will begin to challenge even that. Formal institutions are always being supported or undermined by these more elementary processes. Power, or as we call it, authority, acquired by showing others how to acquire rewards for themselves is probably the most important of all forms of power. Men would have a low capacity to get social action from others if they had to rely only on the sanctions they personally were able to control.

In summary, Talcott Parsons, in his definition of the word *power,* refers both to what we call authority and what we call power. In his inimitable prose he writes: "Power then is generalized capacity to secure the performance of binding obligations by units in a system of collective organization, when obligations are legitimized with reference to their bearing on collective goals and where in case of recalcitrance there is a presumption of enforcement by negative situational sanctions—whatever the actual agency of that enforcement" (Parsons, 1963b: 137). The reference to binding obligations and legitimation by collective goals points to the element of authority; the reference to negative sanctions points to the element of power. Remember that the collective goals may be those, for instance, of a gang of thieves, and the binding obligations may be the well-known honor among thieves.

Summary

In the example of social exchange we introduced in the preceding chapter, we assumed that the profits—the rewards less the costs—made by Person and Other, the two parties to the exchange, were equal. We began this chapter by relaxing this condition. We brought in a third person (the Third Man), who was similar to Person in being unskilled and who therefore, like him, would be rewarded by advice. Under these circumstances, Other controlled a scarce good, one which two persons now demanded but which only he could supply. We showed that this gave him less profit from, less interest in, continuing the exchange than it gave to either of the others, and that his lesser interest in turn gave him power in the sense that the others would be likely to change their behavior so as to make it more rewarding to him. The rule that the person with the least interest is the person with the greatest power is very general and applies to coercive exchanges as well as noncoercive ones.

We then made a distinction between power and authority. In the former, control is internal to the exchange, in that the powerful person himself controls the outcomes of the other party or parties. In the latter, control is external to the exchange, in that the person in authority cannot himself control the outcomes of the other. But if the other, for any reason, does in fact follow the advice, suggestions, or orders of the person in authority and finds as a result that his action is rewarded by the external environment (physical or social), or even by his living up to his obligations and ideals, he is likely, by the stimulus proposition, to follow the advice, etc. coming from this person on later occasions. The capacity thus acquired to give advice, suggestions, or orders that others will obey is what we mean by authority.

We ended by showing why, though we can separate power and authority analytically, the two tend to be associated in the behavior of concrete persons.

5 Cooperation, Conformity, Competition

WE HAVE TRIED TO APPLY THE GENERAL PROPOSITIONS TO THE explanation of increasingly complex social behavior. We first applied them to exchange between two persons, each offering only one kind of reward to the other and each making the same profit from the exchange. We then considered the effect on the original exchange of new exchanges, which the persons concerned were apt to enter upon if they repeated their original exchange. That is, we considered what consequences were apt to follow when a relationship became less impersonal. We next took up the condition in which one of the parties received at first a greater net reward from the exchange than the other did and therefore had less power than the other. To account for this inequality we had to bring in a third person and, with him, the notion of a scarce good, one for which the demand was high relative to the supply. Finally we extended the notion of power to apply to the threat of punishment as well as to the promise of reward, and we tried to differentiate authority from power. We shall now use these ideas to explain various features of interaction among a number of persons larger than the three we have brought in so far. These persons we shall call a *group*.

Groups

There is no need to strain for great precision in defining the word *group*. Let us say that a group consists of a number of individuals, its *members,* each of whom during a given period of time interacts with some of the other members more often than he does with other individuals, who by this definition are considered outsiders. Or at least he is able to interact in such a way, whether he does so in fact or not.

Let us comment briefly on this definition. We bring in the "given period of time" in order to include such groups as a department in a factory, whose members are together only eight hours a day. Of course, there are other groups, such as a hunting band, whose members are together almost continually. The reason for the relatively high frequency of interaction between members may be that they are isolated from other groups by physical barriers or by the nature of a task they share with one another but not with outsiders. Yet though the members of many groups have been assigned tasks in common or have set tasks for themselves, we do not require that in order to constitute a group they must have a common task. For some groups, indeed, it is not easy to say what the common task *is*. What is the common task of a group of friends who dine together from time to time? For that matter, what is the common task of a band of hunters? Perhaps just to keep one another alive, or at least to keep some of their number alive. Again, we make no distinction for our purposes between formal groups, constituted by the action of some larger organization, such as a business corporation, and informal ones, such as a number of young men who hang out together on the same street corner. Nor do we assume that a group must always have a leader or leaders, though we shall have much to say about leadership later. We do not even require that the members recognize they form a group, though surely they almost always do, or that they are called by others, or call themselves, by a special name. The only essential criterion is the interaction of members with one another.

The definition is relative to what unit we are interested in. That is, a group may be part of a larger group, which itself satisfies the definition of being a group. If we are concerned with the characteristics of the larger group, we shall speak of it as *the* group *par excellence* and of the smaller groups as subgroups within it. Thus a group of workers placed in the same part of a room and specializing in a particular job may, if they interact often with one another, as they are apt to do, constitute a subgroup within a factory department, which is itself a group. But if we are specially interested in what would otherwise be called a subgroup, we shall speak of it as *the* group in question. For this reason we shall not try to set any definite upper limit to the number of members beyond which a group would cease to be a group but become a social unit of some other kind, though it is obvious that, the larger a group becomes, the more difficult it is for each member to be able to interact with every other. Nor, of course, do we assume that a particular person must belong to one and only one group at any particular time. Thus during his eight-hour day in a factory, a foreman may be a member of his own department and also of a group of foremen from his own and other departments. Groups may, or may not, have interlocking memberships.

Above all let us make it quite clear that social behavior need not occur only in groups. A woman who goes shopping from one store to another is not behaving as a member of a group, though assuredly her behavior toward the salespersons in each store conform to the laws of social behavior. Yet to deny that all social behavior is group behavior is not to deny the importance of groups in human affairs. For hundreds of thousands of years, the largest human societies were probably bands of hunters and gatherers, each band numbering no more than a few dozen members. Our genetic characteristics themselves may have been acquired in groups like these.

Norms in Exchange within a Pair

In order to understand behavior in groups, we must now bring in the notion of a *norm*. To do so, let us first go back to the original exchange between Person and Other. Suppose that as a result of repeated exchanges Person has come to expect to get advice regularly from Other, and then suddenly, if only for the time being, Other refuses to provide it. By the aggression-approval proposition, Person may react with some degree of aggression against Other. He may perhaps refuse to enter into further exchanges, thus denying approval to Other. Person's anger, by making his threat credible, may increase his power, even though by carrying out his threat he would be cutting off his nose to spite his face. So far as Other values future exchanges with Person, he will be rewarded if he can avoid giving him occasion for anger. And Person himself will be rewarded if he can forestall Other's temporary refusal of advice before it occurs.

To avoid Person's anger, Other must know what Person expects, but how can he know? In time he may learn by painful experience what makes Person aggressive, but there is naturally a quicker and cheaper way. Whatever else men may be, they are at least great talkers. When Other presents stimuli suggestive that some other activity than continuing to give advice might begin to give him greater reward, Person may learn to say: "You've always done this for me; you can't stop now!" or "It isn't fair not to help me!" or "I've done a lot for you, you ought to do this for me." When Person or Other uses words like *ought* or the equivalent, it is a sign that he is stating what social scientists have come to call a *norm*. A norm is a statement specifying how a person is, or persons of a particular sort are, expected to behave in given circumstances—expected, in the first instance, by the person that utters the norm. What I expect of you is what you ought to do.

When Person states what he expects of Other, he is presenting a stimulus or signal to the latter. The presentation of a stimulus, including the statement of a norm, is itself an action; and the propositions of behavioral psychology apply just as much to this sort of action as they do to others. It is highly likely that Person has in the past taken the action of stating a norm. Indeed it is apt to have been one of the earliest things he did after he learned to use language at all. If the action was rewarded with success, he is apt to repeat the action on a new occasion, such as the present one. If, moreover, the action was successful, it will tend to generalize, and the probability that Person will not just state a single kind of norm but a wide variety of them is apt to increase. A generalized way of behaving is apt to be maintained in some strength, just because it is generalized, just because it is performed on many occasions, so that the chances of its being successful on at least a few of them are good. If on the present occasion Person does state that Other ought to give him advice, and Other complies, Person is rewarded in two ways: he gets the advice and he avoids the very real costs of his own possible aggression. In short, men state norms, as they perform other actions, because the results are often rewarding.

Now let us turn back to Other. When Person states what he expects of Other, he is, as we have said, presenting a stimulus to Other. Other in the past is highly likely to have acted on the occasion of this kind of stimulus. As soon, indeed, as he began to understand language, norms are apt to have been among the first things he heard from his mother and father. And if for Other in the past the statement of a norm by somebody else has been the occasion on which his own action in conformity to the norm has been rewarded, perhaps by a hug, or his disregard for it has been punished, then by the stimulus proposition, he has some tendency to conform to what he recognizes as a norm on the present occasion. If the rewards for some alternative action are great enough, he may still disregard the norm, but at least he will not do so by sheer inadvertence. Person has put him on notice. He knows that if he fails to comply, he will have to reckon with Person's anger. He will, as we say, have to think twice before he acts. This sort of result of the statement of a norm—and it may be the result of any kind of norm—is often as great an advantage to him as it is to Person. Let us now elaborate somewhat our definition of a norm: a *norm* is a statement specifying how one or more persons are expected to behave in given circumstances, when reward may be expected to follow conformity to the norm and punishment, deviance from it.

But we must be careful not to imply that the avoidance of a particular person's hostility is the only reason why a man might conform to the norm the other has enunciated. Generalized values may be acquired through being paired with the acquisition of more specific ones, and if in a man's past experience, perhaps in his family, his performance of actions called fair or right has been followed by specific rewards, then being fair or doing his duty may come in time to be, as we say, rewarding to him in itself. Then he may, especially if appealed to, be ready to incur some extra cost in order to do justice and right for their own sakes, without consciously reckoning whether they would bring him any further gain.

Group Norms and Collective Goods

In direct interaction between man and man, especially when it occurs often, each may be able to learn what the other expects by trial and error and without either one's saying a word. Then they do not need a norm to help them avoid punishing one another. But when one or more men would find it rewarding that not only their own behavior but that of a large number of others, such as the members of a group, should conform to a norm, and when their expectations, if only by reason of the large number of others, cannot easily be discovered by trial and error, then some members may find the explicit statement of a norm even more rewarding than it is in exchange between two persons and so become even more apt to make such statements. This is especially apt to be the case when the behavior to be governed by the norm is not directed by the members to one another but to outsiders. For these reasons we postponed consideration of norms until we were ready to deal with behavior in a group.

There are at least two kinds of norms, differing in their origins and therefore differing also in the problems of their enforcement. The first kind takes its origin from the fact that most members of a group tend under certain circumstances to behave in a particular way "naturally." They will behave that way without being told to do so and without any threat that they will be punished if they do not. Sooner or later the members recognize what many of them are actually doing, state their observations in the form of a generalization, and go on to state that this is what all of them ought to do. What is, is always becoming what ought to be. Such a norm is the rule of *noblesse oblige*. For reasons we shall go into later, many persons of high status will naturally behave "better" than those of lower status, even in respects other than those which originally won them their status. The fact that many will behave in this way naturally gives rise to the statement that all ought to do so; that is, it gives rise to the norm. (The celebrated incest taboo, the rule against sexual intercourse between the members of a nuclear family other than between the father and mother, will, we believe, turn out eventually to be a norm of this sort. Most persons will naturally obey the incest taboo, which then becomes a norm which many will feel that all ought to obey and violations of which will fill them with horror. But we shall not pursue this highly controversial question further here.)

Once norms of this sort are stated, they have a back effect on behavior —they produce further changes in, react upon, behavior. Most persons to whom they apply will obey them naturally, and therefore the problem of enforcing them is not as difficult as it is for norms of the other sort. But the past history and present circumstances of individuals produce so much variation in their behavior that not all will obey naturally. The statement of the norm, with its implication that violators will be punished, may make these others a little more likely to comply. For those who comply naturally with such norms will resent those who do not, if only because they are "different," and try to coerce them into compliance. And the existence of the norm may make potential violators feel a little more guilty. Yet no norm, not even the incest taboo, is obeyed by all. Once we have drawn attention to their existence we shall say no more in this chapter about norms of this sort.

A norm of the second class also calls upon all persons in certain circumstances to behave in a certain way. It differs from a norm of the first class in that there is no reason to believe that many of these persons will behave in that way naturally, before the norm has been stated. The evidence for this is that many of them do in fact behave contrary to the norm until others tell them how they ought to behave. Let us turn at once to an example of such a norm. It is common in many groups of factory workers paid by the piece, paid piecework wages, for some members to say that no member ought to turn out more—or much less—than a certain number of pieces per unit of time, the hour or the day. There are all sorts of variants in such a norm, which we need not describe here. Management often calls the practice "restriction of output," though the number of pieces the workers produce may not be much less than the number they could produce if working at top speed. The reason for restriction workers most often put forward is that, if they produce much more than the informal norm, the management will "cut the rate," that is: decrease the price paid per piece, so that the workers will wind up doing more work than they did before but for about the same amount of take-home pay. Let us not worry here whether this reason is valid. Today rate cutting is ruled out by the provisions of many contracts between companies and unions. But it certainly did occur in the past, and it is enough for us that many workers believe that it may still occur.

The action called for by this norm incurs obvious costs for the man who carries it out: he gives up, at least for the short run, the piecework wages he could gain by working as fast as he was able to work and exceeding the norm. The alleged reward for the action is that it avoids rate cutting on the part of management, but this is a result that becomes rewarding only in the long run. Note that if management does not cut the rate, even if it does so for reasons that have nothing whatever to do with restriction, some members of the group have still been rewarded for their restriction and so they will continue to restrict. To this extent we may call their behavior superstitious. Restriction of output is not the only human activity that is maintained in this way.

Yet restriction has much more important features than these. Here the actions of the members of the group, unlike the exchanges between Person and Other, are not aimed directly at other members but at out-

siders. Their actions—or nonactions, if you will—are aimed at management, so that they reward other members only indirectly. Moreover the
members must collaborate in their action if any single member is to be
rewarded: the larger the number of members that fail to restrict, the
less effective is the group in avoiding rate cutting. By restricting production they are collaborating just as surely as they would be if they combined their strengths to move an object no one of them could move
singly. What the norm does in cases like this is state the conditions under
which members of a group can achieve a collective goal, a collective reward or, as it has also been called, a collective good, whether real or
imagined.

In order not to complicate further an analysis that in any event will
become complicated enough, we shall confine ourselves in this book for
the most part to collaboration or cooperation that has the characteristics
of restriction of output. These are, first, that each member contributes,
if the norm is obeyed, what is essentially the same kind of behavior. We
shall not consider the division of labor, in which members contribute
different kinds of behavior to the attainment of a collective good, except
in the case of that most important kind of specialization, the emergence
of leadership. Second, the good achieved is collective in the special sense
that it cannot be divided among the members. Whereas a contractor can
divide among his workers in the form of wages part of the sums he will
receive for the construction of a house, no one can thus divide among
the members of an industrial group the rewards, if they are rewards, of
restriction of output. Each member must take what comfort he can from
the fact, if it is a fact, that management has not cut the rates. A better
way of putting the matter is that, once the result is achieved, no member
can be denied the reward it brings. Norms that state what each member of a group shall do in order to attain a collective good present, as
we shall see, special problems of enforcement. That is what makes them
interesting.

Types of Conformers and Nonconformers

We now turn to a question that has much exercised social scientists:
Who conforms to the norms of a group or deviates from them, and why?

Before we begin we had better enter a disclaimer. We should not be
required to do so, but conformity is so emotional an issue for some persons that, if we do not, they will misunderstand what we say. Though
they may still misunderstand after they have read it, at least that shall
happen through no fault of ours. We do not take any moral stand about
conformity here, one way or the other. The members of a group may say
that all of them ought to conform to its norms, but we do not say so.

Nor do we say that they ought not to conform. In point of fact, we observe that many persons who make a virtue of not conforming to one set of norms are among the most faithful adherents to another. Indeed it is difficult to understand how a man can take part in social life without conforming to something. But for our present purposes, that is neither here nor there. Nor do we assume that the norms we are interested in must be accepted throughout a society, so that we should be justified in holding a deviate in contempt because he is not a good citizen. We are just as much interested in conformity to norms held by small groups made up of persons who are themselves deviates within the larger society: there may be, after all, honor among thieves. In short we are interested in studying behavior and not in making moral judgments. If in fact a norm has been asserted by some members of any group, whether or not it is a "good" norm or a universal norm, we are interested only in why some members conform to it and others fail to do so.

In the attempt to answer the question let us take a group at some initial point of time, when one or more members have just claimed that all members ought to behave in a particular way. We shall use our earlier example of a factory group, some of whose members have told the rest that nobody should turn out more than a certain number of units of production in the course of a working day. Then let us follow over time the response to the norm by five different categories of members, all of which we assume to be represented in the group at the beginning. These categories are: (1) those who find the results of conformity rewarding and conform from the beginning, (2) those who find the results of conformity rewarding, but do not themselves conform from the beginning, though they come to do so later, (3) those who do not find the results of conformity rewarding but come to conform later, (4) those who do not find the results of conformity rewarding, never conform, but do not leave the group, and (5) those who never conform and do leave the group. Each of these categories except (4) contribute to the growth of conformity in the group, even (5), for nonconformers who leave the group increase the percentage of conformers among the remainder. Let us take up each of these categories in turn.

Category (1) is the easiest to deal with. In our example these are the members who believe, as a precipitate of their past experience, immediate or vicarious, that unrestricted production at piecework wages will result in a cut in rates; who fear this result; who believe that conformity to an output norm will be successful in avoiding it; who therefore conform themselves and call on the rest to conform too. Let us call them the *true believers*. Since they have learned to find the same kind of behavior rewarding, they are apt to have undergone experiences in the past that have been in some respects similar—that is, they are apt to be similar in background. In general, the more similar in background are the members of a group, the more likely they are to be able to agree upon a group norm and to enforce it. We shall not explain further the behavior of the true believers but turn to the effects of their behavior on the behavior of other members, who do not conform from the beginning but come to do so later.

Category (2) is in some ways the most interesting of all, but it is often overlooked in studies of conformity. It is made up of persons who believe almost everything that the true believers do. Until we think about it, it might seem strange that a person who believes that conformity to a norm will bring about results rewarding to him should nevertheless fail to conform to it, but we all know such persons. These are the persons who believe—that is, they may confess they think so when pressed on the question —that there are enough true believers to gain the collective good without their help, and that, once it is gained, they cannot be denied their share of it. Accordingly they are free to pursue some action other than conformity that may bring them reward, including, in our example, fairly high production and therefore high earnings. These are the persons who believe in the same action that George believes in, but who let George do it. They propose to eat their cake and have it too. Let us call them the *freeloaders.*

In his theoretical analysis of this kind of situation, Olson (1965: 33–35) asserts that, because of the possibility of freeloading, the members of a group will not jointly put out optimal action to obtain a collective good, when the only reward they get for the action is the collective good itself, unless "there are members who would be better off if the collective good were provided, even if they had to pay the whole cost of providing it themselves." Olson argues that this condition is unlikely to obtain except in very small groups, and that in larger groups, if adequate action, which means in our example, sufficient conformity, is to be secured, the collective good must be supplemented by noncollective goods—that is, rewards or threats of punishment for particular members. Indeed Olson points to a tendency toward "the exploitation of the great by the small," so far as collective goods are concerned. That is, those that do most to obtain a collective good for the group do not get, out of that collective good itself, a reward proportionately greater than that gotten by those that do least. So far as this kind of reward is concerned, they are, according to our earlier analysis, in a position of lesser power. But let us not get sorry for them too soon: their extra costs may be made up to them in other, noncollective kinds of reward, particularly in status.

Pressures to Conform

Let us now examine how, in many groups, individual rewards appear just, as Olson would say, when they are needed to supplement the collective good, and bring some members to conform who would not otherwise have done so. Not only do they induce some of the freeloaders to conform but also some of members of category (3), whom we call the *skeptical conformers*. In our example, these are the members who, unlike the true believers and the freeloaders, believe either that management would not cut the rate under any circumstances or that, if management were prepared to cut the rate, restriction would not be an effective way of preventing it, but who nevertheless end up by conforming to the group norm.

Suppose the freeloaders and the skeptics did not conform. They would then threaten to deny to the true believers a result the latter value. Indeed the true believers may feel that a single person who surpasses the norm and thus reveals to management how much the workers could produce if they tried does as much damage to their cause as many such persons. Accordingly, the nonconformers may, by the aggression-approval proposition, expect to be attacked in some way by the true believers, and attacked the more fiercely, the higher the value set by the true believers on the results of conformity. At its worst, the attack may take the form of physical violence. Short of that, the true believers may withdraw from the others the social rewards that are already being exchanged in the group. They may send them to Coventry, refuse to interact with them at all. If the freeloaders and skeptics conform, they avoid this result, and avoiding it is a reward. They may even gain a temporary bonus in social approval, on the theory that there is more joy in groups, as in heaven, over one sinner that repenteth than over ninety and nine just persons who need no repentance. Note that the avoidance of social isolation and the gaining of approval are individual and not collective goods. They produce more conformity in groups than one would expect if collective goods were the only rewards members could obtain.

It follows that a member is more likely to conform, the more valuable to him are the rewards he receives from other conforming members, relative to those he receives from alternative actions. The rewards of social interaction may be of various kinds. If one purpose of the group is discussion, the reward may be the interest of the subjects under discussion. It may be the exchange of help with other members. It may be casual "social" interaction: small talk, stories, gossip, jokes. It may be the liking that accompanies successful social exchanges of any kind. Whatever it is, the higher the value members set on rewards, other than the collective good itself, that are obtainable within the group, the more likely they are to conform to the norms for obtaining the collective good, since they have the more to lose by not conforming. We are now talking about the rewards a member receives from other conforming members in general, not the specially valuable rewards he may receive from a particular member, which give the latter power. But of course the threatened loss of these special rewards may be a further reason for conforming.

In the above argument we are not really saying anything new. Indeed the price paid for generality is disillusion: the charm of novelty fades as both the new and the old are subsumed under a few universal principles. As Malinowski (1959: 71) wrote: "Systematic study takes up the miraculous only to transform it into the natural." All that we have done is extend to the diffuse exchanges within a group what we have already said about "balance" in the last chapter. There we showed that, if an initial exchange between two persons were rewarding enough, they would tend to become more similar to one another in a second exchange. Now we have shown that, if multiple individual exchanges among the members of a group are rewarding enough, that fact may increase the similarity among members in the sense that more of them conform to a group norm than we should have expected if the direct reward of conforming, that is, the attainment of a collective good, were the only one at work. Some at least of the freeloaders and the skeptics will join the true believers in conforming, provided that the latter form, so to speak, a critical mass—that they are large enough in number so as to be able seriously to deny individual social rewards to persons in the other two categories. We have also supported Olson's argument that, in order to ensure the effective collaboration of members of a group in attaining a collective reward, the collective reward itself will not be a sufficient inducement and must be supplemented by individual rewards. More generally, enduring structures of relationships among men depend on multiple and not just single types of exchange among them.

Now let us go back one step further. The probability that a man will perform a given action depends not only on the value to him of its result but also on his past history of success in getting that result. Before the threat of losing the individual rewards of social interaction can be effective in increasing the number of conformers, members must have learned by experience that they have something to lose. This they learn by repeated successes in getting rewards from other members, and this process takes time. Accordingly, we should not in general expect a newly formed group to be able to exert as much control over its members as one that has been in being for some time. A wise military leader, who wishes the interpersonal relations established in his unit to support its collective morale in battle, knows that he had better keep its members (aside from proven misfits) together, keep the turnover of personnel as low as possible. Such is the way of the world: it gets us hooked on our social relationships and then keeps us in line by the threat of losing them.

By the same argument, the less fully a person has entered into exchanges with other members, the less he has to lose from any breakup of these exchanges, and therefore the less likely he is to become a conformer if he was not one from the beginning. Any one of a number of reasons may have prevented such a man from entering fully into social exchange with others in the group. He may be placed in an isolated physical position, making social interaction more difficult for him than for the others. What we call his background may be different from theirs, and we have already seen that dissimilarity can be a great initial barrier between persons. Anything that inhibits a person's full membership in a group, that puts him in a group but not of it, tends to decrease its hold over him. We shall postpone to a later chapter consideration of what effects differences in status have on conformity.

The Power of the Group

Let us assume that, by the processes described, more and more of the freeloaders and the skeptics come to join the true believers in conforming. As they do so they may become true believers themselves. In our example they may come in time to say and sincerely believe that rate cutting is a real danger, that restriction of output is an effective way of preventing it, and that all members, including themselves, really ought to restrict. By the process called the reduction of cognitive dissonance (Festinger, 1957), people are unlikely to go on indefinitely expressing opinions with which their actions are at variance. Get them once to act as conformers, and their attitudes will fall into line.

More important, they will tend to join the true believers in their behavior toward the nonconformers who are still holding out, and of these there will be fewer and fewer. But if an increasing number of members of a group are prepared to act in the same way towards a deviate, denying him liking and social interaction, it is as if they were acting as one man and as, moreover, a man who monopolized an increasingly scarce good. In the last chapter, we saw that control of a scarce good, scarce in relation to demand, gave a man potential power over others. For the same reason the members of a group, if they will act in unison, have increasing power over a deviate, a nonconformer. So far as a deviate sets any value on liking and social interaction, then the larger the number of other members who would deny him these, the scarcer and hence, by the deprivation-satiation proposition, the more valuable these rewards become for him, the more he has to lose by continued nonconformity, and the more likely he is to conform. The larger, therefore, is the initial nucleus of true believers, and the larger is the number of freeloaders and skeptics they have converted to their views, the larger will be the total number of members who act in unison toward deviates, and therefore the greater will be the likelihood that at least a few further members will conform too.

Much depends, then, on the degree to which the conformers monopolize social rewards and thus are able to deny them to deviates. If there is even one other member who will also hold out against the group, and

thus provide for a deviate an alternative source of social reward, including support for his opinions, the evidence suggests that the deviate is apt
to remain one. He becomes what we shall call a *holdout*. Though it be
misery to be a deviate, companionship in misery helps preserve deviance.
Again, some persons persist in violating the norms of a group even at
the risk of being forced out of the group altogether. They are more likely
to persist if there is some other group to which they can escape and in
which they can find rewards similar to those their original group would
deny them. Let us call these persons the *escapees*. In this case the group
has lost, so far as these persons are concerned, its monopoly of social
reward and hence its power to control their behavior. If there is no such
alternative group, the power of the original group is enhanced. Groups
from which their members cannot easily escape, such as some primitive
tribes and small outcast groups in larger societies, are notable for the
degree of control they are able to exert over their members.

The Holdouts

In any group there may well be a few members who persist in not
conforming in spite of all the pressures that the others are able to bring
to bear on them. What can we say about such persons beyond what we
have suggested already—that for one reason or another they have not
entered fully into exchanges with the rest, that they have found companions in their deviance, or that there are outside groups they can
escape to if the pressures put on them become intolerable?

The little we can say could not be more obvious. They value results
which can only be obtained by actions incompatible with conformity to
the norms of the group, and they value these results highly. If a number
of members deviate from the norms of a group in the same way, they
must hold similar values. Since many values are learned, they are likely
to have gone through similar learning experiences, which means in turn
that they are apt to have similar backgrounds. At any rate, nothing is
better established as an empirical rule than that persons who deviate in
similar ways are apt to be similar in their backgrounds.

Thus to return to our example, it has been found in the United
States that persons who violate the output norm of a factory group, the
so-called "rate busters," are especially likely to have one or more of the
following background characteristics: to come from farms, to be brought
up as Protestants, and to have ancestors that came from one of the na-
tions of northwestern Europe (see especially Dalton, 1948). To some extent the characteristics overlap one another. One explanation offered
for this correlation is that persons with this background are apt to have
learned the set of values Max Weber (1930) called the Protestant Ethic

and therefore to place, compared with other workers, a relatively high value on individual hard work, provided it fetches them good material rewards. Such a value would make for action incompatible with conforming to a norm of restriction of output. A person who values individual hard work would get a greater reward from what he gained by not conforming—high piecework wages—and incur a lesser cost from what he lost—social interaction with others—than would a person of different background.

Similar background, then, is often the cause of similar deviation. But what is cause can become effect. Persons who were not similar in behavior to begin with are apt to become so if they persist in their deviation. Their rejection by the rest makes them more dependent on one another for social reward. Accordingly, for fear of losing this reward, some of them will tend to change their behavior, for instance, a few of their expressed opinions, so as to make it more similar to that of the other deviates and therefore more acceptable to them. This is again a direct application of the theory of balance to the problem of conformity and deviance in a group.

As the deviate persists in his deviance, the conformers will try to bring him into line by punishing him more severely. They will be the more apt to do so, the higher the value they set on his conforming. But increasing punishment may boomerang. Any punishment is apt to arouse some anger in a man, and increasing his punishment may arouse disproportionate anger in the deviate, especially when he sees it as more and more out of line with his crime. We shall have more to say later about justice in the distribution of rewards and punishments. All we can do here is recognize that what men feel to be justice or injustice makes a difference to their conformity or deviance. In his anger against unfair punishment a nonconformer may come to deviate from the norm of the group even more than he did at first; for frustration breeds aggression against its source, in this case the conformers; and what better means has the deviate of attacking them than his denying them the very thing they are showing more and more that they want most—his conformity? Accordingly beyond a certain point increased punishment may produce more deviance rather than less. To put the matter another way, punishment that has failed to get a man to conform must become not just a little more severe but immensely more severe to be effective. The conformers may be unwilling to pay the price of greatly increased severity, and then they will not continue the punishment, for punishment that fails, like any action that fails, will sooner or later be abandoned. They may leave the deviate severely alone, but they will cease to punish him more actively than that. If a group has done its worst to a member, and the worst has failed, it has effectively lost control over him. It has nothing more to take away from him, and so he has nothing more to lose by not conforming. The cost of his not conforming has vanished.

The deviate may be likened to a marble rolling in a bowl. As he deviates more and more he rolls up toward the edge of the bowl, and the forces pulling him back towards the bottom and middle grow stronger and stronger. But once these forces are overcome, and the marble reaches the edge, everything then conspires to get it out of the bowl altogether and quickly.

A Summary Quotation

At the end of this long discussion of conformity, let us sum up, not in our own words but with a wise quotation: "The greater and more valued the reward, the oftener it is achieved through conformity behavior, the more conformist the behavior is likely to become, and the more likely it is to become a generalized way of behaving in new situations. The person need not be aware of these effects" (Walker and Heyns, 1964: 98). This statement rightly treats conformity as a type of action, an activity, which is subject to the laws that govern all action. The remark about the effect of the value of the reward refers to what we have called the value proposition. The remark about the effect of "the oftener it is achieved" refers to the success proposition. The statement also applies to conformity the tendency of all successful actions to generalize. Is conformity so simple a matter that it can be summed up in a statement as short as this? The problem of conformity is not a simple one but its complexity does not reside in the general propositions that are needed to deal with it. It resides rather in the circumstances to which the propositions must be applied. These circumstances include not only the rewards and the successes of an individual conformer or nonconformer but also the rewards and the successes, and hence the behavior of other members of the group and indeed of outsiders, for these determine in part the behavior of the conformer or nonconformer himself.

Differentiation in the Group

Let us now consider what our arguments both in this chapter and in the last imply about the structures toward which groups tend at equilibrium, remembering that no structure remains stable forever. They imply, we believe, first, that most groups will contain a relatively small number of members who are individually powerful, though not necessarily equally so, and who therefore take part in much interaction and are held in high esteem. We measure a man's *esteem* by the number of other members of his group who accord him approval or respect. In the last chapter we considered power as distributed among only three persons, of whom only one was powerful. If we extend the argument to natural groups larger than our artificially small one, we should expect that several members might emerge as powerful, but that their number would still be small in relation to the total membership. To be powerful a man must have the capacity to provide for others rewards that have high value because the supply of them is small in relation to demand. He must have not only the capacity but also the willingness to supply such rewards. When other members see what one of their number can get in return for supplying them, some of these others, if they have the capacity, may become willing too. As an economist would say, they may be drawn into the market for power and esteem. But we should still not expect the men of individual power to be large in number, for if many persons could and would provide for others the rewards in question, these rewards would not be scarce, and the members who supplied them would therefore not be powerful.

Our arguments imply next that there will be a larger number, perhaps a much larger number, of members who may collectively be powerful if they will all act in unison, but who are not individually powerful since they cannot singly provide scarce rewards. This does not mean that they cannot provide any rewards at all but only that they cannot provide scarce ones. And they certainly do not actively hurt the others by failing to conform to the norms of the group. There may not be much to be said in their favor but there is certainly nothing against them. Naturally there will still be differences in behavior between them, though perhaps minor ones. For convenience in presenting the argument, we have assumed so far that people either live up to a norm or fail to do so. But in most real groups members may conform to a norm more or less well while still not altogether setting it at naught, and so we should count on finding differences in this respect even among members who are at bottom conformers. There may also be several group norms and not just a single one, so that members may differ in the number of norms to which they conform. Still, in a first approximate account of group structure, we may not go far wrong if we lump the ordinary conformers together in a single class and assert that there is apt to be a large number of them.

The first two tendencies we have described would together produce a pyramidal structure, with a few specially able and willing men at the top and a much larger number of ordinary good fellows below them. Some groups may display such a structure but certainly not all do. Our arguments imply, finally, that a group is apt to contain a small number of deviates, persons who resemble the ordinary conformers of the middle class in possessing no rare capacity to reward but who differ from them in actively violating one or more of the norms of the group. There is little to be said in their favor and there is something definitely against them. We should expect their number, like that of the individually powerful, to be smaller than that of the ordinary conformers, if only because, were their number greater, they would be the ones to set the norms for the group. They would be the conformers and the present conformers, the deviates. Or the group would split into two hostile sub-groups. The other members may have tried to punish these deviates and, for reasons already suggested, have failed either to bring them to con-form or to drive them out of the group altogether. In failing, the others have lost control over them. Active punishment of the deviates may have ended, unless some withdrawal of social interaction from them be considered active punishment. A dull disapproval of them persists but is without effect in changing their behavior. Accordingly, we should ex-pect the structure of many groups to resemble a diamond more than a pyramid, though a diamond with its greatest width nearer to its bottom than its top. Such, we believe, is the sort of structure our arguments, as developed so far, would lead us to expect in many groups, but naturally we have not said our last word on the subject.

Cooperation and Individual Work

We have so far treated conformity to a norm as a form of cooperation between members of a group. But the type of members we have last considered, the persistent nonconformers or holdouts, are obviously not cooperating with the others, certainly not in maintaining the norm in question. At the end of this chapter we shall say something about non-cooperation, first about merely individual work and then about positive conflict or competition.

In discussing cooperation we have assumed that members of a group cooperated because they could not otherwise have attained results re-warding to at least some of the members. But there are some kinds of tasks that can be carried out successfully either by cooperation or by individual work. One of them is the solution of intellectual problems, and the question arises which method is more efficient for this purpose. Accordingly, some social psychologists are fond of setting up experiments in which they ask groups and individuals to solve the same problems and then compare their success in doing so. In these experiments it often turns out that, on the average, groups solve the problems more rapidly than individuals do, or are "better" than individuals by some other criterion. This result is not surprising, if only because a group may contain several members who are able to contribute ideas toward the solution of the problem, while the individual has only himself. In other words the more members, the more ideas. Nevertheless the investigators, usually biased in favor of groupiness and against the self-sufficient individual, whom they suspect of being undemocratic and even authoritarian, get enormous pleasure from these results. They speak too soon if they go on to imply that all such tasks ought to be assigned to groups rather than to individuals. Although groups may reach a solution more quickly, they also tie up the time of more persons in doing so, time that they might have employed on alternative and rewarding activities. When the costs of giving up these alternatives is included in the calculations in the form of even the crudest estimates—and these the investigators seldom make—it becomes far from clear that all such tasks are more efficiently assigned to groups. The solving of problems by groups might be able to bear the costs incurred, provided that the collective reward from getting an excellent solution quickly were high enough, or that success depended on each of the members supplying information or ideas that only he possessed.

We shall not pursue this question any further here. Nor shall we ask further why some people are ready to cooperate and others are not, except to make one general point. Even if individuals can only secure by cooperation results that would be rewarding to all of them, they may still not cooperate, if they have had no rewarding past experience of doing so. This conclusion follows from the most elementary considerations. A group, a nation, can possess no greater asset than the mutual trust of its members, based on actual past experiences of cooperation in which everyone—or almost everyone—did his part, and in which a result rewarding to everyone was in fact attained. Such trust is a form of capital which may allow new ventures to get off the ground that could not otherwise have done so.

Competition

Individual work has obviously different social effects from cooperation. In the latter, at least some of the persons concerned reward one another. In the former, they do not, and so individual work provides no basis in itself for sentiments of mutual liking and approval. But it provides no basis for sentiments of hostility either, except for the case in which one man's individual work, if successful, deprives another man by that fact of the reward of the latter's individual work: they cannot both get the reward. This is the case of competition. Since to deprive another of an expected reward frustrates him, competition tends, by the aggression-approval proposition, to create hostility between the two. The difficulty we meet in keeping competition friendly—even in games—shows how powerful this tendency is.

In Chapter 3 we showed why in general we might expect persons who interact with one another frequently also to like one another. The reason is, of course, that persons who interact with one another tend to reward one another and mutual reward increases mutual liking. But the generalization has obvious exceptions and one of them, as we have already suggested, is rivalry for advancement within an organization. For instance, two officers of a company have to work together, although they know they are rivals for promotion. Here the external rewards which they get from the company and which they are unwilling to forgo, such as high salaries, may keep them interacting, but they are not apt to like one another very much. No doubt some sets of rivals have managed to like one another, but they have had much to overcome.

In the last chapter we described how one man in a three-man group acquired power over the others by providing them with rewards that were valuable because they were scarce in relation to demand. In larger groups, of course, more than one such person may appear, and they may become rivals for power over the others. Such rivalry is no more apt to foster liking between them than is competition between men for promotion in a company.

Finally, of course, groups as well as individuals may compete against one another. In this case, the fact that the members of one group are threatening to deny reward to members of another not only tends to increase the hostility a member of either group tends to feel for members of the other, but also, by relatively increasing the reward he gets from members of his own group (often called the ingroup), tends to increase his liking for them. He becomes more dependent on them for reward. The degree of the increase probably varies with the success of his group in its rivalry with the other. Leaders of groups have been known to try to exploit this tendency. They have tried to increase the hostility between their own groups and others in order to increase at the same time their followers' dependence on, and loyalty to, themselves.

Horizontal and Vertical Divisions

In our discussion of conformity earlier we showed that deviates in a group by their violation of a norm might well deny reward to the others and thus earn their hostility. We also showed why deviates might come to hang together among themselves. Should the deviates then be considered not just as deviates but as members of a different and competing group? More generally, how should we distinguish between a division of persons into social layers or strata and a division of them into subgroups? In the former, the lines of division are, so to speak, horizontal; in the latter, they are vertical.

In actual cases it is often difficult to decide, and no doubt in real social life divisions may occur in all sorts of mixtures and at any point along the spectrum from one extreme to the other. Yet consider the following possible differences between a set of deviates, as we have described them, and a true subgroup. First, the deviates are generally fewer in number than the conformers: if they were equal, it would be unlikely that a single set of norms could have become dominant in the group. Second, though the deviates certainly deny rewards to the conformers, they do not compete with them for the same rewards. Third, the deviates do not, by our assumptions, include members of high individual power. If they did, the norms they favored would have become dominant in the group, or at least, again, no single set of norms would have become dominant. To the degree that these conditions are realized, we should probably not speak of subgroups but of divisions into layers or strata, the lines between which are horizontal. To the degree that these conditions are not realized—that the numbers of the two (or more) social units are more nearly equal, that the units are in competition, and that they all include members of high individual power—we should probably speak of subgroups, the lines between which are vertical. Of course a subgroup may itself have its deviates. And an unsuccessful rival for high individual power among the conformers may come to side with the deviates and try to turn, in effect, what was a horizontal division into a vertical one.

Summary

In this chapter we increased the number of persons whose interaction we were prepared to study, and we called them a group. We then defined a norm of a group as a statement made by some of its members specifying how they and others ought to behave; and we asked what determined conformity to norms, especially norms obedience to which rewards the members by obtaining for them a collective good. Except in very small groups, individual rewards, including the avoidance of punishment, must supplement a collective good if enough members are to be induced to conform. In every group there are apt to be some members, the true believers, who would conform in any event. Some others are led to conform in order to avoid losing the social rewards that the true believers would deny them if they continued to deviate. It follows that the larger is the number of true believers, and the more valuable to the others are the rewards they have to offer, the more likely are the others to conform. As more and more members conform and act in unison in denying rewards to the nonconformers, the more scarce and therefore more valuable these rewards become for the latter and lead still more to conform. But if deviates manage to hold out against this pressure, there comes a point where their nonconformity begins to increase instead of decreasing, and the group has lost control over them. They are more likely to hold out if at least a few other members do so too and provide them with companionship in misery, or if there are other groups they can escape to when too hard pressed. Deviates are likely to resemble one another in values and therefore in background; they also tend to become more similar in behavior if they persist in their joint deviation. The explanation of both conformity and nonconformity may be looked on as an application of balance theory.

We then considered what our arguments in the preceding chapter and in the present one would lead us to expect in the way of differentiation within a group. We should expect to find a few members who are able to offer rare and valuable rewards to the others, a relatively large number of conformers offering ordinary rewards and doing no positive harm, and a smaller number of deviates.

Conformity to norms is one form of collaboration between members of a group. We turned finally to competition between individuals and between groups. Since, in competition, the success of one party in obtaining reward denies reward to the other, competition tends to produce some degree of hostility between the parties. We considered the conditions in which we might properly consider a group to be divided into subgroups rather than into superimposed layers.

6 Experimental Research

IN THE LAST FOUR CHAPTERS WE HAVE CARRIED OUT SEVERAL tasks. We have stated the general propositions we proposed to use in explaining social behavior. We have then applied them, at first to rather simple given conditions and then to ones of increasing complexity, in order to derive further, less general, more nearly empirical propositions about social behavior—for example, persons who deviate from a group norm are apt to resemble one another in respects other than their deviation itself. But for the most part, we have tried to avoid breaking the flow of our argument in order to cite evidence from research that might support it more or less well. We speak of "support" since we can hardly claim that the evidence "proves" beyond the shadow of a doubt the propositions we have derived. In the next few chapters, before we embark on topics of a somewhat different kind, we shall pause to look at some of the evidence.

The number of pieces of research that might serve our purpose is enormous and seems to increase exponentially with time. No one can possibly digest all of them, and textbooks of social psychology are apt to become unbearably tedious, and thus to fail of their intended effect, by consisting of little more than catalogs of research results. We propose to review only a few studies. We shall therefore have to be highly selective, and there is no doubt others might cavil at our choices. We shall now review some of the results of experimental research on interpersonal influence, and in Chapters 7 and 8 some of the field research on conformity and esteem.

Experimental and Field Research

In experimental research the investigator brings together the persons to be experimented on, usually called the "subjects," by artificial means

—they had not previously formed a group—and artificially manipulates their behavior—it would not have occurred naturally. In field research the investigator studies groups already existing in society by means of observation, the administration of questionnaires, and so forth, without attempting to manipulate their behavior. The distinction between the two cannot be made absolute. For instance, it is sometimes possible to conduct experiments with natural groups, and these are often the most fruitful experiments of all. But the distinction serves very well in a first rough approximation.

Of the two kinds of research, we set somewhat more store by field research. The typical experimental social psychologist has used as his subjects the undergraduates of American universities. Usually he has brought students into his laboratory who, so far as he could arrange it, were no more than barely acquainted with one another before the experiment began, and he has kept them together for at most an hour or two. He has subjected them to experimental conditions and manipulations that were seldom identical with, though often similar to, the conditions they encountered in their daily lives. His experimental manipulations have often required him to deceive his subjects, though he has usually explained to them after the experiment was over the nature of the deception and the reasons for it. Since other undergraduates learn about the deceptions when they read the reports of the research in textbooks or hear it described in lectures, they expect, when they in turn are asked to serve as subjects, to be deceived like their predecessors, and they become wary. We may be rapidly exhausting our supply of that priceless article, the truly naive undergraduate subject, who will respond ingenuously to our experimental manipulations. Finally, and perhaps most important, the investigator has seldom been able to establish experimental conditions that make a big difference to his subjects, so that they care very much whether they behave in one way rather than in another; and their lack of motivation tends to produce a large amount of fairly random behavior, which for that reason cannot easily be explained.

In contrast to the experimentally created groups, persons in real groups usually have previous experience of one another. The members stay together for some length of time: days, weeks, or years; they are seldom exposed to deliberate deception; and they usually care deeply about what they do under the conditions that face them. Accordingly, the question has often been raised whether the results of experimental social psychology should not be disregarded as irrelevant to the behavior of real persons in real social life.

We will not go so far here. The real advantages of the experimental method in the social as well as in the physical sciences, provided no claim is made that it should be the only method of research, ought not to be forgone without strong reasons. Human behavior in the laboratory is still human behavior, and if the propositions of behavioral psychology are universal, behavior in the laboratory should illustrate them as much as behavior anywhere else. Should the findings of the laboratory differ from the experiences of real life, the reason lies in no fundamental intellectual contradiction but in the fact that the two were established under different given conditions. But we are far from agreeing that the laboratory findings do always differ from those of real life. Much depends on what side of real life we have in mind. By its inherent characteristics, experimental social psychology is more apt to demonstrate how persons behave when they have met for the first time and have only just begun to influence one another than how they behave when their mutual influence has done its worst (or best) and they have settled down to more or less repetitive and well-established relationships. To understand the latter we need field studies of real groups.

With these warnings let us look at a few of the experimental studies of influence. We shall limit ourselves to the work done by a single group of men with a single, more or less consistent, point of view. Since each of the men—Stanley Schachter, Kurt Back, H. B. Gerard, and others—worked at one time or another with Leon Festinger, we shall speak of them collectively as the Festinger group.

Approval and Compliance

In an early experiment (Schachter, Ellertson, McBride, and Gregory, 1951), the investigators divided the female subjects into groups of three. That is, they persuaded each subject that she was a member of such a group. In fact she was put in a room by herself and set to work on an arbitrary and repetitive task, which she believed the others were working on too. The members of half the groups were told that "there is every reason to expect that the other members of the group will like you and you will like them." These were called, for reasons that will appear later, *high-cohesive* groups. The members of the other groups were told that the investigators had not found it possible to bring together a congenial group and that "there is no particular reason to think that you will like them or that they will care for you." These were called *low-cohesive* groups.

The investigators encouraged each subject to write notes for delivery to the other members of her group. These a messenger collected but substituted for them and delivered instead a series of standardized notes, which purported to come from other members but which in fact the investigators had prepared themselves. After an initial period in which the subjects' production rate at the repetitive task was allowed to settle down, the notes delivered to the members of half the groups urged them to speed up their production, whereas those delivered to the other half urged them to slow down. Since the investigators could easily measure a subject's production, they were able to determine how much it changed after she received these notes. Crudely stated, the results were that, on the average, a subject's rate of production changed more if she was asked to increase it than if she was asked to decrease it, perhaps because in our society we always look on harder work as praiseworthy, but that, regardless of the direction in which she was asked to change, she changed it more if she was a member of a high-cohesive group than if she was a member of a low-cohesive one.

The psychologists of the Festinger group often speak of *cohesiveness,* which they define as follows: "This property of groups, the attraction it has for its members, or the forces which are exerted on the members to stay in the group, has been called cohesiveness" (Back, 1950: 21). In our language it is the value of the rewards that participation in the group provides for its members. The reward may lie in sheer social interaction; it may lie in the sentiments of liking members convey to one another; it may lie in the practical results the group is able to accomplish; it may lie in a number of other things. But whatever the reward or rewards may be, the higher their average value to the members of a group, the higher, according to the definition, is the cohesiveness of that group.

In this particular experiment the reward in question was the approval, the liking members received—in fact were led to believe they received—from other members. In the experience of many persons, a group whose members like one another is apt to have been a group whose members have performed actions rewarding to one another. Accordingly, to be told that one is a member of such a group is to be given a stimulus under which one is apt to perform actions rewarding to the others. Compliance with what the others are asking you to do, another word for which is conformity to a norm, is such an action. Accordingly, we should expect to observe a larger number of compliant actions in high-cohesive groups than in low-cohesive ones, and the experiment revealed just that.

In groups, moreover, whose members already like one another, a member has more to lose by not conforming than he does in less cohesive groups, and hence, in response to a stimulus of this sort, he is more likely to conform in the former than in the latter. An additional reason for the relationship to exist is that a person who has already received liking from others, as had the members of the cohesive groups, owes the others compliance as a fair return. We do not insist on this last interpretation here, since only in a later chapter shall we reach the subject of distributive justice, and then we shall find that notions of justice, of a fair return, themselves depend on more primitive relationships. There is probably more than one reason why a group that has much to offer its members has much control over their behavior, but the fact that it does so is a reasonable conclusion from this first experiment.

Cost and Profit

Yet we need not be greatly surprised or impressed with the foregoing results, and we do not propose to review the large number of other experiments carried out by members of the Festinger group that revealed variations of the same general finding. One element that was missing from the design of the first experiment contributes especially to our mild dissatisfaction with it. We believe that the probability of a man's performing a particular action varies as the perceived value of its result, less the cost of getting that result, defined as the reward of an alternative action forgone in performing the first. We believe also that the presence of alternative persons from whom these rewards may be obtained increases the cost of a particular action directed to a particular person, since an action that has no alternative has no cost. In the experiment just considered, the subjects were asked by other members of their groups, or thought they were asked, to change their behavior so as to make it more valuable to these others. The experimental manipulations made clear the reward they might expect to get from changing, in the shape of more or less valuable social approval; but the cost of changing, what they had to forgo by doing so, was much less clear, and the investigators made no attempt to vary it experimentally. Thus a member of a high-cohesive group who was asked to speed up might expect to get social approval (or not to lose it) if she did so, but what she gave up by increasing her production was not evident: the job does not even seem to have been very fatiguing. We turn now to an experiment that begins, not altogether by design, to suggest how a change in behavior depends on the relation between reward and cost. This study was carried out by H. B. Gerard, a member of the Festinger group (Gerard, 1954).

The investigator brought his subjects into the experiment in groups of six. He gave the members of each group a case history of a labor-management dispute to read and asked each member to indicate his opinion on the probable outcome of the case by checking a point on a seven-point scale, which ran from "the union will be adamant" at one end, to "the union will give in immediately," at the other. Thus each member committed himself to a particular opinion. The investigator then broke up the original groups of six, and out of the whole population of subjects formed new three-person groups of three different kinds. One kind of group was made up of subjects who had expressed opinions on the outcome of the case that were in close agreement with one another, another kind of group made up of subjects in mild disagreement, and a third made up of subjects who strongly disagreed.

The investigator further subdivided the groups of each kind into two subclasses. He told members of half the groups that they would find one another very congenial, and he told the members of the other half that they would not get on well together. In short, he created experimental groups of six different kinds: High-Attraction, Agree; High-Attraction, Mildly-Disagree; High-Attraction, Strongly-Disagree; and Low-Attraction, Agree; Low-Attraction, Mildly-Disagree; Low-Attraction, Strongly-Disagree.

Each of the three-person groups then met for a face-to-face discussion of the case. The investigator observed the discussion and, at the end of it, asked each man to indicate his current opinion on the outcome of the case. Accordingly, he could determine how much change in opinion the discussion had brought about.

Finally, about a week later, the investigator called in each man individually, ostensibly in order to represent his group in a further discussion of the case with a member of another group. In fact this "member of another group" was, unknown to the subject, a paid participant, coached to behave in a particular way. In the new discussion he took a position on the outcome of the case that was, so far as possible, two steps removed on the scale from the last opinion expressed by the subject, and removed in a direction that would, if his persuasion was successful, pull the subject further away from the opinions expressed by at least one other member of his group. The investigator told each subject that he would only find the paid participant fairly congenial. Once more the investigator observed the discussion and at the end asked the subject to indicate his final opinion on the outcome of the case. He could thus determine how many subjects changed their opinions toward that expressed by the paid participant, which represented a clear alternative to group opinion.

As for the results, members of high-attraction groups made more attempts to influence others in the initial discussion than did members of low-attraction ones; and these attempts seem to have been more successful, for at the end of the discussion the opinions of members were more nearly alike in the former than in the latter. This latter finding is similar to that of the study by Schachter, Ellertson, McBride, and Gregory (1951) we considered earlier, and serves to confirm it. We shall be more interested in some further findings of the Gerard study, which seem to suggest something new. These findings are summed up in Tables 1 and 2.

One word to explain the meaning of these tables. The figure 44, for instance, means that of all members of high-attraction, strongly-disagree groups, 44 percent changed their opinions in the direction of those held by some other member of their group. Comparing the sums of the rows in these two tables, we see that high-attraction people were more apt to change toward someone in their group than were low-attraction ones, and that low-attraction people were more apt to change toward the paid participant than were high-attraction ones. This is in accord with the

Table 1   Percentage of Subjects Changing
toward Someone in the Group

	AGREE	MILDLY-DISAGREE	STRONGLY-DISAGREE
HIGH-ATTRACTION	0	12	44
LOW-ATTRACTION	0	15	9

Table 2   Percentage of Subjects Changing
toward Paid Participant

	AGREE	MILDLY-DISAGREE	STRONGLY-DISAGREE
HIGH-ATTRACTION	7	13	25
LOW-ATTRACTION	20	38	8

argument advanced earlier: if a group is giving you much, in this case
liking, you are under pressure to give it much, in this case a change of
opinion toward agreement with its views. By the same token, if a group
is giving you little, you will be little apt to give it agreement. Indeed you
may be tempted to vex the other members by changing your opinion so
as to depart from agreement even further, which in this case means in
the direction of the paid participant.

So far so good; but when I first scanned these tables I was less struck
by the differences between them than I was by their similarities. In both
tables members of the same type of group showed similar tendencies
simply to change their opinions, whether the change was toward the
opinion of the group or that of the paid participant. Thus in both tables
the persons who changed least were the members of high-attraction, agree
groups and low-attraction, strongly-disagree ones, while those who
changed most were the members of high-attraction, strongly-disagree
groups and low-attraction, mildly-disagree ones. Members of groups of
the other two types displayed medium propensities to change.

The investigator confesses himself unable to account, or rather to
account fully, for these different propensities. He says, for instance, "The
8 percent figure for the low-attraction, strongly-disagree condition is per-
plexing. The figure is too low to be accounted for by chance. There
seems to be no reasonable explanation for this inordinately low figure."

Since the investigator is unable to provide one, let us see if we can
provide an explanation. Two kinds of questions need to be answered:
Why do different subjects change or fail to change their actions, in this
case their expressed opinions? and, If they do change, why do they
change in one direction rather than another, toward the group or to-

ward the paid participant? In the present experiment the answer to the
second question is less interesting than the answer to the first.

Let us assume that subjects could get at least three different kinds of
rewards for changing their opinions or failing to do so. The first was
social approval by members of one's own group, which was purchased by
agreement with them. The investigator takes for granted the existence
of this reward; the design of his experiment called for giving it a higher
value in the high-attraction groups than in the low-attraction ones, and
we too shall not find it difficult to accept. The second reward was the
value some men find in agreement for its own sake and apart from any
social approval it may get them. As Festinger argues, disagreement with
others is, at least on the face of it, not consonant with the truth of a
man's own opinion: if his opinion is correct, it is absurd that others
should disagree. Conditions like this, in which some of the facts before a
man are incongruent with other facts, Festinger calls *cognitive dissonance,* and he claims that dissonance is often painful and its reduction
rewarding (Festinger, 1957: 13, 18–19). But consonance may be purchased
at too high a price, and accordingly the third reward available to a subject in this experiment was the maintenance of his personal integrity,
achieved by sticking to his own independent and publicly expressed
opinion on the issue of the case. The investigator does not mention this
reward, but we cannot make sense of the results without it, or something
much like it.

In different degrees for different subjects, depending on their initial
opinions and the kinds of group they belonged to, these rewards were in
competition with one another: some subjects could not get one without
giving up one of the others. Now according to the argument we presented in Chapter 2, when a course of action requires a man to give up
one reward in order to get another, we speak of the cost of the action
as the value of the forgone alternative. Cost is negative value, and the
higher the cost of an action, the less likely he is to perform it. We introduced the definition:

$$\text{Profit} = \text{Reward} - \text{Cost}$$

And we argued that the less was a man's profit from a particular action,
the more likely he was to change and perform an alternative one. Remember that, by this definition, as his profit approaches zero, a man
does not become more apt to do nothing but rather to switch to another
kind of action. Though we certainly implied that a person was apt to
choose the one of two alternative actions that offered the greater profit,
we were skittishly careful not to commit ourselves to the somewhat
stronger view that a man acted so as to maximize his profit.

In the light of this argument, consider the members of the different
groups in the present experiment. The high-attraction, agree people got

cognitive consonance; they got much in the way of approval from the group, and they had to give up for it little or nothing in the way of personal integrity, for their independent views were already in agreement with those of the other members. Their profit from their current behavior was high, and accordingly they changed little. The low-attraction, strongly-disagree people were getting much in the way of integrity and they were not giving up for it much in the way of valuable approval, for they belonged to groups whose members did not find one another congenial. Reward less cost was high for them too, though not perhaps quite as high as it was for the high-attraction, agree people, for they were not getting consonance; and they too changed little. This is our explanation for the low figure of 8 percent that changed their opinion, which the investigator was at a loss to account for. But note that the low-attraction, strongly-disagree people and the high-attraction, agree people made high profits for opposite reasons. For the latter, approval was the reward, forgone integrity the cost—in their case little or nothing. For the former, integrity was the reward, forgone approval the cost, which in their case too was little or nothing.

The high-attraction, strongly-disagree people were in a very different position. They were certainly not getting consonance; they were perhaps getting much in the way of the maintenance of their integrity, but their costs in doing so were high too, for as members of high-attraction groups they were in danger of losing much that was valuable in the way of social approval. Their net profit was low, and so they were very prone to change their opinions. We cannot say that their profit before change was zero, for our measures are not of the sort that yield absolute figures, but we can reasonably argue that their profits were less than those of the groups so far considered. The same was true of the low-attraction, mildly-disagree people. They did not get a great deal of visible integrity, for their opinions were only in mild disagreement with those of others in their groups; but neither were they giving up much in the way of potential approval, for they were members of low-attraction groups. Unlike the high-attraction, strongly-disagree people, who had both high rewards and high costs, the low-attraction, mildly-disagree people had low rewards and low costs. But they resembled the former in that their net profit—the difference between the two—was low; and accordingly they too were prone to change. The members of groups of the remaining two kinds had medium profits and also medium propensities to change.

Once we have explained the different tendencies to change, the question comes up why subjects should have changed in one direction rather than another. By the terms of the experiment, no one that changed his opinion could have made it at the same time less like that of a member of the group and less like that of the paid participant; any change would have had to be toward agreement with someone, for the paid participant always took a position on the opposite side of the subject's own from that taken by other members of his group. He represented a source of consonance and social approval alternative to the one provided by other members of the group. He was not a particularly valuable source, since he was only "fairly attractive," but he was better than nothing, and some subjects must have felt that by moving toward agreement with him they were not abandoning all their integrity: at least they were not abjectly giving in to the group. If subjects changed, the evidence is that they changed so as to get the more valuable reward: members of high-attraction groups toward agreement with the group, members of low-attraction ones toward the paid participant. As we have said, this last finding is in accordance both with the first experiment reported in this chapter and with the theoretical arguments presented in earlier chapters.

For the first time in the experiments we have been examining, we have evidence here for a person's alternatives to complying with influence exerted on him by his group. We have an alternative reward (the maintenance of integrity) and an alternative person (the paid participant) from whom social approval may be gained. It is the presence of alternatives that allows us to introduce the notion of profit. If profit is defined as the difference between the reward of a particular course of action and the forgone value of alternative courses, the evidence suggests that, the less their profit, the more likely people are to change their behavior, and to change it so as to increase their profit. And if whenever a man's behavior brought him a balance of reward and cost, he changed it away from the action that got him the lesser profit, there might well come a time when, other circumstances remaining the same, he would not change his behavior further, because he had successively abandoned all the actions that brought him less profit. That is, his behavior would be stabilized, at least for the time being. And so far as this were true of every member of a group, the group would have created a social organization in equilibrium. Don't tell us that this is no problem. Many sociologists spend years describing and analyzing social structure without once asking themselves why it is that behavior persists long enough for them to describe and analyze it at all. Structure is not a given: it is itself the result of a social process.

Alternative Sources of Reward

In the last experiment we were forced to consider evidence on the effects of alternatives to a particular course of action. The existence of alternative rewards and alternative actions that may secure them tends to raise the cost of any given action and so render more probable the performance of an alternative. In the same way, the presence of an alternative person from whom a particular kind of reward may be obtained—

an alternative source of the reward—tends to raise the cost of obtaining it from any given person. In the experiment, a subject could get from the maintenance of his personal integrity an alternative reward to the approval of his group, and in the paid participant he had an alternative source of agreement and approval. In the study of social behavior we are particularly interested in the latter kind of alternative. We wish to understand, for instance, the conditions that make a person more likely to violate in word or deed the norms of a group. In the last chapter we argued that one such condition was the presence of others from whom the potential deviate could obtain rewards denied him by the general body of conformers. Even a single such person might have a disproportionate effect in encouraging his nonconformity; and at the extreme a deviant subgroup might form, made up of persons similar to one another in respects other than their nonconformity itself. We turn now to an experiment that points to a general condition tending to produce alternative persons from whom a particular member of a group may get reward.

This experiment was carried out by Festinger and Thibaut (1951). The investigators formed a number of groups of from six to fourteen members each, who met for discussion sitting around a table. They gave the members of each group a problem to consider, half of the groups getting a problem in football strategy and half getting a problem on what should be done about a delinquent boy. After a member had read the case as written out by the investigators, he made public to the others his opinion about it by putting up a card in front of his place indicating his position on a scale of possible opinions. Then the investigators gave each of the subjects a sheet purporting to contain new information on the problem—half of the members getting information that would tend to push their opinion toward one end of the scale, and half getting information tending to push it toward the other end. The investigators did this in order to get a wide dispersal of opinion and hence an active discussion.

The investigators asked each member after he had read the new information to indicate his current opinion; and they drew attention to each member's opinion so that everyone would be aware of the differences. Then they told the members to discuss the case with one another not by word of mouth but by writing notes. The members handed their notes to the investigators, who logged them in their record and then delivered them. In this way the investigators got a measure of the quantity of communication (interaction). At the end of the experiment they asked each member to indicate, as before, his current opinion on the problem.

Besides giving them different problems to work on, the investigators differentiated the groups in two further ways. They told half the groups that the members "were selected in such a way that we believe you all will have about an equal interest in this problem and about equal knowledge about it." And they told the other half that members were chosen so as to be as different as possible in their interest and knowledge. These they called the *homogeneity* and *heterogeneity* conditions, respectively.

The investigators further told one-third of the homogeneous groups that they were interested in observing how a group reached a unanimous decision, one-third that there was somewhat less need for uniformity, and one-third that there was no need at all. They created a similar division among the heterogeneous groups, except that for the first third they said that instead of unanimity a plurality would be enough. In short, the investigators tried to create six different experimental conditions: Homogeneous, under High, Medium, and Low Pressures toward Uniformity, and Heterogeneous under similar differences in pressure.

Now for the results. First, with increasing pressure toward uniformity, there was in fact greater change of opinion in the direction of uniformity. The investigators asked for different degrees of uniformity and by and large they got what they asked for. This result will hardly surprise us. Naive Americans are good people, and they will give investigators what they want so long as they themselves incur no great cost in doing so. As for the quantity of communication (interaction) measured by the number of notes written, more communication was directed at members holding extreme opinions than at those closer to the mode. To get agreement with his opinion is rewarding to a man, but once he has gotten it from some of his companions, the conversion of others who still disagree becomes relatively more valuable to him: there is little to be gained from preaching to the converted. Since the converted in the present experiment were by definition those who held opinions close to the mode, while the unconverted were those who held out for extreme opinions, more communications in the form of efforts at persuasion were directed at the latter than at the former. But in the heterogeneity condition, especially in groups under medium and low pressure toward uniformity, this tendency to communicate to the extremes became steadily less marked as the discussion went on. The reason undoubtedly was that, as we shall soon see, efforts to get agreement were less successful in heterogeneous groups than in homogeneous ones, and that, no matter how valuable a reward may be, a man will not indefinitely persist in action that has turned out to be unsuccessful in getting the reward.

Much more interesting than the effects of differences in pressure toward uniformity were the effects of differences in homogeneity: the changes in the direction of uniformity of opinion were fewer in the heterogeneous groups than in the homogeneous ones. We interpret this result as follows. Persons who are similar in any one respect, including any of those summed up by the word "background," are apt either to be already similar or to become so in other respects, including similarity in conforming to a group norm in word or deed. If the number of such persons in any group is large, their power, we have argued, to convert still further members to conformity is high. The chances are good that efforts to convert holdouts in such groups will be successful. Since many persons have actually experienced these effects, the investigators, by describing some of the groups as homogeneous, presented to their members a stimulus under which those of them who held modal opinions were apt to persist in attempts to convert the others, because such attempts were apt to be successful; and, conversely, those who held extreme opinions were apt to allow themselves to be converted, since in homogeneous groups there would be few if any persons who would support them in their opinions by providing them with alternative sources of reward. In describing other groups as heterogeneous, the investigators presented a contrasting kind of stimulus with contrasting results. A heterogeneous group is one in which a man who holds unorthodox opinions is likely to persist in them because, through the very variety of the membership, he is apt to find someone who will be different from the majority and so able to support him in his dissidence. This is what the investigators mean when they say that the members of heterogeneous groups were more likely than the members of homogeneous groups to see that the formation of subgroups was possible. A subgroup is a place where a man can find support against the rest. In the present experiment, heterogeneity played the same part implicitly that the paid participant played explicitly in the last one.

Similarity as a Source of Reward

In the next experiment we pursue the same issues that we did in the last. But in this one the investigators went still further toward artificially creating a particular distribution of opinion—or the subjects' belief that there was such a distribution—and they were able to observe still more precisely the reactions to it. The experiment was carried out by Festinger, Gerard, Hymovitch, Kelley, and Raven (1952).

The investigators formed groups of from six to nine members each, told the members of half the groups that they would find one another congenial (high-cohesive groups) and the members of the other half that they would not do so (low-cohesive). They made other experimental divisions among the groups, but we need not go into them.

The members of all the groups read a case study of a labor-management dispute, no doubt the one we have heard of before (page 119). After reading the case, each member wrote down on a slip of paper a letter identifying himself and indicated on a seven-point scale his opinion on the probable outcome of the case. These opinions were not made public as they had been in the earlier experiment. Instead the investigators collected the slips in such a way that no member knew the opinions of the others.

This left the investigators free to create a fictitious impression of the distribution of opinion, which they did by handing to each member a slip of paper purporting to show the opinion of every other member in relation to his own. About two-thirds of the members of each group were led to believe that they were "conformers." Each conformer received a slip showing one member of the group holding an opinion three steps removed from his own on the scale, two members (one member if the group had only six or seven members in all) holding an opinion only one step removed, and the rest agreeing exactly with his own opinion. Each "deviate," on the other hand, received a slip showing that he was alone in the opinion he held, that one or two members held opinions two steps removed from his own, and that the rest of the group agreed on an opinion three steps removed.

Suppose that a man's identifying letter was "D," that he actually held opinion "4" on the scale, and that he was a member of a seven-person group. Then Table 3 shows, first, the kind of slip he would get if he were treated as a conformer, and, second, the kind he would get if treated as a deviate.

Table 3   Apparent Distribution of Opinion

OPINION	GIVEN TO CONFORMER	GIVEN TO DEVIATE
1		
2		
3		
4	D B C F G	D
5	A	
6		A
7	E	B C E F G

After the investigator had given out the slips and everyone knew the apparent distribution of opinion, each member again wrote down his current opinion and the degree of confidence he felt in it. This information allowed the investigators to determine how much effect the members' perception of the distribution of opinion had in changing their actual opinions or their confidence in them. Then the investigators told the members that they might write notes to others about anything they liked, including the case itself. These notes were collected but not delivered, and, in the number of words written, furnished the investigators with a measure of the quantity of communication (interaction) directed by each of the members to each of the others.

Now for the results. First, deviates showed greater readiness to change their opinions than did conformers, and less confidence in them. A person who perceives that the majority of his group agrees on an opinion different from his own is in a state of cognitive dissonance: the information he gets from the others is in conflict with the belief that his own opinion is correct. Many people find it rewarding to escape from dissonance, and so deviates are more likely than conformers to change their opinions, which does not mean that all deviates do change in fact. Second, somewhat more change occurred in high-cohesive groups than in low-cohesive ones. Besides a reduction in dissonance, a deviate had more to gain in the way of social approval by giving in to the majority (or more to lose by continuing to disagree with them) in a high-cohesive group than in a low-cohesive one. Third, more communication occurred in the high-cohesive groups than in the others. But results like these and the reasons for them we have encountered in earlier experiments; the nuances of communication are more interesting. Deviates that changed their opinions communicated less than either conformers or nonchanging deviates (holdouts), for a man who has chosen to be changed has by that fact less need to change others. In the high-cohesive groups conformers and holdouts communicated, on the average, about equally; but in the low-cohesive groups the holdouts communicated less than the conformers, as if they doubted not only the possibility of changing members that did not like them but also the value of doing so.

Still more interesting were the different persons to whom conformers and holdouts addressed their communications. In both high- and low-cohesive groups, conformers communicated more to the extreme deviates —that is, to members holding opinions three steps removed from their own—than they did either to members only one step removed or to those that already agreed with them. Besides seeing a good chance of changing the opinion of a man who was alone in holding it, they may have found it more rewarding to preach to the still unconverted.

The behavior of the holdouts, at least in the high-cohesive groups, was quite different. Though the conformers communicated most often to them, they did not reciprocate. Instead they communicated most to the few members that held opinions only two steps removed from their own—in other words, to those whose opinions most nearly resembled their own. A deviate may have "seen"—that is, a common type of past experience may have taught him—that it would be more difficult for him to change the opinion of a member of a conforming majority, especially in a cohesive group and when their opinion was quite different from his own, than to change the opinion of a member who for the moment had no one else to support him and whose opinion more nearly resembled the deviate's own. At any rate, the results of the experiment suggest, in agreement with our earlier argument, that when members of a group perform different activities, any one member may find in another whose activities are similar to his own a source of reward alternative to the other members of the group, and that his finding the alternative source may help him hold out against the rest.

Note that in explaining the behavior of the subjects in this experiment as in others, we have always referred, at least by implication, to their presumed past experience, particularly their social experience. We have, for instance, just assumed that, in the past experience of many persons, a stimulus to the effect that a majority holds a uniform opinion has been the occasion when efforts to change the opinion of a member of the majority are apt to have been unsuccessful; and we have used this assumption to explain why the deviates made few efforts to change the conformers. We social scientists are in the curious position of trying to demonstrate the truth of our propositions by experiments on people who already, for all practical purposes, know some of the propositions and govern their behavior toward others in accordance with them. The fact that the behavior of men is always partly determined by their past experience means that the report of an experiment in social science can never include all the information needed to explain its results. Indeed in the absence of information on the past histories of the particular subjects in an experiment, we are forced to fall back on common knowledge about the usual experiences of people in some way like them. We could escape this necessity only by experimenting with subjects who had no social experience or whose experience we had been able to form and record ourselves. Since social experience begins with birth and since scientists are not allowed to control the experiences of men as they are those of rats and pigeons, our subjects, by the time they are undergraduates, have already acquired an enormous amount of social experience, the details of which are largely unknown to us.

Our only comfort is that we are not alone in this difficulty. Even in physics, scientists have found that the past histories of the materials they work with may make a difference in their present behavior. For example, consider iron—and the hull of a ship may be considered a single piece of iron. The present magnetic characteristics of a ship's hull are determined in part by its past history: where and on what heading it was built, what latitudes it has sailed through, and what buffetings it has taken from the sea. Since a scientist never has adequate information on these matters, he can never predict except very grossly what the present magnetic characteristics of the hull will be. In World War II, this complicated the problem of making ships safe from magnetic mines.

When Influence Fails

The next experiment we shall consider is concerned with the end of the process of influence. It deals less with the stimulus conditions under which people comply with the demands others make of them than with the way others react when they fail to comply. It is concerned with what happens when influence fails. The experiment is the work of Stanley Schachter (1951).

The investigator formed a number of groups, each having from eight to ten members, and set them all to work reading and discussing the case of a juvenile delinquent, the question at issue being what should be done with him. On this question a number of opinions might be held, running all the way from "All he needs is a little more love" to "He ought to be sent to jail." The investigator also saw to it that the groups differed in cohesiveness, but since the details of how he did so would take more time to describe than the result would be worth, all we shall remember here—and it is only approximately correct—is that a cohesive group in this experiment unlike some of the others was not one whose members were persuaded that they liked one another but rather one in which they discussed something they were all really interested in.

Into each group the investigator introduced three further persons, treating them just as if they were ordinary members. In fact and unknown to the other members they were paid participants, coached by the investigator in advance to behave in certain ways in the course of the discussion. The so-called "mode" supported an opinion in agreement with the most commonly-held opinion as it began to emerge in the group. The "slider" began by taking an extreme position, usually in favor of sending the delinquent to jail, and then slowly shifted toward the mode, as if the other members' arguments had persuaded him. And finally the "deviate" maintained an extreme position unchanged throughout the discussion.

The investigator observed the course of the discussion, recording the number of communications (including attempts to influence) that each person addressed to each of the others. Then at the end of the session he administered two tests to the members, designed to reveal the degree of social approval each accorded to the others. First, he told the members that at a future meeting of the group it might be necessary to leave somebody out, and so he asked each member to list the others in rank order beginning with the person he would most like to have remain in the group and ending with the person he would least like to keep. This the investigator called the *sociometric test*. Second, he explained that for the purposes of a future meeting it might be necessary to form subcommittees of the group. These committees—Executive, Steering, and Correspondence—he so described that the first seemed the most attractive, the second next, and the third least. He then asked each member to write down the names of the other members that he would like to see serving on each committee.

Now for the results. As might be expected, the two measures of social approval showed the same tendency. At the end of the experiment, the deviates were named as persons who ought to remain in the group less often than were either the modes or the sliders, and this tendency was even stronger in the more cohesive groups than in the less. The deviates also received more nominations for the "worst" committee and fewer nominations for the "best" than did the others. As we have argued before, a man often finds it valuable that another should agree with his opinions. Should the other persist in not agreeing, he is not apt to give the other any action that rewards the other's behavior, whether it is social approval or the opportunity to do an interesting job. But as usual this was not the whole story, and undoubtedly a sense of justice was at work also. If another is giving a man little agreement, crude justice demands that he give the other little approval in return. In failing to agree the other may, moreover, be withdrawing a reward that the man has come to expect, and he may accordingly meet the withdrawal not just with indifference but with positive hostility. Since a man is more apt to expect agreement with his fellow members in highly cohesive groups, he is also apt in these groups to be more angry when he does not get it.

As for the quantity of communication, more was addressed to the deviate than to either the mode or the slider, and this was in accord with the results of experiments reported earlier. It took a little time for the general group opinion to jell out of the discussion, and accordingly a little time before the others recognized the deviate for what he was. As they began to do so, the number of communications addressed to him tended to increase, whereas the number addressed to the mode or to the slider remained more nearly steady. But the increase did not go on indefinitely. In the more cohesive groups, when it appeared that the deviate was not going to submit to the influence brought to bear on him, the number of communications addressed to him tended to fall off. In ordinary language, the majority gave him up as a bad job. In our language, a man will not continue forever to perform actions that have gone unrewarded. The state toward which these groups tended at the end of the meetings was one in which the deviates received little interaction and little positive sentiment, and in which, by the same token, the conformers, holding the majority opinion, gave relatively more interaction and approval to other conformers—that is, to persons whose actions were similar to their own. We must emphasize this final situation, because as sociologists we must be particularly interested in groups that have reached a relatively stable structure. These are groups in which, at least for the time being, power and authority have brought about all the change they are capable of. They are able to keep the members doing the things they are already doing but not to induce them to undertake new ones. In the next chapter we shall turn to field studies of groups that have approached this state.

Cooperation and Competition between Individuals

To parallel our theoretical discussion in the preceding chapter we shall end the present one by considering an experimental study contrasting the effects of cooperation and competition. The findings of the study are not particularly surprising, but it is good for the record to have them experimentally established at least once.

The experiment was carried out by Morton Deutsch (1953), whose subjects were about fifty students taking a course in elementary psychology at the Massachusetts Institute of Technology. Before the experiment began, the investigator had every subject take certain personality tests. Using the results of the tests, he formed ten groups of five men each, each group matched with the rest in its members' range of ability and personality. He then had each group discuss a problem in human relations, gave it a score on the productivity of its discussion, and then formed two sets of five groups each, each set including the same proportion of high- and low-scoring groups. Having matched groups and sets of groups, he was ready for the experiment proper.

Each group in both sets met separately once a week for a number of weeks. At each session the investigator gave the members two problems: a logical puzzle and a problem in human relations. The members were to discuss each problem, reach a solution, write it up, and turn in the report to the investigator. Since the logical puzzle admitted of a single solution, while the human-relations problem did not, he expected that each would bring out a different sort of discussion.

So far the investigator had treated the two sets of groups in the same way. Where they differed was in the way the members were to be rewarded for their work. In every one of the five groups that got the *cooperative* treatment, he told the members that every week he would give them a score, as a group, on how well they worked together in solving the puzzle problem, and that every member of the group achieving the highest average score for the whole series of meetings would be excused for writing one term paper for the course but would nevertheless receive the highest grade he could have gotten for the paper. In the same way, the investigator would score, for quantity and quality, the discussions and solutions of the human-relations problem. Every member of the group that received the highest average score would receive the highest grade; every member of the group that received the next highest score would receive the next highest grade, and so on. In short, in the cooperative treatment every member of a group would receive the same reward for his participation, and the value of the reward would depend on how well his group did.

In the *competitive* treatment, the investigator told the members of each group that he would rank each member every week on the amount he personally contributed to the solution of the puzzle problem, and that the member who achieved the highest average score for the whole series of meetings would be excused from one term paper but get the highest grade. In the same way, he would rank each member on his personal contribution to the discussion of the human-relations problem, and would give the member that received the highest average score the highest grade, and so on. In short, in the competitive treatment the reward obtained by each member would depend only on his individual activity and not at all on how well his group did. Moreover, a high score received by one man necessarily meant a lower score received by others. Yet just like the members of a cooperative group, the members of a competitive one were required to turn in, as a group, written solutions to the problems set before them.

The investigator naturally expected the two different conditions to produce different kinds of behavior. To discover what the differences were, he set four observers to watching each meeting of each group, recording certain specific kinds of behavior while the meeting was going on and, after the meeting, making certain overall ratings of the members' behavior. When a meeting had ended, the investigator also asked the members to answer a questionnaire, and then again, one week after the final meeting, to answer another questionnaire about the experiment as a whole. We need not describe the observations and questionnaires in detail, but only look at some of the more interesting results.

One of our main propositions says that the more valuable the reward a man gets by performing a particular action, the more often he will perform it. In the cooperative groups, a member was to be rewarded for any action that contributed to his group's doing well; in the competitive groups, each member was to be rewarded only for his own skill. True, he did not get the reward during the course of the experiment itself: it was to come later. But it is much to the credit of American teachers that the occasions in the past on which they have promised rewards have generally been occasions on which the appropriate behavior on the part of their students has in fact been rewarded—in short, they have kept their promises—and therefore their promises are apt to stimulate their students to appropriate action on the next occasion. It is, then, hardly surprising that members of cooperative groups displayed much cooperative behavior, and members of competitive groups much competitive behavior.

Specifically, the two sets of groups did not differ in the "involvement" of their members, as rated by the observers, or in their interest in the task, as rated by their own answers to the questionnaires. But they did differ greatly in other ways. Members of cooperative groups were more likely to express interest in the ideas of their fellow members—and, after all, the ideas of the others might contribute to their own success. The observers also rated the members of these groups as more "group centered" and better at working together—and, after all, they were rewarded for working together. Members of competitive groups, on the other hand, expressed a greater desire to excel others—and, after all, they were to be rewarded if they excelled others. In short, the investigator got from each set of groups the kind of behavior he was prepared to reward, and it would have been startling if he had not.

Less directly obvious but still thoroughly in line with our general propositions were the findings that members of cooperative groups expressed greater friendliness for one another than did members of competitive ones, gave others more encouragement, and expressed less aggression toward them. As we have seen over and over again, social approval is a generalized reward that a man may use to render more probable the performance by another of any action that rewards *him*. In the cooperative groups, almost any idea that a member put forward might contribute to the solution of a problem. Therefore it was apt to reward his fellow members and bring out their approval in return. In the competitive groups, on the contrary, the good ideas that a member expressed would help him but hurt his fellow members. His good ideas, by getting him a high score, would withdraw reward from the rest. Hostility is a common reaction to the withdrawal of a reward, and therefore in the competitive groups friendliness was at a low ebb and aggression was high.

We must now consider findings that are still less obvious until we come to think about them—but something that takes thinking about before it seems obvious is not obvious at all. Two men reward one another, and thus cooperate with one another, when each provides the other with a service that he could not do for himself at all or could not do at such low cost. Sometimes the services the two men provide are similar, as when two join forces to move a rock neither could move alone. But often the services are different, which means that each man becomes a specialist so far as their cooperation is concerned. Thus in our earlier example, Other became, in effect, a specialist in giving help and Person a specialist in giving approval. Competition, at least under the conditions we are interested in here, is much less likely to promote specialization and the division of labor. People who compete with one another are after the same reward, and when, as is often the case, the reward can be obtained by only one kind of activity, the activities of competitors are apt to become similar rather than different. Some business firms make this a conscious rule of competition. If a competitor is selling two lines of goods, the firm must sell goods in the same two lines. To leave the other an unchallenged market in one line and compete with him only in the other is to hand him a better overall competitive position, and thus the goods sold by the two firms tend to get more alike. In short, and as a gross simplification, cooperators may be more likely than competitors to differ from one another in the kinds of action they perform.

How did this difference show itself in the experiment? The observers kept a record of the total amount of time every member contributed to the discussion of the problems. That is, they recorded how much he interacted with other members of his group. They reported more "communications difficulties" in the competitive groups than in the cooperative ones—and, after all, the members of the former could not get much reward from listening to their competitors' ideas. The observers also found that competitive groups did not differ from cooperative ones in the total amount of interaction, at least in the discussion of the human-relations problems; and this finding runs counter to our general expectation that, other things equal, competitors, since they are not rewarding one another, will interact with one another less than cooperators will. But in the present case the other things were not equal. In the competitive groups, members were to be rewarded for the quantity and quality of their individual contributions. What they were contributing to was supposed to be a discussion; that is, they had to speak up and announce their ideas to the others before they could get any individual credit for them at all. Though they had no need to listen, they certainly needed to talk, and for this reason there was as much interaction in competitive groups as in cooperative ones. This was more true of the human-relations problems, for which there was no single best solution, than it was of the logical puzzles, in which a member of a competitive group could get a high score by saying nothing and thinking quietly until he was ready to come up with the one correct answer.

Although the two sets of groups did not differ in their total amounts of interaction, they did differ significantly in the way the interaction was distributed among the members. Members of competitive groups were more nearly alike in the amount they interacted than were the members of cooperative ones. In the competitive groups a man could hope to get a high grade only if he himself talked; he could not afford to let anyone else do all the talking. Accordingly, discussion in these groups tended to find all members participating more or less equally. In the cooperative groups, on the other hand, a member who had nothing useful to say could shut up, let better men talk, and still hope to get a good grade. His grade was the grade of his group, and anyone who could raise the level of the group's discussion could reward *him,* just as he could reward the others by merely keeping still. He also served by only standing and waiting. For this reason, members of cooperative groups differed greatly among themselves in the amount they interacted.

A division of labor means differences in labor. A man who shuts up and lets others talk is differentiating his behavior from that of the others. He is not the less a specialist for the fact that his specialty is keeping still. This tendency for members of cooperative groups to show greater differences among themselves in the ways they behaved than did members of competitive groups showed itself also in the way they went about writing up the solutions to the problems. In these groups, particularly in the human-relations problems, two or more members would be writing up different parts of the solution at the same time. In the competitive groups, though, it was more usual for each member in turn to take over the job of writing up the whole solution, while the others gathered around and told him what to write. Once again, the members of these groups tended to make their contributions similar and equal. Moreover, the written solution made little difference to members of a competitive group. Though they were required to turn one in as a group, it could not reward them. Only their individual contributions, not their joint contributions, could reward them, and for this purpose it was better to talk than to write.

We turn finally to the vexed question of the differences between the two sets of groups in what the investigator calls their productivity. The cooperative groups solved the puzzle problems more rapidly than did the competitive ones, whose members had little to gain by helping one another out. For the human-relations problems, since they admitted of no single best solution, there could be no such clear-cut measure of productivity as the time taken to reach a solution; but at least the cooperative groups wrote more words in the reports they turned in to the investigator than did the competitive ones, to whom, as we have seen, the report in itself made little difference. Another and very different measure of productivity brought results that must have saddened the heart of the high-minded investigator. From the grades that the students received in the first term paper following the experiment, there was no evidence that the members of cooperative groups had learned any more psychology in the course of the experiment than had the members of competitive ones. However much the cooperators may have helped one another in other ways, they were not particularly successful in helping one another to learn.

Summary

In the present chapter we turned from abstract argument to a review of some of the research supporting the propositions put forward in earlier chapters. In the first instance we turned to experimental rather than to field research. We reviewed studies showing the following: that the more the members of a group like one another, the more they are able to influence one another; that increased costs in the form of alternative rewards forgone and alternative persons from whom reward may be obtained increase the capacity of individuals to resist the influence of their group; that heterogeneity in the membership of a group, by providing a potential deviate with alternative sources of reward, increases his capacity to resist group influence; that persons who are similar to one another are apt to turn to one another for support in their nonconformity; that when members of a group attempt to change the behavior of deviates and fail, they will sooner or later give up their attempts, and therefore in the end will direct little interaction as well as little approval toward deviates; that if members of a group are rewarded for cooperative or competitive behavior, they will tend to behave cooperatively or competitively respectively, but that cooperative groups solve certain kinds of problems more rapidly than do competitive ones. We do not say that these research results are surprising in themselves or surprising in the support they provide for arguments we advanced in earlier chapters. We only say that they do in fact support them.

7 Field Research

IN THIS CHAPTER AND THE NEXT WE SHALL CONTINUE TO RE-
view selected researches whose findings seem to us to support the arguments we have presented so far, in the sense that they seem to follow,
under the conditions given in the research, from the general propositions
we started with. But from now on we shall be reviewing field rather than
experimental research.

Tendencies toward Balance: The Acquaintance Process

We review first an investigation carried out at the University of
Michigan by T. M. Newcomb and his associates (Newcomb, 1961). We
have chosen to begin with it for three reasons. First, it is largely concerned with the process of balance, which was one of the earliest subjects
we considered. Second, this process precedes and moves toward the relatively steady states of interpersonal relationships that we call social structures. Third, the method used in the investigation is transitional between
experimental and field research. It resembles experimental research in that
the investigator himself chose the subjects to take part in it. It resembles
field research in that, once he had chosen them, they lived together as a
real group for a long period of time and were subjected to little experimental manipulation. The investigator used this procedure because he
felt that the results of many psychological experiments were irrelevant
to real social processes so long as their subjects' contact with one another
was ephemeral.

To be specific, the investigator acquired a house in Ann Arbor, Michigan, large enough to house seventeen students. He offered to students
transferring from other institutions to the University of Michigan the
opportunity to live in this house rent free for one year, on condition
that each student agreed to serve for four or five hours a week as an

informant and subject in psychological experiments. He chose the students in such a way that none knew any of the others in advance: no two had even come from the same town or city. He did so because he was specially interested in studying how social relations develop from the beginning among persons who are strangers to one another. Besides providing rooms for the students, the house also had its own kitchen, where a hired cook prepared meals which the students served. This was the only task they carried out in common. After living together for one academic year (1954–55), the original seventeen students were replaced for another year by a second seventeen, chosen like the first so as to be unknown to one another but matched with the first in various background characteristics. For instance, they contained the same proportions of Protestants, Catholics, and Jews.

The findings of the research come largely from the responses the students made to questionnaires, tests, and interviews that the investigator and his assistants administered to them, apparently at least once a week. The findings are many, varied, and interesting. We shall review only the more obvious ones here.

The two main variables of the version of balance theory we are interested in are the degree of liking or attraction of two persons for one another and the degree of agreement between them on at least one topic. In the usual research on balance, the variables take only two values: each person either likes or dislikes the other and either agrees or disagrees with him. The theory says that the behavior of a number of pairs in contact with one another will change over time in such a way that the overall correlation between attraction and agreement tends to increase, *both* because liking will bring about agreement, or agreement, liking, *and* because disliking will bring about disagreement, or disagreement, disliking.

The investigator developed and administered questionnaires from the results of which he could measure the attraction of any member of the group for any other member and the changes in his attraction over time. He also developed measures of both the perceived and the actual agreement between any two members on a number of subjects: their liking for other members, their opinions on various political and social issues, and their generalized "values," for instance: the value set on cooperating with others.

In general the results of this prolonged research bore out the predictions of balance theory. Since the members of the group were wholly unacquainted with one another at the outset, it took them some weeks of living together in the house to discover what the opinions and values of the different members were and whether or not they found one another attractive. But once a member had begun to get acquainted with another, he was more likely to perceive he agreed with him, the more highly he was attracted to him (see especially, Newcomb, 1961: 102, 120).

As for the correlation between the mutual attraction of two members and their actual agreement, it tended to increase with time, but more rapidly in the first weeks of acquaintanceship than later, when it leveled off and stabilized, after the forces working toward balance had apparently produced all the change of which they were capable (see 206–207). Finally, as might be expected from the findings about individual pairs, a member whom many others found attractive, who was popular, tended to be one whom many others agreed with (see 202–205).

In the relation between attraction and agreement, either one may, as we have suggested, be a cause and either an effect, depending on the circumstances. A person's previous experience of favorable exchange of rewards with another increases his liking for the other and also the probability that he will later agree with him. In this case, liking precedes and determines agreement—and disliking, disagreement. On the other hand, the experience of agreement, since it is itself a rewarding exchange of opinion, increases liking. In this case, agreement precedes and determines liking. The present investigation seemed to show that the latter process was more powerful than the former in certain conditions. In the course of their acquaintanceship, few pairs of subjects showed much change toward agreement about topics other than their judgments about particular persons. In view of the general tendency toward more balanced relationships, this fact implied that two members who liked one another and agreed about impersonal topics must have held similar views on these topics before they became acquainted. When they did meet and found they agreed, their liking for one another increased. Here agreement must have preceded and determined liking (see 79–80).

Persons who are in initial agreement with one another are apt, for reasons we gave in Chapter 3, to be similar to one another in background characteristics. Accordingly, we should expect that, as members of a group become acquainted and balanced relationships increase, members who are attracted to one another will turn out to be similar in background. In the present research there was some evidence to this effect. Among students living in the house during the first year, those who had become highly attracted to one another by the end of fifteen weeks of residence were likely to be similar in age and in type of residential origin; that is, students who resembled one another in coming from big cities were statistically likely to be attracted to one another, as were students who resembled one another in coming from small towns (see 86–92).

For the most part we have stated the argument as it applies to the two persons forming a pair. But it is obvious that, in real groups, pairs may be linked in clusters, cliques, or subgroups, all of whose members agree with one another, like one another, and interact with one another often. This follows from the assumptions of balance theory in its stricter forms, in which persons can either agree or disagree about a single subject and can either like or dislike one another: neutrality and indifference are not allowed. Then if *A* likes and agrees with *B*, and *B* with *C*, it is very difficult for *C* not to like and agree with *A*; hence a clique is formed. Moreover the persons they dislike and disagree with will like and agree with one another. For if the number of members of a group is limited, to dislike and disagree with some of them automatically means that one likes and agrees with others: one has only these others to turn to for support. Indeed there are theorists (Cartwright and Harary, 1956; Davis, 1963) who argue that, if the processes postulated in the stricter forms of balance theory were the only ones determining social structure, a group would wind up split into just two subgroups, the members of each subgroup liking and agreeing with one another and disliking and disagreeing with the members of the other.

This result does occur in real groups, though not always; nor need the groups be equal in size. If similarity of background tends to encourage agreement and liking, then any inequality in the number of members with similar backgrounds would tend to prevent the division of a group into subgroups of equal size. Agreement and disagreement, moreover, are not the only rewards and punishments exchanged in most real groups, especially not agreement or disagreement on a single subject; nor is one man's agreement of the same value as another's. If one or a few members are able to supply other rewards of specially high value, if, that is, they possess great power, and if they happen also to be in agreement with one another, they are probably able to induce a disproportionate number of lesser members to agree with them and like them, and so again prevent the division of their group into the two equal parts.

When groups do divide into subgroups by balancing processes, it follows from the argument as applied to pairs that members of a given subgroup are apt to be similar in one or more background characteristics. In the second year of the operation of the house studied in the present research, the students could be separated into two "clusters," marked by agreement in values among the members of each cluster and their disagreement with the members of the other cluster. Thus the values of Cluster *A* tended to be those of what we used to call real, corn-fed, American boys, who had a great interest in sports. The clusters also differed in the background characteristics of their members. "All but two of the ten Cluster *A* members were enrolled in the Engineering School, and all but one of Cluster *B* in the Arts College" (Newcomb, 1961: 231). Cluster *A* also included all four of the war veterans, older and more experienced than the others. As for the six members of Cluster *B*, the others tended to refer to them as "Eastern sophisticates." The investigator goes on to say: "All but one of Cluster *B* were in fact from urban centers in Atlantic seacoast states, and only two from Cluster *A*, and these exceptions are revealing. They suggest that the perceived agreers in Cluster *A* included every one who was not an urban Easterner, except two subjects who associated frequently with those who were, together with one Eastern urbanite who was mature, socially extroverted, and a good athlete" (232–233).

These clusters were marked by their members' agreement on values. But in this case mutual agreement was not highly correlated with mutual attraction. There was much mutual attraction among the members of Cluster *B*, but a good deal less among the members of Cluster *A*. Indeed the members of Cluster *A* were more attracted to those of Cluster *B* than to one another, though not to a statistically significant degree. We are warned again, if we needed warning, that no empirical generalization in social science holds good in all circumstances.

Proximity and Friendship

The study we shall next consider formed part of a larger research reported by Festinger, Schachter, and Back (1950). Immediately after World War II, the Massachusetts Institute of Technology built two sets of temporary buildings to help house the influx of married students and their wives. The first of the sets to be built was called Westgate and the second Westgate West. The investigators carried out research in both sets. We shall first consider their study of Westgate West.

The buildings of Westgate West were placed in parallel rows all facing in the same direction. Each of the buildings was identical in design to the others and consisted of two floors with five flats on each floor. Each flat was occupied by a married couple, the husband being a student at M.I.T. On each floor the doors of the flats opened on a porch or gallery that ran the length of the building; the top-floor porch lying directly above the ground-floor one. From the ends of the ground-floor porch stairways ran up to the ends of the top-floor one. Figure 2 shows the layout and gives numbers to the flats for ready reference.

In the study of Westgate West we shall be particularly interested in the findings obtained from a single question the investigators asked of

Figure 2   Schematic Diagram of Westgate West Building

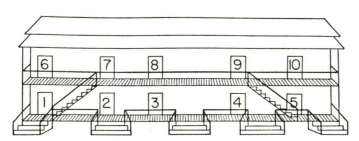

every couple. The question was: "What three people in Westgate or Westgate West do you see most of socially?" The question was addressed to the "social" interaction of the couples and not to their interaction with others in classrooms, laboratories, or elsewhere. People may interact with one another without liking one another, if they are forced to interact by such things as the necessity of collaborating on a job; but since the social interaction of the couples at Westgate West was not so constrained, we shall assume, as the investigators themselves certainly did, that the interaction was accompanied by favorable sentiments, and that any couple naming another couple as persons they saw much of looked on them also as friends.

The findings about Westgate West that we shall be chiefly interested in are those relating the physical layout of the buildings to friendship choices. When the investigators plotted the choices that couples made and received against the position in the buildings of the flats occupied by these couples, they discovered that, statistically speaking, a couple was most likely to choose another whose flat was an immediate neighbor of its own, one unit of distance away, next most likely to choose a nearest neighbor but one, and so on. The nearer a couple lived to another couple, the more apt it was to become friendly with the other.

The next finding was a little less obvious. The investigators examined the way in which couples on a particular floor distributed their choices to others on the same floor, and discovered that couples in the central flats—Nos. 3 and 8—were chosen as friends more often than other couples. When we say that these flats were central, we mean that the average distance from them to all other flats on their floors was less than it was for any of the others. Again, physical proximity was governing the choice of friends.

Let us now ask how we are to explain these findings. Geographical proximity is obviously a universal determinant of social relationships, one of the crucial given conditions to which the general propositions must be applied if we are to explain concrete findings about social structures. People cannot form relationships with others unless they can make contact with them, and physical proximity in one form or another determines the chances that they will make contact. The nearer people are to one another in their life and work, the more apt they are to meet and exchange some amount of activity, however little and however trivial, such as comments about the weather. Of course their nearness need not consist in sheer proximity measured in feet or miles. It may also lie in the likelihood that their paths will cross. Even when a person has made contact with several others, the chances that he will go on to develop relationships with some of them and not with others are affected by proximity, since distance in general increases the costs of interaction with others, so that, if the rewards of interaction with two persons are the same, a man is more likely to interact with the one who is the nearer.

Once thrown together under these circumstances, once they have exchanged some action not positively punishing, they are apt to repeat the exchange and ultimately develop what we have called a relationship, a repeated exchange of rewarding actions of different kinds. That is, they will be apt to do so if their interaction is not constrained, if each is free to avoid interaction should any of the exchanges turn out to be punishing. And once particular relationships have been formed, they render progressively less likely the development of further ones, since people are limited in the amount of time they can devote even to social interaction.

Accordingly, proximity is apt to encourage the development of favorable relationships between persons—provided that other conditions do not interfere. The other conditions may be summed up as the absence of other persons who may be alternative sources of a reward that is sufficiently great in value to more than make up for the increased cost in distance covered to obtain it. This general condition appears to have been met in Westgate West. All of the couples were new to the project and largely to M.I.T. itself. Thus, the development of new relationships could proceed without interference from already established ones. If the housing development had been studied at a later period of time, when some of the couples would have left and others replaced them, the effect of sheer proximity on the patterning of relationships would not have been nearly so clear.

The investigators tell us nothing about the background characteristics of the couples in Westgate West, but they must have been grossly similar in background, more similar indeed than the students at the University of Michigan who were the subjects of the research previously considered. Besides being well-educated, middle-class Americans, they were all, unlike the Michigan students, interested in the same subject, engineering. Since people who are similar are apt to reward one another —particularly in "social" interaction—the presence in Westgate West of clusters of persons similar to one another but sharply different from other such clusters might likewise have masked the effects of proximity: in the development of relationships, the rewards of similarity might have been great enough to more than make up for the possible costs of distance. Surely there must have been individual similarities and differences in background among the couples at Westgate West, and they must have had some effect. After all, the correlation between friendship and proximity, while statistically significant, was not perfect—proximity was not the only influence at work. Yet the differences do not appear to have been great; at least the investigators do not report what they were. In any event, it takes time for people to discover their subtler similarities in values and interests which stem from their similarities in background. They must first make contact, and they do so for reasons other than similarity itself. Westgate West was brand new, and its inhabitants had not lived in it long at the time they were studied. Compared with other influences, sheer proximity may have its greatest effect in the earlier stages of the development of social structure.

The final finding about Westgate West that we present really follows from the earlier ones but is far less obvious. It is shown in Table 4. Row 1 simply indicates the apartment positions on the ground floor, as given in Figure 2. Row 2 takes the total number of choices given by lower-floor couples to upper-floor ones and shows which flats on the lower floor these choices came from. Specifically, the high figures, 13 and 11, show that couples occupying end flats on the ground floor were more likely to choose people on the upper floor than were couples occupying other flats. Since the end flats lay at the feet of the stairs leading down from the top floor, people living in them had an especially good chance to come into contact with upper-floor people. As the investigators say, they were structurally closer to them. Yet couples in the central flats (3) were more likely to choose upper-floor couples than were the occupants of flats 2 and 4, even though the central flats were further from the stairs.

Table 4   Geographical Location and Sociometric Choice

1. Apartment Position	1	2	3	4	5
2. Choices Given to Upper Floor	13	5	8	6	11
3. Choices Received from Upper Floor	14	3	12	4	15

Row 3 tells the same sort of story. It shows how couples on the upper floor distributed their choices among the flats on the ground floor. End apartments were most likely to get choices from above, just as they had been to give them. The central flat came close behind, but flats 2 and 4 got few choices.

The reader will of course have noticed that the number of flats on each floor was only five, and yet the choices given and received were far more than five. The reason is that Westgate West consisted of seventeen identical apartment buildings, and the figures in the different cells of the table represent the sums of all the choices given or received by couples occupying the corresponding positions in the individual buildings. What, for instance, does the figure 15 in row 3 indicate? $17 \times 5 = 85$ couples occupied top-floor flats. Of these 85 couples, 15 chose (said they "saw most of socially") couples occupying No. 5 flats on the ground floors, of whom there were, of course, seventeen. That is, about one-sixth of all couples living on the top floors chose couples living in flat 5. This may not seem a high percentage, but it was significantly higher than the percentage of couples choosing the inhabitants of flats 2 and 4. The table of course represents an aggregate or overall tendency. A single building taken by itself might not, for one reason or another, have displayed the pattern that stood revealed when the figures for all the buildings were taken together.

How shall we explain the pattern? The large number of choices given and received by couples in flats 1 and 5 requires no new argument to account for it. These were the apartments lying at the feet of the stairs running up to the top floor. Accordingly there was a particularly good chance that upper-floor people would meet the people who lived in these flats and hence eventually establish social relationships with them. The relatively large number of choices given and received by the couples occupying middle flats on the ground floor (No. 3) requires a more indirect attack. After all, this was physically and functionally the flat on the ground floor that was, on the average, furthest from the flats on the top floor, and so the effect of geography cannot directly account for this feature of the pattern. And yet geography does come in. If we consider only the occupants of ground-floor flats, we shall remember that its centrality made couples living in No. 3 flat most likely to be chosen as friends by other couples on that floor. And if in turn these couples had any friends on the top floor, they were particularly likely to bring the central couples into contact with top-floor people. We may imagine small parties that brought three or four couples together. That is, we must make an assumption about indirect relations between people: if *O* is a friend of *P*'s, and *P* is a friend of *Q*'s, then the chance of *O*'s becoming a friend of *Q*'s increases. And thus, in spite of the physical and functional distance between them, central couples on the ground floor would be apt to have many friends on the top floor.

Cohesiveness and Conformity: A Housing Study

We now take leave of Westgate West and turn to Westgate, the second of the two projects for housing married students at M.I.T. The research at Westgate reached findings of a somewhat different kind from those reached in Westgate West.

Westgate was the older of the two housing projects and it differed in layout from Westgate West. The married couples lived in flats in buildings of one story, not two, and the buildings, instead of facing all in the same direction in parallel rows, were grouped into nine courts, each given a name. The houses in a court faced one another across a grass plot.

Early in the life of Westgate, the students set up an organization to look after their interests as tenants, especially in dealing with the university administration. As part of their research, the investigators interviewed every couple living in Westgate and among other questions asked how each one felt about the tenants' organization (whether the couple was favorable toward it or not) and how much time they devoted to its activities (whether they were active in it or not). According to their attitude toward, and activity in, the organization, the investigators placed the couple in one of four possible classes: favorable-inactive, favorable-active, unfavorable-inactive, and unfavorable-active. For obvious reasons, there turned out to be no members of the last class, which left three classes to be considered.

The investigators next examined the distribution among the Westgate courts of the couples belonging to the different classes and discovered that in nearly every court an absolute majority of the couples belonged to a single one of the three classes. The position of the majority might differ from one court to another—in one it might be favorable-active, in another unfavorable-inactive—but there was a definite majority position in every court but one, and even in that court a single class held a strong plurality. The investigators did not inquire why the majority in any court held one position about the tenants' organization rather than another; but the fact that majority positions existed was exceedingly unlikely to have occurred by chance: a social process by which majorities were formed must have been at work. Accordingly the investigators felt justified in referring to the position taken by the majority or plurality in each court as the *court standard*. We should call it a group norm.

That a majority of couples living in a particular court conformed to a particular norm of opinion and behavior in regard to the tenants' organization did not, of course, mean that every couple did so. The investigators referred to the members of the majority in any given court as *conformers* and to the members of the other two classes as *deviates*. Let us make sure we understand just what this means. A couple that was unfavorable to, and inactive in, the tenants' organization and that lived in a court whose standard was unfavorable-inactive counted as conformers; whereas the same couple, had they lived in a court whose standard was favorable-active or favorable-inactive, would have counted as deviates. It is clear also that the deviates in any court could depart from its standard in more than one way. The courts differed a good deal in the percentage of conformers among their members, the figures ranging from 77 percent in the most conformist court to 46 percent in the single court in which the standard was followed by only a plurality of the members. The percentage of conformers in a court (or its reciprocal, the percentage of deviates) is one of the two main variables that the investigators related to one another in the study of Westgate.

The other variable was constructed from answers to the question about friendships that was asked of couples in Westgate, as it was asked of couples in Westgate West: "What three people in Westgate or Westgate West do you see most of socially?" The answers to this question showed the same general relationship between friendship choices, on the one hand, and physical and functional distance, on the other, as were found in Westgate West, and we shall have more to say about it later. The particular variable we are immediately interested in was of a different sort. From the raw data, the investigators readily calculated a score expressing the number of friendship choices made by couples living in any one court and given to other couples living in the same court as a percentage of the total number of choices made by members of that court. The scores of the different courts ranged from 67 to 47 percent. This constituted the second variable, which the investigators, as members of the Festinger group, called the *cohesiveness* of a court.

The investigators thought of the percentage of in-court choices among total choices as a measure of the social unity of a court. But this measure might, as they recognized, give similar scores to social situations quite different from one another. Suppose that half the couples in a court chose one another, that the other half also chose one another, but that no couple in one half chose any couple in the other half. The measure the investigators used would then show the court to be highly cohesive, whereas in any ordinary sense of the word it would be hardly cohesive at all but deeply divided into two, probably antagonistic, subgroups. For this reason the investigators introduced a correction into their measure of cohesiveness, the details of which we shall not go into here, so as to insure that the measure would not mask the presence of hostile subgroups and would really tap the degree to which friendships were widely diffused within a court.

There remained only to relate the two variables, conformity and cohesiveness, to one another. The investigators put the courts into rank order on each of the two variables and then calculated the correlation between the two. They found it very high: "The more cohesive the court (that is, the greater the proportion of 'in-court' choices), the smaller the proportion of people who deviated from the court standard" (Festinger, Schachter, and Back, 1950: 93). The correlation was even higher for the corrected measure of cohesiveness than it had been for the original one.

This finding reached in Westgate was not reproduced in Westgate West. It was not that in the latter project the direct relationship between cohesiveness and conformity reversed itself. Rather, there was no correlation between the two variables at all. Indeed there were proportionately far fewer of the buildings at Westgate West that had established any majority position at all in regard to the tenants' organization. In effect, no group standards about this matter had developed; and where there is no norm, the question of conformity does not arise.

But why had norms not developed at Westgate West? Of course there was a difference between the two housing projects in physical layout. The Westgate West buildings did not face one another around courts.

That is, the physical conditions for the development of large and cohesive groups may not have existed there: the individual building, housing only ten couples, was the effective social unit if anything was. Probably more important was the fact that Westgate West had been built and occupied more recently than Westgate, and though social ties between individual couples had certainly developed, there may not have been enough time for the processes of influence to work themselves out that both create group norms and bring people to conform to them. Whatever the reason, let us take note of the fact that here, as so often elsewhere, the relationship between two variables may itself depend on the value of a third variable, and that as its value changes, the original relationship may disappear or even reverse itself.

The positive relationship between cohesiveness and conformity found under the conditions obtaining at Westgate is just what we should have expected from the argument put forward in Chapter 5. The members of the Festinger group define cohesiveness in effect as the degree to which participation in a group rewards its members. The rewards may be of many different kinds: the one studied in Westgate was friendship. If a group can offer much in the way of friendships to its members, it can exert much control over them, since it can deprive them of much if they do not conform. We must also remind ourselves that a change in the value of either variable, in-group friendships or conformity, may effect a change in the value of the other in a continuous feedback loop or spiral. The existence of positive ties between persons tends to make them become more similar in respects other than the activities that led to the original formation of the tie: in the present case, similarity in attitude and behavior toward the tenants' organization. This similarity reacts in turn upon the positive ties and, since it is often rewarding, serves to foster them still further.

In examining the research at Westgate West we have so far encountered only an overall correlation between the proportion of conformers in a court and proportion of in-court friendships. The argument put forward to account for the correlation tacitly assumes that individual members of a court were more likely to choose conformers as friends than they were to choose deviates. That is, individual conformers were rewarded with friendships, or had friendships to lose if they did not conform; and the larger the number so rewarded, the larger the number of conformers. But the assumption may be contrary to fact: it is conceivable that the overall correlation could subsist, even though individual members chose conformers as friends no more often than they did deviates. Were that the case, we should have to find some other explanation for the correlation than the one we have offered. Happily it was not the case. The investigators examined the number of friendship choices *received* by individual conformers and deviates—each couple, of course, *gave* the same number, three—and they found that individual conformers received, on the average, more choices than they gave, and the deviates fewer. This implies, of course, that deviates often chose conformers as friends, but conformers chose other conformers. This pattern of choice held good not only within courts but between them: deviates in one court, if they made any choices of couples in other courts, tended to choose conformers rather than fellow deviates. Of course, since the courts differed in their norms, a deviate in one court might think and behave in the same way toward the tenants' organization as a conformer in another.

The Westgate West study related geography to friendship; the Westgate study related friendship to conformity. A final discovery at Westgate closed the ring, so to speak, by relating conformity to geography. Although most of the Westgate buildings faced one another around courts, a few corner buildings faced away from the courts, and the entrances to the flats in these buildings opened onto the street at the back and not, like the other flats, onto the central plots of grass. The investigators discovered that deviates were especially likely to come from these corner buildings. We cannot be sure why they did so, but we may risk a guess. Because of their isolated location, couples in these buildings were less likely than those more centrally located to form friendships within their own courts. Probably, therefore, other members were less likely to try to get them to conform to court standards, and they themselves had less to lose by not conforming: if nonconformity put an end to friendships, they had fewer friendships that might be ended. For both reasons, these couples were likely to be deviates.

In this connection it is interesting that those few couples who did not conform even though they lived in centrally located flats on the inside of courts received even fewer friendship choices than did the deviates in the corner building. Such couples must certainly have been exposed to attempts to influence them. In failing to comply, they were withdrawing from the others, much more conspicuously than the corner deviates, who geographically were hardly members of their courts at all, a reward that the others thought they had reason to expect. Hence the hostility toward them was greater. If all the outward signs show you to be a member of a group, but you do not behave like one, the other members may get even more down on you than on someone who behaves just as badly as you do but whom they had no reason to consider a member. You are a traitor; he is not.

Besides friendships and conformity, the investigators in the course of their interviews learned many other things about the students' social life. For some couples, social life centered within the housing projects; for others, the parties they went to and the friends they visited lay mostly outside. The investigators found, as we might have expected, that deviates were much more apt than conformers to get their social life outside the projects. Once again we know the facts but not the reasons for them, which might be of two different kinds. Before they came under the influence of fellow members of their court, a couple might already have formed outside ties. Commanding this alternative source of social reward, they would find the approval they might get from fellow members relatively less valuable, and accordingly they would have less inducement to conform. In this case, their outside ties would be the cause of their deviance.

There is another possibility. A couple might have formed no outside ties before coming into the housing project. If nevertheless they failed to conform to the court standard, the other members would deny them social reward, and this in turn would lead them to look for it on the outside. In this case, their deviance would be the cause of their outside ties. No doubt both processes were at work at Westgate, but all we know for sure is the mere fact of the correlation between deviance and social life outside the project. What is more, this confession may be a sign that we have milked the M.I.T. research dry.

Explanation and Causal Chains: A Digression

What we have learned from the M.I.T. research gives us an excuse for making a methodological comment that has a wider bearing than the research itself. Suppose we have learned that, in the conditions prevailing in Westgate, the geographical position of a couple "caused" its social acceptance, and its social acceptance in turn "caused" its conformity to the court norm. There must of course have been other reasons for a couple's social acceptance besides its accessible location and other reasons for its conformity besides its social acceptance, but the causal relationships as stated did hold good statistically. If, moreover, social acceptance "caused" conformity, conformity also "caused" social acceptance, in a typical feedback loop or favorable spiral. Let us assume for purposes of argument that the research established a "causal chain" of variables which we may diagram as follows:

Geographical Location $\longrightarrow$ Social Acceptance $\rightleftharpoons$ Conformity

It is one of the purposes of social science, as of other sciences, to establish such causal chains, and social science has become increasingly effective in establishing their statistical validity. Indeed it has succeeded in establishing chains far more complicated than the one diagramed here, and in so doing it has achieved much. We do not question the achievement; rather, what we question here is the habit some social scientists have fallen into of calling a causal chain an explanation. They would claim they had explained the distribution of conformers among the courts of Westgate by establishing the chain of variables that led up to it.

Anyone is free to define the word *explanation* in any way he pleases. All we wish to do here is point out that this definition of explanation is not ours (see Homans, 1967). In the first place, what is to be explained is always for us a relationship and not a set of values taken by a variable, as it is in the definition of explanation as a demonstrated causal chain. For us, for instance, a typical *explicandum* is the relationship between social choice and conformity, not the distribution of conformers among the courts of Westgate. In the second place, the relationship is, in our view, explained only by showing how it follows from more general propositions, under specific given conditions, as the conclusion of an argument, a deductive system. Those who look on explanation as a demonstrated causal chain often neglect to make the deduction explicit, though often showing implicitly that they know what it ought to be. (For a discussion of the place of causal chains in social theory, see Blalock, 1969: 10–16.)

In our view of explanation, it is not enough to establish a causal chain, however great a research achievement that may be in itself. It is also necessary to provide the argument from which each link in the chain, each causal proposition, follows. In the Westgate study there are three such propositions: central location tends to lead to social acceptance; social acceptance tends to lead to conformity; and finally, conformity reacts so as to produce still further social acceptance. To explain the chain as a whole, we must provide arguments from which each of these causal relationships follows, and indeed we have tried to do just that.

The distinction we have made here between two meanings of the word *explanation* applies to all causal chains, no matter how complicated.

Cohesiveness and Conformity: An Industrial Study

The next investigation we shall examine is the work of Stanley Seashore (1954). We shall limit ourselves to that part of his research most nearly comparable to the M.I.T. study. The results of the two investigations are much alike, although they were carried out in very different settings.

The research was carried out in a large factory in the Midwest making heavy machinery and employing between ten and twenty thousand workers. The smallest recognized unit of human organization in the plant was the "section" of from ten to thirty men assigned to a particular manufacturing job. Sometimes duplicate sections followed one another on successive shifts. For the investigator these sections were the groups to be studied, just as the courts were the groups studied by the investigators at Westgate. For various practical reasons, such as his failure to get reliable production records for some sections, the investigator was forced to leave some of the sections out of his study. He wound up studying 228 sections with a total of 5871 members.

One of the main variables in the study was the productivity of workers. For those jobs in which output could be measured—and these were the jobs included in the research—management had set up standards of production by time-study, and informed the workers every day of their production expressed as a percentage of the standard. If a man produced four pieces of work a day on a job for which the standard called for five, his productivity was 80 percent. This procedure allowed the investigator, as it did the management, to compare the productivity of workers doing wholly different jobs. One man might be welding, another machining, but their productivity was the same if each produced 80 percent of the standard for his own job. The investigator got a record in this form of the average productivity for three months of every worker in the sections he studied.

The second main variable was the cohesiveness of the group, just as it was in the M.I.T. study, but in the present one the investigator measured it in a more complicated way. He asked all the workers in every section studied to answer a questionnaire that included, among others, the following three questions: Do you feel that you are really part of your work group? If you had the chance to do the same kind of work for the same pay, in another work group, how would you feel about moving? How does your work group compare with other work groups in the factory on each of the following points: the way the men get along together, the way they stick together, and the way they help each other on the job? From the answers to such questions the investigator calculated a score for each worker and a score for the average cohesiveness of the members of a section. The larger the percentage of men in a section that said they felt part of the group, wanted to stay in it, and thought it was better than other comparable groups, the higher the section scored on cohesiveness. It seems quite fair that the investigator should call this an index of cohesiveness, as it was evidently designed, like other measures of cohesiveness, to gauge the reward workers got from associating with others in their group.

Now that we have seen the way the underlying variables were measured, let us look at the relationships between them. The more cohesive a section was, the more likely it was to show little variability in the productivity of its members. That is, the greater the liking members expressed for their association with other members of their section, the more similar they were in productivity. The investigator did not take time to make a firsthand field study of any section, but no one familiar with American industry would doubt that sections whose members were similar in productivity must have been sections whose members had adopted, and largely conformed to, an output norm such as we described in Chapter 5. If this interpretation is correct, the first finding the investigator reached in the factory study was exactly the same as that of the M.I.T. study: the more cohesive is the group, the larger is the number of its members that conform to a group norm.

Someone familiar with American industry would also guess that in the more cohesive groups production as reported in the output records may not have been quite the same as actual production. Workers that adopt an output norm are often in a position to control their output records by reporting in the short run more or less work than they have really completed; and their norm is not just that their actual output should be the same but that their reported output should be so. Should this have been the case, it would not invalidate the findings of the investigator, for a norm of reported output is just as truly a norm as a norm of actual output, and conformity with it is just as truly conformity.

When the investigator said that the members of a cohesive section were apt to be similar in productivity, he implied nothing about the level at which they were similar. One section might have adopted for its norm a high level of production, say 120 percent of standard; another might have adopted a much lower one, say 80 percent. Why a section adopted the particular level that it did the investigator could only have explained if he had made a detailed study of each section, especially the past history of its relations with management. But this formed no part of his design. So long as the members' output clustered close to 120 percent in one section and close to 80 percent in another, the two were alike in the aspect of behavior that interested him. In this he resembled the investigators in the Westgate study, who cared little what particular standard a court might have adopted so long as they could count the number of members that conformed to it.

From the finding about within-group similarity in productivity a finding about between-group similarity followed directly. The investigator divided the total range of sections into two parts, putting the high-cohesive sections in one and the low-cohesive sections in the other. And he found that the between-group variability in productivity was greater in the high-cohesive sections than in the low-cohesive ones. But let us put this finding more clearly. The productivity score of a section was the average productivity of its members. Compared with one another, the productivity scores of the low-cohesive sections scattered themselves less widely over a range of possible scores than did those of the high-cohesive sections, again compared with one another. Part of the reason for this we have already seen. High-cohesive sections were those whose members all tended to cleave to an output norm, but the absolute level at which they set the norm could be anywhere: high, middle, or low. Accordingly, a comparison of the scores of such sections might show them widely dispersed over a range: their between-group variability was high.

Unlike those of a high-cohesive section, the individual members of any single low-cohesive one tended to be widely dispersed in their productivity. Instead of clustering near a norm, their individual production records might be low, middle, or high. For this very reason, the productivity score of the section as a whole—the average productivity of its members—would tend to fall near the middle of the possible range. And since the same condition tended to hold good of other low-cohesive groups, whose scores also fell near the middle of the range, the dispersal of their productivity scores was low—or at least lower than that of the high-cohesive groups. The high-cohesive sections were low in within-group, but high in between-group variability. Of course these two findings are not independent of one another: they are the same finding looked at in different ways.

In the present study as in the one at M.I.T. we have found conformity associated with cohesiveness. It is a reasonable guess that in both cases the two variables were associated for the same reasons. A cohesive group is one in which many members reward one another. Accordingly, if some degree of ostracism is the penalty for failing to conform to a norm, a potential deviate has more to lose in such a group than he does in a less cohesive one, and therefore there are apt to be fewer deviates in these groups than in the others. Thus cohesiveness tends to encourage conformity.

The direction of causality can run in the other direction too. So far as there are members of a group that set a high value on conformity to a norm, they are rewarded by any members that conform to it and tend to reward these others in turn, thus contributing to the general exchange of rewards which is measured by the investigators as cohesiveness. The two variables act and react upon one another.

Both studies, moreover, suggest conditions that tend to produce more initial social acceptance for some persons than for others and accordingly more initial cohesiveness for groups whose membership includes many such persons than for other groups. In the M.I.T. researches, where all of the residents were fairly similar in background, social background does not seem to have made much difference to social behavior, and the crucial initial condition became instead the geographical location of persons in the buildings and courts. In the factory research, where the workers were much less similar to one another, the background variable did make a difference. Sections that contained a larger number of workers similar to one another in age were more apt to be cohesive than sections that contained a smaller number. The reason is that persons similar to one another are apt to be able to reward one another: to have learned to carry out and enjoy the same kinds of actions or to speak, as we say, the same language. Similarity is certainly not the only condition that facilitates the exchange of rewards, but it is a prominent one. Persons who are similar are also apt, as we shall see in later chapters, to be equals in status and thus to escape from some of the constraints on social interaction that inequality is apt to produce. Accordingly, groups many of whose members are similar to one another are often groups whose members are especially able to reward one another and thus to control one another's behavior. Similar to begin with, the members tend to become even more so through their conformity to the group norm.

In the factory, moreover, the groups that were more cohesive tended to hold higher status as measured by skill and pay than those that were less cohesive. Workers in high-status groups were, of course, likely to have high seniority in the factory and thus to have learned by experience the risks of departing from traditional norms of production. But there may have been a more general influence at work, though in mentioning it we anticipate the argument of later chapters. Membership in a group to which others accord high status is rewarding. Accordingly, if such a group can threaten to exclude a member who does not conform to its norms, it exerts much control over his behavior.

In short, we may construct for the factory study, as for the M.I.T. study, a causal chain leading up to conformity:

And as in the M.I.T. study we have advanced explanations for every causal link in the chain.

The Distribution of Power and Esteem

The investigations we have just been reviewing have much to say about the collective power of members of a group over other members. We turn now to an investigation that is more concerned with individual differences between members in the power they exert over others. This study is a famous early example of modern social science and is reported in two books, one by J. L. Moreno (1934), who initiated the research, and the other, giving more detail, by Helen Hall Jennings (1950), who did much of the actual work. We shall rely on the latter.

The investigator worked in the 1930s at the New York State Training School for Girls at Hudson, New York, whose inhabitants were more than 400 girls between twelve and sixteen years of age, committed by the Children's Courts for sexual delinquency. At the end of their stay, the school hoped to turn them out as useful citizens, able to support themselves; for this purpose it provided academic and vocational training, but relied above all on the way of life of the school itself. Although the girls were mostly children of poor parents, they were not otherwise unrepresentative of the population at large. No girl was committed that was known to be psychotic, below the normal range in intelligence, or in any other way unlikely to benefit from the training given.

The girls were used to psychologists and to taking psychological tests, and so it was with no overmastering anxiety that they met to take a test of a new kind. The investigator asked every girl to write down in order, without consulting the others, the names of the other girls she liked or disliked in each of four aspects of life at the Training School: living, working, studying, and spending leisure time. This test the investigator called the *sociometric test*. In no absolute sense of the words was it any more social or more metric than any other measure of social behavior that might be devised; but inventors may call their inventions what they will, and *sociometric test* has stuck as the name of questionnaires like those used by the investigator at Hudson.

To be more specific, let us take up the "living" criterion. The living quarters at the school consisted of a number of houses, in each of which roomed a group of from twenty to thirty girls, jointly responsible for its housekeeping and other matters of house concern, under the supervision of a housemother. In the sociometric test, each girl was asked to name the other girls she would like to live with in the same house, whether or not she was in fact living with any of them at the time. When one girl named another, the investigator spoke of her "choosing" the other. The questionnaire at Hudson did not limit a girl's choice: she might name as many others or as few as she wished. In the same way, each girl was asked to name the others she would not like to live with in the same house. This the investigator called "rejection."

The school gave vocational training in shops that also provided useful services to the community: a laundry, a beauty parlor, and the like. In each of these shops seven to fifteen girls worked together, not necessarily the same ones that lived together. In the sociometric test, each girl was asked to name the others she would or would not like to work with in the same shop (choice or rejection on the working criterion). The test did not require that a girl's choices on different criteria should overlap: she was free to choose a girl for working that she had rejected or simply failed to name as someone she would like to live with; but, as we might expect, there was in fact a certain amount of overlap. The same rules applied to choice and rejection on the two other criteria: spending leisure time with a girl and studying with her. On the studying criterion, the girls made rather few choices, and choices for living tended heavily to overlap choices for working. Therefore, in presenting her results, the investigator paid no further attention to choices for studying;

combined in a single set of figures the choices for living and for working; and thus was left with two criteria: living-working and leisure.

In order to explain the findings of concrete research, to show that its findings follow from general propositions under specified given conditions, it may be necessary first to show that the measures employed in the research do in fact correspond to, are in fact examples of, variables that appear in propositions of a higher order of generality. It is quite easy to be mistaken in this matter: the procedures actually used may have measured something different from what the man who does the explaining would like to think they did. In the case of the research at Hudson, we assume that the sociometric test was a measure of social approval, though a crude one. It showed, in three values, how much social approval, each girl gave to every other one. Let us also call social approval "liking" for the moment, though the word *liking* may turn out to have connotations which, while they overlap with the connotations of *approval,* do not wholly coincide with them. Each girl either liked (and chose) another, remained relatively indifferent to (and failed to name) her, or disliked (and rejected) her.

In the test, the girls expressed their sentiments to the investigator and not to the other girls. Although the research has nothing to say on the matter, we have no doubt that they expressed roughly the same sentiments to one another, and that the sentiments were recognized. There may well have been a girl or two who was not herself aware of her popularity with all the other girls who in fact chose her on the test. But studies that have gone into the perception of social choice as well as choice itself have found that, while the correlation is seldom perfect, there is generally a significant correlation between the persons that a person thinks will choose him and those that actually do (see Tagiuri, 1952). At any rate we assume here that the sentiments expressed in the sociometric test were also real rewards exchanged by the girls at the Training School—and real punishments, for rejection must have amounted to punishment.

Besides the sociometric test, the investigator also questioned the girls about their social contacts. She asked each girl to list all the other girls she took the trouble to speak to on her own account and not just because the others spoke to her first, and to list them without regard for her sentiments toward them (friendly, indifferent, or hostile). Since this *social-contact test* was a measure of interaction, we shall pay no further heed to it until we come back to that subject.

The findings of the Hudson research were many: we shall mention only a few of them, and we mention the first only to get it out of the way. The investigator administered the sociometric test on two occasions eight months apart. Because girls were getting discharged from the school and others admitted all the time, the girls who took the first test were not all the same as those that took the second. Indeed most of the findings that the investigator reports have to do only with the 133 girls who were on hand to take both tests and who lived in the same house on both occasions. Of these girls, the sociometric data showed that each occupied much the same relative, if not absolute, social position on the occasion of the second test as she had on the first. For instance, each received about as many choices and rejections on the first test as she did eight months later. This does not mean that no change took place but only that there was some measure of social continuity: the Training School had reached a fairly stable social structure. Indeed the evidence is that when a girl first came to Hudson she formed her opinion of others, and others theirs of her, pretty soon, and neither changed much after that.

The number of others a girl chose depended only on herself and might not mean much socially, but the number of others that chose her depended on these others and meant a great deal. In our terms, it was a measure of the *esteem* in which she was held within the community: it was a measure of her position relative to the others in what she received from them in the way of social approval. As such it was one measure—not the only measure—of her *status* in the community. Since status, as we shall see, is a matter of perception, we must assume again that the way the girls distributed approval in their answers to the sociometric test agreed in gross with the way they distributed it, and perceived themselves as distributing it, in their actual behavior. Esteem is something the girls received; we shall consider later the differences between them in what they gave to the others.

The investigator might have used a more elaborate measure of esteem, for she had asked each girl not only to name the others that she liked but also to put them into rank order of how much she liked them. The investigator might have taken these data into account by multiplying every choice by a figure indicating whether it was a first, second, or third choice, and so on. This would have had the effect of increasing the differences in esteem, for girls that received many choices also received many first choices (Jennings, 1950: 88). But perhaps because the rank orderings would have introduced statistical difficulties, the investigator paid rather little attention to them and in measuring esteem gave all choices an equal weight.

In looking at the results of the research at Hudson, we begin, therefore, with the distribution of the 133 girls present for both tests, according to the number of others by whom each was chosen on the living-working criterion. We shall consider later the distribution of choices for leisure time. We give the results of the first sociometric test; the second showed the same general kind of pattern. The distribution is plotted in Figure 3 from the table given in the investigator's report (Jennings, 1950: 46).

Along the vertical axis are plotted the number of girls choosing a

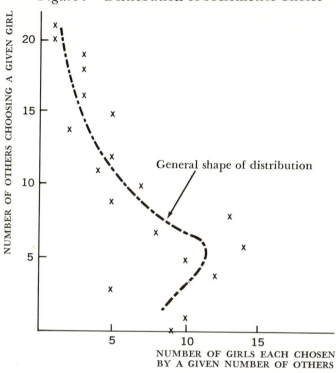

Figure 3   Distribution of Sociometric Choice

given girl and along the horizontal axis the number of girls chosen by a given number of others. Thus the highest point on the graph indicates that one and only one girl was chosen by 21 others; the point furthest to the right indicates that 14 girls were chosen by 6 others each, and the point at the bottom indicates that 9 girls received no choices at all.

Now consider the shape of the whole distribution. It is not what statisticians call a "normal" distribution, forming a symmetrical bell-shaped curve. Instead it tapers toward the top and bulges toward the bottom like a beet or radish. This means that choice tended to focus on a small number of very popular girls, but that indifference (or failure to choose) did not focus nearly so sharply: more girls were chosen little than were chosen much. In other words, the number of girls held in high esteem were, as we might expect from the argument presented in Chapters 4 and 5, relatively few, and the largest number of girls, the ordinary "good citizens," were those chosen by only a few others each. Most girls had found someone to love them: there were more of that sort than there were of girls that nobody chose. Since similar distributions have been found in other sociometric studies (see Bronfenbrenner, 1944), we have reason to believe that some general tendency had made its presence felt.

The distribution of rejections plotted in the same way does not yield the same kind of curve. True, a small number of girls were each rejected by a large number of others, but from then on the curves diverge. The rejection curve does not bulge in the lower middle like the choice curve. Instead the numbers increase fairly steadily and are greatest at the bottom, the largest number of girls being those rejected by no one or by only one other each. That is, while rather few girls found no one to choose them, a very large number found no one to reject them.

What pattern is revealed by the combined distributions of choice and rejection? In the first place it is clear that rejection was not the same thing as low positive choice. If it had been, many girls would have received many rejections, whereas in fact only a few did. To be positively rejected, a girl must have conspicuously violated whatever norms were current in the school, and in her peculiar way she must have been as rare a creature as a very popular girl. In the second place, a girl who was chosen just a little was not a girl who was also rejected just a little: she was more apt not to be rejected at all. For a girl that merely conformed, without being outstanding in any other way, would not have been rejected; and, while she might not have gotten much positive choice, she would assuredly have gotten some. There must have been many girls in this class of the inconspicuous and inoffensive, who had nothing much for them but certainly nothing against them. People who have nothing in their favor but common human goodness are the largest class in any society. In short, the combined pattern appeared to be the following: a few girls were chosen by many others; a few girls were rejected by many others, and many girls were chosen by few others but not rejected.

So far we have considered the distribution among the girls of what they received from others in the way of approval or rejection. We now turn to the distribution among the girls of what they gave to others. The investigator divided the distribution of positive choices into three parts, each containing about the same number of girls. She called the top third of the distribution, consisting of those girls each of whom was chosen by a large number of others, the class of the *over-chosen*. The membership of this class gave the investigator confidence that the residents at Hudson had answered the sociometric test sincerely, and that popularity as revealed by the test corresponded to popularity in the everyday life of the school, for eighteen out of the twenty elected members of the school council turned out also to be among the over-chosen. The investigator called the middle third of the distribution the class of the *average-chosen,* and the bottom third, which consisted, of course, of those girls each of whom was chosen by few others or by none at all, the class of the *under-chosen.*

The investigator then studied the kinds of activities performed by members of the three classes. Specifically, she interviewed every house-mother, and in the course of the interview she talked over with her every girl living in her house. The investigator constructed a rough classification of the kinds of behavior that housemothers complained about—such as quarrelsome, irritable, nagging, nervous, or rebellious behavior—and a similar classification of the kinds of behavior that housemothers praised—such as cooperative behavior, behavior that did not require supervision, evenness of disposition, willingness to do more than one's share of the work, and an ability to plan. Then in the course of the interviews, the investigator noted down which girls the housemothers mentioned as displaying the approved or disapproved kinds of behavior. The tabulated results revealed that the housemothers had, for every kind of approved behavior, mentioned far more members of the over-chosen class as displaying it than they had members of any other class. They had mentioned the average-chosen next most often and the under-chosen least. For most kinds of disapproved behavior the order of the classes was reversed: the housemothers mentioned the over-chosen least often, followed by the average-chosen, then the under-chosen. But, significantly, this was not true of all kinds of disapproved behavior. For rebellious, initiatory, retaliatory, and reticent behavior, the housemothers mentioned more members of the over-chosen than of any other class. In short, with these exceptions, the housemothers found the behavior of the over-chosen more rewarding than that of the average- and under-chosen.

But what do we care about the housemothers? It was the girls, not the housemothers, who answered the sociometric test, and we want to link the choices the girls themselves made with their own evaluation of the different kinds of behavior. We can make this connection if we argue that activities valued by the housemothers must often have been activities valued by the girls as well. The argument seems reasonable, and the investigator herself accepts it. Cooperative behavior, evenness of disposition, willingness to do more than one's share of the housework—all of which the housemothers praised, all of which they most often mentioned the over-chosen as possessing—must also have been activities that the girls themselves found rewarding in their companions. The very exceptions prove the rule. The few kinds of behavior that the housemothers disapproved of but mentioned the over-chosen most often as displaying—these were just the kinds of behavior that the girls themselves were apt to have looked on much more favorably. Thus rebellious behavior, described as "refusing to do what is requested by a person in authority," initiatory behavior ("behavior considered as too self-directive and too self-confident"), and reticent behavior ("does not bring personal problems to the housemother") were surely characteristic of independent girls, ready to lead and support their followers in standing up to the housemothers on occasion. If, in short, the housemothers found rewarding most of the activities performed by the over-chosen, the girls probably found all of their activities rewarding.

Note that the under-chosen, according to the method used by the investigator, included among their number the few girls who were often rejected. Therefore these rejected girls were likely to have displayed behavior disapproved of both by the housemothers and by the girls themselves, not, like the over-chosen, behavior disapproved of by the former but not the latter.

We must point out, finally, that the behavior of an over-chosen girl tended to be viewed as rewarding not just on one count but on a large number of counts, if not on all. If we had not thought about the matter, we might have expected that a girl found to be, for instance, "cooperative" would not necessarily have also been found to be, for instance, "solicitous of the welfare of new girls," but in fact she was apt to be. Perhaps she did not possess some special ability but a rather general one, which manifested itself in many ways. Perhaps what psychologists call the "halo-effect" was also at work here: the tendency for a favorable or unfavorable judgment that a person makes of another on one count to spill over and color the judgments he makes of him on other counts. Perhaps the finding resulted from what we shall call in a later chapter *status congruence.* Or some combination of these influences may have been operating. Let us take note of this fact, note also that we have not explained it, and pass on.

It should be obvious that the findings of the research at Hudson are those we should have expected from the general argument about social exchange presented in earlier chapters, though of course the correspondence may exist for reasons quite other than the ones offered there. In exchanges with the others, a highly chosen girl was able to offer services that, under the conditions obtaining at Hudson, and indeed under many other conditions, were highly valuable to the others—highly valuable because the demand for them was high in relation to the supply. In return, she was able to get from many other girls the reward of social approval.

By the very fact that the services they performed were in short supply, the girls who were able to command high esteem must have been relatively few in number. More numerous were the girls who could not offer the others services of so high a value but who were otherwise inoffensive. Such girls could not command a high degree of approval from many others, but neither were they rejected. Finally there were a few girls that the others actively rejected. These must have been girls who not only had little to offer the others but whose behavior positively hurt them. Such deviates must in any group be less numerous than the ordinary conformers, because deviation is a relative matter. The conformers must usually be a majority if they are to reject the deviates successfully. Should the rejected become the majority, they are no longer deviates but conformers. Indeed some of the previous conformers are then likely to change their behavior to match that of the former deviates.

Without further ado we shall say that a girl at Hudson who provided highly valued services and received high esteem was perceived by the others as enjoying high *status,* and a girl who neither gave much nor received much was perceived as holding correspondingly low status. In similar fashion, the investigator in the factory study assumed that workers who held relatively skilled jobs and received high pay had high status in the factory. Let us accept for the moment and without further question these *ad hoc* meanings given to the word *status* in different investigations. In a later chapter we shall take up the questions: What general meaning should be assigned to the word *status?* How does status develop? What is status congruence? And what back-effects does the development of status have on other behavior?

So far, moreover, we have only reached a gross view of the distribution of social choice at Hudson. The further and more detailed findings on this subject raise issues that had better be taken up in separate chapters. For instance, we have not considered the relationship between choices on different criteria. It turned out that the average girl chose fewer others to spend her leisure time with than she did to live and work with, that she tended to choose girls for leisure who were her social equals on the living-working criterion, and that her leisure-time choices were more apt to be reciprocated than were her living-working choices. Findings of this sort we shall take up again and attempt to explain in Chapter 13 on stratification.

Nor have we considered how girls of given status themselves distributed their choices. It turned out that mutual choice occurred most often among girls who were themselves highly chosen, that mutual rejection, though occurring less often than mutual choice, also occurred more often at this level than at any other; and that mutual indifference (no choice) occurred most often among under-chosen girls. These are matters that we shall take up in the chapter immediately following the present one.

Summary

In this chapter we continued to examine research findings that appear to bear out the conclusions of our more theoretical early chapters, but we turned from the findings of experimental to those of field research. We saw that students hitherto unacquainted who were brought to live together in one house behaved as we expected and increased the number of balanced relationships among them. At the same time, they tended to divide into two subgroups or cliques, the members of each subgroup sharing similar values and backgrounds. Among young married couples living in flats in a new housing development, we saw that, the shorter was the physical or functional distance between their flats, the more likely two couples were to become friendly. In a similar but older housing development, we saw that, the larger were the number of friendships between couples living in a group of houses, the larger the number of couples conforming to a group norm was apt to be. Couples living in isolated positions were particularly apt to be nonconformers, presumably because they were less likely than the others to be drawn into the web of friendships. We saw also from a study of working groups in a large factory that the members of highly cohesive groups (groups whose members were relatively highly rewarded by their membership) were more likely to conform to a group norm than the members of less cohesive groups. The high status of members or their similarity in age seemed to encourage cohesiveness. Finally we learned from a study of a residential community of delinquent girls that girls who received social approval from many others were those who were willing and able to provide rare and valuable services for the others; that is, they held high power.

8 Structures of Sentiment and Interaction

SUPPOSE THAT WE HAD RESTATED—NOT DISCOVERED, REMEMBER, but restated—some of the general propositions holding good of the behavior of men, and suppose further that we had shown how some rather gross empirical propositions about their social behavior followed from the general propositions under simplified though commonly realized given conditions—propositions such as that cohesive groups, groups that can offer their members much in the way of reward, are groups that are apt to contain many conformers. If we had done this, we should have done something. But a social science must sooner or later hope to accomplish more. It must hope to show how the propositions combine in the behavior of particular kinds of individuals under specific external circumstances to produce the unique structures of single groups. The solution of this kind of problem becomes specially difficult when, as must often happen, a small change in the characteristics of the membership or in the external circumstances may bring about big changes in group structure. To put the matter more crudely: analysis in this field may be difficult enough, but synthesis will be far more difficult. It may be easier to explain the fundamental social processes than to explain the results of their combination in particular cases.

Even if we had enough confidence in our propositions to set up problems of this sort and had set them up in some mathematical formulation, we should still until recently have been unable to solve them. Only the development of the high-speed computer has made their solution a practical possibility.

Matrices of Interpersonal Relationships

Here we shall provide neither the mathematics nor the computation, but we still wish to suggest some of the problems of synthesis by laying out simplified models of relationships in a group, or what we shall call toy societies. These models take the form of matrices, though they are not the same as the payoff matrices we introduced in Chapter 3. We· shall use them to help explain some of the patterns of interpersonal choice found at the Hudson State Training School for Girls by generating the patterns artificially and later to explain in the same way the patterns of interaction found in some other real groups. We shall not be escaping from the empirical to the artificial but rather using the artificial to explain the results of empirical research.

Specifically, let us set up a model group or toy society somewhat larger than our former group of Person, Other, and the Third Man. The new group will have six members: O, P, Q, R, S, and T. We then make the following assumptions about their behavior. Each finds rewarding the same kind of activity directed to him by other members. O provides this activity in its rarest and most valuable form—he or she may, for instance, be the most helpful member—and the others in alphabetical order provide a progressively less and less valuable service. Since this is a very small group and we can examine it closely, we allow each member to give a more detailed expression of his or her approval than the investigator allowed a girl at Hudson. Instead of either choosing or failing to choose others, he gives approval worth 5 to the member he likes most, 4 to the one he likes next most, and so on. (We shall not count the approval he gives to himself.) Finally, in accordance with the argument laid out in Chapter 4, we assume that each member can get from every other approval proportional to the rarity and value of the activity he performs for the other. Thus every member would give O approval worth 5 and so on. Under these assumptions, the way in which each member distributes approval to other members, and the differences between the members in esteem as measured in total amount of approval received are represented in the accompanying matrix (Table 5).

Let us be sure we understand what a matrix like this means. The figure 4, for instance, in the cell formed by the intersection of column P with row Q means that member Q gives to member P approval worth 4. The cells along the major diagonal are left empty because they can only represent the approval each member gives to himself. Since in the very way we set up the matrix we necessarily made the subsidiary assumption, which may turn out to be quite unrealistic, that members are equal in the total value to others of the approval each gives to them, the figures in the "Total Given" column are all 15. But we have made no such assumption about the total value each *receives*. The sums of the columns, marked "Total Received," indicate the amount of approval received by each member from the other members and thus correspond to the differences between members in esteem. Thus member O enjoys the highest esteem, followed by the others in alphabetical order.

Simple and straightforward as this matrix is, simple and straightfor-

Table 5   A Model Sociometric Matrix

			APPROVAL GIVEN TO					TOTAL GIVEN
		O	P	Q	R	S	T	
	O		5	4	3	2	1	15,
APPROVAL GIVEN BY	P	5		4	3	2	1	15
	Q	5	4		3	2	1	15
	R	5	4	3		2	1	15
	S	5	4	3	2		1	15
	T	5	4	3	2	1		15
TOTAL RECEIVED		25	21	17	13	9	5	

ward as were the assumptions on which it was constructed, it may still help us answer questions about the detailed distribution of sentiment in a real group. At the end of the last chapter, for instance, we asked how a member who was himself highly chosen would distribute his own choices. The matrix now tells us that, if the assumptions on which it was constructed were correct, he would tend to give his highest choices to other highly chosen members. Thus *O*, whose esteem is highest in the group, gives his first choice to *P*, who is in second place in esteem.

The matrix in fact generates the finding reached at Hudson and in other researches that mutual choice is highest among members themselves highly chosen and lowest among the under-chosen (Jennings, 1950: 87). How does the matrix do so? Let us assume that the conditions under which members of our toy society choose others are similar to the conditions under which the investigator allowed the girls at Hudson to take the sociometric test. We have had each of our toy members put the others in rank order of the approval he gives them, whereas the real girls at Hudson either chose others or failed to do so. To make our toy society fit this condition, let us say that any of our members who took a sociometric test would have chosen another if he gave the other approval worth either 4 or 5. Since three of our members gave one another approval worth this much, three of our members by this standard made mutual choices: *O* - *P*, *O* - *Q*, and *P* - *Q*. All three of these choices include *O* and *P*, our equivalents of the over-chosen girls who made up the top third of the sociometric distribution at Hudson, and none of them includes the under-chosen girls *S* and *T*. In short, our toy society does reproduce or generate the finding.

Why it should do so takes a little thinking. Suppose as our matrix assumes for our toy girls, that each real girl at Hudson chose others in something like the rank order of the value to her of the services these others rendered. Suppose further that many of the girls shared the same values, such as friendliness and cooperativeness in their companions. Under such conditions, many girls would choose the same other girls for much the same reasons, and this would be as much true of girls themselves highly chosen as it would be true of the rest. Accordingly, a girl herself highly chosen would be apt to choose another highly chosen girl, and the other to choose her in return. The probable result would be much mutual choice among the highly chosen. By the same token a girl herself chosen little would be apt to give her choices to girls that many others had chosen and so *fail* to give her choice to another under-chosen girl. The result could scarcely be other than little mutual choice among under-chosen girls.

Though our matrix and the assumptions on which it was constructed succeed in generating this finding of the Hudson study, they may do so for the wrong reasons. Or rather, our assumptions may not be so much wrong as incomplete. Let us consider one way in which they may be incomplete. We assumed that the members all set the same value on the activity each of them provided. But this assumption may become increasingly unrealistic as we move from the bottom of the group toward members held in higher esteem. Suppose that a girl won high esteem because she was helpful to other girls. But if she was able to be helpful, she must have been experienced and competent; and if she were competent, she would not in fact set the same value on receiving help herself as would the girls of lesser esteem: she would not need help as much as they would, and to this extent our assumption may be unrealistic. Indeed we might go on to argue that a girl of high esteem would not value the services of another such girl as much as would a girl of lower esteem, and that therefore we ought not to expect a large number of mutual choices among girls held in high esteem. But this would be contrary to the finding.

There is something to be said for the argument, but other developments are apt to compensate for any failure on the part of persons held in high esteem to reward one another for this particular reason. It is not just that behavior described, for instance, as "helpful" includes a number of different specific activities, and that two girls of high esteem might reward one another by helping one another in different ways. Another sort of development may take effect. The esteem in which they were held was one element in determining the status of the girls at Hudson. In the very process of winning high status through their primary capacity to provide rare and valued services to others, girls acquired a secondary capacity to reward. If they associated with others or, better, allowed others to associate with them, they provided these others with the outward and visible sign that these others were of high status too. This symbolic process would be particularly apt to provide mutual reward and thus mutual choice between girls themselves of high status. For association between a girl of high status and one of low would reward the latter but not the former: the latter would be symbolically raised in status, the former lowered. Association, on the other hand, between two girls both of high status in other respects would tend to reinforce the status of both. But we are anticipating subjects about which we shall have more to say in later chapters.

Rivalry and Hostility in the Upper Class

We have offered reasons why girls held in high esteem should choose one another often. But the investigator at Hudson, we must remember, also found that mutual rejection, though not as common as mutual choice, was nevertheless more common among the over-chosen than it was among either the average- or the under-chosen. This phenomenon was almost certainly the result of competition and rivalry. In Chapter 5 we saw that competition between individuals, since it brings the threat and, if successful, the fact that some of them will deny reward to others, is apt to lead to hostility between them. Of all its forms, competition for people may be the most savage. Two girls who are rivals for popularity, status, and power are not apt to like one another much. In the nature of the case, only the over-chosen at Hudson could qualify for this kind of contest: an over-chosen girl and an under-chosen one were much less apt to be rivals, and therefore mutual hostility was more rife among over-chosen girls, girls held in high esteem, than among the others. The finding obviously does not say that all the girls of high esteem hated one another—the contrary was true. But there were good reasons for both mutual choice and mutual rejection to occur most often among the over-chosen. Why the relationship between any two such girls went one way rather than another, why some became rivals while others did not, why some became mutual friends and others mutual enemies, we could not tell without knowing more about the individuals in question than the investigator at Hudson tells us.

Solidarity of the Lower Class

At Hudson, the under-chosen girls were apt for the most part to look on one another with mutual indifference rather than with either mutual liking or mutual hostility; and the assumptions on which our original toy society was constructed specify the conditions under which we might expect this finding to obtain. But even this finding did not hold good to the last drop. In a few of the cottages the investigator found especially tight little cliques. She called them "closed and overlapping formations": "closed" in the sense that each member chose all the others and "overlapping" in the sense that each member chose the others for both living-working and spending leisure time. These cliques shared another characteristic: housemothers were particularly apt to complain that their members displayed "rebellious" behavior (Jennings, 1950: 87–88).

Cliques of this sort appeared at both the top and the bottom of Hudson society. Some were made up of girls held in very high esteem, and it is not difficult to imagine the conditions under which an upper-class clique might form in rebellion against its housemother. We shall have no more to say about them. More interesting, in view of the general tendency for girls of low esteem to be indifferent to one another, is the finding that the rest of these cliques were made up of girls whom almost nobody else chose except the other members of the clique. By a perhaps unjustified analogy with conditions that sometimes obtain in larger societies, we shall call this phenomenon "the solidarity of the lower class" in opposition to the remainder of a group.

Roughly similar findings were reached by Lemann and Solomon (1952) in a sociometric study of three dormitories in a women's college. We represent their results approximately in a second toy society (Table 6). To facilitate comparison with the first toy society, we have again

Table 6   Sentiment Matrix: Solidarity of the Lower Class

| | | APPROVAL GIVEN TO | | | | | | TOTAL GIVEN |
		O	*P*	*Q*	*R*	*S*	*T*	
APPROVAL GIVEN BY	*O*		5	4	3	2	1	15
	P	5		4	3	2	1	15
	Q	5	4		3	2	1	15
	R	4	4	3		2	2	15
	S	3	2	2	3		5	15
	T	1	2	3	4	5		15
TOTAL RECEIVED		18	17	16	16	13	10	

given the group six members and have allowed each of them a total of fifteen units of approval to distribute. Allowing the members an equal number of units corresponds to the fact that the investigators who carried out the present research, unlike the investigator at Hudson, assigned each girl the same number of choices to *give*. According to the number of choices a girl *received,* the investigators assigned her to one of three status classes (high, middle, or low) represented in our toy society by members *O* and *P*, *Q* and *R*, *S* and *T*, respectively. Presumably the investigators divided the population into three because other social scientists so often talk as if modern societies were divided into three main classes, whether or not they are in any sense so divided in fact.

Comparison of this matrix with our earlier one on p. 169 shows that the differences are greatest at the lower levels of esteem. Upper- and middle-class members behave much as they did in the earlier matrix, except that the middle class gets a little more choice from, and gives a little more choice to, the lower class than it did before. But the lower class (members *S* and *T*) behaves quite differently. Whereas in our first matrix persons themselves of low esteem tended to give much approval to persons of high esteem and little to one another, such persons tend in the present matrix to do the opposite, to give little approval to persons of high esteem and much to one another. In so doing, they tend of course to reduce the absolute amounts of esteem these others receive compared to what they received in the earlier matrix, but without changing the rank order of the members.

We must now ask ourselves what possible sets of given conditions, different from those we assumed in constructing our first toy society might, together with the same general propositions, have produced the pattern or structure we have called the solidarity of the lower class. The discussion in earlier chapters suggests several possibilities. Besides failing to reward the other members or even positively punishing them by failing to conform to the norms of the group, the girls of low esteem may have lived near one another in the dormitories and thus, in accordance with the argument put forward in the last chapter, have developed rewarding exchanges with one another. Another possibility is that the girls of low esteem resembled one another in their background characteristics and hence in some of their values more than they did other members of their dormitories. They may, for instance, have been members of the same ethnic group. Again, we have seen in earlier chapters the reasons for a relationship between similarity and mutual reward. Deviance, combined with either geographical proximity or similarity in respects other than the deviance itself, could have drawn the girls of low esteem toward one another and away from other members of their groups.

The investigators seem not to have inquired into the background characteristics of the girls or the location of their rooms in the dormitories, and they offer no explanation for the solidarity that they discovered in the lower class. But one of their further findings suggests that the explanation would have to bring in something more than just similarity of background or closeness of location, though these may well have had an effect, either jointly or severally. The investigators asked the girls to name those they rejected as well as those they chose, and they found that members of the upper class not only chose members of the lower class little but rejected them much. And members of the lower class behaved in much the same way toward members of the upper. Not just failure to approve but active resentment was at work between the two. Did the very fact that they were assigned low rank, perhaps as a result of failing to conform to the norms of the rest, arouse the active resentment of members of the lower class because they found it unjust or unfair? We shall have more to say about justice in a later chapter. If it did, their resentment could have led to their deviating still further so as to get back at their oppressors, according to the familiar vicious spiral. And there is nothing like a shared hatred of the same other persons to draw men (and women) together.

Given Conditions and Structure

In the case of this latest investigation, we are not for once interested in determining which is the correct explanation of the findings. The investigators do not provide us with enough information to let us decide. Instead we have been interested in suggesting something more general. By means of choice-matrices we have presented two characteristic types of social structure, to each of which the behavior of some real groups approximates. We might have presented many other such structures, such as a group divided vertically into subgroups instead of horizontally into classes, as in the "solidarity of the lower class." What we have suggested is that the explanation of these and other patterns does not require a new set of general propositions but rather the recognition of different given conditions within which the same set of propositions applies. We have considered some of the possible given conditions, not present in the first structure we looked at, that may have produced the "solidarity of the lower class." A single set of propositions applied to many different sets of givens yields many different structures of relationships.

The given conditions themselves can sometimes be explained or their presence predicted in advance. But that is not essential. The social scientist may not be able to explain at all why certain given conditions are what they are, but if at least he knows what they are—if they are given him in this sense—he can use them in connection with a set of general propositions to explain his empirical findings. These points may be obvious but cannot be too often repeated.

Because a great variety of empirical propositions may be derived from a single set of general ones, depending on what is taken as given, a social scientist should hesitate before he claims that any of his findings contradict any of his colleagues'. Nature plays rough but not dirty, and

Claude Bernard argued that there were no such things as contradictory findings (Bernard, 1952: 113):

> In effect, starting from the principle that there are immutable laws, the experimenter will be convinced that the phenomena can never contradict themselves if they are observed under the same conditions; and he will know that, if they show variations, this must follow from the intervention or interference of other conditions, which mask or modify these phenomena.

Let the social scientist look well to the conditions of his experiment, both those he planned to establish and those he did not plan but established nonetheless. It may be that something about the experiment, hidden because it lies in plain sight, makes it quite unlike the one it seems to contradict. Let him do so not just because he is rightly reluctant to give a colleague the lie, but because apparent contradictions point to the unsuspected presence of new phenomena—phenomena that may have made the difference between the experiments. Contradictions should not destroy old findings but lead to new ones.

Let me add a personal word. What we have called given conditions here are the same as what I called in another book (Homans, 1950) the *external system*. I now feel this term is too pretentious and suggests what is not true. If "system" means that the parts of a set are related to one another, the givens sometimes do constitute a system: the geographical layout, the specializations, and the flow of work in a factory department are givens for the social organization of the department, and they are related to one another. But givens do not always form a system. Geographical givens and the givens we have called the *background* of individuals need not be related at all. If the word *givens,* on the other hand, is not pretentious enough to suit the reader's taste, let him try some other phrase such as *parameters* or *boundary conditions,* the boundary being the arbitrary and imaginary line dividing particular social processes from what, for the purposes at hand, we choose to consider their physical and social environment in time and space.

Interaction and Approval

So far in this chapter we have been concerned with the value to individual members of a group of the activities that the other members perform and its relation to the way in which they distribute their approval to one another. In so doing, we may have temporarily lost sight of another kind of variable, the frequency with which an action is performed regardless of its content or kind. This variable has been crucial to us from the start: the general propositions relate the value of the result of an action, the success of the action in attaining that result, and the stimuli attending it, to the frequency with which the action is performed. When the action is social, that is, when the action of Person is rewarded by the action of Other, we speak of the frequency of *interaction* between the two persons. In the latter part of this chapter we shall look at matrices of interaction between members of a group.

We shall approach these matrices indirectly, by considering the evidence for a proposition we first suggested when we examined the effect of what is called balance on the development of relationships between persons (see Chapter 3). This is the proposition that associates two men's liking for one another with the frequency of their interaction with one another.

Quite apart from balance theory, there are good general reasons why this relationship should exist. By the success proposition, if two men reward one another by their actions, they are apt to interact often. And by the aggression-approval proposition, if they reward one another under "fair" conditions, they are apt to express approval (liking) for one another. It follows that if they interact often they are apt to like one another. But we must always remember that the relationship does not hold good under all conditions. It does not hold good when the interaction is constrained, as when two rivals for promotion in a company are forced to cooperate if they are to keep their jobs. Nor, as we shall see in a later chapter, does it hold good when one of the two men is under the authority or command of the other: at least the word *liking* may not accurately connote the sentiment of the subordinate for the superior.

We must also remember that, within a group, the association between interaction and liking may only become conspicuous when interpersonal relationships approach stability. As we saw in the experiment reported in Chapter 6 (Schachter, 1951), if a member begins to deviate from the norms of a group, the other members may direct a great deal of comment, persuasion, and threat toward him in an effort to bring him back into line. In that sense the others interact with him often, though they do not approve of him. Only when it becomes clear that he will not change, that their efforts are unsuccessful, will they give up interacting with him. That is, as relationships stabilize, the association between interaction and liking becomes closer: the conformers will then give the deviate both little liking and little interaction compared to what they give to other conformers.

Though we must be mindful of these warnings, much research suggests an empirical association between liking and interaction. Let us consider briefly a number of examples rather than concentrating at length on one or two, as we have been doing in recent chapters. In an experiment reported by Potashin (1946), the investigator used as his subjects the children in three grades of a primary school. He gave them a simple sociometric test, and then put them together in pairs of two different kinds. The two members of every pair in one set were children that had chosen one another sociometrically; the two members of every pair in the other set were children that had not chosen one another. The investigator then gave each pair a standardized subject for discussion, and observed the interaction that followed. He found that the amount of uninterrupted discussion was greater in pairs of friends than in pairs of non-friends. He also found, which may interest us later, that the differences between the two members in the amount each talked, and in the frequency with which each originated discussion, that is, began talking after a pause, was less for friends than it was for non-friends.

The main finding, that friends interacted more often than non-friends, can hardly surprise us. Friends are certainly people that have rewarded one another in the past: to meet a friend as the other member of one's pair in a new situation is to expect that his behavior will be rewarding, and so one is apt to interact with him often, which gives him the opportunity to be rewarding in fact. A person who is not a friend presents no such stimulus; indeed one may not even allow him an opening for showing how rewarding, for once, he might be.

In the Potashin study of the relation between interaction and sentiment, the independent variable, the one manipulated by the investigator, was favorable sentiment. He put together pairs of children known to be friendly and pairs known not to be friendly, and then watched the differences in interaction that resulted. We shall soon see that the frequency of interaction may be treated as the independent variable, an increased frequency leading to more favorable sentiment. On what grounds might we expect this to be true?

Suppose that two persons are, as we say, thrown together, that interaction between them is made easy and likely because they live near one another or work on the same job. If they interact at all, and if no special factor, like rivalry, is present that might bias systematically their values or their actions, the chances are that each will find some of the other's actions rewarding, if only because they may be obtained at less cost from him than from a third party at a greater distance. And to the extent that each rewards the other, each is apt to express favorable sentiment toward the other. For this reason, an independent increase in interaction between persons is apt to be associated with an increase in liking between them.

Let us now look at a couple of experiments that treated the frequency of interaction as the independent variable. In a study by Bovard (1951), the investigator began by forming four groups of college students, each group to discuss the same set of problems under the chairmanship of a man appointed by the investigator. He trained the chairman of two of the groups, which he called "leader-centered," to monopolize the discussion, so that all comments and questions would be addressed to him and answered by him, and little communication would pass between the members themselves. He trained the chairman of the other two groups, which he called "group-centered," to behave quite differently. The chairman was to ask few questions, make few comments, and, if comments and questions were addressed to him, to turn them back to the members for discussion among themselves.

At the end of the meetings the investigator administered a sociometric test and found that the number of choices given by members to other members of the same group was less in the "leader-centered" discussions than in the "group-centered" ones. In our terms, he had experimentally discouraged interaction between members in the first kind of group and encouraged it in the second. And as we should expect from our argument, the liking of members for other members was less in the first than in the second. Naturally we do not claim that the interaction directly produced the liking. Instead, when the chairman of a "group-centered" discussion encouraged interaction among the members, he gave them an opportunity to reward one another, and the reward produced the liking. The investigator showed that, practically speaking, one of the ways of getting people to like one another is to make them interact with one another. It is a method that works—other things equal. It is also one that many Americans believe in without benefit of psychology: if they can only get Tom and Bill together, the boys are sure to like one another. They tend to forget the conditions that, unless they are somehow neutralized, may prevent the relationship from holding good. What if Tom is white and Bill is black?

Interaction and Rivalry between Groups

A famous and more complicated study was one made by the Sherifs at a summer camp for pre-adolescent boys (Sherif and Sherif, 1953). For a time at the beginning of the season, the investigators allowed all the boys to go around together in a single group. At the end of this period, they got them to answer a sociometric test, and then divided them into two groups, equal in size and, so far as possible, equal sociometrically. That is to say, the investigators chose the members of the groups in such a way that any one boy would now find in his own group and in the other group about the same number of the boys he had chosen. The investigators then separated the groups for a time, each one playing and camping by itself. When they again administered the sociometric test, choice had shifted, and now the choices made by any one boy tended overwhelmingly to go to other members of his own group. Once again, increased interaction between some persons had increased liking between them, and decreased interaction between others had decreased their liking.

But this was not all that happened. A further factor encouraged and complicated the shift in choices. Not only did the two groups camp and play apart for a time, but they also came to be rivals over which was to be considered the better group. Now a rival is someone who threatens to deprive you of a reward; accordingly you are apt to meet him with some hostility; and if your rivals are members of another group, your hostility toward them is apt to increase your friendliness toward members of your own group: they are now the only people who can reward you. In the summer camp, the boys' liking for members of their own group was fostered by their hatred for members of the other. Hatred is not too strong a word: the hostility waxed so great that the investigators decided their experiment had gotten out of hand and they broke up the groups. It is interesting that the rank-and-file members of each group, those that received few sociometric choices, were more eager than the leaders to express hostility toward the other group, as a group. Vying for full acceptance, they behaved as if exaggerated hostility toward the others would win them approval from their own gang. At any rate, the increased hostility between groups and increased friendliness within each of them was the effect not only of their isolation from one another but also of their rivalry. The experimenters had produced experimentally a state of affairs that occurs only too often in real life.

The association between interaction and social approval is often observed in everyday experience. If, for instance, you watch the behavior of three persons in the same room and discover that two of them interact more often with one another than either of them does with the third, you can bet that the two will be ready to express more liking for one another than they will for the third, and you will win far more often than not. As Newcomb (1956) says: "So widespread and so compelling is the evidence for the relationship between frequency of interaction and positive attraction that Homans has ventured to hypothesize that 'If the frequency of interaction between two or more persons increases, the degree of their liking for one another will increase' (Homans, 1950: 112). Actuarially speaking, the evidence is altogether overwhelming that, *ignoring other variables,* the proposition is correct in a wide range of circumstances."

Interaction, Esteem, and Power

We have begun by stating the relationship between interaction and liking as if it applied to only two persons. Let us now ask what it implies about the patterns of interaction in a group of more than two members. If we think of a group as made up of a number of pairs, we may go on to argue that, the larger the number of members that like other members, the more frequent is the total interaction in the group;

and as we have recently seen, for instance, in the experiment by Bovard, this is true. It should follow as a further corollary that, the larger the number of other members who give social approval to any given member —that is, the higher the esteem in which they hold him—the more frequent the interaction he receives from other members.

A great deal of evidence supports this corollary. Two famous field studies of small groups: the Bank Wiring Observation Room (an industrial group) and the Norton Street Gang (a group of corner boys) both showed in an impressionistic way that the more popular members tended to receive most interactions (see Roethlisberger and Dickson, 1939, and Whyte, 1943, analyzed in Homans, 1950). But let me cite an investigation I made myself (Homans, 1954)—a field study using techniques a little more quantitative than those used in the earlier ones.

The investigator was studying a clerical department in a large public utility, which he called the Eastern Utilities Company. Of the members of the department ten girls were each doing the same job, called cash posting. For present purposes all we need know about the job is that a cash poster went from one filing cabinet to another and pulled certain cards out of each one. The posting job required no collaboration between the girls and, unlike many jobs, allowed great freedom of movement. As the girls moved around the room from file to file, they had plenty of chances to meet and talk to one another. These features of the job are worth emphasizing, for if a girl's freedom to interact with others had been curtailed by the need to collaborate with a particular other girl or to stay in one place, the investigation would not have yielded the same results.

The investigator wanted to get a record of interactions in the department for a period of at least two working weeks; but since fifty persons were present all told, he found it physically impossible to record every contact and took a sample instead. Every fifteen minutes during the working day he allowed his eyes to sweep the room, and he checked off which girls were talking to which other girls at that time. He could not determine by this method which of the girls had started a conversation or which had contributed most to it. But he could readily count the sheer number of times each girl had been seen talking to every other girl and thus the total number of times a girl had taken part in conversations with others.

Analysis of the results showed a strong tendency for girls to talk to other girls in their own job group within the department more often than they talked to members of other job groups. That is, cash posters were particularly apt to interact with other cash posters. Where there were exceptions they were likely to be girls who talked to others formerly in their own job group and only recently promoted out of it. For the moment, we shall pay no further attention to this finding and concen-

trate instead on differences between cash posters in the number of interactions each received.

In the course of a long interview, the investigator asked each girl the
sociometric question: "Who are your close friends in here?" She might
name as few or as many friends as she pleased. In the investigator's experience a general question like this was just as apt to yield reliable
results, to correlate with other ways of measuring liking, as were more
specific sociometric tests, such as those used at Hudson, which named
definite criteria for choice. He then put the cash posters in rank order
according to the number of others that named each girl as a friend—that
is, in order of esteem. He put them also in rank order according to the
number of conversations each took part in—that is, in order of the interactions each received. And he found a high correlation between the two
rank orders. This finding is in accordance with our corollary.

Yet a critic may fail to be impressed. He may say to the investigator,
"When a girl named another as her friend, all she meant was that she
associated with her often, and so it is hardly surprising that there should
be a correlation between choices and interaction received." There is this
much merit in such criticism, that when the investigator asked a girl
what she meant when she called another her friend, she might indeed
refer to the fact that "she saw a lot of her." But this was not all she
would say. She would also say that "she liked her a lot"; that is, she
would refer to what we call sentiment, and then go on to explain what
it was about the other girl's behavior that she found rewarding. In short,
in their discussions of friendship, the girls, like the rest of us when we
are not being social scientists, would recognize implicitly the relationships between interaction, activity, and sentiment that we are trying to
make explicit here.

Though there is much evidence that differences between persons in
esteem are positively related to differences between them in interactions
received, we should be making a great mistake if we assumed that esteem
was the only determinant of the latter variable. Or rather, the two are
related to one another only because each is in turn related to a more
fundamental variable. Let us go back to our original small group consisting of Person, Other, and the Third Man. Under the conditions we
assumed to hold good for that group, Other received more interactions
than either of the other two, since both Person and the Third Man went
to Other (and not to one another) for advice. Other also received more
approval, and so interaction and esteem were positively related in this
group. He got more approval, we argued, because the others were ready
to offer him approval in return for his advice and because, through his
monopoly of this scarce reward, he had more power than the others and
so could command a greater return. But suppose that instead of getting
approval in return for advice Other had insisted on getting money. He

would still have received more interactions than the others. That is, power and not approval is the fundamental variable determining the rank order of the members of a group in the number of interactions they receive. Or rather, instead of power, let us speak of what power generates when used—that is to say, differences in status. The higher the status of a member, the more frequent is the interaction he receives from other members. But we must postpone a detailed discussion of status to the next chapter.

The Matrix of Interaction

We are now in a position to do for interaction what we did for approval earlier in this chapter; we shall set up matrices suggesting possible patterns in the distribution of interaction among members of a group. Let us revive our toy society made up of six members: O, P, Q, R, S, and T. Then, taking the word *status* for the moment to mean what we intuitively take it to mean in everyday speech, let us assume that the members are agreed on the way they rank one another in status. Thus every member ranks O highest, P next highest, and so on. We assign every member fifteen interactions, such as going to talk with another member, that he can *give* within an arbitrary period of time, and finally assume that he distributes them to the others in proportion to their status: the higher the status of the other, the more interactions each member gives him. Since interaction is by definition social we do not count the contacts a man may make with himself. The resulting matrix is shown in Table 7. The figure 1 in column T, row O means that O gives T one interaction within the arbitrary period of time. It is not, of course, the absolute size of the figures but their size relative to one another that is important here.

Now let us consider the properties of this rather obvious matrix. First, the pattern of interaction is the same as the pattern of approval shown in the first matrix (see page 169), which is scarcely surprising, since we have seen that interaction and approval often vary together. Second, it illustrates, as we hoped it would, the proposition that the higher a member's status, the more interactions he *receives,* such as others coming to him with requests; for the total interactions received by each member are shown by the sums of the columns, and their rank order is also the rank order of the members in status. Third, the reciprocal or mutual interaction between two members is higher, the higher the average status of the two. Compare the figures 5 and 5 for the interactions between O and P with the figures 1 and 1 for the interactions between S and T.

Plausible as it may appear at first glance, our matrix does not correspond to any real state of affairs, and that for a very obvious reason. It

Table 7 A Model Interaction Matrix

| | | | INTERACTIONS RECEIVED | | | | | TOTAL GIVEN |
		O	P	Q	R	S	T	
INTERACTION GIVEN BY	O		5	4	3	2	1	15
	P	5		4	3	2	1	15
	Q	5	4		3	2	1	15
	R	5	4	3		2	1	15
	S	5	4	3	2		1	15
	T	5	4	3	2	1		15
TOTAL RECEIVED		25	21	17	13	9	5	

shows, for instance, member T addressing interaction to member O five times, but O addressing interaction to T only once. But is this a realistic result? If we assume, as we are free to do—for the matrix is after all only a toy—that T's five interactions were mostly attempts to get some valuable service out of O, then O's single interaction with T shows that the attempts were not very successful. In real life we should expect, as the group moved toward greater stability, either that O would increase the returns he made to T (else he would forfeit the high approval T might have given him), or that T would decrease the number of requests he made to O (for if an action goes unrewarded, a man will in time cease to perform it). In either case the two members would become more nearly equal in the interactions each addressed to the other. We can put it even more simply: most interactions between men take the form of talking. If I talk to you, you will find it difficult not to talk back, and so the interactions each of us gives to the other will tend toward something like equality. For reasons that will appear later, we do not insist on absolute equality.

If what might well happen in any one pair happens also in other pairs in the group, we should expect that members who receive much interaction will also give much. And since members who receive much are ones that stand high in status, we should expect members of high status to be high givers of interaction too. So obvious is this conclusion that we shall not bother to review the evidence supporting it, which is plentiful. For instance, in the Hudson study, the higher the esteem in which a girl was held, the larger was her *social contact range*—the number of other girls she spoke to (Jennings, 1950: 51). Yet the conclusion is not embodied in our matrix at all: whereas the members of our toy society are definitely unequal in the number of interactions they receive, they are equal in the number they give.

Let us, therefore, make an assumption that will bring the matrix more closely into line with real life. Let us assume that the more interactions a member receives, the more he also gives, and correct the matrix accordingly. We do this by multiplying the figures in each row, which represent the interactions given by each member, by a figure representing his rank in interactions received. Thus each of the figures representing interactions given by member O should be multiplied by 6, since O holds top rank in interactions received. The corrected matrix is shown in Table 8.

Table 8   Corrected Interaction Matrix

| | | INTERACTIONS RECEIVED | | | | | | TOTAL GIVEN |
		O	P	Q	R	S	T	
INTERACTIONS GIVEN BY	O		30	24	18	12	6	90
	P	25		20	15	10	5	75
	Q	20	16		12	8	4	60
	R	15	12	9		6	3	45
	S	10	8	6	4		2	30
	T	5	4	3	2	1		15
TOTAL RECEIVED		75	70	62	51	37	20	

In the new, corrected matrix, the rank order of the members in status is their rank order not only in the number of interactions received but also in the number given. Moreover the two members of many pairs are much more nearly equal in the number of interactions each gives to the other than they were in the original matrix. For instance, T still gives 5 interactions to O, but he gets 6 back instead of only one. Yet absolute equality we have not achieved. In fact a close inspection of the matrix shows that in every pair the member higher in status gives more interaction to the other than the other gives to him. On all these counts, except perhaps the last, the new matrix is more realistic than the old one.

In their research on small groups, investigators have obtained matrices of interaction that have many points in common with our toy. Let us look at one of them, without asking for the moment whether it resembles ours because the members of the group in question behaved in accordance with our propositions—without asking, that is, whether we were right for the right reasons. The matrix is shown in Table 9.

Table 9   Aggregate Matrix for Eighteen Sessions of Six-Man Groups

		1	2	3	4	5	6	TOTAL TO INDI-VIDUALS	TO GROUP AS WHOLE	TOTAL INITI-ATED
			TO	INDIVIDUALS						
	1		1238	961	545	445	317	3506	5661	9167
FROM INDIVIDUALS	2	1748		443	310	175	102	2778	1211	3989
	3	1371	415		305	125	69	2285	742	3027
	4	952	310	282		83	49	1676	676	2352
	5	662	224	144	83		28	1141	443	1584
	6	470	126	114	65	44		819	373	1192
TOTAL RECEIVED		5203	2313	1944	1308	872	565	12205	9106	21311

This matrix is the product of research by R. F. Bales and his asso-ciates (Bales, 1953: 129). They formed six-man groups that met for about an hour at a time and tried to reach by discussion some solution to prob-lems set by the investigators. Note that the members of each group had a task to accomplish in common—a condition that certainly does not hold for all human groups. Aside from giving them the problem and requiring that they meet in a special observation room, the investigators did not restrict the members' behavior in any way. From a special ob-servation booth, which let them see and hear the members without the members' seeing and hearing them, the investigators, among other things, recorded every act in the discussion as being made (initiated) by a par-ticular member and directed at (received by) another member or the group as a whole. A unit act consisted for the investigators of any word, set of words, or gesture, no matter how short, that made sense by itself in the context of the discussion. In some circumstances the word "Oh?" alone might express doubt about what had just been said and so count as a unit act.

From these records the investigators could make a count of the num-ber of interactions (unit acts) addressed by each member to every other one and to the group as a whole. The present matrix represents the aggregate of such figures for eighteen separate sessions of six-man groups. First, the investigators constructed a matrix for each separate session as follows. They arranged the members in rank order of the number of interactions they initiated, the No. 1 man being the most frequent initia-tor, the No. 2 man the next most frequent, and so on. Then they filled in the cells of the matrix by indicating how many acts No. 1 had directed to No. 2, how many to No. 3, and so on for him and then for the other members. Having thus constructed a matrix for each of the eighteen sessions, they arrived at the aggregate matrix simply by adding together the figures in the corresponding cells of the original matrices. Thus the figure 1238 is the total number of times that the eighteen different No. 1 men initiated acts directed at their respective No. 2 men.

Remembering that only relative magnitudes and not absolute ones are of interest to us, let us compare this matrix with our own artificial one. In both, the more often a member receives interaction, the more often he initiates it too. But the members that initiate often do so proportionately a great deal more often in the Bales' matrix than in our own: the frequent talkers do a great deal more to monopolize the discussion. The reason lies in part in the simple 6, 5, 4, . . . series that we used in constructing our matrix. Though it is a natural series to use, it need not correspond closely to the way interaction is distributed in real life. The tendency for the high initiators to monopolize the discussion is even more marked when acts addressed to the group as a whole are included. In constructing our matrix we made no allowance at all for this kind of act.

Both in the Bales' matrix and in ours the interactions given by each member of any pair to the other member tend toward equality without reaching it. But there the resemblance ends. In any pair in our matrix the member higher in total interaction gives more interaction to the other member than the other gives to him. The reverse is true of the Bales' matrix: close inspection shows that in almost every pair the member lower in total interaction gives more interaction to the other than the other gives to him. Thus the No. 6 man in initiations gives 470 interactions to No. 1, while No. 1 gives 317 to No. 6. There are a few exceptions to this rule, for instance, the pair made up of Nos. 3 and 4, but the general tendency is pronounced. The reason for this difference probably lies in the interactions addressed to the group as a whole, which were possible in the Bales' groups but which we did not allow for at all in our toy society. In the Bales' groups, some of the remarks addressed by low interactors to high ones the latter answered indirectly—by talking to the group as a whole. Interaction tended to go upward—from low interactors to high—in pair relations, and thence downward from high interactors to the group as a whole. No chairman of any kind was appointed or elected in the Bales' groups. In many real discussion groups, such as committees, the institution of a chairman formalizes the tendencies informally present here: members conventionally address the chairman, and the chairman addresses the group as a whole.

Remember that the Bales' matrix was an aggregate matrix. Not every one of the eighteen single sessions would have revealed the pattern so clearly: it stood out only when the figures for all of the sessions were summed up; yet we may guess that it represents a strong central tendency in groups of this kind. These were discussion groups: each had a single problem to consider as a group, and each member could easily talk to every other. If these conditions had not been met, if, for instance, there had been no single task set for the group or the physical layout of the room had made some members easier to talk to than others, we should not have expected so neat a pattern nor so heavy a concentration of interaction on a few talkative members.

In the same way, we do not argue that every real group matches our model matrix, which is no more than the pattern our proposition about the relationship between status and interaction predicts under a very special condition: that in assigning status every member ranks the others in the same way. There is no reason to believe that this condition always obtains in real groups, though it often does so. We shall use our matrix only as a kind of benchmark for comparison.

The Bales' matrix bears a strong family resemblance to ours, and yet the resemblance may be factitious. The former was constructed by arranging the members of the groups in rank order of their initiation of interaction: it made no assumption that this rank order was also the rank order of members in status. But in constructing our matrix we did make just this assumption. Unless we can show that it also held good of the Bales' groups, we have no right to cite his matrix as evidence in support of our argument. The horrid fact is that we are able to do so only in part. As we shall see later, in Chapter 13 on stratification, the high initiators in the Bales' groups did indeed stand high on one possible dimension of status: the others often named them as having done most to help their group complete its task. On the other hand, they were not particularly well-liked. We may be forced to distinguish between different kinds of social approval, instead of lumping them all together as we have done so far. In particular, we may have to distinguish between an ingredient of approval that most of us would call "respect" and another that we would call plain "liking." We only raise the question here; in later chapters we shall have much more to say about it.

The Origination of Interaction

When Bales and his associates say that in one of their groups a member *initiates* interaction, all they mean is that he addresses an act to another person or to the group as a whole. Indeed all they usually mean is that someone says something to someone else. They do not try to give *initiation* any stronger sense, as when we say someone takes the initiative in starting a conversation. That is, by defining *initiation* as they do, they specify nothing about the place of the act in a series of interactions. It may have been the first of a series: one member may have asked another to do something for him; but it may also have been the last: the other may have complied with the request and thus brought the series of inter-actions to a close. The action that starts off a series of exchanges between two or more persons after a period, long or short, in which no interac-tion has taken place between them, we shall speak of as the *origination,* rather than as the initiation, of interaction (see Chapple, 1940).

Unless the two persons are within easy speaking distance of one an-other, it may be necessary, if one is to originate interaction with the other, for him to move into the presence of the other, as when Person leaves his own desk in the office and goes over to Other's to ask him for help. It may be worthwhile asking whether there is any rule that de-termines in circumstances like these which member of a pair is the more likely to originate interaction with the other.

According to the argument presented in Chapter 4, the person who is apt to originate, to make the first move, is the one who values what the other has to offer more than the other values what the first person has to offer in return. That is, the person who is apt to make the first move is the person with the lesser initial power. As we shall soon see, he is also the person with the lower status. In this connection it may be significant that, both in the Bales' matrix and in the matrix we shall present next, the person of lower status tends to give to the person of higher more interaction than he receives from him. But note that this only holds good of exchanges in pairs. As far as interaction directed at the group as a whole is concerned, the higher the status of a member, the more often he initiates action. We shall have much more to say on this point when we reach Chapter 12 on leadership.

The social processes we have considered so far tend to produce natu-rally a pattern of interaction between members of a group such that inter-action between some members is greater than we should expect by chance and interaction between others less. Specifically, interactions both given and received tend to concentrate, focus on members of high status. Thus social processes occurring naturally tend to produce something much like the set of channels of communication coming together at the apex of a pyramid, which is laid out by design in a formally organized bureaucracy. No doubt the artificial pattern was originally modeled on the natural one.

Interaction with Equals

Let us finally look at an interaction matrix that has something in common both with Bales' and with our own latest one and yet differs from both. The matrix resulted from research by Riley, Cohn, Toby, and Riley (1954).

The investigators studied the girl students, some 1500 in all, in the ninth and tenth grades of eight New Jersey high schools. No doubt each grade in each school formed a true social group, but all the grades together obviously did not form one, and the results the investigators report represent an aggregate, like that of Bales. Nor probably did any single grade have the sharp focus for interaction that the discussion of set problems provided for Bales' groups. The opportunities for interaction were much more diffuse.

The investigators asked every girl to answer a question in which she was to name, out of the other girls in her grade, a certain number (say three) that she considered the most "popular." Then she was to name the three she thought were most "liked," and the three she thought were most "admired." Out of the results of this questionnaire the investigators put the girls in each grade in rank order of "status." Note that "status" here is not the same as esteem, for each girl was not asked to name the others she personally liked most but rather the others she perceived as being generally best-liked. No doubt real esteem would have correlated with perceived esteem, but the research report tells us only about the latter. The investigators next divided, by arbitrary cut-off points, the whole distribution of status scores into six different status classes, the highest being status 6 and the lowest status 1.

The investigators then asked every girl to answer a new questionnaire, designed to discover how much she was apt to talk to every other girl in her grade. They gave her a series of seven possible topics of conversation ranging all the way from relations with the opposite sex to problems of right and wrong—a long distance, we must agree—and asked her to name the other girls she would be apt to talk with about each topic. The larger the number of topics a girl said she would be disposed to talk about with another, the higher was her score on communication with the other. From these individual scores, it was easy to calculate the average disposition to communicate between girls in any status class and those in another. Note that the investigators studied verbal expressions of a disposition to interact and not interaction itself. How much the girls' answers represented reality and how much wishful thinking we cannot tell; but even if they represented nothing but wish, the way that wished-for interaction was distributed would still be interesting. At any rate, the matrix is shown in Table 10 (see next page).

In examining this matrix we should, as usual, pay no attention to the absolute scores but only to the relative ones. Thus the significant fact about the figure 1.36 is not that it is a particular quantity but that it is the highest figure in the matrix. It means that girls of status 6 (the highest status) felt more disposed to talk with other girls of the same status than they were to talk to girls of any other status; indeed that there was more talking between girls of this class than there was within any other status or between any pair of statuses. In Bales' matrix and in

Table 10   Status and Disposition to Communicate

STATUS	COMMUNICATION CHOICE RECEIVED						AVERAGE GIVEN
	6	5	4	3	2	1	
6	*1.36*	.66	.39	.25	.16	.04	.47
5	.88	*.81*	.52	.33	.19	.05	.46
4	.81	.76	*.62*	.36	.18	.07	.47
3	.69	.54	.42	*.38*	.20	.07	.38
2	.60	.47	.34	.26	*.26*	*.11*	.34
1	.49	.41	.26	.22	.26	.07	.29

(left label: COMMUNICATION CHOICE GIVEN)

AVERAGE RECEIVED .81   .61   .43   .30   .21   .07

ours the cells on the major diagonal were left empty because scores in them could only represent a person's talking to himself. In the present matrix they are filled because there were many girls in each status and they could perfectly well talk to one another.

The matrix displays many of the features of the Bales' matrix and ours. The higher the average status of any two status classes, the higher is the disposition of members of these classes to interact with one another. The more often the members of a class receive interaction, the more often they give it too, though the difference between statuses in interaction given is very small—proportionately much less than the corresponding differences in the Bales' groups. Moreover the tendency toward equality between any two status classes in the exchange of interaction with one another is much less marked than it is in the Bales' matrix. Even more marked, on the other hand, is the tendency for the lower status to give more interaction to the higher than it receives from the higher. The reason for both these differences is, of course, that the present matrix shows perceived and not actual interaction: girls of high status were under no such pressure to respond to a disposition to communicate with them on the part of girls of low status as they would have been under in real life.

For our immediate purposes the present matrix has one great advantage over Bales'. In the latter the rank order of members in receiving interaction was simply taken as given and not related to any measures other than those of interaction itself. In the present matrix, on the other hand, we can see that the rank order on receipt correlated with the independently measured status of the girls. Thus the present matrix provides more direct evidence than does Bales' in support of our corollary: the higher is a member's status, the larger is the number of interactions he will receive.

Yet there is one feature of the present matrix that appears neither in

Bales' nor in ours. Look down the columns. In every column but one the highest figure lies on the major diagonal, making the series 1.36, .81, .62, .38, .26. The only exception to the rule is the figure .11 in the last column, column 1, and that is only one cell off the major diagonal. If, moreover, we scan the other figures in each column, we see that they drop off steadily on either side of the highest figure, unless as in column 6 the highest figure is at one end.

What does this well-marked pattern mean? The rows indicate whither each status gives its interaction; the columns, whence each status receives it. The rows show that the higher the status, the more interaction, or rather the more expressed disposition to interact, another status gives to it. But the columns show something more. They show that so far as interactions received, not interactions given, are concerned, the members of each status receive more interaction from other members of their own status than from any other. More than this, the nearer any two statuses are to one another, the more interaction the members of one receives from the members of the other. Thus the members of status 4 receive most interaction from members of that same status, next most from statuses 5 and 3, and so on.

The differences between the present matrix and Bales' were probably made possible not only by the different method used in the present research—questionnaire instead of observation—but also by the different nature of the groups. These were not discussion groups, whose members met for only an hour or so and focused their communication on a single problem, but rather grades in school, whose members shared many different curricular and extracurricular activities in the course of months and even years spent together. No doubt these differences in the nature of the groups will sooner or later help us explain the differences between the matrices. But all we shall do here is note that the present matrix displays not only what we expected and what Bales found—a tendency for persons of high status both to receive and to give much interaction—but something more: a concomitant tendency for equals in status to interact often with one another. Only later, in Chapter 13 on stratification, shall we try to explain this last finding.

Summary

In the present chapter we have tried, citing both field and experimental research, to show what some of the propositions explained in earlier chapters implied about the detailed distribution of sentiment and interaction in particular groups. With the help of model matrices, we suggested the conditions under which members held in high esteem would tend to choose one another often and those held in low esteem to choose one another seldom, and then the different conditions under which something like the reverse would occur and members held in low esteem—the "lower class"—would be solidary with one another. We also gave reasons why mutual rejection as well as mutual choice would be common among members held in high esteem and why rivalry between groups would tend to increase liking within them.

We examined evidence for the generally positive association between liking and interaction, and then went on to look at the distribution of interaction between members differing in status, one characteristic dimension of status in many groups being the esteem in which members are held. Members of high status tend both to direct much interaction to others and to receive much from them in return. They also interact often with members of their own status, whereas members of low status interact seldom with others of the same status. Finally, interaction tends to flow from members of lower to those of higher status in pair relations, but then from the latter to the group as a whole. We tried to explain why this pattern of relationships should exist. Finally we showed that, within this overall pattern, some groups displayed a further tendency for equals in status to interact with one another. We left to later chapters both a general discussion of the nature of status itself and an explanation of this last finding.

9   Status

IN RECENT CHAPTERS WE HAVE FOUND OURSELVES USING THE word *status* more and more often. So far we have not tried to define it, but have taken it without definition as meaning what we intuitively believe it to mean when we use the word in everyday life. The time has now come for us to try to give the word and the subject a more rigorous and analytic treatment.

As we have gone on, we have also found ourselves more and more often describing and explaining how and why members of a group respond toward differences between themselves in activity, conformity, power, and esteem. They are often inclined to say, not just that one member is different from another in one or more of these and other respects, but higher or lower, better or worse than he. That is, they rank the differences. And finally they tend not to keep a member's rankings on the different counts separate but to conflate them into a single ranking, which social scientists, and following them the ordinary citizens, tend to speak of as a ranking of the members in status. Indeed social scientists use few words more often than *status,* and few words they leave more often undefined. In this chapter we shall try to make clear not only what we shall mean by *status* but also, and more important, how we believe a status ranking might arise in a group.

Power and Status

Let us go back to our original model group whose core members were Person, Other, and the Third Man. We say "core" members because we shall now add others, whom we introduce for the moment only as spectators of, as audience for, what the original three are doing. None of the members can assess the "subjective value" to the others of the rewards they receive and the costs they incur in interaction with one another. Thus Person and the Third Man cannot judge what it means personally to Other to receive approval or to take time off from his own work. But they certainly can perceive—and he can too—that both of them go to him for advice, that both give him approval in the form of hearty thanks, and that he takes much time from his own work to advise them.

That is, persons interacting with one another do not simply reward or punish one another's actions but also, in so doing, present visible and other stimuli to one another. They also present them to members of the audience who are in a position to watch or listen to what is going on. This book cannot be a treatise on perception, but it certainly assumes that members of a group are able to perceive these things and very often to perceive them accurately: what they say is going on is often going on in fact. (Much social science, by the way, seems to be concerned with showing that people misperceive situations and with explaining why they do so. No doubt they often do, but not all *that* often. The emphasis has had the practical effect of making out ordinary men and women to be greater boobs than they really are.) This book also assumes that, in social interaction, the stimuli presented by other persons are the most important stimuli of all, that paying attention to such stimuli is itself an action, which like other actions a person will perform more often if he is rewarded for doing so, and that he often is so rewarded. If, for instance, people can learn rewarding behavior by watching the behavior of successful models (see Bandura, 1969: 143–167), even members of the audience may be rewarded by paying attention to Person, Other, and the Third Man: they may learn which of the three to go to if they themselves need help.

We also assume that the members of a group compare these stimuli, both the ones that others present and the ones they themselves do, along a number of dimensions. Thus Person and the Third Man can and do compare themselves with Other on the dimensions of advice and approval, what he gives and what he gets in exchange with them. They can see that he gives more advice than they do and gets more approval. And he, of course, can also compare himself with them. What is just as important, other persons present in the office, the audience, may also be able to make the comparisons. Although they may not themselves ask Other for advice, they may still compare him with themselves and judge that he is more knowledgeable than they are.

Status always begins with such comparisons, but status also implies a ranking—from top to bottom, from good to bad. Accordingly, if status is to develop in a group, it is not enough that men shall compare themselves along a number of scales. They must also establish the direction in which each scale runs. One man may have more of something and another less, but which is "higher" or "better," to have more of it or to have less?

The answer to the question is not quite as obvious as it looks. Suppose that in our little group Other is recognized by all members as holding higher status than Person and the Third Man—a supposition that certainly accords with our everyday experience of the way in which men assign status to others. Now we know that Other gives more advice and gets more approval than do the other two. They, on the other hand, give more approval and get more advice than he does. If our minds were utterly innocent—as I fear they are not—we might well ask why the fact that Other stands higher in the first two respects should give him the higher status. Why should not the fact that Person and the Third Man stand higher on the second two give it rather to them?

Apparently the answer is that in the circumstances advice is, as we have so often claimed, a scarce good, and that both Person and the Third Man set a high value on getting it, while Other does not: he, so to speak, can provide his own advice, while they can not. Other may, on the other hand, set some value on approval, but approval, unlike advice, is not in the circumstances a scarce good: any member of the group can supply it. The initially crucial, though not the only, determinant of the direction in which men rank others along the different dimensions of status is the relative value of the goods men exchange with others, value being determined by scarcity in relation to demand. The general rule seems to be that men will perceive a person as being of higher status than another, if in exchange he *gives* more of the good that is *scarce* in relation to demand, and can be seen to be so, but *receives* more of the good that is comparatively *plentiful*. Conversely, they perceive a person as being of lower status than another if he *receives* more of the *scarce* good and *gives* more of the *plentiful* one. Of course what is scarce or plentiful in one situation may not be scarce or plentiful in another.

In formulating this "rule," we have assumed that every member of the group was a net giver of one kind of good and a net receiver of another and not that he was both a giver and receiver of a particular good. But in some kinds of groups and, more important, with some kinds of goods a man may be both a giver and a receiver. Money, as a generalized reward, is the prime example of such a good. With money the rule simplifies: the man who both receives and gives more money than another, who has both higher income and higher expenditure, is the man of higher status as far as this dimension is concerned. But even here the man who receives much money is often also able to provide scarce goods other than money.

To be perceived by others as having high status, a man must be able to satisfy the rule consistently over a period of time and not just now and then. Let us look at one example. Remember that such things as the capacity and the willingness to kill others are often goods and scarce ones at that—goods in the sense that the capacity to kill is also the capacity to spare, and scarce in the sense that a few men may command much better capacities to kill than many others do, especially if armament is expensive. Accordingly, a rare capacity to kill ought to be able to win a man high status. But we must be careful to distinguish between situations.

Just because a man with a gun is able to hold you up once does not give him a higher status than your own. On the next occasion he may not be able to do so, if only because there are too many policemen within easy call. But if he were regularly able to hold you up and take your money from you, his status would sooner or later be recognized as higher than yours. Indeed it would in time be acknowledged that he had a right to hold you up, for instance, to make you pay rent. Many aristocracies, such as that of feudal Europe, originally won their position in something like this fashion.

The fact that a good is scarce in relation to demand usually implies that few people are able to supply it. Accordingly, the higher any given status in a group, the smaller, in general, is the number of persons who occupy that status. But this generalization may not hold good over the whole range of statuses. In some groups, as we saw in the last chapter, the number of persons in the very lowest status is smaller than the number in the levels just above the lowest.

As we have gone on, it should have become more and more clear that we have been repeating ourselves. All this talk about members of a group who are able to supply goods that are scarce in relation to demand should have reminded us of our earlier discussion of power. Nor should this have been surprising. For differences in status are fundamentally, if we disregard the secondary elaborations of status that we shall consider later, the result of differences between men in power. (See Lenski, 1966: 63.) And the reason for our rule of thumb that what a man has to give in exchange, rather than what he receives, is the prime determinant of his status is that what he has to give determines his power directly, whereas what he receives determines it only indirectly, if at all.

We must be careful here. As we have conceptualized power, initial differences between men in the power they command tend to disappear in the course of repeated exchanges. That is, each man can get the others to persist in the changes in behavior that his power has brought about, but cannot get them to change further. Yet the fact that power tends in this sense toward equality does not mean that status does so too. The initial differences between men in power produce changes in the direction of inequality between them in what they give and get in social exchange; the equalization of power tends itself to maintain these inequalities, and they provide the elements of a ranking by status.

Consensus on Status

Yet for a phenomenon to exist that we may properly recognize as status, it is not enough that members of a group should rank others from top to bottom or from good to bad on a number of different dimensions.

For different members might not choose the same dimensions or rank others along them in the same order. If what we call status is to correspond at all well to what people ordinarily mean by it, the members of a group must rank one another in pretty much the same way. There must be some degree of consensus among them on this subject, though not necessarily perfect consensus.

There is one good reason why we should expect some degree of consensus. The origins of perceived differences in status are actual differences in power. As we have repeatedly insisted, men are powerful when many want what they, the few, are able to supply or many fear what they, the few, are able to withhold. When many want or fear the same things, they must to some extent be in similar circumstances. Accordingly, if there are any differences in power between the members of a group, there will be a relatively large number of members who will scarcely be in a position to deny that what they want or fear is relevant to their ranking of other members, or to deny that others, who can provide what they want or withhold what they fear, are of higher status than they are themselves. If they try to deny these things, they will in fact be claiming higher status for themselves than their actual power can make good, and others, their actual equals in power, will challenge them. Thus at least some nucleus of members of a group will provide a basis for consensus on status. To this extent the realities of the situation will keep breaking in.

But this process need have no effect on other persons—members of the group in the sense, perhaps, of being present in the same room as the rest—who do not happen to want what the few are able to supply, and who accordingly are not themselves subject to the power of the few. Such persons do not have the same reason for agreeing with the others that the few do indeed hold high status. Yet in many groups we find them agreeing also. Why should they do so?

So far we have talked as if members of a group "perceived" others to be ranked along various dimensions of status. But what do we, outside scholars and observers, care about what they perceive? It is our perceptions and not theirs that count for science. We do not perceive their perceptions; what we do perceive is what they say. The members of a group will talk spontaneously about other members; or we outsiders can get them to talk about them in interviews and questionnaires. As they talk, they will come right out and say that some members are "better" or "higher" than others in some respect, or they will make remarks that indirectly imply a ranking. And, as we have pointed out, they often agree with one another in what they say about the way other members are ranked.

If status is in large part revealed through the use of language, one of the forces making for consensus about status, consensus in the way members of a group rank one another, is a force that helps bring about consensus in the use of language generally. Uttering a particular form of words is an action like any other, and a man is unlikely to repeat such an action indefinitely, if it does not succeed in getting assent or apparent understanding from others. Suppose that the members who need not themselves accord high status to the few talk as if the latter were no more than ordinary members of the group. What they say may not command the assent or even the understanding of their listeners, who may not, as we say, know what they are talking about. Accordingly such members, in speaking about the others, will tend to shift to a form of words that does succeed in communicating. In so doing, they contribute to forming consensus about the status of members. In this respect they resemble the members of a group who conform to a norm because by so doing they get the approval of others and not because they find conformity rewarding in itself.

Thus a person may talk as if another were generally recognized as holding high status, without himself agreeing in the least that he ought to hold it. Even revolutionaries continue to speak of the upper class while doing their best to see that it shall not be upper for long and that they themselves shall replace it. (Actually in the United States few people, even revolutionaries, speak of an upper class: the highest class people refer to is usually an upper middle class. The reason for this behavior is not altogether clear.) That is, a rough consensus about the way men are in fact ranked by status does not in the least depend on a consensus that the ranking is morally justified. And what we have called *esteem* is not the same thing as status, though investigators have sometimes talked as though it were. Esteem may, of course, be one of the dimensions on which a man is ranked, but it is not status in itself; and, depending on the characteristics of the group in question, a man may hold high status without being held in high esteem—in fact, he may be feared and hated.

The fundamental dimensions of status are those along which men can be ranked according to what they give to others and what they get from them. The capacities of persons that produce differences between them in power and therefore in status vary in detail from group to group; but of course some such capacities have been very common bases for power in a large number of groups and societies. Some of them have been: intelligence and education, if these imply the capacity to find solutions to problems; command of physical force; command of material goods; the presumed ability to control physical phenomena, such as rain; capacity to restore physical or spiritual health. Corresponding to this variety in what men can give to others is the variety in what they get from them. Some of the things that men get in many groups and societies are: money and other forms of wealth; esteem, which we have already made so much of; deference; and obedience, which we shall have more to say about later. Persons that have these things to give and get these things in return become recognized as holding high status not only in their immediate groups but in society at large. Note how the two main dimensions stand out even in the very generalized status systems of large modern societies. What counts most here are a person's occupation (what he gives) and his income (what he gets).

The Accretion of Status Dimensions

In accordance with our policy of beginning with what we believe to be the simpler and more primitive phenomena, we have begun with the relative status of persons as established in their own eyes and in those of the audience by immediate and direct exchanges between them. Thus we have emphasized status as determined by the observable things a man gives to others and gets from them. But to these fundamental dimensions of status others become attached by accretion.

Suppose that in groups of a particular kind many powerful persons, persons who therefore are apt to have acquired high status in these groups, have in an overwhelming number of cases been older or of longer service in an organization than persons of lower status. The fact that they are older contributes nothing in itself to their power; it is their knowledge, let us suppose, which gives them that, though of course their years of experience allowed them to acquire their knowledge. The contingencies thus established make it likely that for many members of these groups a man's age is a stimulus in the presence of which a request for help or advice will be rewarded. Under these conditions, age becomes in effect another dimension, besides what they actually give and get in exchange with others, along which the status of persons may be ranked. And members of such groups will come to expect that a person who stands high on the dimension of age will also stand high on what he can give, say his skill, and what he can get, say esteem from his work group and pay from his company.

We take age to be a characteristic dimension that may accrue to the more fundamental dimensions of status. But we all know of others, at work in the past in one group or another, or still at work today: sex, race, ethnicity, education, ancient lineage. Thus in parts of the United States there still lingers, wholly apart from the black-white division, a status ranking of ethnic groups, with the Yankees (descendants of Protestant immigrants in colonial times) still precariously on top. The accepted rankings on dimensions of this sort may persist for long periods of time, but there is nothing that requires that they remain forever the same. They respond, though with a lag, to changing realities. The ranking by sex, with the males on top, is much less firmly established today than it was in the last century. If women come in fact to have the same skills and occupations as men and get, on the average, the same returns, the sex dimension will cease to be significant for status.

We do not discuss the development of status just because it is interesting in the abstract. We discuss it because it makes a difference to social behavior. According to the stimulus proposition, the reappearance of the stimuli once accompanying a rewarded action makes it more likely that a person will repeat the action. The crucial stimuli to social behavior are those presented by persons, and a person's status is a set of such stimuli. If, for instance, many people have established through their experience that older and more senior persons are more apt than others, at least in certain kinds of groups, to provide scarce rewards—if, that is, age is established as a sign of high status—then members of these groups who need help may not ask for it from a man who looks young, though he may in fact command the required skills. Accordingly, he may not soon get the chance to establish his power, win approval, and raise his own status. In social behavior what does not happen is just as important as what does.

On the other hand, a person who does happen to stand high on such an accrued dimension of status may be approached—and approached in place of a person who does not present the appropriate stimuli—by some member of the audience who, though he has not needed help so far, does need it now. Then such a person will get a chance to extend his power and win still more esteem, should he find these things rewarding. That is, the development of status introduces new rewards (and, as we shall see, possible costs) over and above those originally present in social exchange. What we often say is that acquiring and maintaining high status becomes rewarding in itself. What we mean is that status becomes an acquired value by becoming paired with, by becoming a means to the attainment of, more fundamental rewards.

Status Congruence

In the exchanges among Person, Other, and the Third Man—which, we shall remember, were also viewed by an audience—we saw that the status of each party was determined by his rank on two dimensions: what he gave to the exchange and what he got from it. We also saw that, in this case, the place of each member on one of the dimensions was the same as his place on the other. Thus Other stood higher than the other two both in what he gave, advice, and what he got, approval. Person and the Third Man were lower than Other on both dimensions and incidentally equal to one another. This coincidence of his place in the rank order on one dimension with his place in the rank order on the other made it easy for all three and for the audience to rate Other's overall status as higher than that of Person and the Third Man. Suppose also that, in this group, age or seniority had become, for the reasons suggested earlier, a significant further dimension of status, and that Other was older than the other two men. Then on advice, approval, and age— all three—Other would stand higher than the other two, and on all three the rest would stand lower than Other. The rank of every member of the group on any one dimension would be "in line with" his rank on the other dimensions, relative to the ranks of the other members. This condition has been called by a number of names: status crystallization, status congruency, status consistency. We have called it in the past and shall still call it *status congruence*—not that the name makes any differ- ence if we are agreed as to what we are talking about (see Hughes, 1945). To the extent that the condition is *not* realized we shall speak of status incongruence.

In groups like our model, where, we assume, exchange works itself out without interference from outside agents, the condition of status congruence in the relation between the members follows naturally from their underlying differences in power. Since what actually happens to persons tends to establish what they expect will happen and since enor- mous numbers of persons throughout human history have belonged to groups of this sort, mankind has, we believe, come to expect that what happens in fact in such groups will be the rule in all groups. That is, many persons have come to expect that they will normally be congru- ent in status with respect to those with whom they interact, that this will be the normal relationship between the stimuli each presents to the other. Incongruence, then, represents the unexpected, the signal of a difficulty of some sort. To speak more simply, a man whose status is in- congruent presents to others stimuli for conflicting types of behavior to- ward himself. A man's greater age is congruent with his possessing greater skill than oneself. What, then, if a particular person turns out to be more skilled, but younger? His skill suggests one type of behavior toward him; his youth, another. The status, moreover, of a person who presents incongruent stimuli is ambiguous or marginal; the status of a person who presents congruent ones is to this extent unambiguous or established. One knows where one stands with a congruent person, and he knows where he stands himself. One's response to him can be more integrated than one's response to an incongruent person. The state of incongruence, then, is to some extent one of uneasiness or anxiety both on the part of the incongruent person and on the part of those who interact with him. They may get over the uneasiness, but there is some- thing to be gotten over.

As we have said, the direct exchange of rewards between members of a group tends naturally to produce congruent relationships of status be- tween them. Incongruence is much more likely to occur when the ranks of members on some of the dimensions of status are determined by their exchanges with outsiders, as when a person's pay or seniority is deter- mined by his past history in the factory in which he works and his present terms of employment as negotiated with the management. Suppose, for instance, in a New England factory of the not too distant past, a worker was an older man, highly skilled, highly paid, of much seniority, a high-school graduate, and a Yankee. His rankings on the different dimensions of status—sex, age, skill, pay, seniority, and education—were in line with one another. Even his ethnicity (to use that dreadful word) was in line, for in the unavowed ranking of ethnic groups in New England, the Yankees (who today would be called Wasps) stood high. Naturally this did not mean that all Yankees held high status—far from it— but to be a Yankee was at least to stand high potentially on the ethnic dimension of status. Since all the stimuli such a man presented in social interaction were in keeping with one another, people faced no unusual conflicts in dealing with him. Then consider another sort of worker—and there were some such: incongruence is not rare. She was a woman of Syrian origin, holding a highly skilled job with much pay and seniority. The stimuli she presented, ranked on the different dimensions of status, were incongruent indeed. In a factory setting, her sex and her ethnicity were badly out of line with her other characteristics. It looks, by the way, as if incongruence of this sort, which can neither be changed nor disregarded, is often the object of joking. The skilled Syrian woman was more likely to have jokes directed at her by others, and to joke with them in response, than the skilled Yankee man. Indeed humor generally appears to be a response to, and indeed to rely upon, incongruent stimuli.

Congruence, Similarity, and Productivity

Perhaps we had better look now in some detail at actual data on the effects of congruence and incongruence. People seem to find that there is something natural and appropriate, something "right," about congruence. Accordingly, when they are working together as a team, we might expect that the degree to which they are congruent would make a difference to their effectiveness. If they are highly congruent over against one another, at least one possible source of disturbance to their collaboration has been removed. We turn to a study showing how success or failure in establishing status congruence made a difference to the relations between the workers and to the success of individual units within a commercial company. The study was made by J. V. Clark (1958) under the auspices of the Harvard Graduate School of Business Administration, and it was concerned with eight supermarkets belonging to a larger chain of stores.

The investigator devoted most of his time to two of the eight supermarkets and, in them, to the "front end" of the store where the checkout counters stood side by side in a long line. In a fashion now familiar to most Americans, a customer wheeled up to one of these counters a cart filled with the goods he had chosen from the shelves. There an employee took the goods from the cart, added up on a cash register the sum due for them, and packed them into a bag or bundle for the customer to take away after he had paid for them.

The number of customers that come into a supermarket, like any other food store, varies greatly from day to day and from hour to hour; therefore the need for employees in a supermarket varies greatly, and its manager hires a great many part-time employees. In the markets studied in the research, about two-thirds of the nonsupervisory personnel were part-timers, each working from ten to thirty hours a week.

When there were not many customers, only a few checkout counters were manned, and each was manned by a single full-time cashier who carried out all the operations of the counter, both "ringing" (adding up on the register the sum due from the customer, taking his payment, and making change) and "bundling" (taking the goods out of the carts and putting them into bundles for the customer to take away). When the customer load became heavy, more counters were manned, and, to speed up the through-put, each was manned by two workers, one to ring and one to bundle. The extra cashiers and bundlers were drawn partly from full-time workers usually busy in the "back end" where the merchandise was laid out on display, and partly from part-time workers, some of whom spent all their working hours at the front end. The question that came to interest the investigator most was what made an efficient team—ringer and bundler—at a checkout counter. In the supermarkets, a ringer and a bundler had to work together, if only in the timing of what they did to put a customer past the counter.

Besides casually observing what went on, the investigator carried out preliminary interviews with eighteen workers in the two supermarkets, chosen so as to represent the different categories of workers. These first interviews were fairly "nondirective," designed to give the investigator a quick general impression of workers' attitudes toward their jobs. Later he interviewed the same workers at greater length, and this time tried to test out systematically the ideas he had picked up earlier. Among the other questions he asked was this: "If you were suddenly called upon to go to the front end and bundle, arrange these people in the order in which you would *like* to bundle for them." Note the use of the word *for* here. In the workers' parlance, if you bundled *for* someone, that someone was a ringer: you were working *for* him or her as a subordinate.

The investigator then showed the worker a series of cards, each card describing a particular category of person. For instance, one such series was the following: full-time male, part-time male, full-time female, and part-time female employee. The worker was to put the cards in the order in which he would prefer to bundle for the type of person described on each. Some of the dimensions of preference that the investigator examined by means of other such series were age, marital status, education (whether in high school or college), and educational intentions (whether planning to go to college or not). He brought in these last two because most of the part-time help was of high school or college age. Indeed all of the dimensions were ones that the investigator had come, through his first interviews, to believe were particularly significant to the workers. When the worker had put the cards in any series in order, the investigator asked him to explain why he had put them in that order. Besides the information from the interviews, the investigator secured from the personnel office the usual background data about each worker: pay, seniority, job title, and regular job assignment.

We are now ready for the congruence problem. Bundling was the job that, if it was a worker's regular assignment, got the lowest pay. It was probably also the most monotonous and least responsible. Yet at times of heavy customer load, men from better jobs were moved into it, and this created one kind of ambiguity: people working on jobs that were "beneath" them. But it was not the only kind of ambiguity or the most important one. If one went onto bundling, it made a difference whom one bundled *for*. This expression, regularly used, of bundling *for* someone showed that the employees felt the cashier was superior in responsibility and authority to the bundler, and indeed as a regular job cashiering got more pay. But at times of peak load people from other jobs were moved onto ringing as they were onto bundling, and then the question was bound to come up what combinations of different kinds of workers made pleasant or appropriate ringer–bundler teams.

From his interviews the investigator came to the conclusion that the following rules, not always explicitly stated, described the conditions the workers felt should obtain when two of them collaborated:

1. A person should be able to talk comfortably with whomever he works beside.
2. The status factors of a person's job should all be in line.
3. A person's job status (which is determined by the amount of pay, responsibility, variety, and autonomy) should be in line with his general social status (which is determined by his sex, age, education, and seniority).
4. A person should work *with* someone else of his own social status (sex, age, education, seniority, and religion).
5. A person should not bundle *for* a cashier of lower social status than his own.

Actually there were only two main questions that these rules answer. First, whom is it legitimate that I should bundle for, as a subordinate? And second, whom do I enjoy bundling with, as a companion? For cashier and bundler are at once companions and superior and subordinate. The answer to the first question is that I should bundle for someone the characteristics of whose regular job and social background are congruent and superior to mine in other respects besides the superiority of ringing to bundling. And the answer to the second question is that I enjoy bundling with someone who, because his background is like my own, has many things in common with me, so that we can talk comfortably. We have already considered the effect of similarity on social relations. In the supermarkets the similarity factor combined with the congruence factor to make the preferred cashier someone who was legitimately superior to the bundler but not so far superior as to be utterly unlike him.

Let us now tie down these points in detail, quoting from the interviews. First, cashiering (ringing or checking) was socially superior to bundling. As one male cashier said:

> You know I feel sort of silly saying it, but in the scheme of things in this store, when you are checking you feel superior to the people who are bundling and to the stock boys, and this superiority is because of the responsibility of the job.

In the supermarkets as elsewhere, one job was more responsible than another if more damage could result if it were done wrong. But if as a job cashiering was superior to bundling, then status congruence required that the cashiers be superior to the bundlers on some other count besides the job itself. Accordingly we hear that:

> It would be a very bad situation to have even a 20–29-year-old bundling for a 16–19-year-old ringer. That's a *must* for good personal relations. Another way of saying that, is that high school guys should bundle for college guys. The college guy would naturally feel superior, and it would induce friction if he bundled for a high school guy. You see, he would *feel* superior as a person but *be* in an inferior position on the job.

That is, ringing had a higher job status than bundling, and so the ringer should have higher social investments than the bundler—in this case more age and education. Of course this does not mean that the condition of legitimacy was always realized in practice. Girls were thought of as having lower status than boys, at least boys of about the same age, and yet girls often rang the cash register and boys bundled "for" them—an ambiguous situation never considered wholly legitimate. Even in that most modern of American institutions, the supermarket, congruence still requires—or required when the study was made—that the man have a better job than the woman.

The reason, of course, why girls were often assigned the "ringing" and boys the "bundling" job may have been that the latter was heavier work, especially if the bundler carried the package to a customer's car.

But the fact that there is a good reason for an ambiguity in status need not prevent the existence of the ambiguity.

As two employees worked at a checkout counter, a little talking helped along an essentially dull job, especially in the intervals between passing customers through the slot. And though the condition of congruence was satisfied if a high school boy who was also a part-time worker bundled for a cashier who was an older man and a full-time worker, the bundler might not find him particularly easy to talk to because his background was too much unlike the bundler's own. Congruence, then, was a necessary but not a sufficient condition for a good ringer–bundler team: the two should also be similar in background. Accordingly, the investigator heard statements like this:

> I'd like to bundle for the regular high schools kids. [The speaker was one himself.] You could talk to them, you know? . . . The college kids would be too smart for *me*. You always like to bundle for someone your own age and class.

The resultant of the two demands for legitimacy and similarity was that a bundler most liked to work for a cashier whose social investments were higher than his own, but not so much higher as to put comfortable talking out of the question. Especially suitable was someone whose investments the bundler himself expected to attain in due course. Such a team might match a cashier who was already in college with a bundler who resembled the cashier in all respects except that he was not yet in college but aspired to go there: he was taking the college preparatory course in high school. Such a pairing of bundler and cashier met the specifications for both congruence and congeniality.

Perhaps the combined effect of the two requirements was best described by a part-time employee who was also a high school boy planning to go to college:

> I always prefer to bundle for the male if he's a friend. Not all of them are your friends, though, and I'd want to bundle for those that are. In general, I'd bundle for the younger person first because you're more apt to be friendly with younger fellows than older people. But between a high school cashier and a college cashier, I'd bundle for the college person first. If a person is older, you look up to and respect him more. I'd bundle for the high school girl before I'd bundle for the college girl, though. I'd have more in common with a younger girl than with an older one.

Note that, though he would bundle for a college boy, he would prefer not to do so for a college *girl,* on the grounds that she would have too little in common with himself.

We turn now to the investigator's final discovery about the supermarkets. A cashier and a bundler worked together in putting customers through a checkout counter, and we might expect any failure in the congruence and congeniality of the relationship between them to have some effect on their joint efficiency. Indeed one girl admitted that when she was forced to bundle for a cashier of lower status than her own, she purposely slowed down the speed at which she worked. The investigator succeeded in getting systematic evidence on this point.

The costs of manning the checkout counters formed a very large part of the total labor costs in the supermarkets. The investigator began by studying intensively two stores in the chain, Nos. 6 and 58. The former was much less efficient in its use of manpower than the latter: grocery department man-hours per $100 of sales were 3.85 hours in the former but only 3.04 in the latter; and operating gain as a percentage of sales was 3.89 percent in the former but 5.67 in the latter. The investigator also had the impression that of all possible bundler–ringer pairs, fewer in No. 6 store could meet the conditions of congruence and congeniality than could do so in No. 58. That is, the evidence suggested to him that labor efficiency and number of suitable bundler–ringer pairs might be correlated. He decided to test this hypothesis, not just for the two stores but for a larger sample of stores in the chain.

The investigator knew that the part-timers did most of the checkout work: about 80 percent of all customers were checked out by them, so it was largely for them that matching the members of the checkout team in congruence and congeniality was a problem. Although he did not have time to study the other stores at first hand, he knew that their jobs were the same as those of Nos. 6 and 58, and he had access to their personnel records. From these records, he gave each part-time worker in the other stores a score on each of a number of different dimensions: for instance, a boy scored higher than a girl on the sex dimension, a college boy higher than a high school boy on the education dimension, and so on for the other relevant dimensions of an employee's job and background, such as pay.

Since each part-time worker might be assigned, at one time or another, to work with every other one at a checkout counter, the investigator calculated for eight different stores—by a method too complicated to be described here—the percentage of all possible pairs of part-time workers that could realize the conditions necessary for a good team: similarity of background and job characteristics, on the one hand, and legitimacy in the form of status congruence, on the other. And he discovered that the rank order of the eight stores on this measure, which he called a measure of *social ease,* correlated almost perfectly with their rank order on labor efficiency (man-hours of labor used per $100 of sales): the greater the social ease, the greater the efficiency. If the rank order of the stores in efficiency was 1, 2, 3, 4, . . . , their rank order in social ease was 1, 2, 3, 5, 4, 6, 7, 8. The two stores that were fourth and fifth in efficiency reversed that order in social ease, and this was the only departure from a perfect correlation.

The investigator was also able to show that none of a number of other possible explanations accounted for the differences in efficiency nearly as well as did differences in social ease. He then added a fascinating final twist. Of the two supermarkets he studied at first hand No. 6 had, when he first studied it, a lower score in labor efficiency than had No. 58. Later No. 6 went through a spell of heavy labor turnover, which may itself have been a sign that employees were dissatisfied with the social conditions they encountered. The investigator was able to show that the employees who came in as replacements possessed characteristics more apt to make them members of congruent and congenial pairs than did those who had left. And as the replacements came in, the labor efficiency of supermarket No. 6 rose. Congruence and congeniality in the relationship between two men working together can make a difference to their productivity.

Congruence, Liking, and Effectiveness

At least one other study reaches conclusions similar though not identical to those of the supermarket research. Stuart Adams, to whom we owe the term *status congruence,* studied the effectiveness of Air Force bombers in relation to the congruence of their crews (Adams, S. N., 1953). He gave each member of each crew a score on a number of different dimensions of his background, his job in the bomber, and his social position—the dimensions being age, education, length of service, flying time, combat time, rank, the importance of his position in the crew, his reputed ability, and his popularity. His scores on the two last dimensions were determined by a simple sociometric test. Thus, to be obvious, an older man got a higher score on age than a younger one. From these scores on particular dimensions the investigator was able to develop a status congruence score for each member. Thus an older man with long service would be highly congruent as far as his scores on these two dimensions were concerned. And from these scores for individual members it was an easy matter to construct a measure of the average congruence of each bomber crew.

The investigator then correlated the crews' congruence scores with their effectiveness as measured by the number of hits they got in practice bombing, and also with the results of two questionnaires—on the degree to which members felt confidence in, and friendship for, one another. Congruence correlated highly with both confidence and friendship: the greater the congruence of a crew, the greater the average friendship of its members for one another, which is just what the supermarket study would lead us to expect, if social ease encourages friendship. On the other hand, effectiveness as measured by scores in practice bombing correlated negatively, though not highly so, with congruence, which is not what the supermarket study would lead us to expect, if effectiveness is equivalent to efficiency in the use of labor.

A closer look showed the investigator that the relationship between congruence and effectiveness was really *curvilinear*. That is to say, a bomber whose crew had very low congruence was apt to be a rather ineffective one. From then on an increase in congruence was associated with an increase in effectiveness until *medium* congruence was reached: the most effective bombers were those of medium congruence; but after that any further increase in congruence meant a sharp falling-off in effectiveness, until at the other end of the distribution a very congruent bomber was apt to be a very ineffective one. It was as if the members of such a crew were, by reason of their congruence, so much at their social ease that they spent their time enjoying one another's company instead of tending to business. It was as if, in the supermarkets, bundler and ringer had spent so much time talking to one another that they neglected to put the customer through the slot. Although the pressure from the customers was enough to prevent anything like that from happening in the supermarkets, there are plenty of other situations in which the adjustment of workers to one another may become so smooth that it gets in the way of work. Unfortunately the man who studied the bombers does not give us enough information to let us decide whether this explanation of the results is correct.

Congruence and Job Assignment

In the supermarket study, the workers certainly preferred to be assigned to jobs in such a way that their relationships with those they were to work with would be congruent. But they themselves had no power to bring this condition about: management made the assignments, apparently without giving much thought to congruence but only to what workers happened to be available; whether or not the assignments were congruent seems to have been a matter of chance. But sometimes, of course, the leader of a group or its members as a body are able to require one of their number to undertake some task for the group, and then we can see them making congruent assignments.

For an example, let us turn to the Bank Wiring Observation Room, last of the celebrated researches carried out by Elton Mayo and his colleagues in the Hawthorne plant of the Western Electric Company (Roethlisberger and Dickson, 1939; 379–584; Homans, 1950; 48–155).

The two principal jobs carried out in the room, wiring and soldering, need not be described here. It is enough to say that the pay rate of the wiremen was higher than that of the soldermen; they were presumed to be more skilled and held more seniority. Of the nine wiremen, six worked on so-called connector equipment and three on selector equipment. The differences between the two jobs were slight, but the connector wiremen were a little senior to the selectors and were assigned a slightly higher pay rate. There were three soldermen in all, one for each set of three wiremen, and they soldered in place the wires that the others had previously connected to terminals on the equipment.

In social activities two cliques had arisen, one centering in the connector wiremen and one in the selectors; and in these activities—as in skill, pay, and seniority—the first clique held itself to be somewhat superior to the second. To the first, or connector, clique but in a subordinate position as befitted his inferior job status belonged Steinhardt, the solderman for the first three connector wiremen. To the second, or selector, clique in the same sort of position belonged Cermak, who had replaced another man as solderman for the three selector wiremen. Matchek, the solderman for the middle group of wiremen, suffered from a speech defect and was hardly a member of Observation Room society.

All the men ate lunch in the room, sending out one of their number to pick up their food and drink from the plant restaurant. The question was who should be the "lunch boy"—note the word "boy." The lunch boy did not perform a very valuable service; anyone could have done it for himself, and it was menial: the lunch boy was a servant for the others. At the time the men were first assigned to the room Steinhardt had reluctantly agreed to do the job. But as soon as Cermak came in as a solderman for the selector wiremen and was accepted as a member of their clique, Steinhardt was relieved and Cermark took over as lunch boy.

Why was it appropriate that he should do so? He was a member of the "worse" clique; he was a solderman, and soldermen held the lowest job status in the room; of the soldermen he was the least senior and the last to come into the room. On all the dimensions of status, both those of his background and of his formal job assignment, he ranked lower than the others. Accordingly the group assigned him the least distinguished activity at its disposal: his menial job was in line with the other features of his status. No doubt when Cermak should have served his time as lunch boy and acquired, again with time, higher pay, seniority, and skill, and when someone should have come into the room who stood still lower on all these scales than he, then he would be able to shove the lunch-boy job off onto the newcomer.

We have treated this case as an example of status congruence, because it illustrates how the members of a man's group may keep what he does in line with the other features of his status. But we might also have used it later, in Chapter 11 on justice. The question for distributive justice is whether what a man gets, his reward, is in line with what he gives in social exchange. If it is in line, the condition of distributive justice is realized. Since the others gave the lunch boy an unrewarding job, and he, for his part, did not otherwise contribute much to the group, he met the requirements of distributive justice. Since they share the problem of bringing the ranks of persons on at least two dimensions of status in line with one another, congruence and justice are overlapping phenomena.

Status Symbols

So far in this chapter we have suggested that men find status congruence in their relationships with others with whom they are in contact to be an appropriate and comfortable state of affairs; and we have suggested how members of a group might act so as to bring the activity of one of their number over whom they have some power into line with the other features of his status. We turn now to the actions a person himself might take, without being forced to do so by others, to maintain congruence in his status, and to the reasons he might have for doing so. But in order to maintain status congruence for himself, he must be able to manipulate the observable features of his status, he must be able to control the stimuli he presents to others, and he may be able to do so only in part.

We considered earlier how various dimensions along which men may be ranked, dimensions that have no necessary relevance to their status, might nevertheless become relevant by accretion to the fundamental dimensions of status, which are always what men give in social exchange and what they get. According to the circumstances of the group or society in question, these assimilated dimensions of status might include such things as sex, race, age, ethnicity, seniority, education, etc. Now a man cannot easily control his rank on dimensions like these. Even his education, though it certainly results from action he has taken in the past, is not something he can do anything about quickly. Such stimuli may well affect the behavior of others toward a man, but he often presents them willy-nilly.

Yet there are other stimuli, which resemble the former in that they can be placed in rank order and which, though not necessarily relevant to status, may become relevant to status, but which differ from the former in that their presentation is within a person's control: he is able either to present them to, or, if need be, hide them from, other persons, his audience (see Goffman, 1959). His presentation (or failure to present) stimuli of this sort becomes itself an action like any other in the sense that he is more apt to perform it if it is followed by reward. Since being accorded high status is a reward, either in itself or through its further effects, a person will often, if he is able to do so, present stimuli that have this result. Such stimuli must, by the stimulus proposition, be ones under which the persons to whom they are directed may expect their own actions to receive reward or avoid punishment. Accordingly their characteristics must be in keeping with the assumption that the person who presents them has scarce rewards at his disposal, is getting much in return for them, and finds many people coming to him for help and protection. That is, the stimuli must be in line with, assimilable to, the two fundamental dimensions along which status is ranked. Manipulable stimuli of this sort are often called *status symbols*.

So much has been written about status symbols in both popular and technical literature that we need not dwell at length on them here. Sometimes the link between the symbol and the substance of status appears to be wholly arbitrary. But if we look closely we can usually find the unconscious logic that links the two. Take a famous historical example. Why, in the Roman and later in its successor the Byzantine Empire, should the topmost status have been associated with the wearing of purple robes rather than with those of some other color—so much associated that persons not of this status were forbidden to wear the purple? In many societies persons of high power are apt also to be persons of wealth, both because great wealth, being a scarce good, confers power and because, even more often, power confers wealth. In classical antiquity the purple dye was the rarest and costliest of all dyes, and purple robes were therefore the costliest of all robes. Accordingly, purple was an appropriate symbol of wealth and power, and of the status wealth and power bring; and the emperors and their close kin wore purple clothes on state occasions.

The fact that they were symbols of the topmost status need not, of course, have prevented people from finding purple robes beautiful and attractive for their own sake. But their sheer aesthetic appeal would not have been enough to make them symbols if they had not also been costly. Indeed as symbols they did not survive the discovery of cheap but good purple dyes. The technology that has made so many physical objects far cheaper than they were in the past and the progressive taxation that has made people more nearly equal in income than they were in the Roman Empire have tended to eliminate many kinds of goods as effective status symbols. Status symbols today are apt to be inconspicuous, recognizable only by those in the know, unlike those of the classical and medieval periods, when they were flaunted before the eyes of the merest peasant. Today, being in the know is itself the real status symbol, and conspicuous consumption is all too likely to attract the attention of the tax assessor. But let no one claim that status symbols have disappeared. In any modern organization, for instance, the size of the desk assigned to an officer is apt to vary directly as the officer's rank, even though the higher officers, who do not use them for writing because they have secretaries, may need big desks less than the lower officers do (see Roethlisberger, 1941: 79–80).

Since the display of a status symbol is an act that, like other acts, becomes more probable the greater the value of its reward, we should expect such display to occur most often where it made most difference—at the higher levels of status. We should also expect it to occur most often where status in other respects is most uncertain. If a man's status in a group is so firmly established and so visible in the fundamental dimensions that neither he nor the other members can entertain any doubt about it, he can afford not to worry about the external trappings of status. But alas! anything can become a status symbol if the circumstances are propitious, and a conspicuous lack of concern about status may be the best symbol of all. The honest determination of some great men not to "pull rank" may only give them more rank to pull. Finally, a man should be most likely to display a status symbol when the actual employment of the rare capacities that confer high status is most risky. Let us examine this issue more closely.

Once the association between a symbol and a status is established, a man of high status may become especially careful to display the symbol for fear that a failure to do so will throw his status in doubt, and that a doubt about his status may encourage a further doubt about his underlying power. Consider, for instance, a man—and there have been many in the past—whose power and high status rest, among other things, on his command of physical force. A person in contact with such a man may be more ready to risk action that would usually entail punishment, if the man of high status fails to display the symbols of his capacity to punish, such as conspicuous armed guards. In these circumstances, the person in question may be more ready to challenge, as we say, the authority of the other. To defeat the challenge the latter may be required actually to use the force at his disposal, and such action is in general costly. Rightly or wrongly, fairly or unfairly, punishment may arouse the resentment of the man punished, and his resentment may arouse him to renewed attacks. The resources that give power must always be husbanded, and especially the capacity to punish. An effective threat of punishment is much cheaper than punishment itself, though should actual punishment never occur, the threat may become incredible. The trick is to keep the actual use of force as infrequent as possible. For these reasons it is rewarding to a person of high status that others should avoid challenging his power at all, and his display of appropriate symbols may render a challenge less probable. Like the proclamation of a norm, it renders less likely any challenge made by inadvertence, by a lack of awareness on the part of a challenger of the risk he runs.

We end this section with a further illustration of the process by which status symbols get connected through a series of quasi-logical links to the substance of power. Consider the assumption made in many groups and organizations that, if a superior and a subordinate have something to discuss, and the two are in different places, the subordinate should meet the superior at the latter's place, such as his office, rather than the superior at the subordinate's. Here the direction of physical movement has become a symbol of status, but why this particular direction rather than the other?

We suggest that the answer runs as follows. In interaction, the person with the lesser interest has the greater power: Other has more power than Person, if Person wants what Other has to give more than Other wants what Person has to give. In these circumstances, by the value proposition, Person will do more to get what Other offers than Other will do to get what Person offers. If getting it requires physical movement, Person is more apt to go to Other than Other to go to Person. That is, the less powerful person goes to the more powerful one. Since power is the ultimate, though not always the immediate, determinant of status, the inferior in status tends to go to the superior. This appears to be the logical process by which one man's physical movement toward another becomes a symbol of the other's higher status.

Once this relationship is established in the experience of many persons, it makes possible new kinds of social action. If you can then, for instance, maneuver another man into coming to you before you go to him, you have established for all to see the outward and visible sign of your social superiority to him; you have presented a stimulus to the effect that your status is the higher and thus presumably your power the greater. This kind of maneuvering is a favorite sport in some bureaucracies: if you can get another man, hitherto considered your equal, to come to your office to discuss some problem instead of your going to his, you are to that extent one up on him. If you are about to bargain with him, you have won half the battle, the symbolic half. But you had better be careful: there is always a counter ploy. If he is smart enough to show no reluctance about coming to your office, as if this kind of social climbing were wholly beneath him, and he makes this plain to any observer who may be on hand, including yourself, he has turned the tables on you; for the man who shows no anxiety about status is apt to have the highest status of all.

By the same "symbolic logic," persons who are equals in status are apt to go about equally often to one another's places, or, if they are negotiating as recognized equals, they may meet at neither of their own places but at some neutral spot.

The secondary mechanisms of social behavior ride on the backs of the primary ones. Men learn new kinds of behavior whose rewards depend on the fact that they recognize certain other social relationships as already established.

Back Effects of Status on Exchange: Noblesse Oblige

We began this chapter by considering how a status ranking gets established, first on the basic dimensions of what a person gives and what he gets in social exchange and then on other, assimilated dimensions. We also considered how the expectation might arise that a man's rank on one dimension would be in line with, in keeping with, congruent with his rank on other dimensions. But as the chapter has gone on, we have become more and more concerned with what happens after the rankings and the presumption of congruence have become established. If we began by showing how the process of exchange gives rise to status, we end by trying to show how status, once established, reacts upon the exchange process itself, by altering the rewards and the costs of the participants.

Let us consider first the case in which a person is already established as another's superior in some dimensions of status but not in all. In particular, let us assume he is superior to the other in what he receives in social exchange. (Later, in Chapter 11 on justice, we shall consider the case in which what a man gives, not what he receives, is taken as initially fixed.) Let us assume also that he is able to change his ranking on some of these other dimensions, especially in what he gives; and that, since high and secure status is a reward, he will try to establish his status congruence at the level of his rank on the dimension on which he stands highest: he will try to bring up his overall status rather than lower it. Then he will, other things equal, try to raise his rank on these other dimensions.

For an example let us go back to the supermarkets. As we have seen, they employed both full-time and part-time workers. The full-time workers received higher pay and generally held greater seniority than did the part-timers. But sometimes the two were assigned to work together on the same job. In this situation, as one of the full-timers pointed out (Clark, 1958):

> A full-timer has got to show the part-timers that he can work faster than they can. It's better to work with them than against them, but he's got to show he's a better man.

No doubt it is only just—and we shall have more to say about this when we get to distributive justice—that a man who gets greater rewards than another should also incur higher costs in hard work, but it is also congruent that he should do so. For him to act otherwise is to cast conspicuous doubt on his higher status. A worker's superiority to another in pay and seniority is congruent with his superior ability to do a job; the full-timers were superior to the part-timers in the former respects, and so they had to show they could do the work better than the part-timers too, even if it required them to work harder than usual.

This is in fact a homely example of the phenomenon called *noblesse oblige*. We are far from arguing that the nobility, or what passes for it in any particular group, does always oblige. We know better than that. Depending on the particular situation, the costs of obliging may outweigh the reward. All we are arguing is that the reward is there: the reward of maintaining one's overall status in one's own eyes and in the eyes of an audience—or, what amounts to the same thing, avoiding a fall in one's status—by showing that one is superior to others not just in a few respects but in all.

We laugh at the language of the public-relations industry and its preoccupation with the "image" its clients present to the public; but many men, not all of them cheap *arrivistes,* have good reason to act as if their image, that is, the stimuli they present to others, made a difference. The public need not necessarily be the loser when they do so, since if they really try to behave in keeping with their preferred image, they may behave better than they would otherwise have done.

Note that in this case the development of status brings into play a process that tends to maintain what has already developed and establish it still more strongly. This phenomenon of development in the direction of greater stability is characteristic of many other social processes. Without it we should never see as much persistence in the forms of social structure as in fact we do see. It is not a question of some unexplained force of inertia on the analogy of physical inertia. It is rather a question of specific mechanisms that work toward stability. Other circumstances, particularly changes in the external circumstances of a group, are always destroying the stability, but the tendency toward it remains.

It is not, of course, always possible for a man to act so as to establish congruence between his ranks on all the dimensions of status, and in such cases various kinds of compromises may be worked out. Consider one example (Whyte, 1948: 47–63). A person who is superior to a second in other aspects of status is apt to be superior to him in authority too. In many American (and other) restaurants, the cooks are older men, with greater skill, seniority, and pay than the waitresses, who are women to boot. That is, the cooks are superior to the waitresses on several dimensions of status. Yet the waitresses must pass the customer's orders on to the cooks; in this respect they control what the cooks do, and control is the very marrow of authority. In this situation cooks and waitresses are in a notably incongruent relationship with one another. Perhaps as a result of a long process of unconscious adaptation, waitresses often give their orders to the cooks through a small window or over a high barrier, where the two can see one another with difficulty if at all, and the consequent impersonality seems to take some of the curse off the incongruence: one cannot, so to speak, feel incongruent with a bodiless voice or with an order written on a piece of paper and stuck on a spike. Persons who are in a strongly incongruent relationship may avoid one another (an example may be mother-in-law avoidance), just as persons in a weakly incongruent relationship may joke.

Back Effects of Status: The Maintenance of Equality

We have first looked at the phenomenon of *noblesse oblige,* in which a man, already superior to another in one or more dimensions of status, and especially in what he receives, acts so as to maintain his superiority on still another dimension and thus remain congruently superior. Let us now look at the situation in which a man, already equal to another in one or more dimensions of status, acts so as to maintain his equality on still another dimension and thus remain congruently equal.

Let us begin by looking at some illustrations, and first at the relation between equality and the exchange of physical goods. Here the great classic is Marcel Mauss' little book, *Essai sur le don* (1954). The book is concerned with exchange in the so-called primitive societies, but that does not make it irrelevant to our interests. Ours is the old doctrine that "human nature is the same the world over." Not that actual behavior is the same in every society—it would be absurd to claim that. But some of the propositions about behavior are the same. For instance, members of different groups may have come in the course of their different histories to value different things, but in any society a man who is able to provide others with scarce and valued rewards—whatever they may be in that group—is apt to hold power and win status.

Mauss pointed out that primitive people—and many not so primitive —try to act according to a "norm of reciprocity." (See Gouldner, 1960.) If a person gives something to another, the other is expected to return something of equal value. Remember that the word *value* here does not have the same meaning as *value* when it appears in our general propositions. The latter refers to what is sometimes called "subjective value," the former to "value in exchange," that is, value as determined by some convention accepted by members of a group or established by some mechanism such as market price. The two meanings are not unrelated to one another, but they are not identical.

In many primitive societies, indeed, if Person covets one of Other's possessions, he will try, just like a wheeler-dealer in our own society, to force a gift on Other and thus establish a claim on him. He will even withdraw the gift if the claim is not met—behavior that the pioneers of North America, already accustomed to more impersonal types of exchange, called "Indian giving." Person is often in a good position to force Other to accept the gift, for to refuse it is a refusal to enter into exchange and is equivalent to a declaration of hostilities: the person who refuses has deprived the other of what he wants and, under the norm of reciprocity, expects to get.

Should he accept the gift, Other ought to return to Person an object of at least equal value. He may even try to return one of slightly greater value, especially if some time has gone by before he is able to make the return. This tendency gives rise in primitive societies to something like interest. And just as failure to accept a gift implies hostility, so taking the gift and making a fair return implies the reverse. It implies that the two men are friends and that their exchange will be repeated. Should either party later break off the series of exchanges, he has declared hostilities just as much as if he had refused a gift in the first place. With the primitives as with us, an exchange of rewards between two persons tends to lead to their friendship and further interaction. But the primitives have gone further than we have done in turning what often happens into a set of rules about what ought to happen. Where we have done more than they have to institutionalize the impersonal market, they have done more than we to institutionalize the personal gift.

Mauss says that the primitives hold to a norm of reciprocity. But no norm enforces itself. What sanctions bring about some degree of conformity to the norm? Something very much like the behavior in question would undoubtedly occur even if the norm had never been explicitly stated. By the success proposition, a man is unlikely to go on rewarding another if the other does not sooner or later reward him in return. But there is more to the matter than this. Should Other take the gift and make an equal return, he shows himself to be not only a friend of the giver but his equal in status: each party holds the same rank on the dimensions of giving and receiving. But what if Other accepts it and fails to make a return? Should they be in any sense members of the same group, he then confesses himself, not only to the giver but to any other beholder, to be neither the giver's enemy nor his friend but his social inferior. He may even, in becoming the giver's inferior, become his subordinate too: the only way he can work off his debt may be to accept the orders of his creditor.

Since status is a relative matter, the same act that brings one man down in the world brings another up, and some givers may use the norm of reciprocity to enhance their own status. With deliberate intent they may press on others gifts they believe the others cannot repay, in order thus to humiliate them and make them out to be their inferiors. The most extreme example of this perversion of primitive gift-giving was the *potlatch* of the Indians of the Northwest Coast of North America. Two men of high status, usually in fact two groups, tried to snow one another under with gifts, to compete in the number of gifts they pressed upon third parties, indeed at the worst to compete in the number of goods they could afford to destroy. The person or group whose presents failed to match the other's in value lost face, fiercely resented the victor's triumph, and vowed social revenge. But the potlatch only exploited to a bizarre degree a possibility that is implicit in all primitive gift-giving—and much that is not so primitive.

Since comng down in the world is a punishment for most men, it provides a powerful sanction enforcing the norm of reciprocity. Most men will try to comply with the norm in order to avoid losing status—unless, of course, the value of the alternative to compliance is so great as to outweigh this cost. Other may need what Person has to supply so much, may value it so highly in our first sense of the word *value* that he will accept it even if he cannot make a return of equal value in the second sense of the word.

For some persons, on the other hand, the cost of failure to comply with the norm may itself be low. It costs one nothing to lose status if one has no status to lose. So far we have tacitly assumed that the person who accepted a gift and failed to make a return of equal value was already established as at least the giver's equal in rank on other dimensions of status. Such a person certainly has something to lose by violating the norm. But what if a person is already well established as the giver's inferior? Then his acceptance of gifts that he cannot repay in kind is in line with his status in other respects and can do his status no damage. Accordingly, such a person will be more ready to accept gifts of this sort than will the other. The problem of compliance with the norm of reciprocity is a problem in status congruence.

We have considered Marcel Mauss' study of gift-giving and the effect of departures from the norm of reciprocity in primitive societies. Let us now look briefly at a couple of analogous phenomena in our own society. In a certain machine shop described by Zaleznik (1956), there were two main classes of workers, recognized by different job titles, the machinists and the operators. As the titles suggest, the machinists ranked higher than the operators in seniority, pay, and, at least in theory, skill. Operators often borrowed tools from machinists and went to them for advice and help in coping with mechanical difficulties in their work: their asking for help was congruent with their inferiority to the machinists in other respects. But machinists hardly ever borrowed tools or asked help from other machinists. For a machinist to have done so would have been incongruent with his equality with the others and would have cast doubt upon it. And when, as occasionally happened, a machinest did ask another for help, he tried to conceal that this was what he was really doing. He pretended that it was not advice he wanted but only an opportunity to compare notes, to discuss with a fellow expert a technical problem of interest to both. Even if no one was really fooled by the disguise, it may have saved a machinist a little face by letting him avoid an open confession of his inferiority. Just as in the case of *noblesse oblige,* when a person is established as superior to another in one respect, he acts so as to maintain his superiority in others, so in cases like this, when a person is established as equal to another in one respect, he acts so as to maintain his equality in others. In both cases the tendency is *toward greater stability of social structure.* Stability may not in fact be achieved; other tendencies may prove stronger than this one, but at least they will have something to overcome.

With the understanding we have just acquired, we are enabled to go back and clear up an earlier step in the argument of this book. The processes of social behavior act and react upon one another simultaneously, but a verbal argument is ineluctably linear, so that, in explaining the processes, some points must be taken for granted at the beginning and accounted for only much later. Thus when we first introduced our two protagonists, Person and Other, the unskilled man and the skilled one, and discussed their exchange of approval for advice, we assumed that both men, besides getting rewards from the exchange, also incurred costs. We further assumed that for both men the chief cost was time taken from their own work. Now we must confess that this may have been much less true of Person than of Other. For according to the stage of the argument we have now reached, one of the chief costs to Person in asking Other for advice must have been the confession of inferiority to Other that he thus made, a confession that not only the parties themselves but others present in the office may have been able to observe. The cost to Person would naturally be the greater, the more fully the outward signs of his status, his seniority, for instance, or his job title, already established him as equal to Other. If he were observably inferior to Other, as the operators were to the machinists in the research just considered, his cost would be much less, and therefore, other things equal, the likelihood much greater of his asking Other for advice.

In the *potlatch* of the Northwest Coast, the two parties are frankly antagonists, each an aggressor against the other. Each is trying to establish by superior giving his general social superiority to the other. In other cases closer to home the giver is trying to do no such thing but finds himself, to his dismay, resented as an aggressor nonetheless. Suppose that a friend of yours gets into financial difficulties and you offer to help him out by lending him some of your money. His difficulties themselves imply that he will not be able to repay you soon, if he will ever be able to do so at all. You make the offer from the noblest of motives and are surprised to find that it is met, not with gratitude, but with ill-disguised signs of resentment. You should have remembered that your friend, by the very fact of being your friend, is also your equal in status, and that by offering to make him a gift he cannot repay, you have put that equality in danger. You have threatened to lower his status relative to your own. Montaigne (1958: Book III, Essay 9) put the matter thus: "As giving is an ambitious quality and a prerogative, so is accepting a quality of submission." See also what Emerson (1903) had to say on the subject in his essay on "Gifts." And real, if unintended, threats are apt to meet with real, if again unintended, resentment. Your charity would have been accepted with a better grace by someone frankly your inferior. You may still be able to get your friend to accept your gift, but it will take much of your tact, and that implies there is a danger to be avoided. It will take still more of your tact to keep his friendship afterwards.

Our argument may now appear to be getting us into a contradiction. Earlier, in our model case of social exchange, we argued that, if Other helped Person, he got Person's approval, even his admiration. Now we seem to be implying just the opposite: that if Other helps Person, he gets Person's resentment. How can both things be true? We believe they both can be true, but only under different conditions, and sometimes a fine line separates one condition from the other. The first statement appears to hold good when Person is already established in other respects as inferior to Other, or they have met so recently that the question of relative rank has not yet come up, and when it is Person that takes the initiative by asking for help rather than Other by offering it. In so doing Person indicates that he has discounted the costs he will incur in the exchange, and that, though his pride may suffer, he will find nothing to resent in Other's behavior. The second statement appears to hold good when Person is already established as equal in status to Other, and when Other takes the initiative by thrusting help on Person. This is, in effect, an act of aggression and so may arouse resentment. "The superior man," the Chinese tell us, "will never make another feel inferior." Excellent advice, but like so much excellent advice, difficult to carry out.

Doing Favors

Let us look briefly at another situation in which doing something for another may arouse his hostility, but for somewhat different reasons from those we have just considered.

Suppose that a person with whom you regularly associate does you a favor at your request, helps you out as Other helps out Person with advice at the office. You get the help on good terms and in return you make the emotional response of according him approval, even admiration if the favor has cost him much. In so doing you also accord him, at least in this respect, superior status. Then suppose he himself makes some claim on you later in return for the favor. Indeed you may discover that he did the favor only to put you under obligation to him, only for the purpose of making the later claim. But to ask a favor in return for a favor is to treat you as an equal, whereas you had been treating him as a superior. He has already received your approval and now he wants his favor to boot. But this is more than he has a right to by the standards of distributive justice; he managed to get your approval under false pretenses, and you will have some tendency to be angry with him (see Whyte, 1948: 251).

A person who recognizes the possibility of this reaction will adjust his behavior accordingly. If he is another's superior in some respect, if, for instance, he is the other's boss, he may well do the other a favor if the other asks for it. Such behavior is in line with his superiority in other respects. But he will not do a favor and then make a claim for a counter favor later. He will do it out of pure kindness. Not only will such a later claim arouse the other's anger, it will also tend to bring the superior's status down to the level of the other, and that may have further unfortunate consequences for the superior. It may conceivably make the other less likely to obey his orders. In such intricate ways are status and justice related.

Back Effects: Deference

We have considered the effects of congruence and incongruence, as a status system becomes established, on the behavior first of superiors toward inferiors and then of equals toward one another. Let us end this chapter with a brief look at the behavior of inferiors—some inferiors—toward superiors. We have suggested that, if men try to achieve status congruence, they generally do so by bringing up their scores on dimensions in which they rank low rather than by bringing down their scores on dimensions in which they rank high. But this is not always true, and some inferiors become congruent by bringing some aspects of their behavior down to the level of other aspects. A person who is already established as another's inferior on one dimension of status may be able to exploit that very inferiority to his own advantage—an advantage of sorts—in exchange with the other. He may display deference—symbolic inferiority—toward him. Since some men are rewarded by receiving indications of their superior status, and since deferential behavior accomplishes just this, the inferior is able to provide the superior with an additional reward, and so may himself be able to get in return rewards, perhaps material rewards, that would otherwise have been out of his reach. By exploiting his inferiority he has secured resources for exchange that he would not otherwise have controlled. He has, of course, secured them at a price. Since his deferential behavior is congruent with his initial inferiority in other respects, and since congruent status tends to be established status, he has fixed his inferiority to the other more firmly than ever before.

Summary

A person's status in a group is a matter of where he and others perceives he ranks in comparison with the rest of the members along a number of dimensions. Since the basic determinant of status is power, the crucial dimension is that on which a person is ranked by what he gives in social exchange, for what he gives determines his power. When exchange between members occurs without interference from "outside" agents, a person's rank on what he gets in social exchange, the second dimension of status, tends naturally to fall into line with what he gives. To these fundamental dimensions, other dimensions along which a person's background characteristics are ranked, such as his age or his ethnic group, tend to accrue. For a status system to exist in a group, there must be some degree of consensus among the members as to which dimensions are relevant to status and where members rank along the different dimensions. The fact that in many groups a number of members can hardly fail to acknowledge the superior power of a few provides a basis and a nucleus for such a consensus.

Particularly when a person's rank on certain dimensions is influenced by agents outside the group, his rank in relation to other members on some of the dimensions may be different from what it is on others. We then call his status *incongruent*. Since a person of incongruent status is, in effect, presenting contradictory stimuli to others, it is not easy for them to respond to him in an integrated way. They may feel some uncertainty, some anxiety, in his presence and he in theirs. In mild cases of incongruence, the contradiction may be eased by mutual joking and, in severe cases, by avoidance. We presented evidence that the number of incongruent relationships in a group might be inversely related to the productivity of the group, and that, when members of a group were able to assign a special job to one of their number, they did so in such a way that the job was congruent with his status in other respects.

The rank of a person on some of the dimensions of status may be partly within his own control. Naturally this is more true of what he gives in social exchange and of what he displays in the way of status symbols than of what he receives, which he can control only indirectly. Since the stimuli a person presents may affect the behavior of others toward him, and since his rank on any dimension is such a stimulus, a person's action in manipulating his rank may, like any other action, become more probable if it is followed by results favorable to him. Such results may be his eliminating any doubt in the minds of others about his overall status, or his establishing his status firmly by making it congruent on any one dimension with the highest rank he already holds on other dimensions. We looked particularly at what a person may do to bring or keep his rank on what he gives into line with what he receives, using as illustrations the phenomena of *noblesse oblige* and the exchange of gifts. Even a person of low status may, by displaying deferential behavior toward them, receive from those of higher status rewards he would not otherwise have obtained, though at the cost of establishing his low status still more firmly.

10 Satisfaction

THERE ARE TWO MAIN KINDS OF DIMENSIONS ALONG WHICH A person and others who observe him assess his status. He is ranked on what he does himself—that is, on what he gives in social exchange—and on what he gets from others. In the last chapter we began to be concerned with the relations between the two. First we considered the condition in which we take his rank on one or more of the dimensions of status, and especially what he gets, to be initially fixed, and then ask how he responds in what he gives. The answer seems to be that he acts, if he can, so as to bring his rank on what he gives up at least as far as his rank on what he gets.

We turn now to the other condition, in which we take his rank on what he gives in social exchange to be initially fixed, asking then whether what he gets is in line with it, and, if it is not, what his response is apt to be. This is the problem, as we shall see, of *distributive justice*. Note that the second condition is not the mirror opposite of the first, since a person cannot respond to it in a diametrically opposite way. He can directly change what he gives, since what he gives are his own acts, but he can only indirectly change what he gets, since what he gets are the acts of others, though naturally his own acts may influence theirs.

We shall approach the study of distributive justice only indirectly; in Chapter 11, we shall study it in more detail. We shall begin by asking the more general question: What determines a person's satisfaction with the rewards of his actions? In the study of satisfaction we plunge directly into the study of emotional behavior. Of course we have never wholly lost sight of it. Thus we argued that the approval a person rendered to another might well be in part an emotional response to what the other gave him, though at the same time it might also be an instrumental response or operant.

Usually we first learn about a person's satisfaction or dissatisfaction through what he says about the reward he receives rather than through his wordless actions, whether expressive of elation or anger. We usually get some warning. In the end, a student of social behavior must be more interested in what men do than in what they say about what they do. He is a little like a general who does not care whether his soldiers grumble so long as they will fight. Yet there are good reasons for devoting a chapter to satisfaction, provided its length is not out of proportion to the importance of the subject. With all its ambiguities, men will talk about it. Other things equal, responsible leaders would rather have their subordinates happy than not and may even believe that a satisfied subordinate is also a productive one. A great deal of research in social science is concerned with what people say about their satisfactions and dissatisfactions, and with the determinants of what they say. Moreover the study of satisfaction brings in again, in a new and perhaps interesting way, some of the variables we have already worked with in other connections.

Now we shall try to do three things. First, we shall try to establish what satisfaction is *not,* for there is much confusion on this point; second, we shall look at evidence that suggests what the main determinants of satisfaction are; and third, we shall ask what relation, if any, there may be between a man's satisfaction with a reward and the amount of activity he will put out to get that reward.

What Satisfaction Is Not

Though both have to do with reward, the variable, *satisfaction* with a reward, is not identical with the variable we have called the *value* of a reward. To speak crudely, a man may find the result of an action rewarding, and so continue to perform it, without liking the result in the least. Remember the case of the bandit (page 79). His victim hands over his money, saves his life, and is thus rewarded, but he is hardly satisfied with the result.

Take another case of the simplest sort. Let us suppose a man is performing an activity in small, more or less regular, units, and, as he does so, is being rewarded in regular units. Let us suppose, in fact, that he is cutting up a steak and eating it in successive chunks. He starts hungry and has as yet eaten no steak. Therefore the first piece of steak he swallows has a high value for him, but, by the satiation proposition, with every successive piece he chews up the value goes down, until at the end, since we shall assume there is plenty of steak, the value to him of eating any further steak is zero, and he is apt to say, "he could not eat any more if he tried," though of course in a few hours he may feel quite differently. He is satiated with steak, and this is just the point at which he is most apt to say that he is satisfied with the amount of steak he has had. This is not surprising, since the words *satiation* and *satisfaction* share the same element, the Latin word *satis,* "enough." Accordingly the value of the reward is lowest when satisfaction with it is highest, and the example shows us that the two variables cannot be identical, cannot even, in general, vary concomitantly, though they may do so in special circumstances.

But if value cannot be directly related to satisfaction, the other variable we have called the frequency of reward or degree of success can be. For the amount of steak a man has eaten may be considered a measure of his success in getting steak, and therefore his satisfaction is high when his success has been high.

Note, finally, that when the man has finished the steak, and the value of further steak has reached zero, he will, by the value proposition, be unwilling at least for the time being to do any further work that is rewarded by steak. Let us briefly savor this point but not pursue the matter further. We shall return later to the question of the relation between satisfaction and productivity. All we have done so far is demonstrate that value is not satisfaction.

The Determinants of Satisfaction

If value is not the same variable as satisfaction, if value alone certainly does not determine a person's satisfaction with a reward, what does? The best recent discussion of the determinants of satisfaction appears in Nancy Morse's book, *Satisfactions in the White-Collar Job* (1953), and we shall begin by considering some of her findings.

Remember first that satisfaction is at best a slippery concept. No doubt there are satisfactions and satisfactions. There is the satisfaction that attends the completion of a single, prolonged, and difficult task finished once and for all. Here the value of the result may for once be directly related to satisfaction, together with the escape from punishment that completion brings. Somewhat different, no doubt, is the satisfaction obtained from an ongoing set of activities, ever renewed, like those that make up an ordinary job. We shall limit ourselves to the latter sort of case, but even here there are different kinds of satisfaction. Indeed there are satisfiers and dissatisfiers (see Herzberg, 1956). A dissatisfier is a condition that creates dissatisfaction if it is not present but no particular satisfaction if it is. One will be dissatisfied with one's place of work if it is not warm in winter, but if it is warm one will simply take the fact for granted. As for the satisfiers, a job may offer intrinsic interest; it may offer the opportunity for interaction with others; it may carry with it some degree of status; and it usually offers pay. A person who holds the job may be more satisfied with some of its rewards than with others, and he may be able to weigh the different satisfactions together so as to reach some judgment about his overall satisfaction with the job.

One of Morse's more specific findings will serve to introduce her most general conclusion about the determinants of satisfaction. Among her other researches carried out among the white-collar employees of a large American corporation, she studied by questionnaire the degree to which certain workers were satisfied with promotions in the company. She found that they were likely to be more satisfied, the better they believed their actual chances for promotion to be. She then divided these workers into classes whose members assessed their chances for promotion as about equally good, and found further that, within each class, the employee was less likely to say he was satisfied with promotion, the more "important" to him he felt promotion to be. We must remember that all employees do not yearn for promotion with equal passion, since promotions usually require them to undertake greater responsibilities, that is, costs they are not all equally ready to incur.

In short, the investigator found two kinds of determinants of satisfaction with promotion: one that tended to increase satisfaction, and one to decrease it. Summing up the results of this and other similar studies, she states the following general rule about satisfaction with any particular kind of reward: "The greater the amount [of the reward] the individual gets, the greater his satisfaction and, at the same time, the more the individual still desires, the less his satisfaction" (Morse, 1953: 28).

Let us be scrupulous to recognize that the variables the investigator brings into her generalization are not quite those she actually measured in her study of the employees' satisfaction with promotions. She did not measure the number of promotions they had in fact received but rather the number they expected to receive in the near future; and she did not measure the amount of promotion they still desired but only how "important" to them they felt promotion to be. Accordingly we cannot unreservedly accept her generalization, if it is founded on her study of promotion alone. Yet there may be some degree of correspondence between the respective variables in the actual finding and in the generalization. Let us suspend for the time being any skepticism we may feel about the latter and go on to examine its implications.

The investigator states her generalization as it applies to the behavior of a single individual. Suppose that for this individual the amount of reward he still desires is measured by the degree to which the amount of reward he has actually received up to the present falls short of the amount that would satiate him with it; and suppose further that the amount that would satiate him is a constant, if not in the long run at least in the short. (Later we shall have to ask whether satiation in the ordinary sense of the word is really relevant to a person's satisfaction with the more interesting kinds of reward, and certainly to question the constancy of the amount of reward that would satiate him.) Under these suppositions, Morse's two determinants of satisfaction turn out to be themselves related to one another; for the larger the amount of a reward a person has received, the less must be left for him still to desire.

Yet the investigator was not just studying a single individual: she was comparing the satisfactions of several individuals; and as between two persons, it may well take more to satisfy one than it does the other, and so the two may get the same amount of the reward, yet the former be less satisfied than the latter, because he is left with more to desire. Let us accordingly rephrase Morse's generalization in the form of two propositions. First, when two men would be satiated with the same amount of reward, and one has gotten more of it than the other, the one that has gotten more is the more satisfied. Second, when two men would be satiated with different amounts of reward, but have gotten the same amount, the one that needs less to satiate him is the more satisfied. Note that the further a person is from satiation with a reward, the more valuable to him, by the deprivation-satiation proposition, is any unit of that reward; and so we may conclude that, of two men receiving equal amounts of a reward, the one who finds the reward the more valuable will be the less satisfied. Here is another proof, if we want one, that value need not be directly related to satisfaction.

The Determinants at Work: Examples

Now let us look at further studies of satisfaction and its determinants, particularly further studies made by Nancy Morse in the company in which she investigated satisfaction with promotions.

In one of her researches (Morse, 1953: 55–75) she divided the different clerical jobs in the company into four categories and put them into the following rank order: high-level technical, semisupervisory, varied clerical, and repetitious clerical. This was the order of the categories from top to bottom in pay, responsibility, and variety, and also, not surprisingly, their order in status within the company. It also turned out to be the rank order of the jobs in the average degree of satisfaction the persons who held them expressed for the intrinsic rewards of the job itself, such as the sheer interest of the work. If we considered only these results, we should be inclined to believe that the sole determinant of satisfaction was the first of Morse's factors, "the amount the individual gets." The greater was the variety and interest of a job, the greater was the satisfaction of those who did it.

But when the investigator asked the employees in the same categories of jobs how satisfied they were with pay and promotions, the rank order almost reversed itself. In spite of the fact that they drew the highest pay, the high-level technical employees were now the least satisfied, the varied clerical somewhat more so, and the repetitious clerical still more. The semisupervisory employees, as the most satisfied, represented the only exception to a complete reversal of the former rank order. We shall have more to say about them later.

Leaving the semisupervisory employees aside for the moment, let us look at the others. The repetitious clerical workers got less pay than the others and certainly had received few promotions, yet they were the group most satisfied with both. Here it is clear that "the amount the individual gets" of a reward cannot be the sole determinant of his satisfaction. What factor is missing? The order of the jobs in pay and responsibility was naturally also their order in the average age and average seniority in the company of the persons who held them. When employees first came into the company, most of them started out on the lowest and dullest jobs. But most of them were also youngsters, new to the labor market. Though they were far down on the ladder of promotion, at least it looked as if they could climb. Though their pay was relatively low, it was much more than they had gotten before, and as persons who had as yet acquired few outside responsibilities, they had few demands for money put upon them. That is, the amount of pay "they still desired" was relatively low. We shall perhaps agree that, in the abstract, our potential desire for money is infinite; but once this point of doctrine is out of the way, we shall also perhaps agree that most of us would get by very well with somewhat less money than that, especially if we thought we could count on getting just a little more money in the near future.

As employees gained seniority in the company, moved up to more varied, interesting, and responsible jobs, and found more satisfaction in the job itself and in its informal status, they were also apt to acquire wives (or husbands), children, houses, and so forth—so many more demands on them for money. Most promotions entail an increase in pay, but the increases these employees received as they moved up in the company apparently did not keep pace with their increasing need for pay and promotion, the increasing value, to use our term, they set upon these things. In any organization, moreover, an employee's chances for further promotion narrow rapidly as he approaches the top. His need for promotion may still be increasing when his chances of getting it have begun to decrease.

In order to explain variations in satisfaction with pay and promotions, it is clearly not enough to bring in just "the amount the individual gets" of this type of reward. It is also necessary to bring in the second of Nancy Morse's two factors, "the amount the individual still desires." And whereas we naturally began our discussion with the simplest sort of case, that of eating steak, in which the amount of reward that will satiate a man remains pretty constant from one occasion to another, we have now moved to cases where that amount changes with time, age, service, and seniority in a company. It changes because these things usually bring better jobs and more money, and money is a generalized reward, which may be used to realize other values, which are themselves changing. The problem of satisfaction then becomes that of the relative rates of change of the two factors. The fact that employees became less satisfied with pay and promotion, the more pay and promotion they received, is to be explained by the assumption that the amount of these rewards they still desired increased more rapidly than the amount they actually got. On the other hand, the value a person sets on an interesting job and on informal status may remain relatively constant over the years of his working life. Certainly it is less influenced by outside demands than is the value set on pay. Accordingly the satisfaction of employees with the intrinsic interest of their jobs and their informal status increased directly with the amount of these rewards they actually received. Both findings, in their different ways, satisfy Morse's general statement.

Sometimes we are able to see how satisfaction with the two different kinds of reward combine to produce a person's overall satisfaction with a job. In some companies overall satisfaction is highest in the least senior and in the most senior jobs and is lowest in the middle (see Purcell, 1953: 79). The least senior people are most satisfied with things like pay, and the most senior ones most satisfied with informal status and the intrinsic interest of their work, while the people in the middle are not much satisfied on either count.

Finally, let us return to the semisupervisory workers, who, we shall remember, ranked second on intrinsic job satisfaction and first on satisfaction with pay and promotion, and thus constituted an exception to the rule that the rank order of jobs on the latter kind of satisfaction reversed their rank order on the former. To explain their relatively high satisfaction with pay and promotion we must bring in not only a factor we have already considered but also another one which we have not considered so far, their expectation of getting the reward. It happened that most of the semisupervisory workers were women and also unmarried. Since they were unmarried, they probably did not have to shoulder heavy family responsiblities. Accordingly, their need for pay and promotion may not have risen as rapidly as it did for other employees of high status and therefore may not have had the effect of decreasing their satisfaction with this type of reward.

Not only were they unmarried, they were also women. In the recent past in American industry, before the advent of anti-discrimination legislation or Women's Liberation (and who dares say it is not still the case?) women on the average were apt to get worse jobs than men and even to get less pay than men doing the same work. Accordingly, they expected less in the way of pay and promotion than men did, for it is fact and experience that in the long run determine expectations; and since they expected less, they were more apt than men to be satisfied with any given amount of pay. Their lower expectations may help explain the relatively higher satisfaction of the female semisupervisory workers with the pay and promotions they actually received. One might not think that what an individual expects is quite the same thing as Nancy Morse's second factor, "what an individual still desires." Yet they seem to have a similar effect on satisfaction. It may be that the second factor has two kinds of determinants. What one still desires is what one needs to get, as determined, for instance, by the outside demands placed on one. But what one still desires is also what one has come to expect to get. The effect on a person's behavior of what he expects in the way of reward will become of increasing interest to us.

Another and more famous study of satisfaction with promotion suggests the same sort of conclusion, and once again seems to contradict the common-sensical notion that, the more of a reward a person gets, the more he is satisfied with it. In World War II, the Research Branch, Information and Education Division, of the U.S. Army carried out a series of studies on the attitudes, morale, and behavior of American soldiers. Among other things, the investigators studied attitudes toward promotions, and they found, in particular, that soldiers in the Air Force (then part of the Army) were far less satisfied with promotions than were soldiers in the Military Police, in spite of the fact that the actual chances for promotion were far greater in the former than in the latter (Stouffer, Suchman, DeVinney, Star, and Williams, 1949: 250–53).

How shall we explain this apparently paradoxical finding? Note first that it deals with the *average* satisfaction of soldiers in the two branches. Perhaps the soldiers who had just been promoted would have expressed satisfaction with promotions, but the questionnaire was not administered to them alone; it was also administered to soldiers who had not been promoted. Now if there is much promotion in a particular outfit, that fact will lead its members to expect promotions, and accordingly they will be more dissatisfied if they do not receive them than will the members of another outfit, like the Military Police, in which promotions have been few and far between. Even those soldiers in the Air Force who had in fact received promotions may have come to expect still further steps upward in quick succession and so have become dissatisfied even with their actual rate of advancement. In short, the difference between the Air Force and the Military Police in rates of promotion, far from making the difference in satisfaction more difficult to explain, makes it easier, if the relation of fact to expectation, and of expectation to satisfaction, are taken into account.

Another consideration may further help us to explain the difference in satisfaction with promotions. If there is much promotion in a particular outfit, members who have been passed over will have many occasions to ask why others have been advanced and not themselves, to ask what these others have which they themselves have not, and then to wonder whether the promotions were fair. In an outfit, on the other hand, where promotions have been few, such occasions for resentment are much less apt to arise (see Davis, 1959). Promote everybody or promote nobody and soldiers will be satisfied with promotions, the study in question seems to say. Unfortunately neither of these two policies is satisfactory for other reasons. But we are now getting a little ahead of ourselves. In bringing in interpersonal comparisons, justice, and resentment, we have brought in matters that we meant to reserve for the next chapter.

Satisfaction and the Level of Aspiration

In reaching the question of what men expect in the way of reward, we must revise some of the assumptions we made earlier. Nancy Morse stated that a person's satisfaction with a particular reward is determined by two classes of variable: the amount of reward he has received, which, as it increases, tends to increase satisfaction, and the amount he still desires, which, as it increases, tends to decrease satisfaction. We have found no reason to question the first of these variables, but we have steadily drifted toward a definition of the second that is somewhat different from the one we started with. We started by assuming that there was a quantity of the reward in question which, received within a given period of time, would satiate the person with it. Then the amount he still desired was the difference between that quantity and the quantity he had actually received. When we are talking about some specific material reward like steak, it may be more or less meaningful to speak of the quantity that, eaten at a sitting, would glut a man; but when we are talking about generalized or nonmaterial rewards like pay, promotion, variety of work, or autonomy, it is by no means clear what we might mean by satiation. As we have studied satisfaction with rewards of this kind, what we have practically done is substitute the quantity of reward that he expects for the quantity of reward that would satiate a man. The further what he has actually received falls short of what he expects, the more, in Morse's terms, he still desires. The variable as redefined still fits the meaning of her proposition, for the more a person still expects, the less he will be satisfied with what he has gotten so far.

Not only did we assume that there was a quantity of a reward that would satiate a person but that this quantity remained constant. Again, this assumption may hold good of a reward like steak: the amount that would satiate him with it may not change very much from one sitting to another. But it may not hold good of those rewards for which what a man expects, not what would satiate him, is crucial in determining his satisfaction. For what a man expects will happen is largely determined by what has happened to him. What he expects in the way of reward depends on his past success in getting that reward, and on the relation of what he gets to what he gives. As his success changes, his expectation will sooner or later change too. As he works in an organization, for instance, a man's seniority, skill, and so forth usually increase, and as they do, he is apt to expect corresponding increases in such things as his pay. What psychologists call his *level of aspiration* rises: he aspires to better things. If it rises without a corresponding increase in the amount of reward he is getting, his satisfaction will decrease.

For an example of the effect of an increase in the level of aspiration let us return to Nancy Morse's book (1953: 138–40). In the course of her investigations, she studied the differences in job satisfaction between white-collar workers under "general" and those under "close" supervision. Briefly, a close supervisor was one who kept checking up on what the workers were doing, kept "breathing down their necks." A general supervisor, on the other hand, was one who, once he had explained to a worker what he wanted him to accomplish, left him alone to accomplish it by whatever methods he might choose. The investigator knew from earlier studies that, other conditions equal, employees preferred general to close supervision, and so she was surprised to find that, in one department in particular, the employees under general supervision were less satisfied with their pay, status, and even the intrinsic content of their jobs than were the employees under close supervision.

She came to attribute this finding, first, to a rise in the level of aspiration of the employees under general supervision, a rise brought about by their experience of general supervision itself, and, second, to the fact that these employees received no more pay or promotion than did the employees under close supervision. What general supervision meant in this department was not only that the boss did not continually check up on an employee but also that the employee himself took a great deal of independent responsibility in carrying out an important task. But a man who has learned to do a job on his own responsibility has, in effect, learned to do a more difficult job, and so he may come to believe that, in fairness, he ought also to get a raise in pay and a promotion. If he does not get them—and he did not get them in the department in question— he will become less satisfied than his fellow workers down whose necks the boss has been breathing all the time, even though, taken by itself, the latter is the worse situation to be in. Reactions like this have persuaded some people who would prefer to believe otherwise that any effort to satisfy men is bound to be self-defeating: any satisfied desire tends to create an unsatisfied one. But again, when we start talking, not about the amount of reward that would satiate a man or the amount he expects or aspires to, but rather the amount he thinks in fairness he "ought" to get, we are verging on matters that we shall take up more fully in the next chapter.

Note that it is not a person's increased need for a reward but his increased success in getting it that raises his level of aspiration. The value a man sets on a particular reward may increase greatly without doing anything to strengthen his expectation that he will actually get it. The historians have often recognized that people are not very apt to revolt just because they are badly off. They are much more likely to do so when, after having been badly off, they have for some time experienced increasing prosperity, but then the increase has stopped. Their previous experience has raised their level of aspiration, but their actual reward has not kept up with it, and they are angry. In time they will adjust their expectations to the new level of reward, but their adjustment may come too late to prevent revolt. The phenomenon has been called "the revolution of rising expectations."

Productivity and Satisfaction

We shall end this chapter by returning to a question we raised at its beginning: What is the relation between a man's satisfaction with a reward and the rate at which he will work to get that reward? In American industry this is the famous question of the relationship between satisfaction and productivity: Is a satisfied worker one that will work hard? Many Americans have been inclined to believe that he will indeed work hard. Perhaps they believe (much to their credit as optimists) that augmenting one good thing must augment all others too (but then it would be easy to attain the best of all possible worlds). Or they may rely (much to the credit of their view of human nature) on a theory of fair exchange: if management does much to satisfy the workers, the workers will do much to satisfy management. Unfortunately for their optimism and good-heartedness, studies of the relationship have reached ambiguous results; and we have already suggested reasons why we should not expect a generally positive relationship between satisfaction and productivity.

The workers' notion of fair exchange does not always jibe with management's. Indeed their slogan, "A fair day's work for a fair day's wage," they often apply in practice by pegging production at a certain level instead of working as hard as they can. Apart from the possibility, which they will always stress, that working beyond that level will tempt management into cutting the rates for piecework, they may reach a point, if more work brings more pay, at which they find any further increase in pay less valuable than some alternative reward, such as social interaction with others, and then they will turn from work to what seems like play. At any rate, the happy worker is not always a

particularly productive one, nor is the productive worker always particularly happy. These facts seem to provide ammunition for the cynics: in
fact they provide it only for the realists, who need not be cynical at all.

But let us explore the relationship in a more formal fashion, if only
to clarify some of the ideas we have been developing in earlier pages.
Our argument will be highly abstract, as it must be if it is to be at all
general, and it will make use of a simplified model or toy, which should
be taken lightly like the serious thing it is, just as light things should be
taken seriously. At the very least the toy may show how inadequate
our assumptions and formulations are. Readers who are not amused by
toys or prefer not to tax their minds with even the most elementary
mathematics had better skip the next few pages.

Let us assume, as we did in our earlier example of eating steak, that
a man is performing successive units of a single kind of activity and
getting as a result successive units of a single kind of reward, either
from another man or from the physical environment. Let us further
assume that no rewarding alternative is open to him—though in real
life there are almost always alternatives—and that therefore we may
disregard costs. If the man begins without any of the reward, if he starts
from full deprivation, we shall give the label R to the number of units
of reward he receives within a given period of time. The number of
units of the reward that, received within the given period, would
satiate him physically, or come up to what he expects, or fully realize
his aspiration—we may take our pick—we shall call the *satisfaction
quantity, Q,* and assume it to be constant over the period in question.

If we can establish the relationship between each of two different
variables to the same third variable, we can establish their relationship
to one another. Accordingly, we shall attempt to express in terms of R
the two variables whose relationship to one another we are interested in
examining. These variables are, first, the degree, S, to which a man is
satisfied with the number of units of reward he has received, and, second,
his productivity, the number of unit acts, A, he performs in the course
of getting this reward.

Let us begin with the determinants of satisfaction. According to
Nancy Morse's statement, which we shall henceforward call the *satisfaction proposition,* a person's satisfaction with a reward varies directly
with the quantity, R, he has received and inversely with the amount by
which that quantity falls short of the satisfaction quantity: the amount
of fall-short is $Q - R$. For the purposes of our toy we shall asume that
$Q - R$ cannot become negative, that the man cannot or will not receive more of the reward than the amount that would fully satisfy him.
We may accordingly write the equation:

$$S = \frac{R}{Q - R} \tag{1}$$

We turn now to the determinants of productivity, A. According to the value proposition, a person will perform an action more often, the more valuable, V, a unit of the reward is to him; and when we are considering changes in the value of a single kind of reward, rather than comparing the values of different kinds, we take its value, according to the deprivation-satiation proposition, to be an inverse function of the amount of reward he has received. Let us accordingly eliminate the value variable and relate productivity, A, directly to the degree to which the man is deprived or satiated. One possible formulation of this relationship would state that A varies directly with the amount by which the quantity of reward he has received falls short of the quantity that would satisfy him: that is, it varies directly with $Q - R$ and inversely with the quantity he has already received, R. The former represents the degree to which he is still deprived, and the latter the degree to which he has already been satisfied. Accordingly, let us write the equation:

$$A = \frac{Q - R}{R} \tag{2}$$

Note that the expression on the right-hand side of the equation is the inverse of the expression on that side of equation (1).

But productivity, A, is not determined by the value of the reward alone. No matter how valuable a reward is to a man, he will do nothing to get it if he has never in the past been successful in getting it. According to the success proposition, the frequency with which an action is performed varies directly with the frequency with which it has been rewarded. But within this gross and overall relationship, the schedules according to which successive actions are rewarded may differ, depending on the type of action, the type of reward, and other circumstances. Reward may come at regular intervals of time or at variable intervals. It may come at a regular ratio to the number of acts, as when every nth act is rewarded, or at irregular ratios. And there are other possibilities, as we shall see. Each schedule has a somewhat different effect on the frequency with which a man performs the act. Let us choose for our toy the regular-ratio schedule, partly for simplicity and partly because it commonly occurs in real life, as when a man paid piecework wages gets so many cents per completed unit of work. Under this condition we may write the equation

$$A = kR \tag{3}$$

where k is a constant of proportionality representing the ratio of A to R. If k is greater than unity, the man gets less than one unit of reward for any one act; if k is less, he gets more than one unit for any one act, and if $k = 1$, then one unit of action gets one unit of reward, however that is defined.

Now we have enough equations to find the relationship, under the assumed conditions, between satisfaction and productivity. Multiply equation (2) by equation (3). Then,

$$A^2 = k(Q - R) \qquad (4)$$

Eliminate $Q - R$ between this equation and equation (1). Then

$$S = \frac{kR}{A^2} \qquad (5)$$

This equation at least suggests that there is no simple, single, direct relationship between satisfaction, S, and productivity, A, since the relationship between the two variables is conditioned by a third variable, R, the amount of reward received within a given period of time.

Now let us make a further simplifying assumption. Let us assume that $k = 1$: that is, that $A/R = 1$, and each unit of action gets just one unit of reward. Use this formula to eliminate R in equation (5). Then

$$S = \frac{1}{A} \qquad (6)$$

This relationship is certainly simple and single, but it is far from direct. Under the assumed conditions, productivity varies inversely as satisfaction, and the more satisfied the man is with a reward, the less he does to get it. But remember that the assumed conditions are highly simplified compared to those of real life. Our toy is, after all, only a toy.

Let us finally ask what other condition would have to be met if, within the limitations of our toy, the dreams of kindly people were to be realized and productivity were to vary directly as productivity. A simple formula for such a direct relationship is

$$S = A \qquad (7)$$

We must also abandon the constant ratio, k, of action to reward and replace it with a variable ratio, r. Then equation (5) becomes

$$A = \frac{rR}{A^2}$$

That is,

$$r = \frac{A^3}{R} \qquad (8)$$

This means that, if the requirement were to be satisfied, the rate of reward would have to increase much more rapidly than the rate of action. When applied to real life, such a formula suggests that an employer who wanted to keep both the productivity of his workers and their satisfaction with their pay increasing at the same time would be required, instead of keeping his piecework rates constant, to increase them very rapidly with every increase in the number of units of work completed. He would not be able to do so without going broke, unless he was able to decrease his costs or increase his returns per unit proportionately, and at best he would be able to accomplish this feat for only a short time.

Another situation in real life that might satisfy the requirement is the following. Suppose that soldiers have been fighting all day, at first with little apparent success against the enemy. But as dusk approaches, they begin to see rapidly accumulating signs of his imminent collapse. Then they will both redouble their efforts and feel increasing elation as they come within sight of victory. But remember again that we must not ask for too close a correspondence between our toy and real life. Its purpose is only to get us thinking in general terms about the complicated relationships between action, reward, and satisfaction.

Summary

In the present chapter we examined a person's emotional response, in the form of satisfaction or dissatisfaction, to the amount of a particular reward he has received. We first showed that satisfaction with a reward is not the same variable as the value of that reward. Then we examined evidence on what determines a person's satisfaction. His satisfaction seems to vary directly as the amount of reward he has received and inversely as the amount he still desires. What he still desires may be determined by his needs, as when people need money to support their families. But for some kinds of reward, what he still desires may be what he expects to get but has not yet gotten. Since what he expects is often determined by what he has in fact been successful in getting in the past, an increase in his success may raise his level of aspiration for the reward. And if what he gets of it lags behind what he aspires to, his dissatisfaction will increase.

We then examined the relationship between a person's satisfaction with a reward and his productivity—that is, the amount of work he will do to get it—and developed an unsophisticated model to show, first, why we should not in general expect productivity to vary as satisfaction and, second, what conditions would have to be met if it were to do so.

But if a person's satisfaction has no simple effect on his action in the sense of his productivity, it may affect his action in another way. If a person gets less of a reward than he expected to get in comparison with the reward some other person gets—if he gets less than what he considers fair—then the discrepancy may, by the frustration-aggression proposition, arouse his anger and aggressive behavior toward the source of the unfairness and its beneficiary. This is the problem of distributive justice or relative deprivation, which will be the subject of the next chapter.

11 Distributive Justice

IN THE LAST CHAPTER AND IN THE PRESENT ONE OUR TASK IS to examine the emotional and other responses persons make to the amount of reward they receive, especially to the relationship between that amount and other aspects of their status. In Chapter 10 we saw that, as between two persons who received equal amounts of a given reward, the one for whom "the amount he still desired" was greater was the less satisfied. We also saw that one of the determinants of the amount of reward a man still desired was his need for it. But as we went on, we were forced to recognize that in many cases another determinant was what he expected by way of reward. The larger the amount he still expected to get, the less satisfied he was with what he had.

Here we shall carry the matter further. We shall consider the case in which what an individual (or a group) expects in the way of reward is determined by his comparing the reward he gets with what another individual gets. He claims that he not only expects but deserves to get more than, or the same amount as, the other, and if in fact he only gets the same amount or a lesser amount respectively, he feels some degree of resentment toward whoever brought the condition about or benefited from it. A person who does not get the reward he needs feels dissatisfied but not necessarily angry: though he needs more, he may have no reason to expect to get it. But a person who does not get what he expected— and what he expected is always becoming what he deserves—is apt, by the frustration-aggression proposition, to find the results of aggressive behavior toward the source or beneficiary of his frustration rewarding. His frustration brings in a new and highly important value, which may change the terms under which he will take part in social exchange. He may be willing to forgo other rewards in order to get back at his tormentors.

This is the problem of *relative deprivation,* as many social scientists have come to call it: the deprivation of one individual or group with respect to a particular reward in comparison with another individual or group. (See Merton and Kitt, 1950.) Here we shall prefer to call it the problem of *distributive justice,* or rather injustice: injustice in the distribution of rewards between individuals or groups. We do so because we feel we ought to honor our predecessors in social science by using their terminology, so far as possible. Aristotle was the first to develop a general analysis of distributive justice, and we owe the term to him.

An Example

Let us begin with a characteristic case of distributive injustice, injustice at least in the eyes of some of the persons concerned. For this purpose let us return to the Eastern Utilities Company and its Customers' Accounting Division, home of the cash posters, whom we described in an earlier chapter. The posters were only one of serveral groups of employees that carried on, within the same big room, the special tasks of the division. This time we shall be concerned with the relations between the cash posters and the members of the largest group in the division, the so-called ledger clerks (Homans, 1953).

We shall not go into details about the cash posters' and the ledger clerks' jobs. Like the other jobs in the division, they had to do with keeping the company's accounts with the customers who bought electric current and other services. Though no longer carried out by the methods of old-fashioned bookkeeping, cash posting resulted practically in recording on the customers' accounts the amount of money they paid on their bills. The job had little variety; it allowed a great deal of movement from file to file, and the company felt it was the one job in the division that should be kept caught up with: all payments were to be recorded on the customers' accounts on the same day they were received.

Of the ledger clerks' job it is enough to say that they did everything other than cash posting necessary to keep the accounts up to date. They had, for instance, to record changes in customers' addresses and breakdowns of over- and under-payments. Each ledger clerk had a "station," which consisted of a block of files containing the accounts of people living in a particular section of the city, and at the station was a telephone with which the clerk was to answer calls, made either by the customers themselves or by employees of the company, about the state of the accounts. As the investigator put it: "Whereas the cash posters had, in the main, to do one single, repetitive job on a production basis, requiring little thought but plenty of physical mobility, the ledger clerks had to do a number of nonrepetitive clerical jobs on a nonproduction basis, requiring some thought but little physical mobility."

All the cash posters and ledger clerks were women. Because the regular line of promotion in the division was from cash poster to ledger clerk, and many of the clerks had formerly served as posters, they tended to be older than the posters and to have more seniority in the company. But there was some doubt that the promotion was really a promotion, for ledger clerks received the same weekly pay as posters. Some of the posters, indeed, had refused the ambiguous promotion to ledger clerk, giving the reason that the additional responsibility was not balanced by higher pay. Finally we shall remember that cash posting was the one job in the division management felt it had to remain caught up with every day. To make sure of doing so, the supervisor every afternoon took some of the clerks off the stations and set them to work helping to clean up the posting. He did not mind if the ledger work fell temporarily into arrears.

With each of the women the investigator carried out a long interview, in which she was free to talk about her own job and those of others in any way she chose. The women tended to compare jobs as more or less rewarding or costly along a number of different dimensions. They did not all rank the jobs in the same way on every dimension. Thus the older women did not rank the opportunity to move about while at work nearly as highly as did the younger girls. But they agreed on most rankings, or, as some sociologists would put it, they shared most values. Thus all agreed, as would the rest of us, that a job with higher pay was "better," on that count at least, than one with lower. The more important dimensions were pay, seniority, chance for advancement, variety, responsibility, and autonomy. When the women said that one job was more responsible than another, they implied that more harm would be done if it were not done right. Autonomy was the only one of these words the women did not use themselves. In the list of dimensions it represents the investigator's shorthand for the value implied when a woman said in praise of a job that "they [the supervisors] let you alone to do your own work."

In the Customers' Accounting Division, it was largely the ledger clerks who thought they were unjustly treated, and it was the cash posters in comparison with whom they felt the injustice arose. So let us discover how the ledger clerks compared their job with that of the cash posters along the dimensions both groups agreed were relevant. In general, they liked their job: it had variety and interest, certainly more variety and interest than the posters'. They were also inclined to enjoy the opportunity for personal contact with the customers. They did not see much chance for advancement, but then neither did anyone else in the division: as far as promotions were concerned, all jobs were about equally bad, which in its way was a tribute to the company, since it meant that employees seldom quit. And the ledger clerks were satisfied with the absolute amount of their pay, in the sense that they acknowledged they could not get better pay for comparable jobs elsewhere in the city.

Relative pay was something else again. When the ledger clerks compared their job with the cash posters' they complained about the two jobs' getting the same pay when theirs was the more "responsible." They also complained about being "taken off their own jobs and put down to work on posting." Notice the "down": their temporary afternoon assignment to cash posting was a loss in status as well as in autonomy. Finally they complained that their immediate supervisor did not "stick up for them." This meant that he did little to get these injustices set to rights. A typical statement was the following:

> I like the work. There's only one thing I don't like about it. Everybody talks around here as if cash posting was the only job that counted. They take us off stations to work on cash, and they think that the stations can just take care of themselves. The work piles up and you get behind. Of course we've got to get the cash out, but I think the station work is just as important. And it's much more responsible. Cash posting, most of it, is just mechanical, but station work is a responsible job. You have to deal with customers and with the stores, and if you don't do something right, someone is going to suffer. Of course that's true of cash posting too, but there are a lot more things that a station clerk has to do. It's a more responsible job, and yet the station clerks get just the same pay as the cash posters. It seems that they ought to get just a few dollars more to show that the job is more important.

The complaints of the ledger clerks sound like another one of those problems, so frequent and troublesome in industry, of wage differentials—problems not of the absolute amount of wages but of differences between groups in their wage rates. And so it is, for problems of wage differentials are problems of distributive justice.

Before turning to the analysis of this case, let us look at the behavior of the management of Eastern Utilities, which, after all, established the pay rates and other working conditions for the ledger clerks and the cash posters. An outsider might well ask why the pay rate of the cash posters was equal to that of the ledger clerks, when the latter were generally agreed to have the more responsible jobs. The management kept it equal for two reasons. First, in the recent past cash posting, but not ledger clerking, had been a man's job, and at that time men's jobs in the company generally received higher wages than women's. Second, management considered posting to be so monotonous and subject to so much pressure for production that they would not be able to induce women to take it unless they paid fairly high wages. In point of fact, the girls, when they got used to it, did not find it all that demanding.

When the ledger clerks complained to their supervisor about being taken off their own jobs and put "down" on posting, the supervisor said, in effect: "What do you care what work you do? You get paid just the same. When we take you off stations and put you on cash, we don't bawl you out if your station work gets behind." This was perfectly true:

by its lights management was fair. It felt that, since it paid the ledger clerks good wages, it had a right to expect them to do anything lawful it asked them to do. As a principle of fair exchange this was reasonable but lacked, so to speak, detail. The ledger clerks' own principle was more complicated. They were saying: "In return for our hard work, we expect you to pay good wages and, more than that, we expect you, in establishing the conditions of our work, wages included, to maintain proper relations between us and the cash posters and other groups we associate with." Management was expected to maintain justice not only between itself and the different job groups but also between the job groups themselves. It was a tall order, but one more easily met if recognized.

Analysis of the Example

We might argue that the relationship between the ledger clerks and the cash posters reveals nothing that we have not already encountered in Chapter 9 on status. Persons holding one kind of job and persons holding another rank one another's activities along a number of different dimensions and find that one job is in an incongruent relationship with the other: "better" on a number of dimensions but "equal" or even "worse" on others. It is true and important to recognize that cases of distributive injustice are also cases of status incongruence. But not all cases of incongruence are also cases of injustice. What specifically makes incongruence unjust? That is the question we turn to first.

The dimensions of status along which the employees ranked the two jobs may be divided into separate classes. One class was made up of reward dimensions, dimensions on which they ranked what people *got from* a job. In the case considered, pay was obviously a reward dimension, as were the intrinsic interest and variety of the job. Another class was made up of cost dimensions, dimensions on which the employees ranked what people *gave to* a job, or, if we prefer to put it in this way, what they *gave up* in order to do the job. Responsibility was such a dimension. A responsible job might be stimulating, but it was also costly: it meant worry and the risk of making mistakes; it meant peace of mind forgone. Some of the girls found in the responsibility of the ledger clerks' job reason enough for refusing to be promoted to it.

Besides these dimensions along which the employees ranked the job itself, there were others along which they ranked the persons doing the job. In the case considered, seniority was such a dimension. It was not something like skill and taking pains which people gave to a job, though seniority might well imply skill, nor was it something that people received as an immediate reward, though time spent on a job did build up their seniority. Rather it was a background characteristic of the persons doing the job, and a characteristic in which some were "better" than others: they had accumulated more seniority. Since the employees had to "put in" time to acquire seniority, we shall, to preserve the economic metaphor, speak of things like seniority as *investments*.

Now in the case considered, the ledger clerks were superior to the cash posters in investments such as seniority; they were also superior in costs such as responsibility, but as for rewards, though they were superior in some, such as variety, they were no more than equal to the cash posters in the crucial reward of pay and positively inferior to them in autonomy: they were taken off their own jobs and put "down" on posting.

The ledger clerks, then, were superior to the cash posters in investments and in costs, but only equal or even inferior to them in some rewards. It was the fact of rewards being out of line with their rank on the other two dimensions that made their condition one of distributive justice or relative deprivation. They were not driven to open revolt, but they were vexed and they complained. Their complaints, addressed to both the management and the union and still unsuccessful at the time the investigation ended, were directed toward bringing their rewards into line, toward establishing just conditions. That is, they asked for more pay than the posters and they asked that they be no longer temporarily assigned to posting.

Though the ledger clerks certainly felt that they were victims of injustice, they were also concerned about their status. If it really was superior, why did some of the posters refuse promotion to it? There was a highly symbolic element in their demand for more pay. It was not the size of the difference between their pay and the posters' that concerned them, but only that there should be *some* difference, "to show that their job was more important." They were not just being unfairly rewarded: they were being treated in such a way as to throw their superior status into doubt. Perhaps there are no pure cases of distributive injustice; perhaps it always comes mixed with status anxiety.

That men consider the condition in which rewards are in line with investments and costs to be a condition of justice is suggested by other job groups in the Customers' Accounting Division. So far we have only considered the jobs of the ledger clerks and the cash posters, but there were a number of others, among them the so-called Address File. This job consisted in keeping up to date a separate file of customers' addresses by placing new cards in the file whenever information reached the office about a change in address or a new occupant of a house or flat. It was recognized as being the worst job on the floor; it got little pay; it was hopelessly monotonous; it was closely supervised, and it was carried on in a corner cut off from the rest of the floor by high walls of files, so that the address girls could not easily talk to the others. It was, in short, the local salt mine.

The girls on the Address File certainly did not like the job: they were forever grumbling about its dreariness. Yet their complaints were quite unlike those of the ledger clerks. The ledger clerks complained about the rewards of their job relative to those of the cash posters. The address girls made no such complaints about the relative rank of their job over against cash posting, the next job above it in the ladder of advancement. Though in absolute terms they were certainly badly off, they only complained about the job itself. They did not complain of being unfairly treated in comparison with others. What made the difference? Whereas the ledger clerks' job stood higher than the cash posters' on most counts but not on all, the address girls' job stood lower than the posters' on all counts: it got less pay, less autonomy, less opportunity for social life; it incurred vastly higher costs in monotony, and it required even less skill. The address girls were, moreover, the youngest girls and held least seniority in the department. Not only the characteristics of the job itself but also their own investments were all in line and lower than those of the posters. However little they liked the job, the address girls did not question the justice of their having it. Distributive justice does not determine absolute satisfaction with the results of one's activity, but only satisfaction with what one gets relative to what someone else gets. This may be something, but it is certainly not everything.

By this time the attentive reader should have caught us in an apparent inconsistency. We have so far left the inconsistency uncorrected, for by resolving inconsistencies are explanations clarified. The inconsistency is concerned with the notion of cost. We argued, on the one hand, that one count on which the ledger clerks stood *higher* than the cash posters was that of the cost of their job: the former incurred greater costs in responsibility. Then we argued, on the other hand, that one count on which the address girls stood *lower* than the cash posters was that of cost: the former incurred greater costs in monotony. In the one case, it appears, higher costs were associated with higher status, in the other case, with lower status.

The inconsistency can be resolved by recognizing that there are costs and costs, costs that imply superiority and costs that imply nothing of the sort. A job that forces its holders to incur high costs in responsibility accepted, skill expended, anxiety borne, and peace of mind forgone is an important job, a job that, well done, will reward others greatly, or ill done, hurt them much. Relatively high costs of this kind are wholly compatible with, in line with, high investments and rewards. A job, on the other hand, that requires its holders to incur high costs in mere dirt or monotonous drudgery is usually not an important job:

it may reward others, but probably not greatly, since the capacity to perform it is probably not rare. High costs of this kind are wholly compatible with low investments and rewards.

Indeed cost is not really what we are talking about at all. That is, we are not talking about cost or, for that matter, about reward as experienced by the individual, as what we have called value, forgone by him or not forgone. We are talking rather about cost and reward as perceived by members of a group, about the visible, audible, and other stimuli that men present to other men, and that they rank from top to bottom along a number of dimensions. In particular they rank, and he himself ranks, what a man gives in social exchange, which includes his perceived costs, what he gets (that is, his rewards) and what we have called his investments. If his investments and what he gives are taken as fixed and as higher than, or equal to, those of another person, but what he gets (his rewards) are equal or lower respectively, he is a victim of distributive injustice; he will try to bring up his rewards to the level of his investments and what he gives, and he will be angry if he cannot do so. Note the difference between this case and, for instance, that of *noblesse oblige*. In the latter a man's investments and rewards are taken as fixed and higher than those of another person, and he tries to bring what he gives up to their level. In that case his emotional reaction is shame or guilt rather than anger.

The Rule of Distributive Justice

The rule we have found to be implicit in the behavior of the employees of the Customers' Accounting Division we believe to be implicit in the behavior of many persons in many different societies. Nor does it remain merely implicit in behavior; it is often explicitly stated. Thus Jouvenel (1957: 149) writes: "What they [men] find just is to preserve between men as regards whatever is in question the same relative positions as exist between the same men as regards something else." But we ought to consider with special care and veneration the first statement about distributive justice, which we owe to Aristotle. It appears in Book V, Chapter 3, of his so-called *Nichomachean Ethics*, which consists of drafts of his lectures on ethics, put together by himself or, more probably, by his pupils. He distinguishes between corrective justice, such as the proper punishment of criminals, and distributive justice, which is what we are interested in. Of it he writes (Aristotle, 1967: 269):

> It follows therefore that justice involves at least four terms, namely, two persons for whom it is just and two shares which are just. And there will be

the same equality between the shares as between the persons, since the ratio between the shares will be equal to the ratio between the persons; for if the persons are not equal, they will not have equal shares; it is when equals possess or are allotted unequal shares, or persons not equal equal shares, that quarrels and complaints arise.

A little later he goes on to say:

Justice is therefore a sort of proportion; for proportion is not a property of numerical quantity only, but of quantity in general, proportion being equality of ratios, and involving four terms at least.

Let us try to restate in our own terminology what Aristotle is saying here. Distributive justice involves a relationship between at least four terms: two persons, P_1 and P_2, one of whom can be assessed as higher than, equal to, or lower than, the other; and their two shares, or as we would say, rewards, R_1 and R_2. The condition of distributive justice is satisfied when the ratio of the measures of the persons is equal to the ratio of the measures of their respective rewards. That is, if the two persons are equal, they should, in justice, receive equal rewards; if one is better than the other, he should receive the larger reward. That is, the condition of distributive justice is satisfied when:

$$\frac{P_1}{P_2} = \frac{R_1}{R_2} \tag{1}$$

In the fourth century B.C., Aristotle was saying just what was implicit in the behavior of the employees of the Customers' Accounting Division, provided only we recognize that what he calls the measure of a person should include both his investments and what he actually contributes to social exchange.

We believe, though we confess we do so without adequate evidence, that something like the rule of distributive justice is either explicitly stated or stands as an implicit major premise in the arguments and behavior of many men in many, and probably all, human societies. We do not argue in the least that it is the noblest rule of distributive justice a philosopher or saint could devise; we argue only that it represents what many men in fact find fair. No doubt, through their proverbs and, by implication, through their comments on the behavior of themselves and others, members of the older generation in many societies teach the young some form of the rule, as a condition that ought to obtain, but often of course does not. Though, again, we cannot claim to be experts on the development of moral standards in children, we also believe that, even if the rule were not taught to the young, they would discover it anew for themselves every generation.

The reason we think so is that the rule of distributive justice is a statement of what ought to be, and what people say ought to be is determined in the long run and with some lag by what they find in fact to be the case. Now we have seen that ordinary exchanges between people, exchanges such as we have illustrated in our little group of Person, Other, and the Third Man, when they are unconstrained by fear of punishment or by the actions of outsiders, do in fact result in persons who produce superior contributions to the exchange, contributions recognized as superior by the parties themselves, getting superior rewards; in persons who produce similar (equal) contributions getting similar rewards, and so on. Thus, as we have pointed out so often, Other in our little group gives the best advice and gets the most approval. So many people, we believe, encounter this process of distributing rewards so often in their own actual experience that they come to generalize it as the kind of distribution that ought to obtain always.

Unfortunately, the fact that people accept the same general rule of distributive justice need not mean that they will always agree on what is a fair distribution of reward between them. Even if they concede that reward should be proportional to investment and contribution, they may still differ in their views of what legitimately constitutes investment, contribution, and reward, and how persons and groups are to be ranked on these dimensions. Aristotle himself recognized the difficulty. Speaking at the beginning of Book V of his *Politics* (Aristotle, 1967: 371–372) about the conflict between the parties of oligarchy and democracy in the cities of Greece, he stated:

> Thus democracy arose from men's thinking that if they are equal in any respect they are equal absolutely (for they suppose that because they are all alike free they are equal absolutely); oligarchy arose from their assuming that if they are unequal as regards some one thing they are unequal wholly (for being unequal in property they assume that they are unequal absolutely); and then the democrats claim as being equal to participate in all things in equal shares, while the oligarchs as being unequal seek to have a larger share, for a larger share is unequal.

That is, the oligarchs and the democrats, while accepting implicitly the same general rule, differed about how it should be applied. The oligarchs thought property the only legitimate investment. Since they had more property than the democrats, they believed they should have more than the democrats in other respects, such as political rights. The democrats, on the other hand, considered free birth the only legitimate investment. Since in this respect they were the equals of the oligarchs, they believed they should be equal to the oligarchs in political rights. (Presumably both parties agreed that in all respects they were superior to the slaves and should allow them no rights at all.)

What was true of ancient Greece has probably been true of all other groups and societies. In the Customers' Accounting Division, management talked as if only skilled work and good wages ought to enter into the balance of fair exchange, whereas the ledger clerks thought that other features of their job, such as its lack of autonomy, ought to be brought in as well. In industry everyone agrees that promotions ought to be in line with the employees' investments and contributions, but the general rule is not of much help in answering the next question: Which should count most in gaining promotion for a man: his skill or his seniority? Many labor unions have in effect come down on the side of seniority, partly because differences in seniority can be determined more objectively than can differences in skill, and so leave less room for argument.

Moreover, what people agree on counting as legitimate investments change from time to time in many societies. Once upon a time ancient lineage counted as a legitimate investment, but in modern American society it counts officially not at all, though one can sometimes feel it playing its part unofficially. Once upon a time, too, the fact of being a man rather than a woman counted as more of an investment than it does today in America: a man doing the same job as a woman might demand more pay than hers. Today he is much less likely to make such a claim. And the same, of course, was true of being a white rather than a black.

All the arguments about surplus value from John Ball to Karl Marx and his followers amount to one long attempt to prove that what employers and owners count as their investments and contributions ought not to be so counted, and that therefore they get more than their fair share of the returns from economic enterprise and exploit the workers. Naturally none of the arguments prove the point; such things are not capable of proof; they are matters, so to speak, of taste. When someone says that one group is exploiting another, all his words mean is that he personally does not approve of the way in which rewards are distributed between the two groups. They mean no more: there are no objective means of determining whether exploitation is taking place.

Only perhaps for rather brief spans of time or in rather small groups are men fully agreed not only on what the rule of distributive justice is but also on what particular investments, contributions, and rewards should fairly be placed in the scales and at what weights. Men certainly assess their own investments, contributions, and rewards; but to make a rule of justice work, they must assess those of others by the same measures and on the same dimensions. The others, for their part, must agree at every point, which does not make consensus any easier to achieve. The evidence, as we might expect, is that it is easier to achieve among persons who, through similar experience, reflected in similar backgrounds, have acquired similar values; but even here consensus is always in danger of breaking down. This means that there is no just society, though there may be societies and groups that are more or less just, to the extent that their members agree in their evaluations and maintain a rough proportionality between contributions and rewards. By these standards the Customers' Accounting Division was a pretty just place. Except for the ledger clerks everyone believed that she was getting something like her fair share relative to the others, and as for what was happening to the ledger clerks, almost everyone agreed at least that it *was* an injustice—which is more than can be said about injustice in many places.

Justice, Satisfaction, and the Choice of Comparisons

No person can point to an absolute standard by which he can decide whether or not he is receiving the reward he deserves. Instead he must compare what he is receiving with what someone else is receiving, and decide by the rule of distributive justice whether, compared to that person, he is receiving what he ought to receive. The question is always one of *relative* deprivation (or relative advantage).

So far we have not tried to find any general answer to the question what other persons a man compares himself with, or what other groups the members of a particular group compare themselves with. The group thus chosen for comparison is sometimes called a *reference group* (see Merton and Kitt, 1950). But the term *reference group* has been given other meanings: it may not be the group a man compares himself with but—which is rather different—the one he identifies himself with or is a member of. Accordingly, we shall speak here only of *comparison groups* or *comparison persons*.

The general rule seems to be that people are more apt to compare themselves with others they are to some degree close or similar to than with others that are distant or dissimilar. Above all they will compare themselves with others they are in direct and personal exchange with. So far we have not taken up this case from the point of view of distributive justice. Instead we have taken up cases like the relationship between the ledger clerks and the cash posters, who were not rewarded by one another but by a third party, the management of Eastern Utilities, which was responsible for the perceived injustice. Outside of direct exchange, the rule does not specify just how close or similar the comparison persons must be. To be able to compare oneself with another person one must, no doubt, know something about him, and that knowledge presupposes some degree of contact with him, direct or indirect. Also as Merton and Kitt (1950: 61) put it: ". . . Some similarity in status attributes between the individual and the reference group must be perceived or imagined in order for the comparison to occur at all." One's own investments, contributions, and rewards must be at least similar enough to the other's to be ranked along the same dimensions.

There is yet another reason why a man is apt to compare himself with others who are in some respect close or similar to himself. A man does not go on forever making comparisons that show him to be unjustly treated, if he can do nothing about it. Some people, it is true, can nurse a grievance, but most of us cannot keep it up indefinitely. A man is the more apt to complain about his treatment relative to somebody else, the more successful in redressing the injury his action is likely to be. Accordingly, he is particularly likely to complain about unjust treatment relative to others that are similar to him at least in the sense of belonging to the same larger social unit, for only in such a unit is there likely to be some superior power, some mechanism, capable of changing his rewards relative to those of the other. Thus a man is more likely to compare himself with others of his own nation, own organization, or own group than with others belonging to a different nation, different organization, or different group.

There is one especially interesting case of the tendency to compare oneself with others who are similar to oneself in some respect. The fact that the poor are usually more likely to compare themselves with others only slightly less poor rather than with the very rich has often been the despair of radical reformers, who feel that, if only the poor would make it, the latter comparison would force them to be more angry and more capable of revolt. Only when society is badly shaken up are the really big comparisons made, and people begin to ask, like the English peasants when they rebelled in 1381:

> When Adam delved and Eve span
> Who was then the gentleman?

A general tendency for a person to compare himself with others who are in some respect similar or close to himself does not allow us to make very definite predictions about his choice of comparison persons or groups, for it does not specify just how similar or close the comparison person must be. We can do a little better in demonstrating the reciprocal relationships between three variables: the degree to which a person's rewards are in line with the other aspects of his status, his satisfaction with his rewards, and his choice of comparison persons. We are able to do so thanks to a study carried out under the auspices of the Institute for Social Research of the University of Michigan and reported by Martin Patchen, the chief investigator (Patchen, 1961).

The investigators carried out the research at an oil refinery located in Canada near the U.S. border. In the refinery they interviewed a sample of the male, nonsupervisory workers. This sample, 489 men in all, included a third of all such workers and was stratified by job type and pay level.

The investigators were interested in the workers' satisfaction with their own pay in comparison with the pay of others. In every interview with a worker, the investigator first asked him to name two persons he knew, either inside or outside the refinery, whose yearly earnings were *different from,* either higher or lower than, his own. That is, the investigator allowed the worker to choose the other persons whose rewards he was ready to compare with his own. The way the question was phrased did not allow the worker to compare himself with someone whose earnings were *equal to* his own. Later we shall suggest what sort of results the investigators might have obtained if they had allowed the workers to compare themselves with their equals in pay as well as with their superiors or inferiors.

The investigator then asked the worker to describe the occupation of each of the persons he chose for comparison. These occupations were later coded so as to place them in a ranking of occupations ranging from professional at the top to unskilled or unemployed at the bottom. Since the investigators knew from the company records the kind of job held by the person interviewed, this information allowed them to rank each comparison person as higher than, lower than, or equal to him on a dimension of status *other than pay,* in fact, on what each contributed to social exchange, the kind of work he did. They could do so particularly easily if the comparison persons chosen were themselves workers in the refinery.

Finally, the investigator asked the worker he interviewed to record, by choosing a point on a five-point scale, how satisfied he was with his own earnings compared with those of each person he had chosen for comparison.

These were the types of information obtained by the investigators that seem most pertinent to our present interests. They also obtained other types of information, some of which we shall bring in later.

Now for the results of the research. Though they are always interesting, Patchen does not always state them clearly or organize them well. Moreover, he formulates his results in terms of Festinger's theory of cognitive dissonance (Festinger, 1957) rather than in terms of the theory of distributive justice. Though the two do not always apply to the same phenomena, they fortunately do in the present case, where consonance may be translated as justice and dissonance as injustice. In spite of these difficulties, we believe that in what follows we have not misrepresented the findings obtained in the research.

We shall remember that a worker was allowed to choose two comparison persons and that the earnings of each were either higher or lower than his own. Let us first take the case in which he chose to compare himself with someone whose earnings were higher. If the comparison person was also superior to the respondent in occupation, the latter was apt to say that he was satisfied with his wages relative to those of the comparison person. If, on the other hand, the comparison person was equal or inferior in occupation to the respondent, then the latter was apt to say that he was dissatisfied with his wages relative to those of the comparison person.

The first condition is, of course, a condition of distributive justice, and it is, as we should expect, positively associated with the respondent's satisfaction. The comparison person is superior to the respondent both in what he gives to social exchange and, at least so far as pay is concerned, in what he gets; the rankings of the two persons are in line with one another; this is right and proper, and the respondent has nothing to complain of. The investigators asked the workers they interviewed to explain why they were satisfied with comparisons of this sort, and they reported that "what these men seem to be saying, in effect, is: 'I am satisfied to be earning less, because there is some other difference between us which makes the wage difference okay' " (Patchen, 1961: 45).

The second condition is a condition of distributive injustice, and it is, as we should expect, positively associated with the respondent's dissatisfaction: it is unfair that the other should get more than the respondent, when what he contributes is only equal or inferior. We say that injustice is "positively associated with" dissatisfaction, because we cannot in this case be sure that the injustice caused the dissatisfaction. Dissatisfaction may conceivably have caused the injustice, in the following special sense. Since respondents were free to choose their comparison persons, those who were dissatisfied with their lot for quite other reasons may have deliberately chosen "unjust" comparisons in order to nourish their sense of being ill-used. In this case their behavior would have to be explained by the theory of cognitive dissonance as well as by the theory of distributive injustice.

Let us turn now to the case in which a respondent chose to compare himself with someone whose earnings were lower than his own. If the comparison person was also lower in his occupation, the respondent was, as we should expect, satisfied with his earnings relative to those of the comparison person. This condition is, again, one of distributive justice. As for the unjust condition, it could only in this case have been one in which the comparison person was superior or equal in occupation to the respondent, though lower in earnings. Then the respondent would have been the beneficiary of injustice rather than a victim. We have not considered this case so far, at least not as a problem of injustice. What would the reaction of the respondent have been? Hardly the straightforward satisfaction that goes with justice visibly maintained. One sort of person might have reacted with a species of supersatisfaction, or gloating, but he would have been well advised to keep it to himself. Another sort might have felt some degree of guilt. But perhaps the most significant bit of evidence is that few if any of the workers interviewed at the refinery chose comparison persons of this sort. Men may be reluctant to admit that they are the beneficiaries of injustice. Later we shall consider the sort of response by which men can avoid thus benefiting.

The way the question was phrased in the interview did not allow a worker to choose as a comparison person someone whose earnings were equal to his own. From the argument presented so far, we may guess that, had he been allowed to do so, his response would have been one of the following. If he chose someone whose occupation was also equal to his own, he would have expressed himself as satisfied with his earnings. If he chose someone whose occupation was inferior to his own, he would have expresed himself as dissatisfied. And if he chose one who was superior, he would perhaps, as a beneficiary of injustice, have felt supersatisfied or guilty. But we had better admit that we are not sure what the characteristic response to this condition may be.

The relationships among the three main variables—relative occupation, relative pay, and satisfaction—both those actually found in the research and those that might have been found if respondents had been allowed to compare themselves with their equals in earnings, are laid out in Table 11. Note that if the values of any two of the variables are known, the value of the third may be predicted.

Table 11   Relative Earnings, Occupation, and Satisfaction

RELATION OF COMPARISON PERSON TO RESPONDENT		SATISFACTION OF RESPONDENT
In Earnings	*In Occupation*	
Higher	Higher	Satisfied
Higher	Equal or lower	Dissatisfied
Equal	Higher	?
Equal	Equal	Satisfied
Equal	Lower	Dissatisfied
Lower	Equal or higher	?
Lower	Lower	Satisfied

Let us close this section by mentioning a couple of subsidiary findings of the research at the refinery. An interviewer allowed a worker, if he wished, to name a close relative as a comparison person. "Close relatives were defined as brother, son, father, sister, daughter, mother, and corresponding in-law relations" (Patchen, 1961: 30). When a respondent chose to compare himself with a relative whose earnings were greater than his own, he was much less likely to express dissatisfaction with the comparison than he was when he chose a non-relative in the same position. The reason the chief investigator offers for this difference is based on the workers' own explanation of their answers to the questions. Though they were prepared to express dissatisfaction with their earnings compared with the earnings of others, they also recognized that such attitudes laid them open to charges of mere envy toward those who were better off. Envy is indeed often rationalized as injustice (see Schoeck, 1969). And they were especially reluctant to be suspected of envy toward their relatives. Hostile attitudes were inappropriate within the family. Envy was a hostile attitude and should be kept for outsiders.

One of the questions that an investigator asked a worker was: "For men who grew up when you did, how much would you say a man's chances for getting ahead in life depended on himself and how much on things beyond his control?" (Patchen, 1961: 33). It is interesting that, among workers who compared themselves with others earning more than they did themselves, those who accepted a high degree of personal responsibility for their fate were more apt to express satisfaction with the comparison than those who did not. In effect, if a man is earning less than someone whose occupation is equal to his own, so that outsiders might judge him to be suffering from injustice, but he says it is his own fault, he is saying that his investments and contributions are not really what they seem, not really equal to those of the other, and so the condition of justice is realized. A man is angry when what he gets ranks below what he gives only if he recognizes the apparent injustice to be the result of someone else's actions and not of his own.

Injustice and Intergroup Hostility

A person expects to get from others reward in line with his investments and contributions. Injustice for him is the condition in which he gets less than what he expects. Accordingly, by the frustration-aggression proposition, he will feel some degree of anger and display some aggressive behavior toward the source or beneficiary of the injustice. His aggressive behavior may become at the same time an instrumental act by which he tries to raise to a higher and more just level the amount of reward he gets. An inferior's willingness to fight changes the balance of power between him and a superior. We should be much less interested in injustice if it did not lead so often to anger and aggression. In direct exchange between two persons or groups, the source and the beneficiary of injustice are the same. When some third party rewards one person or group unfairly in relation to another, the source of the injustice is the third party, the beneficiary the other person or group. We shall now look at two studies, one of experimental groups, one of natural ones, in which injustice played a part in creating hostility between groups. These studies should be compared with the Sherifs' study of a summer camp, reported in Chapter 8, where rivalry but not injustice created the hostility (Sherif and Sherif, 1953).

We owe the experimental study to Thibaut (1950). His subjects were

boys from ten to twelve years old attached to settlement houses and summer camps near Boston. The boys came to the experiment in groups of
ten to twelve members each, who had known one another and had lived
and played together for some time. The investigator began by asking
every boy to answer a questionnaire in which he was to put down in
order of his preference the four other boys he would most like to have
on his team if his group was divided into two teams to play games. With
the benefit of this information, the investigator did in fact divide each
group into two teams of from five to six boys each. As far as he could,
he arranged each team so that every member would find about an equal
number of the boys he had chosen on his own team and on the other
one. He also arranged that an equal number of the more popular boys
should be on each team. These popular boys—those in the top half of
each team in the number of choices received—he called the *central* members; the rest he called the *peripheral* ones.

The investigator could now go ahead with the experiment proper. He
had the two teams from each group play a series of four games, in each
of which one of the teams had to serve or assist the other, to take the
less interesting and inferior part. "In one game they served as 'human
arches' for the other team to run under, in another they were a 'human
chain' for the other team to buck against, and in the third game they
held the target for, and retrieved, thrown beanbags"—beanbags thrown
by members of the other team. The same teams took the inferior position in all the first three games. These the investigator called the *low-
status* teams; the others, who regularly took the superior position, he
called the *high-status* teams.

After the first three games, an observer encouraged the members of
the low-status teams to protest unanimously to the investigator about the
way they had been treated, and this they were not backward in doing.
With half these teams the investigator accepted the protest and allowed
them to take the superior position in the fourth and last game: he allowed them to throw the beanbags, which was the game the boys found
most fun. But he rejected the protest of the other half and kept them in
the inferior position in the last game, as they had been in the earlier
ones. Thus there were, according to the treatment they received, four
kinds of teams:

1. Consistently low-status.
2. Consistently high-status.
3. Successful low-status (who took the superior position for the last
   game).
4. Displaced high-status (who lost their superior position for the last
   game).

During the games observers kept records of the amounts and kinds
of behavior, verbal or other, performed by the members of each team;

and after the last game the boys answered a questionnaire similar to the one they started with.

Some of the results were just what we might have expected. Before being divided into teams, the members of each pair of teams had all belonged to the same group, and the teams were equal in the number of popular boys each possessed. Nothing, therefore, in the backgrounds of the two teams justified the fact that one of them got preferential treatment. For one team to take the most interesting part in every game clearly violated the rule of distributive justice. Not only was the other team deprived of reward, but unjustly deprived, and its members displayed the characteristic emotional reaction. As it became increasingly clear over the first three games that they were getting unfair treatment, their hostile remarks directed at the high-status team steadily increased in number. After that, the communications of the successful low-status teams—those that had displaced the high-status teams for the favored position in the last game—fell off rapidly, while those of the unsuccessful teams mounted still further but became a little less aggressive, as if the members were beginning to give up hope of bettering their lot as far as the games were concerned and were trying instead to get in with their more favored opponents.

The high-status teams did little to reply to these attacks. Presumably they held the same standards of justice. Though willing enough to take advantage of their favored position, they seem to have felt guilty and embarrassed. There was no rejoinder they could make when the low-status teams complained that they were unfairly treated, for it was an obvious fact. Their emotional reaction, if we may call it that, was to avoid their less favored opponents.

More interesting, because less obvious, were the results of the questionnaire all the boys answered after the last game. Compared with the way they had chosen others before the games began, the members of all teams tended to shift their choices toward members of their own team and away from the other team. This is what we might have expected. But within this overall tendency, there were great differences in the amount by which within-team choice increased, both as between teams of different sorts and as between central and peripheral members. The least increase, and it was so small as not to be statistically significant, took place in the successful low-status teams and in the high-status ones they had displaced in the last game. For these teams something had been done to realize the conditions of justice and to make their status equal by exalting the humble and bringing down the proud—especially as the last game was beanbag-tossing and the most interesting of all. Neither team in these pairs was consistently superior over the whole series of games; neither remained very hostile toward the other, and, accordingly, boys on one team did not remain alienated from their old friends on the other.

We are left with the consistently high- and the consistently low-status teams and with their central and peripheral members. The order of the different categories of subjects in the amount by which they increased the number of their within-team choices was the following:

1. Peripheral members of high-status teams.
2. Central members of low-status teams.
3. Central members of high-status teams.
4. Peripheral members of low-status teams.

Between the first two of these categories the increase in within-team choice was statistically significant.

How shall we explain this rank order? We believe that two sorts of effects, one positive and one negative, tended to increase choice within teams. Positive was the effect of the increased reward a boy got from being a member of a high-status team. Ultimately, of course, he got this reward from the experimenter, but he got it through his association with the other members of his own team, and therefore we should expect his liking for them to increase. Negative was the effect of the hostility expressed toward him by members of the low-status and unjustly treated team, which tended to cut him off from his old friends in that team and thus increase his relative friendliness toward members of his own team. This effect is eloquently described in the words of the old song: "I don't give a damn for any damn man who don't give a damn for me!"

These tendencies had different strengths within different categories of boys. The first of the two effects—the reward effect—was apparently the more generally powerful, for the greatest change toward within-group choice occurred among the peripheral members of high-status teams, and they were just the boys that had gained most by their favored treatment. From ranking as second-class citizens in their original groups they had, in effect, risen into the privileged class. They responded by greatly increasing the liking they expressed for the other boys in whose company they had made these gains. We do not argue that the hostility expressed toward them by members of the other team played no part in repelling them toward their own, but we can only explain the magnitude of their increase choice by pointing to their increased reward.

But the second, or hostility, effect was powerful too. For if the greatest change toward within-team choice occurred among the boys who had gained most, the next greatest occurred among those who had lost most. The experiment brought the central members of low-status teams down in the world. From ranking as first-class citizens in their original groups they had become members of the proletariat. Theirs was the greatest relative deprivation meted out to any set of boys in the experiment, and they repaid with hostility the others who had benefited at their expense. There is evidence from the records the observers kept of behavior during the games that, in return, they provoked many hostile reactions from members of the high-status teams. Thus repelled, they turned their expression of liking inward, toward their companions in misery.

The third largest increase occurred among the central members of the high-status teams. They had benefited from the favored treatment given their teams, but not as much as had the peripheral members, since they, unlike the peripherals, were of high status to begin with. Accordingly, they increased their choices for the boys in whose company they had made these gains, but not as much as did the peripheral members. The increase in liking was proportional to the increase in reward.

Finally, the least increase occurred among peripheral members of low-status groups; it was not statistically significant, and it varied greatly from team to team. If the central members of high-status teams had least to gain from the experimental treatment, these boys had least to lose. They had less to lose than the central members of their own teams, for they were of low status to begin with. At worst they were only confirmed in their position of inferiority: the treatment they received was consistent with their previous position, so that, in effect, little injustice was done them. Though they expressed some hostility toward members of the high-status teams, and increased their liking for members of their own, they did not do so to any great extent. Indeed they tended, according to the observers, to react less with hostility than with efforts to escape. Even before the games began, they were, as peripheral members of the original groups, getting few social rewards; now they were getting even fewer, and the observers noted that, of all the categories of boys, they were the ones who most often tried to get out of the situation altogether by paying no heed to the games or asking the investigator to let them do something else.

On this interpretation, the degree to which the different categories of boys increased the number of friendship-choices they made within their own teams depended primarily on the *amount* by which their rewards changed, for better or for worse, in the course of the experiment: the greater the change in reward, the greater the increase in choice; and secondarily on the *direction* of the change: with the amount of change held constant, an increase in reward produced a greater increase in choice than did an increase in deprivation. The results can be summed up as follows:

1. High-status peripherals—most gain.
2. Low-status centrals—most loss.
3. High-status central—least gain.
4. Low-status peripherals—least loss.

For a "natural" example of the manner in which perceived injustice creates intergroup hostility, let us return to the Bank Wiring Observation Room at the Hawthorne Plant of the Western Electric Company, which we considered in another connection in Chapter 9 on status (Roeth-lisberger and Dickson, 1939; 379–510). We shall remember that the wire-men formed the largest and most important job group in the room, and that they were divided into subspecialties: six men worked on so-called connector wiring and three on selector wiring. The connector wiremen were a little senior to the selector wiremen and very slightly higher in day-rate wages. On the other hand, the difference between the two jobs in the skill they required was so slight as not to be detectable. In short, the two jobs were in a somewhat incongruent relationship with one another.

Presuming on their superiority in seniority and pay, the connector wiremen took for granted in much that they said and did that they were superior in overall status to the selector wiremen. Presuming in turn on their equality in skill, the selector wiremen resented the airs the con-nector wiremen gave themselves. Their hostility was not great, but it seems to have affected their behavior to some extent. Already located near to one another at the back of the room, the selector wiremen drew apart from the others in social interaction, so that they formed a recog-nizable clique; and they got back at the connector wiremen by slightly—not greatly—violating a norm the connector wiremen held dear. The norm stated that no one in the room should complete more than about six thousand wiring connections in a working day: to do more was to be a "rate-buster." But no one should do much less, either, for that, ac-cording to the system of payment by group piecework, would hurt every-one's earnings to some extent. A man who did so was a "chiseler." The selector wiremen were never rate-busters but they did chisel to some de-gree: they regularly produced a somewhat smaller number of connec-tions than the output norm called for. Note that in doing so they con-firmed the view of the selector wiremen that they were inferior socially. Their manner of getting back at the others had made them more, rather than less, congruent in status; indeed it had established their inferior status more firmly (Roethlisberger and Dickson, 1939: 521).

Injustice and Power

Since a person who is more powerful than another is apt by that fact to be able to get rewards he deems just from the other, whether the other agrees they are just or not, the problem of injustice is, as we know, a problem for the weak rather than for the strong and therefore usually a problem created by superiors in status for inferiors.

Yet his anger at the source or beneficiary of the injustice he suffers from may somewhat increase the power of the inferior. He is now ready to hurt the other, and one obvious way of hurting a person with whom one is in exchange is precisely to deny him what he wants from you. Such action incidentally tends to restore just conditions by bringing what he gets from you down into line with what you get from him. But to find reward in denying reward to another is also to move toward a condition of "lesser interest," that is, of relatively increased power. You may, as we have said before, be hurting yourself in the process, but that may be worth your while if you can get back at your oppressor. Certainly when two men or groups are bargaining with one another, a convincing show on the part of one of them that he is so maddened by unfair treatment as not to care what happens to him so long as he gets his revenge may give him great leverage. Of course this is unchristian behavior; we are certainly not saying that men ought to behave in this way, nor are we saying that all men do behave so: some have learned— often the hard way—to turn the other cheek. But many men do behave in this way, and in this book we are interested in how they do behave and not in how they ought to.

Since according to the frustration-aggression proposition a man will feel angry only if his action does not receive the reward he expected, any distribution of reward, however unjust it may have appeared at one time, that does in fact persist long enough—but how long is that?—to become the expected thing will also become the just thing and cease to arouse resentment. We do not agree with Alexander Pope that whatever is, is right, but we have repeatedly insisted that whatever is, is always on the way to becoming right, though it may not long remain so. Then the persons concerned will have no trouble finding new dimensions along which their contributions and rewards are to be ranked or new ranks for these things along old dimensions, until they are ready to claim that contribution and reward are once more in line with one another.

If inferiors in power and status are more apt to suffer from injustice than superiors, then the capacity of redressing unjust conditions is, by the same token, often in the hands of superiors. Indeed, by a mechanism we described in Chapter 9 on status, doing justice may become an outward sign of superior status. Because injustice is apt to bring out aggression, many superiors have learned to avoid injustice in their relations with others: injustice costs too much. We often forget how much of a rough and imperfect sort of justice in the distribution of rewards exists in the world. But of course for many persons in many circumstances, the alternatives to creating just conditions may appear too rewarding, especially if these persons do not assess their contributions and rewards in the same way as those that feel themselves unjustly treated, and consider themselves to be so superior in power that they need not fear the resentment of their inferiors.

Naturally it is not just single superior individuals who may have power to establish just or unjust conditions. If the members of a group will only act together they may develop power greater than any one of their number and may use it to maintain what they believe to be a just proportion between their rewards and his, either by increasing their own rewards or decreasing his. Let us look at one example. The Norton Street Gang, described in W. F. Whyte's book, *Street Corner Society* (1943), consisted of thirteen young men who in the year 1937 used to hang around together in the Cornerville district of what Whyte called Eastern City. Among other things they used to go bowling several nights a week. One of the members who often bowled was Alec. By reason of his performance in other activities he was held in rather low esteem in the group, but he fancied himself as a bowler and from time to time beat other members of the group in individual matches, including Long John, a highly esteemed member and a friend of Doc's, who was the leader of the gang. But when Doc instituted for the first time a regular bowling tournament between all the members, Alec did not do well. Good bowling takes confidence, and Doc and the other members saw to it that Alec's confidence was undermined by friendly heckling. In so doing, they maintained a state of justice. As I said of Alec in *The Human Group* (Homans, 1950: 180):

> In individual matches and when the leaders of the group did not gang up on him, he could do very well in bowling, but in other activities he did not conform very closely to group standards. He was boastful; he was aggressive in trying to improve his social ranking. He spent more time chasing girls than the other Nortons did, and, what was worse, showed that he was capable of leaving friends in the lurch when on the prowl. If his behavior had improved in these respects, his social rank might then have risen, and his scores in intraclique bowling competition might have been allowed to go up. As it was, his rank remained low.

Alec's contributions to the group were not of much value; indeed he violated important group norms, and therefore, when the members were in a position to control the reward he got—and a good bowling score was a valuable reward—they kept it down. They kept the value of what he got in line with what he gave. Note for future reference the preeminent part played by the leader of the group in maintaining distributive justice. But Doc, the leader of the Nortons, did not act alone: the others supported him.

Responses of the Beneficiaries of Injustice

So far we have had more to say about the responses to injustice on the part of its victims than about those of its beneficiaries. It is obviously easier for a person superior in power to treat an inferior unjustly than for the inferior to treat him so: the superior can look out for himself. Yet even a person superior in power may well, as we have seen, go some distance toward treating an inferior in ways the latter considers just, in order to avoid his hostility, which tends to reduce the difference in power between them.

Yet suppose that a beneficiary of injustice has little to fear from the reprisals of his victim. Will he still do something to redress the injustice? Experience shows that people are much more ready to claim they are the victims of injustice than its beneficiaries, and for obvious reasons: the victims may have something to gain from doing so, but the beneficiaries have something to lose. The latter often manage to discover good reasons why they are not profiteers at all but only getting what they deserve. Still, there is evidence that they will sometimes act so as to reduce their advantage, even in the absence of any fear of reprisals. The best recent evidence comes from a series of experiments by Stacy Adams and his associates (Adams, J. Stacy, 1965).

In one study, the investigators seemingly offered students employment as proofreaders. Each student who applied for the job was told that he was to correct the galley proofs of a forthcoming book on human relations in industry. He was to read every galley and mark all the errors, and for this he was to be paid a piecework wage of so many cents for every galley completed. Actually all applicants were given identical galleys, with a given number of errors deliberately placed on each page. Thus the investigators could obtain for every student two measures of his performance: the quantity of work he completed, that is, the number of galleys corrected per hour, and the quality of his work, that is, the average number of errors he found and corrected per galley.

The students were in an exchange relationship with an employer: they gave him their work and got from him their wages. Into this relationship the investigators introduced different degrees of perceived injustice, in the following manner. Before hiring a student, an investigator interviewed him, ostensibly to discover whether he was qualified for the proofreading job. If the student was assigned to the *high inequity* condition, he was told that the standard piecework rate for proofreaders was 30 cents a page, that he was not really qualified to earn that much, but would nevertheless be hired and paid at that rate. That is, the investigator tried to persuade, and apparently succeeeded in persuading, students in this condition that, as an employer, he was paying them more than they deserved. They were the beneficiaries of injustice.

If the student was assigned to the *reduced inequity* condition, he was persuaded by the same method that he was not fully qualified for the job, and that accordingly his employer was not justified in paying him at the standard rate but only at the rate of 20 cents a page. If, finally, a student was assigned to the *low inequity* condition, he was persuaded that he was fully qualified and would receive the standard rate. In the last two conditions, the students were being fairly paid: their pay was in line with their qualifications, though some of them were more qualified than others. The degree of injustice in reward was the independent variable in this experiment, the quantity and quality of work, the dependent variables.

In predicting the relationships between the variables, the investigators made the following assumptions. They assumed, as we do, that the condition of distributive justice in exchange is one in which Person's rewards are in line with his contributions relative to the rewards and contributions of Other. Instead of rewards and contributions, the investigators spoke of outcomes, O, and inputs, I, and they formulated the condition of justice as:

$$\frac{O_p}{I_p} = \frac{O_o}{I_o} \tag{2}$$

Note that this equation is, in effect, the same as Aristotle's, which we stated earlier in this chapter (see equation (1), page 249).

Let us now return to the conditions of the experiment. If a student is Person and his employer is Other, the outcome of the student is his wages, his input, the quantity or quality of his work. And the outcome for the employer is the work done for him; his input, the wages he pays. In the experiment, the high-inequity students, but not the others, were in the situation where

$$\frac{O_p}{I_p} > \frac{O_o}{I_o} \tag{3}$$

since their outcomes (O_p) in terms of their wage-*rates* were labeled as high relative to their potential inputs.

If they were to restore justice in the relationship between them and their employer, they had to reduce the value of the fraction O_p/I_p. They could do so either by lowering the numerator (their outcomes) or by raising the denominator (their inputs) or by both. But their inputs were of two different kinds: the quantity of their work, that is, the number of pages corrected, and the quality of the corrections. Raising the number of pages corrected would not serve to reduce the value of the fraction, since, under payment by piecework, it would also raise their outcomes. Raising the quality of their work, on the other hand, would not have this effect. On the contrary, it would tend to lower their outcomes, since giving special care to thoroughness and accuracy would tend to cut down the number of pages completed. Accordingly the investigators predicted that students in the high-inequity condition, in the effort to restore fair exchange between themselves and their employer, would tend to raise the quality of their work and lower its quantity relative to those of the students in the two equity conditions, who would have no such reason for reducing the proportion that their rewards bore to their contributions.

The results supported just this prediction. Indeed the students in the high-inequity condition tried so hard to make every possible correction in the proofs that they found errors where none in fact existed. As the chief investigator writes: "Generally, these misclassified errors were of a type that permitted minimal or no basis for being perceived as errors. For example, the word 'conceive' was underlined as an error by several subjects, although it was correctly spelled. This gives some indication of the strength of motivation underlying the behavior" (Adams, J. Stacy: 285–286).

In other similar experiments, Stacy Adams and his associates tested the effects of hourly as well as piecework wages on the behavior of the beneficiaries and victims of injustice. As in the earlier experiment they found that high-inequity subjects produced less than low-inequity ones when they were paid by the piece. On the other hand, they produced more when they were paid by the hour. In this situation, unlike the other, they could raise their inputs (and thus the outcomes of their employer) without raising their own outcomes at the same time, since they were not paid for their output but for their time. Here an increase in productivity was an effective way of reducing their relative advantage in the exchange.

The investigators made the assumption that the beneficiaries of injustice in these experiments would act so as to reduce the injustice, and apparently they did so act. But remember that reducing injustice usually entails costs for its beneficiaries: they must lower their rewards relative to those of the persons with whom they are in exchange. In the experiments just reported, the high-inequity students did not have to give up much. Their pay was not high at best; it did not make much difference to them, and in any event they were only temporarily employed. If their costs had been higher, they might not only have failed to reduce injustice but also might have found good reasons for claiming that they were not really treating their employer unfairly after all.

In these experiments, the high-inequity subjects were getting greater rewards than they had reason to expect, not lesser ones. It was the employer who might suffer in this respect, not themselves. Accordingly their behavior was not governed by the frustration-aggression proposition: their emotional response to the situation took, if anything, the form of guilt and not anger. It might, perhaps, be expressed by: "He thinks I'm no good, but I'll show him!" In acting so as to raise their own contributions relative to their rewards, they look a little as if they were acting under the doctrine of *noblesse oblige,* which we analysed in Chapter 9 on status. They really were not: keeping their status in the eyes of the beholder clearly superior to that of their employer, by ranking higher than he both on what they gave and what they got, was not their problem. Injustice was. Yet the problems of maintaining social certitude and of maintaining social justice have much in common. Both are predicated on the assumption that a person's (or a group's) rewards should be in line with, congruent with, his contributions and investments, relative to those of other persons. And in concrete cases a person's motives are often divided between the two: it may be difficult to tell whether his actions are being rewarded by social certitude or by justice, or by both.

Summary

Relative deprivation or distributive injustice occurs when a person does not get the amount of reward he expected to get in comparison with the reward some other person gets. He expects to get more reward than the other when his contributions—what he gives in social exchange—and his investments—his background characteristics—rank higher than the other's, equal reward when his contributions and investments are equal to the other's, etc. Though many men in many societies implicitly accept this general rule, they may still disagree as to whether the distribution of rewards is just in particular circumstances, because they do not admit the same dimensions of reward, contribution, and investment as relevant. In their assessment of distributive justice, persons are more apt to compare themselves with others that are close or similar to themselves in some respect than with others that are distant or dissimilar.

Relative deprivation or distributive injustice does not interest us just for its own sake. It interests us because it is a fertile source of hostility between persons and groups. When a person gets less than he believes he ought to get by the standards of justice, he will, according to the frustration-aggression proposition, feel some degree of anger and express some degree of hostility toward the others who caused the injustice or who benefited from it (if the two are different). Since a willingness to fight adds, in general, to a person's power over another, those who are in a position to do so will often go some distance toward meeting such a person's demand for justice. And when groups are able to control the rewards received by their members, they often distribute them in such a way as to maintain, by their standards, just conditions.

A person is angry if he gets less reward than he expected according to the standards of justice. But what if he gets *more?* What if he is a beneficiary of injustice rather than a victim? Then, if he is able to do so and it does not cost him too much, he is apt to increase what he gives in social exchange and thus increase what the other gets. His behavior has something in common with the phenomenon of *noblesse oblige,* discussed two chapters back. We have come full circle: then as now we take what a man receives in social exchange as given and ask what he does to bring what he gives into line with it.

12 Leadership

IN THE PRESENT CHAPTER WE SHALL TRY TO RELATE WHAT WE said in earlier chapters, particularly in Chapter 4, about power and authority to what we said in Chapter 8 about structures of interaction and in still later chapters about status. We shall be concerned with leadership or, to use a word commensurate in weight with the thing itself, command. A man issues what can be recognized as orders, which need not be official orders or be more explicit than the wave of a hand, to a number of others, who themselves interact with one another to form a group. His action is not a one-shot affair: he issues such orders repeatedly. By reason of both his power and his authority, which need not in the least be official or legitimate authority, the members of the group often, though not always, obey him, and when they do, their actions match up with his orders more or less well, though seldom perfectly. He uses his orders and his followers' obedience to them so as to coordinate their actions toward gaining a collective good, that is, a result which rewards at least some of the members of the group, and which no one of them could have gained by his unaided effort. This man is a leader, a commander, even if no one outside his own group recognizes him as such. We are, of course, aware that even in informal groups there may be different levels of leadership, and that a man who is himself a leader may in turn be led. In this chapter we shall be concerned with the characteristics and behavior of leaders. Our ideas will owe much to Barnard (1938), Jouvenel (1957 and 1963), and Stacy Adams and Romney (1959).

Who Becomes a Leader?

Our first question is how a person becomes a leader in his group. We are not in the least interested in an appointed leader but in one who is self-made. Our concern is with fundamental social processes, those that appear in their simplest forms in what are called informal groups. The appointment of leaders in formal organizations is a secondary development, however important. In any event a leader who is formally appointed is unlikely to be successful unless he has some of the characteristics of the man who simply emerges as a leader in a group or makes himself one.

For a long time psychologists tried to discover some single trait of personality, or single set of traits, the possession of which was apt to make a man a leader. Their results have been meager and ambiguous: no single trait or set seems to make a man a leader with any regularity. The highest correlation links leadership with intelligence as measured by an intelligence test, and we shall find reasons why this might have been expected, but even this correlation is not very high. Recently the psychologists have contented themselves with saying that leadership does not depend on the personality of the leader but on the nature of the relationship between himself and his followers (see especially Browne and Cohn, 1958). But just what does this mean?

Field studies of groups suggest a general rule: the same process that wins a person high status in a group is also apt to win him leadership, if the group has any use for it. As we have seen, a person wins high status in a group by providing the members, not necessarily all of them, with rare and valuable rewards in individual exchanges. So far we have hardly allowed him to get more than approval in return, but there is no reason why he should not ask, implicitly or explicitly, for other kinds of reward, including compliance with his orders, should compliance be rewarding to him for its own sake or as a means to remoter ends. That is, persons of high status may be able to gain leadership through their power in pair exchanges with individual members of their group.

As we cannot reassert too often, followers in some groups find some of the damnedest things valuable. So long as a man can, by hook or by crook, provide his companions with these things, he is apt to win power over them and status. Naturally his ability to provide them depends often on his possession of some general trait of character like intelligence or even sheer energy, but it need not do so always; and in many cases the accidents of a man's past experience and learning put him in command of abilities outlandish in themselves but such as his followers happen at the moment to demand. This is the reason why no single trait of character, not even intelligence, is highly correlated with leadership. One of the more wryly amusing of human experiences is discovering that we, who by definition possess energy and intelligence in abundance, do not become leaders, while others, who conspicuously lack our qualities, make the grade.

Consider also the particular kind of rare and valuable service that wins a man power and status in many groups. Often it is the kind we have had Other providing for Person and the Third Man in the office.

It takes the form of giving good advice, suggestions as to what individuals ought to do for their private advantage. In acting upon the advice, many members of a group have already, in effect, complied with the instructions of a single other person and found it rewarding to do so. By the stimulus proposition, therefore, the likelihood has increased that they will again comply with instructions coming from him, not only when the instructions are concerned with the private good of individual members, but also when they coordinate the actions of many members toward obtaining a collective good. He has told them what to do individually and they have found compliance rewarding; accordingly when he tells them what to do collectively they are apt to obey again. In cases of this sort a man's status is associated with his leadership because he begins by winning status through establishing his power and authority over individual members separately, and power and authority are apt in turn to win him leadership over the group.

Status and Leadership: Empirical Research

Let us now look at some empirical studies of the relationship between a man's status and his ability to control the behavior of others. The first one we cite was carried out by French and Snyder (1959). It was quite straightforward and none the worse for that. Working at an Air Force base, the investigators formed a number of groups each consisting of four men. Three of the men in each group were enlisted men and one was a noncommissioned officer who, quite apart from the research, had official responsibility for supervising the enlisted men. Accordingly, one man in each group had acquired responsibility by appointment, but, as we shall soon see, he exercised actual authority in the experiment only if he had earned unofficial status.

Before the experiment itself began, the investigators asked each member of every group to answer a sociometric question about each of the others. The question was blunt: "How well do you like him?" and the subject was to answer by indicating a point on a seven-point scale of liking. The investigators then presented each subject with a card on which were drawn two similar figures, labeled *A* and *B,* whose relative size was made ambiguous by lines that tended to create an optical illusion. Two of the subjects in each group were shown cards in which figure *A* was the larger of the two, though, thanks to the optical illusion, not obviously so; and two were shown cards in which figure *B* was the larger. The investigators adopted this procedure so that there should be some difference of opinion about the relative size of the figures between two of the men and the other two.

The investigators asked each member to record privately which figure he judged to be the larger, and then threw the question open for discussion among the four members, without, of course, allowing them to settle it by actually measuring the figures. The investigators observed the discussion, recording the number of attempts to influence the others that each member made, and finally they asked the members once more to record their private judgments.

The investigators repeated this procedure three times, using different figures each time, and each time they paired the noncommissioned officer with a different one of the enlisted men by giving them identical cards. Thus each noncommissioned officer encountered each enlisted man in his group once as a supporter and twice as an opponent in the discussions. In this way the noncommissioned officer had an equal chance to show how much he could influence each of the three enlisted men.

The results were just what we should have expected. The investigators referred to the noncommissioned officers as "leaders," which is what they were officially. The first finding concerned the relationship between attempted influence and the results of the sociometric test. The more a leader accepted, that is, the better he liked, the other members of his group, the more often he attempted to influence them in the discussion, and, for that matter, the more they attempted to influence him and one another. Why they should have done so we have attempted to explain in Chapter 5 on cooperation, conformity, and competition. We are naturally more interested here in the degree to which the others liked the leader, that is, the esteem in which they held him. In this experiment the only measure we have of a leader's informal status is his esteem, since we are not told what he had done to earn it. The crucial finding was that, the greater the average liking of the other members for the leader, the more often he attempted to influence them in the discussion.

We have still not reached the heart of the matter, as we are much less interested in attempted, than in successful, influence, though of course if influence fails, it will sooner or later not be attempted. The investigators developed a measure of a leader's effectiveness, which took into account his success in changing his opponents' opinion, as recorded after the discussion, so as to coincide with his own, his success in preventing his partner from switching, and his success in resisting a change in his own opinion. They found that the higher was the leader's average acceptance by members of his group—or, as we should say, the higher his informal status—the more effective he was. Why should this have been so?

As we argued earlier, a man of high status is likely to have made many suggestions to his followers as individuals and to have had many of them rewarded with compliance. Accordingly, he is liable to make further attempts to influence them collectively. But this is not all: for if he enjoys high status, his followers must often in the past have found compliance with his suggestions rewarding, and so they will be all the more prepared to comply with them on some new occasion—in ordinary language, they will have gained confidence in his judgment. In short, status and leadership are apt to be associated, both because a man of high status will attempt to influence many people and because many of his attempts will be successful. Let us not forget a commonplace but vital fact: no attempt has less chance of succeeding than an attempt not made. Nothing venture, nothing have. This experiment incidentally suggests something for which there is a great deal of further evidence: an appointed leader, like the noncommissioned officers here, will be most effective if he does not wholly rely on the authority officially assigned him but goes on to earn unofficial authority by the methods typically used by informal leaders.

In this last experiment we knew that the more influential leaders were also held in high esteem, but we were told nothing about the means they used to earn it: we know what they got but not what they gave. We shall now turn to a piece of research that does give us some information on this point. The characteristics of leadership are primitive: they seem to reappear in groups of youngsters almost as soon as they are able to take part in social interaction at all, and the present research, by Lippitt, Polansky, Redl, and Rosen (1952), studied the way boys won and wielded power and authority in two summer camps. The investigators observed the boys' actual behavior, particularly noting which ones influenced which others by contagion—that is, if one started doing something the other started to do it too, without a word's being said—and which ones influenced which others by direct attempts at influence—that is, one actually told the other to do something and he did it. The investigators also asked each boy to answer various questions about the others, such as: "Who would you like to be with? Who would you like to be? Who is best at getting others to do what he wants them to do?" Finally they asked each boy to rank the others on various criteria: goodness in sports, fighting ability, campcraft, and of course sex sophistication—no modern psychologist would dream of leaving sex alone.

Putting the data together, the investigators found that boys were apt to let their behavior be influenced, through either contagion or direct attempts at influence, by other boys they mentioned in the questionnaire as having high power. Boys mentioned as having high power made more attempts to exert influence than did other boys, and more of their attempts were successful. But this finding only tells us that boys seen as powerful were so in fact. Much more important was the finding that powerful boys were better than the others at campcraft or fighting. That is, they were especially able to perform actions that were rewarding to their fellows or to withdraw actions that were punishing. For the ability to fight is the ability to hurt, and to stop beating a man is in fact to reward him. We must never forget that a leader is often able to maintain his position by negative rewards, such as the threat of physical violence, as well as by positive ones—though if his followers can readily escape to some other group, the negative rewards by themselves will not be enough to maintain his power. In short, the experiment showed that the boys won their high status by their ability to reward or punish members of their group, and that their high status was associated with a high capacity to influence the other members.

Let us now take a quick look at the relation between status and leadership as revealed in a couple of field studies of small groups. In the Bank Wiring Observation Room at the Hawthorne Plant of the Western Electric Company, the wireman Taylor came closer than any other wireman to realizing the group's highly valued output norm (see Homans, 1950: 78). When the men were suffering in their work from wire of poor quality, it was he that left the room and brought back a good supply. Socially he was always ready to take part in a game or conversation, and the men in the room had a standing invitation to play poker at his house. He was much the most popular man in the room, and the others showed their sentiments toward him by helping him in minor ways at his work more than they did anyone else. The help was not of the sort whose acceptance would have undermined his status: what help they gave him anyone could have given; he was conspicuously able to do his own work well, and often failed to return the help he got. As for his influence, he won more arguments than any other man in the room, he gave more advice that was accepted, and he took the lead in putting an end to disputes that were threatening to turn into fights.

To take another example, Blau showed in his study of workers in a federal law-enforcement agency that those agents who received much interaction and much esteem were not only highly competent at their work and so able to give good advice to others but also, which was not true of all the competent agents, ready and willing to give advice (Blau, 1955: 97–179). Note that the help they gave the others was of the rare kind, not the kind that any fool could give. And they also exerted most influence, particularly when many agents were on hand to be influenced and problems affecting all the agents were to be faced. The only occasions when all members of the department were assembled in one group were the departmental meetings, held once a week; on these occasions the agents who had earned highest esteem participated most often in the discussion, and here, as elsewhere, their suggestions were the ones most likely to win acceptance by the rest:

> The superior status of agents who received many contacts also manifested itself in the dominant role they assumed when a small group of officials were engaged in a joint undertaking. They made most suggestions and their suggestions were most often followed, whether the suggestion was where to go for lunch or whether the decision referred to a project on which several agents worked together, as they occasionally did. This was particularly evident in the case of the informal leader. For example, he and two other agents were once appointed to draft a proposal for changes in one of the

regulations. In their conference, he took command of the situation, making the decisions and telling the others what to do. One of them accepted a subordinate position unquestionably, and the other, an exceptionally independent person, also submitted to his directives after some protest.*

Channels of Communication and Command

To make a man a leader it is not enough that he should have power and authority over the members of his group as private individuals; he must also be prepared to give orders to the group as a whole, and the next question is what determines whether or not he will do so. Remember that giving an order is an action like any other, and will therefore be subject to the propositions that state what determines the frequency with which any action is performed. Thus according to the success proposition, a man will tend to repeat the action of giving an order if the action has met with reward. He may ultimately, of course, be rewarded by the results of the members' obedience, the ends they accomplish, but his immediate reward is just plain seeing them obey. This is probably a case of the very general type of reward men get from manipulating nature, from seeing her do what they tried to make her do. Accordingly, the more often people in fact comply with his orders, the more ready a man will be to give orders again. This is the process that makes a person who already holds high status more likely to give orders to his group as a whole. Since his advice in pair exchanges with individual members has often been taken, he is by generalization apt to offer advice to the whole group. If for any reason the members in fact obey, he is on the way to becoming a leader.

By the same token, if a man atempts to give orders to his group as a whole, and the group does not obey, the likelihood that he will make another such attempt diminishes. Indeed experiments can be arranged in which secret confederates of the experimenter differentially reward members of a group for making suggestions to the group as a whole. Suggestions made by certain members the confederates support; those made by others they deliberately disregard. As we should expect, the number of suggestions made by the former increases, the number made by the latter decreases (see Marak, 1964). Remember always that an action not taken is an action that cannot be rewarded, and that a man who never even tries to give orders can never become a leader.

It is not just that he is unlikely to have offered advice to individuals and seen it adopted which tends to keep a member of low status from

* This quotation and those in Chapter 15 are reprinted from Peter M. Blau's *The Dynamics of Bureaucracy*, 1955 (Revised Edition, 1963) by permission of the author and The University of Chicago Press. Copyright 1955, 1963 by The University of Chicago Press. All rights reserved.

offering suggestions to the group as a whole. He may be positively punished for making the attempt. Once the giving of orders has become associated with high status, or, to put the matter more accurately, once the giving of orders has become one of the dimensions along which a member's status is ranked, then a member who tries to give orders but who ranks low on the other dimensions is incongruent in status. Members otherwise his equals may conclude that he is trying by this method to raise his status relative to theirs. "Who is he," they will ask, "to tell us what to do?" They will reject his suggestion without even considering whether it has any merit. They will punish him for his presumption; the punishment may make him less ready to try to influence them on the next occasion, and if he does not even try, he certainly cannot succeed. None of this means, of course, that persons originally of low status never rise to command. We know better than that. It does mean that they have something to overcome first and high costs to pay before they succeed.

Under these circumstances a man of low status will learn that, if he would have any large number of members of his group take some concerted action, he had better not suggest it to them himself. He had better take his idea to the established leader instead and clear it with him. Only if the leader takes up the suggestion and puts it out as coming from him will the others obey. In this manner something very much like legitimate authority builds itself up in even the most informal groups. Here is a further determinant of the pattern we examined in Chapter 8 on structures of esteem and interaction, which showed communication flowing from low status to high in pair relations and then from persons of high status to the group as a whole. A leader who is sensible enough not to rebuff such approaches may get more credit for good ideas than his own native faculties deserve. In this field nothing succeeds like success or fails like failure: "Whosoever hath, to him shall be given; but whosoever hath not, from him shall be taken away even that which he hath." The circles are vicious—or benignant as one chooses to pass judgment on particular cases; they are very difficult to break; and they contribute enormously for good or ill to the stability of relationships in a group.

Participation in Decision-Making

In Chapter 4 we considered a number of the definitions that social scientists and others have given to the word *power*. We paid special attention to two of them: what we proposed to call *power* proper, when the powerful person can himself control the rewards others receive, and what we proposed to call *authority*, when he cannot do so, and the rewards come from the environment, physical or social. Note that both power and authority are concerned with the question whether orders will be obeyed but not with what the content of the orders shall be. A third meaning that many persons give to the word *power* refers to how the content of an order is reached. We are certainly apt to call someone powerful who makes, or has a hand in making, decisions that, when carried out, affect the behavior of a large number of others. This kind of power is power as participation in decision-making. Naturally it is not enough just to reach a decision: the problem of getting it carried out still remains, and that requires the other kinds of power.

We should now be able to understand why this kind of power, in small groups as in large organizations, tends to get associated with the other two in the hands of members of high status. So far as a man's ability to make a sensible decision depends on his getting relevant information, the communications that flow from low-status persons to high-status ones tend to keep the latter better able to reach decisions because they are better informed, though certainly not always absolutely well-informed. And since it surely makes a difference in reaching a decision to know whether it will be embodied in orders and whether the orders will be obeyed, the making of decisions tends to get into the hands of persons of high status, because they possess power in the other two senses and therefore are able, if anyone in the group is able to do so, to issue orders that the members will comply with. It is idle for a man, indeed damaging to his future leadership, to issue an order that he knows in advance will not be obeyed. To use the language of organizational theory, a man's authority to carry out decisions should match his responsibility for making them, and often in fact does so.

We have spoken of the fact that persons of low status are, by the rule of status congruence, not expected to give orders to their group as a whole, and may even be punished by their fellow members if they attempt to do so. The other side of the coin is, of course, that persons of high status *are* expected to reach decisions and give orders, when the occasion calls for them. Should they then fail to do so, their status can fall rapidly. At the peril of his leadership, a leader must lead. Not least of the costs of high status is having to decide, having to act. People think that members of high status get all the goodies that are going in a group. They get many of them but surely not all. O the bliss of not having to decide, not having to act!

Obedience to Orders

Suppose then that a member of a group makes a suggestion or gives an order to others. Let us not worry about words like "suggestion" and "order": in both cases a verbal stimulus has specified an action that ought to be performed. In this sense an order belongs to the same class of thing as a norm. The differences between them are matters of degree not of kind. An order may govern behavior only within a relatively brief span of time; a norm is generally supposed to remain in force without limit of time: it is, as we say, a "standing order." Again, an order emanates from a single person or office, whereas we usually find a norm being stated by a number of members of a group, though even so it turns out that leaders have more of a say in establishing norms than followers do. In any particular case we might find it difficult to decide whether something was properly labeled an order or a norm.

What sort of thing determines whether followers will comply with the order and perform the action it specifies? We ought to know the answers by now, but let us review them here. First, there is the nature of the order itself. Many orders specify a man's action only in the sense of naming the result to be accomplished by the action. Does the person to whom the order is addressed find that he is able to do what he has been told to do, that some action he is able to perform will be successful in getting the result? The answer to the question will depend on how similar the required result is to results he has been successful in attaining in the past, and how different it is from results he has failed to attain. Linked to the question of success is the question whether the result itself would, if attained, yield him net reward, reward assessed in relation to cost—that is, to alternatives forgone. The same rule holds for obedience to orders as for other actions: the more likely obedience is to end in success, and the more valuable the result thus obtained, the more likely it is that the follower will obey.

Second, there is the person who gives the order: he is always a chief part of the stimulus. Has obedience to his orders in the past resulted in success and net reward for his followers? If it has, a follower is more apt to obey him on the present occasion. Hence the crucial importance for a person who is on his way to becoming a leader in a group that he get the other members to obey his orders at least once and find that their obedience does accomplish the intended result and that the result is rewarding. The first may be the most difficult occasion on which to get them to obey: after that every act of obedience gives the leader the opportunity of making further obedience still more likely to occur. Since a person's status is apt to embody his past record of rewarding others, a follower is, as we have seen, initially more apt to obey a person of high status than one of low. A man's informal status plays in informal leadership the part that his official position in an organization plays in his official authority: it creates the presumption that compliance with an order emanating from him will result in net reward, and failure to comply, in net punishment.

Let us be careful as to what we mean by net reward. Obedience to orders by the members of a group may result in their acquiring what we called in Chapter 5 collective goods: goods that, once obtained, no member of the group can be prevented from sharing. Victory in battle is such a good: it is a reward all members of the victorious army can share. But collective goods alone, no matter how often obedience to a leader's orders has resulted in success in obtaining them, are usually insufficient by themselves to secure obedience to all his orders by all his followers. The problem, as we have seen, is that of the "free loader": the member of the group who is delighted to share in the reflected glory and other rewards of victory, while avoiding the costs of personal and energetic compliance with orders. Accordingly, collective rewards must usually be backed up by individual ones, and a person to whom an order is addressed will be more likely to obey if the leader's past record of rewarding him personally for exceptionally able compliance or compliance in especially difficult circumstances—"beyond the call of duty"—and of punishing him personally for failure to comply is well established. That is, the leader must possess power as well as authority. Of course, his ability to reward and punish particular individuals may itself depend on whether third parties will obey his orders.

The two factors—the nature of the order and the record of the person who gives the order—interact with one another. Certain kinds of order no follower will obey, no matter whom they come from: compliance would be too costly. A leader is well advised not to issue such orders, for if he does so, he at once raises the question whether the other orders he issues will yield his followers net reward. On the other hand, certain kinds of persons will not be obeyed no matter what suggestions they make. Such persons are in the unhappy position of never being able to get their authority off the ground, of never being able to show that, had their suggestions been followed, the results would have been rewarding. A suggestion not followed is a suggestion whose worth cannot be tested. Yet in between orders that will never be obeyed and persons that never will be obeyed, there are orders that will be obeyed if one person issues them but not if another does. Under these circumstances, the man who is obeyed is, as we have seen, the man whose past record, embodied in his status, of giving individual advice or collective orders has created the behavioral presumption that further compliance with his orders will result in net reward for his followers. Even though the followers look askance at the terms of the order itself, the fact that it comes from him will tip the scales toward their compliance.

In considering the problem of obedience to orders, we have looked so far at the relations between leader and followers but not at the relations between the followers themselves. Yet these latter ties may directly affect obedience. We have seen that an order belongs to the same class of thing as a norm. From this it should follow that obedience to orders has the same sort of determinants as conformity to norms. In our study of conformity in Chapter 5, we learned that some members of a group may get no reward from the ostensible results of conformity, but will conform nevertheless for fear of losing the approval and companionship of other members, who do find the ostensible results valuable. So it is with obedience to orders. So far as orders coordinate the cooperation of members of a group, direct their combined actions to secure a result no one of them could have obtained by his individual efforts, and so far as some members value these results, a member who disobeys has threatened these others, and accordingly they are likely to try to punish him by withdrawing their approval from him or even driving him out of the group. Then a member who sets no value on the direct results of cooperation, but who does value his position in and membership of his group, may well comply with orders for fear of losing these things. It has often been observed, for instance, that soldiers fight hard in battle at least as much because they are unwilling to let their comrades down as because they want to beat the enemy.

It follows that the more social approval from others members have to lose, the more disobedience will cost them, and therefore the more likely they are to obey. It follows further that, if a high level of good feeling has already been established in a group, if many members like other members, the larger—other things equal—will be the number who will obey the leader's orders, so long as any of them find the ultimate results of obedience rewarding. And as more members actually obey the leader, more come to trust that others will obey him in the future, and therefore they are less tempted to look first after their private interests, on the assumption that the rest will do so too. That is, the more members are bound to one another, the more they control one another, though if they ever come to reject the leader's aims, this very cohesiveness will constitute his greatest danger. Whatever else it takes, at least it takes time to build up the good feeling. It takes time, for instance, for the members of a military unit to develop confidence in one another through actual experience; and therefore no officer should be in a hurry to break up such a unit and reassign its members, if he values its fighting capacity. In short, a leader's control depends not only on his own relations with his followers but also on his followers' relations with one another; and a leader will do what he can to encourage good feeling among his men for his own sake as well as theirs.

The Maintenance of Justice

If the leader can do little positively to encourage good feeling among his followers, he may at least be able to do something to avoid bad feeling and jealousies by maintaining as best he can the condition of distributive justice among them, for injustice leads its victims to resent not only the author of injustice but its beneficiaries. The latter are the other followers; the former they often assume, and rightly, to be the leader himself. If the leader's chief external task is to be successful, his chief internal one is to be fair. "He's fair!" are the words in the mouths of his followers from which all other praises spring.

Nor does a leader often have a choice whether or not he will try to do justice, for the job will be thrust upon him willy-nilly. When two members get into a dispute and find they cannot settle it by direct negotiation, they will be apt to refer it for arbitration to someone of higher status than they are themselves. For to submit a dispute to someone hitherto equal to yourself—unless he is so much of an outsider that his status makes next to no difference—is in fact to accord him higher status, since he now decides what happens to you, but you do not decide what happens to him, and this superior authority is an outward sign of higher status. As matters effecting status may be the very ones in dispute, choosing such an arbiter may upset the social order even more than the dispute itself does; whereas if the parties go to someone whose superiority to themselves is already established, they exalt no new man. We certainly observe leaders that try to maintain distributive justice in their groups. Thus Doc, the leader of the Norton Street Gang, took the chief part in bringing Alec's bowling score into line with his contributions to the group.

The maintenance of distributive justice is not just a matter of the settlement of disputes or of assigning special jobs to members in accordance with their investments. We have spoken of the collective goods a group may acquire. These are the rewards that cannot be divided: no member can be prevented from sharing in them, even if he has made little or no contribution to getting them. One example is an increase in wage rates across the board, which a union may have gained by a strike. No worker in the plant can be denied his share in the raise, even if he has done nothing to support the strike. Or, to take a humbler example, if a group has undertaken to solve a problem by discussion, the rewards of success cannot be differentially distributed among the members: each must take what pleasure he can out of it. This does not mean that the member who has contributed most to the discussion does not raise his status by doing so; he does. But status is a different reward from that of solving the problem.

Yet there obviously are rewards, such as money, for some kinds of collective actions, which can be differentially distributed among the members. The question of their distribution will arise and be dumped, for reasons we have already given, in the leader's lap. One of his chief jobs is that of dividing the booty, whatever it may be, fairly. He will have to hit upon some rule of proportionality between the investments of particular members, their contribution to the successful result, and their shares of the reward. In particular, he will have to decide what shall count for this purpose as legitimate investments and contributions.

In deciding he will do well to forget abstract considerations and adopt those that his followers will in fact accept. Any failure to establish fair shares may lessen the willingness of members to work together in the future, therefore lower their capacity to obtain distributable rewards, and thus lead to still further disintegration.

Leadership as Risk-Taking

A leader's past record of success in coordinating the actions of his followers toward reaching some rewarding result and of justice in his distribution of the reward among them renders it more probable, by the stimulus proposition, that they will again obey orders specifically coming from him. In this light, his record may be looked on as risk capital. It gives him room for maneuver: the next time he issues an order, his followers will allow him the benefit of the doubt, give compliance a try, and wait to see what the result may be. If the result turns out to be rewarding in the end, the leader has replaced and even increased his capital. If, on the other hand, his followers obey him and the result is mere failure, he has lost some of it. But no leader can be successful all the time, and we suspect that, by the rule of intermittent reinforcement, a leader who is often successful will lose little by way of control over his followers from an occasional failure. If a leader is successful often enough, his followers will come to obey him almost blindly, to obey orders coming from him that they would never have obeyed coming from anyone else. If, indeed, we agree that a man earns power and status by providing others with services that they find both rare and valuable, we must recognize that the able leader provides the rarest and most valuable of all services: he has decided what the others are to do, and decided correctly, especially when the correct, that is, the rewarding, decision is not at all obvious. Some men would rather do anything than decide for themselves. But a leader pays a price for being correct: when a problem whose solution is not obvious arises again, his followers will be all the more ready to leave the decision to him, and then he will endanger his leadership just as much by not deciding at all as by deciding incorrectly.

Command and Liking

We must now deal openly with a question that has remained latent in much of the preceding discussion, the question of the sentiments his followers express towards a person in command. We have argued that in informal groups a man earns approval from members by having rewarded many of them in pair exchanges, and that his status, thus acquired, enables him to give orders to the group as a whole. But what do we really mean by social approval? And though a man begins by gaining the approval of members, do not their sentiments toward him change when he comes to exercise command over them? If by social approval we mean liking in the ordinary American sense of the word—the sentiment we express toward someone we approach easily in the expectation that he will reward us without requiring us to incur high costs in fear or inferiority—then it is clear that leaders are not always much liked, though not necessarily disliked. They may be esteemed in the sense of being respected, but liking is another matter. Indeed some persons whose popularity began by earning them a position of command have found that their exercise of command ended by losing them their popularity. Workmen, for instance, who have been elected shop stewards in their factory, have been known after election to complain: "No one is your friend any more." Why should these things be?

When Person asks Other for advice in the office, and Other gives it to him, getting his approval in return, Other has provided Person with something Person directly and immediately values. When Other orders Person to take some action as part of a collective effort, Person's obedience may not gain for him any such direct and immediate reward. In exercising command, a man by his orders directs others toward a result no one of them could have reached by his unaided effort. Yet that very fact may make trouble. We have already met the problem created by collective goods. The followers may well be content to partake in them eventually, but no single follower may be eager to incur the cost of his doing the necessary work now. "Why pick on me?" he may say in effect or in fact. "Let George do it." If the leader insists that he shall do it and not George, he is asking him to incur costs in return for rewards he might otherwise have obtained at no expense.

Moreover, the rewards of collective action are likely at best to be slow in coming compared with the rewards of many individual activities. Their rewards are deferred but their costs are immediate. And so the man who requires you to incur these costs is still in the short run someone to be avoided, someone to be feared as well as liked. He is the more to be feared, the higher the short-run costs and the greater your risk of actually incurring them. Even if success crowns the efforts he directs, including your own, and you come to admire him, the fear may still linger. You would rather admire him at a distance. Though you will readily obey his orders if he can catch you, you would rather not be around when he gives them. He is the lightning, and you cannot tell where it will strike next.

No doubt Person incurs costs, particularly in confessed inferiority, when he asks Other for advice and follows it. But in this case it is at least he and not Other that takes the initiative in making the request at a time of his own choosing, and by so doing he has accepted the costs in advance. In giving orders, on the other hand, it is Other that takes the initiative. He requires Person to forgo, at a time now of Other's choosing, alternative activities whose results, in the absence of the orders, Person would have found more rewarding. Other's orders thus threaten to constrain Person's behavior. What we call freedom of action is itself a reward and its loss a punishment. Person may still obey but he may not like it much. Of course, he always has a choice not to obey but he may feel as if he had none.

Naturally, when a leader is in a position to reward individuals, if only by praise, for obedience to his commands, and when the individuals in question are burning to acquire personal distinction by the skill and courage with which they carry them out—an unlikely condition if the commands call only for routine but necessary work—then his followers may do their best to attract his notice. But the positive inducements to compliance are always in short supply, and a leader must often be required to back up the relative weakness of collective rewards by using individual punishment or the threat of it. Even if his followers try to accomplish what he has asked them to do, he may feel bound to criticize the skill and success with which they do so. Though he may praise, he may also blame, and words, even words that are thoroughly deserved, do hurt as much as sticks and stones. When he sits in judgment in matters of distributive justice, one may get fair treatment from him, but fair treatment may still result in another's gaining at one's expense. And one cannot even be quite sure of getting fair treatment from the leader: to have many opportunities to make decisions is to have many opportunities to make mistakes. He will make them, never fear; no one can be a leader who cannot learn to live with this ineluctable fact. A leader, then, is a man who is remarkably well able to punish his followers as well as to reward them. Just punishment, it is true, punishment that helps a man make his later actions more successful in attaining an ideal reward, may not have the usual effects; and there are men who lick the hand that strikes them. But in general punishment arouses a very different kind of emotional and behavioral response from that aroused by positive reward: punishment is a reason for fearing and avoiding the punisher.

Finally, by his very position as a man of high status, a leader may be standing in your light—you who, but for him, might be top dog yourself: he is depriving you of reward. We have perhaps not had enough to say about envy in this book. It is a particularly vicious emotion, especially when masked as idealism.

In short, a leader may be dangerous, and such men are to be approached with circumspection. He is apt to hurt his followers as well as reward them—indeed to hurt them in the course of rewarding them—and so they will have good reasons for avoiding and fearing him as well as for approaching and liking him. The sentiments they express toward him will accordingly be mixed or, to use the modern word, ambivalent. They will be more mixed, the more serious the costs they may incur by obedience, and the higher the risk of their actually having to incur them. Often the best the leader can do is maintain a surplus of positive sentiments over negative ones. But liking is seldom the proper word for describing the sentiments of followers toward a leader who does any serious leading—perhaps respect, esteem, admiration, or deference, but not liking.

Command and Liking: Empirical Research

Whether or not the reasons we have given for it are the correct ones, the ambivalent nature of followers' sentiments toward a leader is often observed. It is most often observed in the case of leaders whose presumptive right to command—the presumption that they will give orders and that the orders are to be obeyed—has been established by appointment or inheritance. Compliance with the orders of such men is enforced in case of necessity by sanctions coming from outside the group in question: the foreman's orders to his workmen will usually, for instance, be backed up by higher officers in the firm. Accordingly such men are freer to control their followers by punishment or the threat of punishment and so more liable to arouse hostile sentiments than are informal leaders, who usually have to earn at least their initial status, the initial presumption that their orders will be obeyed, by providing positive rewards for their followers.

A good example is provided by fathers in some primitive societies. (Remember that groups of kinsmen are still groups, and that what applies to other groups applies to them too.) In patrilineal societies, for instance, a father inherits from *his* father the right to exercise command over his family and sometimes over his brothers' families too. In the words of an anthropologist like Meyer Fortes, he possesses jural authority: he acquires and wields command according to the recognized norms of the society in question, which means that he will be supported in his actions by the other men of his patrilineage (see especially Fortes, 1949: 12–43). In such societies a son's sentiment toward his father is apt to be far removed from what we usually call liking. He may respect or even admire the old man, but liking in the form of easy friendliness is not the sentiment he displays, and he is even apt to keep clear of his father except when they have a job to do together. The attitude of respect gets more firmly established the more regularly he works with his father and under his father's orders, for instance in tilling the family land, and the more fully his father's means of controlling him are limited to punishment or the threat of it. We must not blame the father, poor fellow, too much for using negative sanctions: they may be almost the only ones at his disposal. In this respect a father is usually at a disadvantage compared with a mother, who especially in a child's early years has many and valuable rewards of a positive sort that she can give him; and accordingly a boy's sentiment toward his mother is apt to be warmer and less ambivalent than his sentiment toward his father.

In certain matrilineal societies, on the other hand, where jural authority over a boy is vested in his mother's brothers and not in his father, the boy tends to take the characteristic attitude of respect toward these authority figures, and then he is free to be much more of a friend and companion to his father than he could have been in a patrilineal society. In societies where many families live in the same circumstances, these attitudes toward jural authority get repeated and generalized from family to family throughout the society, and get enshrined in their turn in its norms. They may also have wide repercussions on behavior toward other kinsmen (see Homans, 1950: 190–280; Homans and Schneider, 1955).

As students of the elementary processes of social behavior, we should not be much interested in reactions to jural authority in primitive societies if the same tendencies were not observed in informal groups in societies of a very different kind. Let us look at an example. We are already familiar with the general procedures R. F. Bales and his associates use in their research in small groups. They put a number of undergraduate volunteers into a room, set them a problem to be solved by discussion, and make a variety of detailed observations of their interaction. Note that they always give the members of the group a joint task, for which they receive a typical collective reward, and that we have no reason to believe just the same findings will be obtained in such a group as would be obtained in one like the cash posters in the Eastern Utilities Company, whose job did not require collaboration.

In the particular research we are now concerned with, Bales and his associates formed four different five-man groups and made their usual observations on a total of twelve sessions of these groups (Bales, 1953: 111-161). In addition, they asked every member at the end of each session to put the members of his group, including himself, in rank order on four different criteria: Who contributed the best ideas for solving the problem? Who did most to guide the discussion and keep it moving effectively? Whom do you like most? Whom do you dislike? Had the answers to these questions been scored in a straightforward way, the sum of all scores on any one question would have equaled the sum of all scores on any other. But the investigators in their report of the research say that they did not in fact treat the data in quite the straightforward way we have described, and as a result the total scores on the different criteria are not in fact equal. Disliking scores, for instance, are much lower than the others, which seem to mean that the general level of dis-liking was low.

We shall remember that in Chapter 8 on structures of esteem and interaction we studied a Bales' matrix made from observations on six-man groups. The present groups had only five members each, but we have no reason to believe that their interaction matrix would have shown a different pattern. We shall also remember that the investigators set up that matrix by putting the members in rank order of the number of unit acts each one initiated, both to other members and to the group as a whole, which turned out also to be their rank order in interaction re-ceived. At that time we complained that the investigators told us nothing about the relationship between the rank of members in interaction and their rank in esteem. In the present research, they made the deficiency good. As before, they put the members in rank order for initiations at each session, but then they tabulated the scores each member got on the four sociometric questions against his initiating rank, and summed up the results of all twelve sessions in the accompanying chart (Figure 4).

Figure 4   Choice in Relation to Initiation Rank

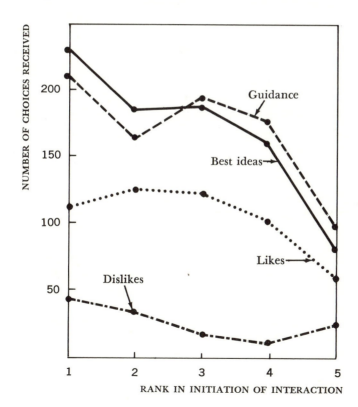

It suggests some central tendencies in the relationship between interaction and sentiment in discussion groups.

From the chart we see first that the curves for "best ideas" and "guidance" are much alike, suggesting that these two criteria are really a single one, which might be called "contribution to the group task." We also see that the more often a member initiated interaction the higher the score he got on this criterion: the more he did in fact contribute to the discussion, in quantity of talk if not in quality, the more often he was named as contributing; but the relatively low score of the No. 2 initiator prevents the relationship from being a completely linear one. As for the No. 1 initiator, the investigators at the end of the whole series of sessions asked the members of each group who had acted as their leader, and they were especially likely to name him.

Much more interesting are the curves for "likes" and "dislikes." The general tendency or slope of the liking curve suggests a positive relationship between interaction and friendship, such as we found among the cash posters. But the relationship was obviously not linear. The second initiator was the best-liked man, followed closely by the third, and the top initiator only got a fair amount of liking. Moreover he was the most *disliked* member, which suggests an ambivalent attitude toward him on the part of the rest, although disliking seems in general to have been less intense than other forms of choice. In short, choice for liking was rather differently distributed from choice on guidance and best ideas, and holding the top position in guidance, initiation, and leadership tended to get in the way of a man's being liked.

Further analysis of the data confirmed these results. Examining the whole set of intercorrelations between the measures they had made, the investigators found that the correlations between liking and the other variables, while positive, were the lowest in the set. Hollander (1964: 66–76) reached a similar result. He allowed the members of a group to choose other members on a number of different criteria. When he calculated the correlations between choices on the different criteria, he found that the lowest correlation was that between choice for leadership and choice for friendship. Members tended not to choose the same person for the two roles.

In the Bales' groups, moreover, the correlation between liking and the other forms of choice tended to decrease with time. For instance, the top initiator was more apt to be also the best-liked member after the first session of a group than after the last. In a sociometric study of a series of group meetings Lippitt (1948) found something of the same sort: choices on the two criteria of working with another member and spending leisure time with him tended to be much more highly correlated at the beginning of the series than they were later. At the beginning, a member named by many others as someone they would like to work with was also named by many as someone they would like to spend leisure time with. As time went on and the members' social standing became better established, we may suspect that choice for leisure shifted toward the Hudson pattern: members began to choose for leisure other members who were their equals in esteem on the working criterion.

The question now is why the top initiator in the Bales' groups, the person seen as contributing most to the discussion, should not have been better liked. First and always we must remember that the investigators gave each group a definite task to accomplish: it was to reach by discussion some solution to a set problem. The top initiator tended to be the leader of the group in the sense that he was most occupied with directing it to its goal and supplying it with ideas for a solution. In Bales' terms he was the task, or instrumental, leader. As leader he necessarily had to evaluate and criticize the contributions of others and even, deliberately or in effect, to choke them off in the middle of speeches that were not pertinent to a solution. In so doing he inevitably and to some extent punished the others, depriving them of rewards in freedom and approval they might otherwise have enjoyed. But to make a man forgo reward, no matter how small, is to arouse his hostility, no matter how little. As Bales (1953) puts it: "The more 'directive' and 'constricting' the quality of activity, the more likely it is to arouse negative reactions."

No doubt the leader's activity rewarded the other members by helping them solve the problems set for the group. The reward may not have been great—they may not have been much interested in solving the problems—but it was probably better than nothing. In return they gave him their respect, as shown by their choices for "best ideas" and "guidance." But in rewarding them the leader also forced them to incur costs, and so they turned their liking choices away from him and toward the others with whom they could interact at lower cost—with whom they were more at ease and less constrained—particularly to the men who were second and third in interaction and in choices for guidance.

This argument is supported by further evidence Bales cites. In a new series of five-man groups he paid particular attention not only to interaction initiated but to the relationship between interaction initiated and interaction received: the receipt/initiation ratio (Bales, 1956). He found that members were much more apt to dislike leaders who talked more than they were talked to than leaders who behaved the other way around and received more interaction than they gave. Indeed leaders whose ratio of receipts to initiations was high were apt to be chosen highly for both guidance and liking, and in their groups the relationship between interaction and liking became linear: the more a man led, the better he was liked. We may be justified in guessing that a leader who talked more than he was talked to was one who spent a particularly large part of his time bossing the group around, telling the members what they ought to think and say—doing, that is, the sort of thing most apt to prove immediately punishing to the members, however effective it might be in accomplishing the group task. Accordingly, such a leader would be particularly apt to arouse some hostility in his followers. On the other hand, a leader who was talked to much more than he talked was apt to be more encouraging to his followers' ideas, more willing to allow them free expression, less constraining to their behavior, and so more rewarding to them. Accordingly, such a leader was more apt to be liked than was the other kind.

As he wins his leadership, perhaps the best a man can hope for is that the things he is liked for should increase a little faster than those he is disliked for. In a sociometric study of students in the ninth and tenth grades of several different high schools, Riley and Cohn (1958) arranged the subjects in classes by order of status, status being measured as it was in another study by Riley and her associates, described in Chapter 8 on structures of esteem and interaction. The investigators then counted the number of traits that other students praised each subject for possessing and the number of traits they blamed him for possessing. The higher the status of a student, the larger, they found, was the number of traits for which he was favorably mentioned, but the larger also the number for which he was mentioned unfavorably. Yet the ratio between the two, the proportion of favorable mentions to unfavorable ones, increased steadily with increasing status. Speaking roughly, we may say that a person of low status, which usually means a low degree of leadership, makes neither many friends nor many enemies: he makes little difference; whereas a person of high status makes many of both: he makes a big difference both for good and for ill. But so long as a man can stand some dislike—and there are people that cannot stand any—a person in command may take it, somewhat wryly, as a sign that he is not doing badly.

The Degree of Ambivalence toward Authority

It is one thing to argue that a leader is apt to inspire some fear and avoidance in his followers, another to show what determines how much of them he inspires. Our argument suggests that there should be two sorts of determinants. The activity on the part of a leader that is most apt to inspire fear and avoidance is his giving orders to large numbers of his followers in the endeavor to coordinate and control their actions toward the attainment of a relatively distant goal. In this case, compliance with his orders is apt to incur costs for his followers in the form of short-term rewards forgone; and in order to insure compliance the leader is apt to resort to implicit or explicit threats of punishment. We should therefore expect that, the more often a leader gives such orders, relative to the number of times his actions immediately reward his followers as individuals, the greater should be their fear and avoidance of him.

We must also consider the goal to the attainment of which the leader's efforts at coordination are directed. Though collective goods may not always be effective in mobilizing the efforts of individual followers, it should still be true in general that, if the goal is attained and proves rewarding to the followers, particularly in comparison with the disasters that have been successfully avoided in the course of attaining it, these conditions will more than make up for the costs the followers incurred. We should therefore expect that, the less successful a leader is in attaining a group goal, or the less rewarding the followers find the goal when attained, the greater should be the followers' tendency to fear and avoid him.

On the first kind of determinant Bales' results have already provided us with some information. Although on the average the leaders in his groups were respected but not much liked, those leaders who spent a particularly large amount of their time directing the group, relative to the time they spent accepting communications from individual followers, were disliked even more than was the average leader. In contrast, those leaders who behaved the other way and spent a particularly large amount of their time accepting communications from individual followers, relative to the time they spent directing the group, were liked much more than the average leader: indeed they got much respect and much liking too.

Sometimes the frequency with which a leader tries to direct his followers depends on the circumstances in which the group is placed. Informal leaders, for instance, in groups that already have formal ones are unlikely to exercise command over a full range of fields of activity; the formal leaders preempt some of the fields, and incidentally attract much of the potential hostility to themselves: they are the obvious targets. Thus in industrial groups, where the formal supervision of manufacturing is in the hands of foremen, informal leaders are less apt to take full control of their followers than they are in more independent groups like gangs. Taylor in the Bank Wiring Observation Room, while giving much help and advice to individuals, did rather little to coordinate the activities of the members toward the accomplishment of a joint task, and this was probably one of the reasons why he was so well liked: his popularity was more prominent than his leadership. For the kind of command that will incur followers the highest costs—costs in criticism received, rewards postponed, and immediate pleasures forgone—is command exercised in coordinating their activities. When people are prevented, as they must be by coordination, from doing just what they want when they want to, they will find the experience to some degree costly. And cost, being deprivation, is apt to arouse some fear and avoidance. Accordingly, we may put the matter bluntly and say that the less a man of high status is also a commander, the more apt he is to be liked.

Now for the second kind of determinant. Even though a leader often coordinates the activities of his followers in accomplishing a group task, he may still be well liked if the result is sufficiently rewarding to the members. Then the immediate costs he has made the followers incur will be swallowed up in the ultimate rewards his efforts have brought them. This, or something much like it, has been demonstrated in research by Theodorson (1957). The investigator studied two pairs of discussion groups, making four groups in all. The two groups in the first pair were artificially formed and met in a social science laboratory; their members discussed problems of family adjustment. The groups in the second pair were naturally formed, in the sense that people attended or failed to attend who happened to feel like doing so, and their members discussed current problems of world politics.

The first variable the investigator examined he called *cohesiveness*, which Festinger and his associates define, as we have seen, as the degree to which members are attracted to take part in a group (Festinger, Schachter, and Back, 1950: 164). In the present instance, the investigator based his measures of cohesiveness on the answers each member gave to questions on how much he enjoyed a meeting, how much he liked every other member, and how much he was "concerned about and willing to sacrifice for the group." Members that expressed high concern in answer to the last question were, we suppose, members that found the group goal more valuable than any incidental rewards; and members that answered the other questions favorably, particularly the first, must have felt the group goal had in fact been attained to a high degree. In each pair of groups, one group was significantly more cohesive than the other on these counts. The investigator did something to make one of the laboratory groups more cohesive than the other by assigning it a desirable meeting place and an observer of high status; he did nothing to make one of the natural groups more cohesive than the other, but one did in fact become more cohesive in the course of time.

As we have seen, the investigator used the liking choices members gave to other members as the basis for one of his measures of cohesiveness: a group was more cohesive the higher was the average level of liking within it. But he also used the choices to put the members of each group in rank order of popularity. And after every meeting he asked each member to rank the others on the amount of leadership each had exercised and on the number of good ideas each had contributed to the discussion. The investigator used the answers to put the members in rank order of recognized leadership and contribution.

He then examined the correlations between group cohesiveness and the rank orders of individual members in popularity, leadership, and contribution. He found that in each pair the more cohesive group showed higher positive correlations between popularity and leadership and between popularity and contribution than did the less cohesive group. On our interpretation, the more rewarding the members found the group task and the more successful they were in accomplishing it, the more likely it was that the leaders who had contributed much to its accomplishment would be popular too. Under these conditions leadership and popularity overlapped. Even though you coordinate the activities of others and so make them incur heavy costs, you may nevertheless recover the esteem you have put in jeopardy, provided that by your exercise of command and their obedience to it you can accomplish a result highly valuable to them. You may then manage to be a leader and be popular too, but you should not count on having this happy condition last. A good example is provided by military leadership. Many officers are not particularly popular with their men; indeed an officer who is merely popular is a little suspect on that account, but an officer who has brought his men successfully through great dangers and so has accomplished a result highly valuable to them, is apt to win something as close to adoration as we are likely to see this side of Paradise.

According to this argument the leaders in the Bales' groups may have found it particularly difficult to reconcile effectiveness with popularity, for they were apt to fall between two stools. On the one hand, there was a group task to be accomplished, and they did a great deal to direct the members toward its accomplishment; on the other, the task may not have been one that brought the members very valuable rewards. After all, the members did not volunteer for the groups because they were interested in the problems under discussion, which were set by the investigators and not chosen by themselves. Thus the leaders exercised much command in accomplishing a not very valuable result, and on both counts they were likely to endanger their popularity.

Familiarity Breeds Contempt

In describing the followers' reaction to the leader, we are in danger of forgetting his reaction to them. If they incur costs in obeying his orders, he incurs costs in issuing them. That the costs are real and severe will come as an unpleasant surprise to a man once merely popular who has been elected or appointed to leadership. Indeed a serious problem in creating successful groups may be that of finding men who can bear the costs of command. For many leaders the chief of these costs may be loneliness. Both leaders and followers have reasons for avoiding one another some of the time, but the reasons come into effect in different situations, so that when one party has no reason to avoid the other, the other party may have one.

We have already seen how followers have some reason to avoid being subject to commands. When there is any danger of a leader's issuing them, some of the followers will be tempted to stay out of the way. On other occasions, however, they will be tempted to approach him, since he has goods at his disposal that they want, and then he may be the one to back off. A man may raise his status by first providing rewards to others as individuals, but once he is a leader and needs to maintain cohesion in his group, he must also distribute the rewards fairly. He cannot yield to the special pleading of particular followers without putting in danger his maintenance of distributive justice. Even allowing particular followers to seem close to him may lead others to suspect that he is playing favorites. A leader can easily become a man whose time is not his own. He too has good reasons at times for keeping some distance between himself and his followers.

A leader must accept the anxiety of making decisions and bear as best he can the guilt of making wrong ones. Nor will he find it easy to be natural and unselfconscious in the face of his followers' ambivalent attitude toward him and his toward them. On the more "social" occasions, such as an office party, which are supposed to symbolize the unity of the group, relations between them may have to be eased by a stylized ritual, on the one hand, and by alcohol, on the other.

Leadership, of course, has its rewards, especially the leader's conviction—sometimes his illusion—that he is getting things done that badly need doing and that others could not do nearly as well. But here we have been emphasizing its costs. From loneliness, from the burden of decision, from the ambivalence or importunity of his followers, the leader will seek occasional escape in the society of persons with whom he can relax and be at ease. In the nature of the case, the only such society open to him is the society of his equals: people who have nothing to ask of him that he may not ask of them in return—for to ask for something is to confess inferiority—and people whom he in turn has no right to command—for to command is to assert superiority. Because leaders in any one group are few in number, a leader is apt to find his social equals in the leaders of other groups; and it is a matter of observation that persons of high status in any one group are apt to have more "outside" contacts and friends than do persons of low status. Should outsiders who are his equals be hard to come by, the leader will be denied even this resource. A good example is the master of a ship at sea.

The leader, then, is apt to stand in some degree of aloofness, both chosen and enforced, from his followers. It may be a burden to him, and yet there is an ancient maxim claiming that even aloofness has its compensations, that at least a man cannot slough it off and remain a successful leader. This maxim is "familiarity breeds contempt."

Few maxims have more aroused the scorn of democratic Americans. Democracy has been uncomfortable with institutions as authoritarian as armies. Americans look on military life as an imposition, and on officers as incompetent until proved otherwise—until they have actually saved their outfit and the Republic. But military officers have been especially fond of citing the maxim, sometimes even to justify "social" distinctions that do not correspond to the realities of American life. Indeed we do right to scorn it if it justifies a man's avoiding other men and so implying his superiority to them on grounds, such as mere birth or money, that our society does not recognize as legitimate. Yet properly translated and circumscribed in its application, "familiarity breeds contempt" only states the facts of social life.

It simply means that command over a man and social equality with him are, in our terms, incongruent. If I am "familiar" with a man I treat him and he treats me as a social equal: we interact often and we are without reserve toward one another, and in this case he has a right to ridicule any pretensions I may advance to hold command over him. If, on the other hand, he has in fact accorded me command, it will make us both uncomfortable to be familiar: my greater power is at odds with the free give and take, the equality in influencing and in being influenced, that is at the heart of familiar friendship. Read again what Chaucer had to say on the subject in the epigraph of this book.

Once the experience of many men has established the incongruence of familiarity and command, someone who persists on treating a subordinate with familiarity or allows himself to be so treated presents stimuli, not only to the subordinate himself but to other subordinates who may be spectators of his behavior, that cast doubt on his own superiority and hence on the presumption that his orders are to be obeyed. To be sure, if he is a man of tact he may be able to remain more familiar with the subordinate and still keep more control over him than another man in his place could have done. Or if he and the subordinate are firmly established in their relative positions on other grounds they may be able to get away with it. A court jester may risk familiarity with a king, but he has to be a fool—someone firmly established as of no account—to do so. All the maxim says is that it will take tact or security: there is a limit to what a man can get away with in defiance of incongruence, and sooner or later he cannot have things both ways. The general point has been well made by Barnard (1948: 223): "Much experience demonstrates that those who are unequal cannot work well for long as equals. But experience also demonstrates that where differences of status are recognized formally, men of very unequal abilities and importance can and do work together well for long periods."

If the success of a group in accomplishing a task depends to some extent on the leader's exercise of command, and if his exercise of command depends on his staying to some extent aloof from his followers, then we might expect the leader's aloofness to be associated with the group's success. There is a piece of research by Fiedler (1958) that may be interpreted as bearing out this conclusion. It is true that studying the effectiveness of formally organized groups, such as those Fiedler worked with, takes us beyond the boundaries of elementary social behavior, but the opportunity to illustrate the results of the leader's aloofness is too tempting to be forgone.

Fiedler studied a number of different types of groups, running from basketball teams through bomber crews to open-hearth steel shops, always choosing groups whose effectiveness he could measure. Within each type he compared the effectiveness of a number of groups identical in organization. Thus he compared basketball teams by the number of games they won, bombers by scores in target bombing, open-hearth crews by the time it took them to make a given amount of steel.

The investigator also took various measurements of the sentiments of the members of the different groups, both the followers and the official leaders, such as the captains of the basketball teams. Besides a simple sociometric test, he used questions designed to get at the leader's "assumed similarity" with his followers. We shall not go into the methodology of the "assumed-similarity" score, but only take the investigator's word that a low score measured "an attitude toward others which may best be described as emotional or psychological distance." We believe that it measured what we have called aloofness.

The investigator then correlated the effectiveness scores of the groups of each type with their members' sociometric and "assumed-similarity" scores. For groups of every single type he found that effectiveness was higher, the more nearly two conditions were realized: first, the followers gave the leader a high degree of sociometric choice, that is, they approved of him highly—though we may suspect that the approval was of the sort we have come to call "respect" rather than the more intimate "liking"; and second, the leader himself had a low score on "assumed similarity," that is, he felt himself somewhat aloof from the others. In a few of the groups a third condition seemed also to play a part in effectiveness, namely that the leader himself gave a high choice to his "keyman," the member of the team who, next to himself, did most to make it effective. If leader and keyman were personal allies the group was particularly likely to succeed in its endeavors.

But the relationship between the leader's emotional distance and the effectiveness of his group is the finding we most want to emphasize here. The investigator was all the more surprised to find it holding good so regularly because it ran counter to his original hypothesis, which was that effectiveness would be associated with the leader's psychological *closeness* to his followers. His original assumption is just the one many American social scientists would have made. Indeed they have had so much to say against "authoritarianism" (which may have little to do with authority) and so much to say in favor of "democracy" (which may have little to do with political democracy) that their students have learned to shudder with guilt if they ever catch themselves giving a man a direct order or standing in the least apart from him socially.

Summary

A leader is someone who repeatedly issues suggestions, orders, and the like to many members of a group and they repeatedly comply. A person who becomes a leader in an informal group is likely to have already won high status in other respects. He wins high status as members discover that taking his advice rewards them individually; and this experience of theirs in turn makes it more likely that they will obey him collectively. A person cannot become a leader unless he at least attempts to influence others. Since making a suggestion, giving an order is an action like any other, he is more apt to make the attempt if his previous attempts have been successful in getting compliance. A leader is also likely to make decisions for the group as a whole, since it is idle for a person to decide what the content of an order ought to be unless he is able to get the order carried out. A member who is not a leader and who wishes the group to take a particular action will not make the suggestion in his own name but take it to someone who is a leader and get him to issue it. Only then will there be some chance that the other members will comply with it.

Ordinary members obey orders for essentially the same reasons as those for which leaders give them: they find that compliance is followed by their getting results and that the results are rewarding. Members are more likely to follow a person whose orders they have obeyed in the past and achieved success as a result than one whom they have obeyed without success or have not obeyed at all. Hence the great importance of a potential leader's getting his followers to obey him at least once: if they never obey, they will never have a chance of finding the result rewarding. But to say these things is only to describe from the followers' point of view, rather than that of the leader himself, the process by which leadership emerges.

An order is the same kind of thing as a norm, and what is true of conformity to norms is also true of compliance with orders. Some members obey orders, not because the results of doing so reward them personally but because these results reward other members, whose friendship they would forfeit if they disobeyed. Widespread good feeling within a group will therefore make it more likely that a man's followers will obey him, and so a wise leader will do his best to encourage the good feeling. By maintaining justice in the assignment of tasks and the division of rewards, he can at least discourage jealousies among his followers.

Since a leader who does any serious leading cannot help incurring costs for his followers, if only by limiting their freedom of action, the sentiments they express toward him are seldom those of easy friendship.

Instead, their sentiments are ambivalent: they may admire the leader but not feel close to him. Once this kind of relationship between leaders and followers is generally recognized, a leader who displays social familiarity with his followers casts symbolic doubt on his superiority to them and hence on his right to have them obey him. Thus both leaders and followers will have some reason to remain aloof from one another. Indeed some degree of aloofness may add to the success of leadership.

13 Stratification

THE PURPOSE OF THE PRESENT CHAPTER IS TO PULL TOGETHER a number of phenomena lightly touched on in earlier chapters and show that they form a single complex or structure. Let us recall what these phenomena are. As we saw in Chapter 3 on relationships and balance, persons who continue to interact with one another tend to become more similar to one another, and, vice versa, persons who begin by being similar to one another tend to increase their interaction with one another. As we saw in Chapter 8 on structures of esteem and interaction, persons tend to direct interaction toward their superiors in status but also toward their equals, the concrete pattern of interaction in a group being some resultant of the two tendencies. As we saw in Chapter 9 on status, persons who are equal in status in one respect tend to become or remain equal in status in other respects, their equality further implying that any goods or services they exchange are in some sense similar. And, as we saw in the last chapter, both leaders and followers have good reason on some occasions for avoiding one another and, by that very fact, for seeking out their equals instead.

Equality and Similarity

Finally, there is the set of findings we wish to begin by analysing. Let us go back to the research at the New York State Training School for Girls at Hudson, New York, some of the results of which we considered in Chapter 7 on field research. We shall remember that the investigator asked the girls at Hudson to make sociometric choices of other girls on three main criteria: living with them in one of the cottages into which the school was divided, working with them, and spending leisure time with them. Choices on the living and working criteria turned out to be much alike in the sense that, if a girl chose another for living, she

299

was apt to choose her for working too, and so the investigator lumped the two sets of choices together. The more choices a girl received on these criteria—that is, the higher the esteem in which she was held—the more likely she was to perform actions rewarding to many other girls under the circumstances in which they lived and worked together. Her ranking on both what she received and what she gave in social exchange made her status high.

As for choices on the criterion of spending leisure time with another girl, we did not consider them in detail. Let us do so now. What were the facts? First, choice for leisure overlapped with choice for living and working much less than the two latter overlapped with one another. Whereas a girl was apt to name the same other girls for both living and working, she named different ones for leisure: of all girls chosen for leisure, 64 percent were chosen for leisure only. Second, a girl chose, on the average, fewer other girls for leisure than she did for living and working, and third, a higher proportion of these choices were mutual choices, those in which two girls chose one another. Finally, though there was little overlap in choice between living-working and leisure, the two were still related to one another in an interesting way.

As the investigator says, a girl in making her choices for leisure tended not to direct them to girls highly chosen for living and working but elsewhere. But the "elsewhere" was not anywhere else (Jennings, 1950: 257–258):

> The "elsewhere" is not very far afield from her own position: it is predominantly to those members of the community's population who have approximately the same choice-status as the chooser herself shows. . . . In other words, although she directs a predominant amount of choices towards a relatively few well-chosen individuals for living-working, when she is choosing for spending leisure time with others she seldom selects those very individuals, shifting instead to those who are more nearly within her "sociometric class" in the official life of the community.

In short, a girl was more apt to choose another for leisure, the more nearly the other's status was equal to her own.

This last finding alone goes far toward accounting for the others. If a girl confined her choices for leisure to those who were roughly her equals in status, she had fewer others to choose from than she would have had if the whole population at Hudson had been open to her choice. And in fact a girl made fewer choices for leisure than she did for living and working. Since any chosen other was limiting her choice in the same way as the girl did herself, and since for both the number of others open for choice was small, we might indeed expect purely as a matter of chance that mutual choice for leisure would be frequent—unless, of course, the number of choices girls made for leisure decreased even more than the number of girls open for choice. And although there was in general little overlap between choices for living-working and choices for leisure, we should expect—which was the fact—that what little overlap did take place was most apt to do so in the mutual choices among girls of high status. Since a girl held high status if she received many choices on the former criterion, including choices from other girls of high status, and since on the latter criterion high-status girls, like the rest, tended to choose their social equals, then it followed that high-status girls were especially likely to choose one another on both counts. Yet we have every reason to believe that the small number and high mutuality of choices for leisure was not the result of chance alone.

The esteem a girl earned depended on the degree to which others found her actions rewarding; and therefore two girls held in roughly equal esteem must have performed actions that were in some respect similar. But, as we have seen, persons that perform similar actions are apt to hold similar values, and so they are apt to be rewarded by one another even more under some circumstances than they are by third parties. To use the current phrase, they have much in common. Let us recall, for instance, the requirements for a pleasant ringer-bundler team in the supermarkets. One of the requirements was that the two workers concerned should have similar backgrounds and so find it easy to talk to one another. Of course people can reward one another by exchanging actions that are different, that are complementary, as well as by actions that are similar. What we are now suggesting is that the former type of exchange is apt to be associated with inequality between them in status, the latter with equality.

The more similar, moreover, are the values of two persons, the more apt they are to reward one another in ways that go beyond whatever earns them status in the larger group. Thus at Hudson a shared taste for, say, bird-watching might not have been relevant grounds for choosing a girl to live with in company with a relatively large number of others. What would count there would have been behavior that helped the whole enterprise go more easily and pleasantly. But we are now talking about leisure, about what people do when their cooperation with a number of others is temporarily at an end. The point about leisure is that it leaves one free to indulge one's idiosyncrasies, and a shared taste for bird-watching might make all the difference in choosing a companion for one's leisure. When we come to think about it, then, the fact that girls of equal status were particularly apt to choose one another for leisure seems perfectly natural, for girls of similar status are apt to be similar in other ways as well. Indeed if the argument presented in Chapters 9 and 11 is correct, they are apt to *become* more similar in the course of maintaining their equality in status. And similars are apt to be able to reward one another.

Whatever the reasons for it, the fact itself was clear. The investigator at Hudson talked informally and unsystematically to the girls about the reasons why they chose others, and she found that they were, indeed, particularly apt to choose for leisure other girls whose values resembled their own. One girl went so far as to say: "You'll think this is a crazy reason but it's the truth. She likes noise like I like noise. I'm always holding myself in in the house, don't yell around or nothing. Susan and I race all over the place in our spare time. . . ." (Jennings, 1950: 260) We cannot tell whether the similarity in values was itself determined by a similarity in the girls' backgrounds, a subject the investigator did not go into. Note that the more idiosyncratic were a girl's values, the fewer people, naturally, she could find to share them—which was undoubtedly one of the reasons why the girls at Hudson made fewer choices for leisure than they did for living and working.

Equality and Escape

A girl at Hudson tended to spend her leisure time with her equals in status not only because they could positively reward her but also because her superiors and inferiors could hurt her. We have just considered the reasons for the first effect; let us now turn to the reasons for the second. If the commonest explanation a girl offered for choosing another girl for leisure was that "she likes the same things I do," the next commonest was that "I can be myself with her." But this very explanation implied that she could not be herself with third parties, that with them she felt under some kind of constraint. In interacting with them she incurred, as we say, costs. Since choice for spending leisure tended to go to social equals, these third parties could only be, on the average, a girl's superiors or inferiors.

What were these costs, and how were they incurred? A person of high status is a person who has provided rewards to others that are rare and valuable because a relatively large number of these others demand them. Accordingly, if more than one field of activity is open to members of a group, the field in which status is won—and lost—is apt to be the most "public" one, the one in which the largest number of members participate. At Hudson this was the sphere of living and working, in the cottages and shops. Here a few girls won high status by providing services much in demand by many others, but here too other girls found their inadequacies exposed. The same process that put some up, put others down: one person's superiority implies another's inferiority. No doubt the rest of the girls were glad, up to a point, to get the services of their superiors, but the price they paid was a tacit confession of their own lower status.

At Hudson, moreover, as in other groups, persons of high status were particularly apt to exercise command, even though it was unofficial command, over the group as a whole, if there was any combined result the members wished to achieve. In the last chapter we examined the costs, as well as the rewards, incurred by obedience to command: the constraint a superior imposes on a subordinate and the criticism he directs at him when he fails to live up to group norms or do his part in reaching goals set by the superior.

The investigator cited the costs a girl might incur in criticism and, more generally, in trying to live up to the standards of the larger group, the group whose members lived or worked together. For instance, she quoted one girl, who had not yet found a companion for her leisure time, as saying of another: "Lena's wonderful in our house but for me she's useless as a personal friend—one minute she says she understands you and the next she's telling you you're just awful." And the investigator spoke of "responsibilities, cares, and awarenesses which come with participation in work relationships or common living relationships wherein the . . . individual may be urged to 'improve,' 'raise the standards,' and, in general, may feel threatened with guilt, the cause of which he may be at a loss to discern" (Jennings, 1950: 270–72).

None of this means that the interaction of persons of different status, of superior and subordinate, in the public activities of a group does not win them rewards, though not necessarily equal rewards. What it does mean is that it also incurs them costs. By the deprivation-satiation proposition, the value of the rewards tends to decrease over time relative to their cost, until finally the cost becomes too high, at least for the time being. Then a member of a group will be ready to escape from the costs of participation in the public field. The subordinate will be ready to escape from the constraint imposed by a superior, and his own subordinates in turn will be ready to escape from *him*. As we saw in the last chapter, the superior will also be ready to escape from the importunities of an inferior, from his demands for personal favors. In the nature of the case, neither has any field of activity to which he can escape except the relatively private field, the field of "after hours," of leisure—the field, as we shall see, of "social" interaction in the special, party-going sense of the word. And in this field neither can count on escaping in the company of any other sort of persons but his approximate equals. This is the reason why at Hudson as elsewhere choice for leisure and choice of equals tend to go together.

Equals are persons who perform equally valuable activities. Accordingly, they can exchange rewards on even terms and thus escape the costs of confessing any inferiority. Indeed, as we have seen, if they do not exchange rewards on even terms, they do not long remain equals. At Hudson a girl's equals could not make her feel inferior, nor could she make them feel so. Only with them, therefore, could she relax and "be herself," free of judging or of being judged, free of the necessity for command or obedience; and only them could she really "like" in the American sense of liking, for "liking" implies an absence of constraint, and constraint is rarely absent from relations between superiors and inferiors.

Mind you, a girl that chose another for leisure seldom called her "wonderful" as she often called the girls she chose for living and working. She was seldom deceived as to her companion's absolute worth: "a poor thing but mine own" was apt to be her apologetic attitude. This was only natural. She could hardly help observing how much—or little— the other girl had to offer the community and how much—or little—esteem she earned there. What made the other a suitable companion for leisure was not that her behavior was highly rewarding in itself, though it might be if the two shared the same special interests. Since it was behavior that became valuable only after the prior and more serious demands of living and working had been satisfied, it was apt to consist of the small change of sociability, though sociability might then, of course, become very valuable indeed. Whatever its inherent value, the crucial feature of the other's behavior was that it resembled the chooser's own, and so could not make her feel small. No matter how little the other had to give, it was at least purchased at a low cost in social inferiority. For even if one's reward from an action is low, one still has a profit and is apt to repeat the action if its cost is lower still.

A Resultant of Superiority and Equality

In earlier chapters and now in the present one we have encountered two tendencies: a tendency for persons to express approval of, and to interact often with, others who are in some sense "better" than they are themselves, and a tendency for them to like and interact with their equals. We now ask how the two tendencies might combine with one another to form some overall pattern. As far as interaction is concerned, one possibility is suggested by the results of the study by Riley, Cohn, Tobey, and Riley (1954) of two grades in eight New Jersey high schools, which we examined in Chapter 8 (p. 190). As for liking, it is at least conceivable that under some circumstances, especially when no sharp distinction can be made between "work" and "leisure," the two tendencies might combine to produce a resultant tendency for persons to express liking for others who are a little "better" than they are themselves but not much better—to choose "up" but only a little "up." To examine this possibility, let us go back to the research by Bales and his associates that we considered in the last chapter (Bales, 1953).

As we shall remember, the investigator found, in observing several discussion sessions of five-man groups, that on the average the member who interacted most often received most choices from the other members on the criteria of "best ideas," "guidance," and "leadership." In fact the relationship between frequency of interaction and a combined measure that might be called "contribution to the group's task" was approximately linear: the more often a member interacted, the higher the choice others gave him as a person who had done much to help the group reach its goal.

The investigator also asked the members to choose others on the simple criterion of "liking," and he found that in this case the relationship with interaction was not linear but curvilinear. The best-liked members were only second and third in frequency of interaction, and the top interactor was only third in liking choices received, followed by the two least frequent interactors. In short, the curve bulged upward in the middle and drooped at both ends, though more toward the low end in interaction than toward the high. (Look once more at Figure 4 on p. 287.) In the last chapter we concentrated on the top leader, and used Bales' data to illustrate the ambivalent sentiments men express toward persons in command, sentiments better called respect than liking: members who contribute little are little liked, and members, such as the top leader, who contribute much but in so doing make the others incur high costs, are both liked and disliked. In this chapter we stop concentrating on the top leader alone and consider the whole shape of the curve.

In explaining his results, the investigator has much to say about the best-liked man, who was also No. 2 in frequency of interaction. Just because the No. 1 man concentrated on getting the job done, the investigator argues that the No. 2 man was forced to specialize in another kind of activity, particularly apt to win him the liking of others: he specialized in what the investigator calls the "socio-emotional" field—patting people on the back, approving without criticizing, and easing tense situations with jokes. Indeed the fact, which is apparent in Figure 4, that the No. 2 man was not named quite as often for "best ideas" and "guidance" as he would have been if the relationship between interaction and choice on this criterion had been perfectly linear does suggest that he may have been performing other services than those contributing directly to the solution of the group's problem. Bales also believes that a particularly stable solution to the struggle for status that often rends the upper levels of a group may be an alliance of personal friendship between the No. 1 interactor who is, in Bales' terms, the "instrumental-adaptive" leader and the No. 2 man who is a specialist in the "socio-emotional" field. Bales' argument is borne out, in part at least, by Fiedler's (1958) finding, which we also considered in the last chapter, that the leader of a successful group is apt to be on particularly good terms with his key man or second in command.

Yet the behavior of the No. 2 man cannot fully explain the pattern of liking in Bales' groups. After all, the No. 3 initiator of interaction received almost as many liking choices as did No. 2, and yet there seems to be little evidence that he too was a "socio-emotional" specialist. Some more general force must have been at work. What we should like to know is not just the total score in liking that each member received, but the way each member distributed his liking among the others. That is, we should appreciate having a liking matrix. Since Bales does not provide us with one, let us choose some hypothesis, construct a matrix embodying it, and then see how close it comes to generating Bales' results. Our hypothesis is that liking choice in Bales' groups resembled leisure-time choice at Hudson and tended to go from a man to his fellow members to the degree that they were his sociometric equals on other criteria, but that when two others were equally near the chooser's own rank, he chose the higher man instead of the lower one. In short, he chose "up" but only a little "up."

The detailed rules for constructing our matrix are the following:

1. *O, P, Q, R,* and *S* are the five members of the group, and this is their order from high to low in frequency of interaction.
2. Each member gives a score of 4 to the man he likes best, 3 to the man he likes next best, and so on.
3. Each member likes best the man whose rank on interaction is nearest his own; second best, the man whose rank is next nearest; and so on.
4. When a member has two others equally near him in rank, as *Q* has *P* and *R* equally near him, he gives more liking to the man who is higher in rank.

The matrix that results from these rules is shown in Table 12.

Table 12 Sentiment Matrix: Equality and Superiority

		O	P	Q	R	S	TOTAL GIVEN
			LIKING CHOICE TO				
	O		4	3	2	1	10
	P	4		3	2	1	10
LIKING CHOICE FROM	*Q*	2	4		3	1	10
	R	1	2	4		3	10
	S	1	2	3	4		10
TOTAL RECEIVED		8	12	13	11	6	

In this matrix the important thing to look at is the bottom row of figures, which shows the total liking received by each member and thus corresponds to the curve showing the relationship between interaction and liking in the Bales data. We submit that the two curves are of the same general character. The best-liked men, and nearly equal to one another in liking received, are the Nos. 2 and 3 interactors. From this high tableland the amount of choice drops off at both ends of the curve but more toward the lower end in frequency of interaction than toward the upper. Our matrix, to be sure, makes liking for the top interactor and task leader even lower than it is in the Bales results: he was better liked in reality than we allowed for in the rules for constructing the matrix. Nevertheless we may guess that the hypothesis embodied in the matrix corresponds to a real tendency in the Bales groups. Indeed O. J. Bartos in an unpublished memorandum has shown that the rules for constructing our matrix will predict actual popularity rankings in ten-man Bales' groups to a rank-order coefficient of 0.76.

In the Bales groups liking choice was the same sort of thing as leisure-time choice at Hudson. Just as the girls there were apt to choose for leisure other girls who were nearly their sociometric equals on the living-working criterion, so the members of the Bales groups were apt to choose others who were nearly their equals in contribution to the group task. The only difference is this: we have no evidence for Hudson that, when members were faced with two others equally close to them in rank, they tended to give the higher choice to the member of higher rank.

We must believe that similar tendencies had similar causes: the increasing costs incurred by men in interaction with their superiors in status make it worth their while to exchange rewards of a different kind with, and to express a less respectful approval for, their equals. Although the design of Bales' research gave the members no opportunity for interaction during leisure time, the kind of behavior he calls "socio-emotional" is in fact the kind that people are most apt to exchange on "social" occasions.

Stratification in Society at Large

The complex of phenomena related to choice and interaction among equals in status in small groups has much in common with what sociologists call in society at large *social stratification* or the development of status systems. Let us review the gross similarities. First, the status of persons in all stratified societies, whether their status is inherited or achieved, is principally determined by their occupations, in the largest sense of that word, and by the incomes their occupations win for them. That is, status in society at large as in small groups is won or recognized through what people give and what they get in social exchange, especially exchange in what we have called the more public field of activity. Second, the more nearly equal persons are in public status, the more apt they are to interact in the private field, the sphere of leisure, of after working hours, of "social" interaction: eating together, playing together, going to parties together. Since marriage is in the first instance an intimate and private relationship, though given public recognition, marriage also tends to be contracted between social equals, even in societies where there is no formal prescription to this effect. Naturally the tendency for persons to interact with their equals in status on "social" occasions does not require, even in a small group, that a man interact with every one of his equals, and in society at large that would be impossible. It only requires that those he does interact with socially should tend to fall into that class. In big societies, this tendency produces a diffuse network of social interaction stretching across the society, with some members of party-going group *A* also being members of party-going group *B*, some *B*s belonging also to *C*, and so forth.

Third, persons who are roughly equal in status tend also to become similar in other respects besides the occupations and income that win them their status in the first instance. And in becoming similar to their equals they become different from their superiors and inferiors. The reasons why frequent interaction between persons should be related to their becoming more similar have already been discussed under the headings of balance and conformity in Chapters 3 and 5. The relationship holds good just as much of persons who interact because they are equals in status as it does of persons who interact for other reasons. At any rate, persons who are equals in status tend—and remember always that we are speaking of statistically significant and not of perfect correlations—to express similar attitudes, to learn similar values, even to develop what are called similar styles of life. If indeed the relationships between similarities and differences of status, on the one hand, and similarities and differences of styles of life, on the other, become sufficiently well established, a person who recognizes another as following a style of life similar to his own may continue to interact with him as an equal, even if the other's rank on some other dimension of status, such as his occupation, should fall somewhat below his own.

The phenomena of stratification are so similar in small groups to what they are in large societies that they must have been produced by the same processes in both places. We have already suggested what some of the processes are. Indeed in many fields of activity no sharp line can be drawn between the phenomena that appear in small groups and those that appear in society at large. Least of all can one be drawn in the field of social stratification.

Speaking of sharp lines, we must here take notice of a possible source of confusion that lies within the word *stratification* itself. Stratification naturally implies strata, that is, layers, and layers in turn seem to imply that one can determine where one layer ends and another begins: there is some breach of continuity between them. Yet the phenomenon usually called stratification could occur—a tendency for equals in status to inter- act with one another on "social" occasions and to behave in somewhat similar ways—without any sharp lines developing between social layers or, as we shall now call them, social classes. The process of stratification could just as well create something like a color spectrum, in which "higher" bands of color—purple would be a good one—could be recog- nized, then somewhat lower ones, like red, and so forth, but in which the changes between the colors would be continuous and no line other than an arbitrary one could mark, for instance, where purple ended and red began.

Both types of stratification occur in societies of the present and have occurred in those of the past. In some societies, one type has changed into the other. Not long ago it was possible on a number of criteria to distinguish unambiguously between an Englishman who was a gentle- man from one who was not. That is, there used to be a clearly defined English upper class, no doubt with lesser distinctions within it. It is not possible to draw any such line today in England, and it may never have been possible to draw one in the United States. This does not mean that there are no persons in the United States who may fairly be called mem- bers of an upper class, any more than that there are no colors that may fairly be called purple. It only means that there are some persons, just as there are some colors, that can only arbitrarily be assigned to one class or band rather than to another.

Let us try to illustrate the matter by another little model. Suppose that there are six members of a group: a, b, c, d, e, and f, and that they are ranked from top to bottom on two dimensions of status, I and II. Consider first the following pattern (1) of rankings on the two dimensions:

I_1	II_1
a	b
b	a
c	d
d	c
e	f
f	e

Here we should be justified in arguing that there were three definite classes, composed of a and b, c and d, e and f, respectively. We should be justified in doing so because a and b have more in common with one another than either has with c and d, and so forth.

Consider next the following pattern (2) of rankings:

I_2	II_2
a	a
b	d
c	b
d	e
e	c
f	f

Here it is not possible as it was in the first pattern to lump any two persons together unambiguously as members of the same class. And yet the rankings in the two patterns are certainly correlated with one another: there is a top and a bottom in both.

We think it only right to raise the present issue, but since we are more interested in the fundamental social processes than in the way they combine in particular cases, we are not going to attempt to specify the conditions under which groups develop one type of stratification rather than another. Even when we talk, as we shall in the next chapter, about upper-, middle-, and lower-status members of groups, we shall not imply, nor will our failure to do so invalidate our argument, that at the boundaries the assignment of individuals to classes is anything but arbitrary: a lower member of the upper class we might perfectly well have called an upper member of the middle. Nor shall we ask whether members of classes are also class-conscious, nor whether class interests are something different from the interests of individual members of the classes. These are questions for sociologists who deal with the characteristics of societies at large.

Social Climbing and the Like

In the field of stratification as in so many others, once the fundamental relationships are established and recognized by the members of a group, this very fact makes possible the secondary development of behavior controlled by new rewards and costs predicated on the fundamental relationships themselves. Thus if equals in status tend in fact to perform similar kinds of activities, then a person who would otherwise be another's inferior but who can, by hook or by crook, imitate the other's behavior, has presented an outward sign that he is the other's equal. Even if he is unable to persuade the person he is imitating that the two of them are peers, he may be able to convince less well-informed third parties who are spectators of the scene, and this result may be rewarding to him: they may accord him higher status. When we use words like "convince" to describe situations like this, we mean, of course, that he presents a stimulus to third parties, under which they may alter their behavior in his favor. Such imitation is one of the well-known techniques of social climbing.

The climber may have to imitate a number of different activities carried out by his superiors. If equals tend to interact with one another socially, and if, as we showed in Chapter 3 on relationships and balance, people who interact with one another frequently tend to become more similar in their activities than they were to begin with, then equals tend to become similar in ways other than those that originally determined their equality. Accordingly, a social climber may have to imitate, not one activity only, but a whole style of life.

Unfortunately the trick can work both ways. What is the use of the climber's imitating a superior if that pulls the latter down rather than the former up? Much depends on which of the two is the more fixed in his status, on which presents to others the more unambiguous and unshakable signs of it. Naturally the climber hopes that the status of the superior is fixed while his own is movable. But what about the superior? The climber, by adopting behavior in some respect similar to his own, may signal to third parties that he now resembles his inferior in status rather than that his inferior resembles him. Accordingly, some superiors—or those that hold themselves to be such—continually attempt, over and above the other tendencies for a body of equals to develop a distinct style of life, to differentiate their behavior from that of their inferiors, to invent new activities, new "in" things to do, which display their status afresh to the initiates, as social climbers progressively discover, imitate, and wear out the usefulness of the old things as symbols of status. Such persons are the more liable to do so, the more insecure is their own status, the fewer, that is, are the other status symbols they present that climbers, for one reason or another, cannot imitate. This may mean that such persons are now, or have recently been, social climbers themselves. The most effective symbol of high and secure status is, of course, showing no indication that one cares about status at all, but it is often a great strain to present it.

Remember that there are two kinds of social climber. There is the man who manages to increase the substance of his power, whereupon "social" interaction with his former superiors and the other outward signs of a rise in his status are bound to follow sooner or later. His former superiors may attempt for a time to deny him the secondary signs of status, but the evidence is that they will fail, and that they are silly even to try. It is unwise, except for a very high price indeed, to tempt the resentment of a person commanding real power. The other kind of climber is the one who, by successfully presenting the outward signs, is accepted as holding high status, but who does not command the substance of power. Naturally, getting himself accepted as a man of high status may itself get him some power. He may also succeed only in getting himself exposed. Upon the whole, his task is more difficult than that of the other kind of climber.

We are far from implying that everyone is a potential social climber, certainly not a social climber of the second class. For most persons the costs incurred are too steep. As persons at a higher level than one's own develop their own distinctive styles of life—and as one's own level develops *its* own—"social" interaction with superiors becomes for many people increasingly uncomfortable. It is not easy to adjust to unfamiliar behavior, and yet one of the chief virtues of "social" interaction, in the special sense of the word "social," should be its easiness. The contempt many of us feel for the second or "bad" class of social climber rests on his apparent willingness to put up with humiliations, to put up with discomforts, which we flatter ourselves we would never put up with. No, we are certainly not implying that everyone is a potential social climber. We are only pointing to the social relationships that a man, if he does happen to be a climber, will have to try to turn to his account.

We turn now to another of these relationships. If persons tend in fact to interact with their equals on "social" occasions, then a person who would otherwise remain another's inferior, but who can manage to get invited to a party or eat a meal with him, and who can be seen doing so, has presented an outward sign that he is the other's equal. The other may not be prepared to admit the fact, but the climber may thus be able to persuade third parties of its truth—third parties who are spectators of the scene but less well-informed. As before, the trick cuts both ways. "Social" interaction between persons hitherto unequal in status may be taken by the superior as a threat to his superiority, and hence he may try to avoid it or to deny it to the other. Our pretended superiors often try to avoid being seen in too intimate a relationship with us on "social" occasions. And superior groups often try to be exclusive, partly for this reason but partly also because, if it is generally true that, the higher the level of status, the smaller is the number of persons occupying that level, then the small size of the group becomes itself a status symbol. Note that these processes make the relationship between equality and "social" interaction even firmer than it would otherwise have been. Alas! that the laws of elementary social behavior should also be the laws of snobbery—but they are.

On the other hand, a man whose superior status is so firmly established that he need not give it a thought, a man who has reached the condition we call social certitude, may allow his inferiors "social" access to him. His status is congruent and superior on so many counts that he can afford, so to speak, to let it be incongruent on this one. Association with him can bring up the ostensible status of others and so can reward them without threatening to bring his own status down. Accordingly he has acquired a new basis for power, a new way of earning their esteem to add to those he controls already. As usual, the man who gets some more is the man who already has something.

The Initiation of "Social" Interaction

In his interesting book, *Social Psychology,* Roger Brown (1965: 96) points to a norm apparently followed in so many societies that it may fairly be called a human universal. The norm states that, if "social" interaction is to occur between persons unequal in status, the superior is the one that ought to initiate the interaction and not the inferior. For instance, the boss (or his wife) ought to be the first to invite the subordinate to his house, not the subordinate, the boss. We agree with Brown that the norm is universal. Of course, like all norms it is a statement of what ought to happen and not what always does happen. Yet it could hardly have become or remained a norm unless there was some tendency for actual behavior to match it spontaneously.

Brown argues that it is a very queer kind of norm. Since the inferior, he says, has more to gain from "social" interaction than the superior, we might expect that the inferior would make the first move toward getting it and not the superior. Yet the norm says that the reverse ought to happen. Brown does not attempt to account for the reversal, though we bet he could have done so if he had tried. Since he did not, we are free to make the attempt. The problem itself is not of the first importance, but it illustrates again how the primary relationships of social behavior give rise to secondary ones, which tend to reinforce the first.

Let us look more generally at the initiation of interaction in pair exchanges. (We shall not be concerned here with the initiation of orders, commands, directed to the members of a group as a whole.) Brown's assumption—that the person who values the more highly the reward to be obtained from an exchange will be the one to initiate it—applies very well to interaction between inferior and superior in what we call the public, or "business," or practical, rather than the "social" field. Thus Other in the office had more to offer Person than Person, at least initially, had to offer Other. Accordingly, Person went to Other to ask for help and in this sense initiated interaction between them. Note that though Other might lose working time when he provided the help, he had nothing to lose socially. Indeed it was by providing help that he won his social position.

But look at what happens after rankings in status have developed. Once it is established that the person who needs what you have to give more than you need, at least at first, what he has to give is your inferior in status, then you, by initiating interaction with him in the sense of forcing on him what he needs and you can well spare, are threatening to lower his status relative to yours. But to threaten another is to stimulate his resentment. Accordingly, superiors often try to avoid giving practical assistance to others unless the others ask for it first. If the others initiate the exchange, they have by their behavior indicated that they have accepted in advance and discounted the costs they will incur in recognized inferiority, and that they have no reason for resentment. Accordingly, the norm, and not just the actual behavior, in exchanges involving personal help, favors, and the like in the business or practical field, is that the inferior takes the initiative.

In the case of exchanges in the "social" field, the norm is just the reverse: the superior ought to initiate the interaction. Yet the same general tendency accounts for the new norm as well as for the old: only the circumstances to which it is applied differ. Once it is established that persons who interact with one another on "social" occasions tend to be equals in status, a person hitherto your inferior, who invites you to join him at a party he is giving, threatens by his action to bring your status down toward his own. Your status may be so secure that you do not feel the threat, but he need not be sure of that. To threaten another is, we repeat, to stimulate his resentment, and a superior, if he is resentful, is apt to be able to do something about it. Accordingly, inferiors often avoid taking the initiative in seeking social interaction with superiors. Thus they escape the risk of receiving a humiliating rebuff themselves, and they leave to the superior his freedom of choice. If, on the other hand, the superior initiates the exchange, he certainly presents no threat to the inferior; he has indicated by his behavior that he has accepted in advance and discounted the cost he might incur in lowered status, and that he has no reason for resentment. If, therefore, anyone is to initiate interaction in the "social" field, it is apt to be the superior, and what many persons are inclined to do naturally tends to become a norm that all ought to follow. If the laws of elementary social behavior are the laws of snobbery, they are also the laws of politeness. Politeness is largely concerned with how to avoid presenting social threats to others.

An inferior may have still another reason for hesitating before he invites a superior to take part in "social" interaction. If the invitation can be observed by his own equals, they may accuse him of trying to curry favor with the boss. In effect, he is symbolically setting himself above them, and his relations with them may suffer as a result. No such result will follow if the superior initiates the interaction, especially if he invites a number of his subordinates at a time. Nor will it follow if the subordinates as a body initiate "social" interaction with a superior; and indeed much interaction between superiors and inferiors begins in one of these last two ways.

In the interests of pursuing an interesting problem in explanation we have undoubtedly made too much of this whole business of the initiation of "social" interaction. Though the tendencies described are present in all societies, they vary greatly in strength from one society to another. They make much less difference—though still some difference—in a society where most men hold a democratic ethos than they do in one where men are highly sensitive about status, as they were, for instance, in the France of Louis XIV.

Links between Alternate Statuses

We have seen that equals tend to like and interact with one another particularly on "social" occasions. But how about people who fall short of complete equality, particularly those between whom some distinction is made, but who are still nearly equal, so that their status relative to one another remains in doubt? Earlier we gave brief consideration to the effects of social certitude and incertitude on the interaction between men, and now we must return to the problem. In this field we possess very few good studies, which gives us all the more reason to consider one whose results were clear-cut, even though it is less concerned with elementary social behavior and more concerned with status as formally recognized in society at large than we should like it to be.

The research in question was carried out by Zander, Cohen, and Stotland (1959). In six large American cities the investigators and their associates interviewed three different kinds of professional people concerned with mental health: psychiatrists, psychologists, and social workers. In all, they interviewed about 150 members of each profession. They first asked each subject to assess the authority and influence of members of the other two professions in comparison with his own authority and influence. As we should expect from our general knowledge of American society, all three professions agreed that the psychiatrists, who of course held medical degrees, had more authority and influence than did the other two groups—though the psychologists and social workers were not quite as sure about it as the psychiatrists were themselves. As for the relationship between psychologists and social workers, these two professions saw themselves as about equal in authority.

The investigators then asked each subject how much he wanted to be respected and liked by members of the other two professions and to have professional and social contacts with them. In accordance with the higher status of the psychiatrists, the other groups were more likely to express such wishes about psychiatrists than the psychiatrists were to express them about the other groups. And in accordance with their higher recognized authority, the psychiatrists were more ready to complain about the behavior of the other two professions than were the other two to complain about the psychiatrists.

Much more interesting and much closer to the elementary processes of social behavior were the differences within each profession. Those psychologists and social workers who saw themselves as holding relatively high authority expressed less desire for   professional or social contact with psychiatrists than did psychologists and social workers who saw themselves as holding little authority. Among the psychiatrists, on the other hand, the relationship reversed itself, and those psychiatrists who saw themselves as holding relatively high authority expressed more desire for contact with members of the other professions than did psychiatrists who saw themselves as holding little authority. We may reasonably guess that most of the persons who believed that they held relatively high or low authority must in fact have held high or low status, respectively, within their professions. And then we may say that the persons who wanted least contact with the other group were the low-status members of the high-status group (the psychiatrists) and the high-status members of the low-status group (the psychologists and social workers). That is, the persons closest in status, provided that they belonged to different groups, wanted least contact. This finding may seem to run counter to our proposition that equals will seek out interaction with one another, but we must remember that we are not concerned with equals here: by the standards of American society, psychiatrists in general are accorded higher status than the other two professions. We are concerned instead with persons who, though relatively close to one another, are still sharply divided by status.

As we saw earlier, a man established as another's equal hesitates to take any step that might suggest his inferiority to the other; but a man already established as the other's inferior shows no such hesitation. In the present case, there is no question of absolute equality, yet something of the same sort occurred. In the presence of two broad status classes, the members of the lower class that stood highest within their class were most anxious to avoid contact with members of the upper class, presumably because such contacts would have given the upper class an opportunity to remind them of an inferiority they were far from feeling within their own group. If frequent social contacts could have ended, as they can in some cases of social climbing, by winning for a psychologist full acceptance as a member of the upper class, no doubt he would, by the success proposition, have been more eager to make them. But only a medical degree could make him a psychiatrist, and in these circumstances he had little to gain and much to lose by mere interaction. In the same way, the members of the upper class who stood lowest within their class were most anxious to avoid contacts with members of the lower class, presumably because they might have found it difficult to maintain, over against these others, a superiority they were far from feeling within their own group. Interaction with members of the other class presented a threat to both these types of person.

But the members of the upper class who were firmly established as high in status and the members of the lower class who were firmly established as low had nothing to lose by contacts with the other group and welcomed them as at least a possibility. These persons were more congruent in status than were the others, who were either low men in a high group or high men in a low group. We are forcibly reminded of the classic peasant who, just because "he knows his place" can speak up to the lord of the manor, and of the lord who can be perfectly at ease with members of the "lower orders" because after all they cannot conceivably shake his effortless superiority. It is the *bourgeois,* the man in the middle, who is nervous about his relations with other classes.

Phenomena like these bear a family resemblance to what anthropologists have come to call the division of a group into alternate generations (see Homans, 1950: 215–16, 251). In some primitive kinship systems, the members of two generations that are closest to one another, like fathers and sons, are apt to express respect rather than close affection for one another and to avoid one another except when required to work together. Remember that the older generation often exercises command over the younger, but that the younger will eventually replace the older. Members, on the other hand, of alternate generations—that is, generations separated by an intervening one, like grandfathers and grandsons—cannot be rivals, and the older may not even have authority over the younger. In consequence they are apt to express close affection for one another and to interact frequently and without constraint. In the one case the differences in status are determined by differences in generation and in the other by differences in profession, but in both cases the persons nearest in status, provided some line is drawn between them, are the persons whose relations are most strained.

Summary

People often make a distinction between their relatively more public and their more private spheres of activity. It is in the public sphere, where services of different kinds and values are exchanged in a network including a large number of the members of a group, that members become differentiated in status. In this sphere members interact often with, and express approval or respect for, others who are "better" than they are themselves in the services they perform. In the private sphere, that of leisure and "social" intercourse in the narrow sense of the term, they are more likely to interact often with, and express a more intimate liking for, members who are approximately their equals in the public sphere. At a time when the rewards of public interaction are temporarily exhausted, inferiors thus escape the costs of their inferiority and superiors, the costs of their superiority. Equals are also likely to be similar in values and abilities and so are often able to reward one another by the exchange of similar activities, activities which by that very fact cannot imply inferiority. By so interacting, equals are apt to become still more alike in their behavior, even to the extent of developing styles of life distinct from those of their superiors or inferiors. By these processes a phenomenon develops in small groups analogous to stratification in society at large.

If no firm distinction can be made between the public and the private sphere of activity, the tendencies to express approval for superiors in the former and for equals in the latter may merge to produce a resultant tendency for members to express greatest liking for others who are "better" but only a little "better" than they are themselves.

Once the primary relationships described above become established and recognized, they create opportunities for members to gain rewards of a new sort. Then a member who can successfully imitate the style of life of his superiors and take part in "social" interaction with them offers, by these facts, evidence to third parties that he is the social equal of his former superiors. But the same evidence that may pull him up may pull his superiors down to his own level. Accordingly, he presents a threat to his superiors unless they are very secure in their status. To avoid making the threat and suffering the reprisals that may follow from it, many persons allow their superiors to make the first advances toward "social" interaction between them, and in many societies this has become a norm of social behavior.

But the rule that approximate equals tend to seek one another out socially does not always hold good. Interaction between persons or groups that are relatively equal to one another but still separated by a line of demarcation in status may threaten both parties more than interaction between persons that are more distant in status. Problems of obedience to authority or incongruence in status are less likely to arise between the latter than the former. This phenomenon bears some resemblance to the close ties between members of alternate generations that appear in many kinship systems.

14 Status, Conformity, and Innovation

As we have moved ahead in this book, the way we have gone to work has gradually changed. At the outset we stated a few very general propositions and drew from them some conclusions about social behavior that were themselves fairly general. Only later did we look for empirical findings that might bear the conclusions out. More recently we have begun to reverse the process. We have started with empirical findings and then asked whether they could be explained by applying to particular given conditions the more general relationships we had, as we hoped, already established. At the outset, moreover, we tried to explain what we called the primary or fundamental relationships. Only later have we tried to explain the secondary relationships, secondary in the sense that they could not have developed until men, in their interaction, had first brought into being and then recognized the primary ones. We have also, of course, moved from simpler toward more complicated phenomena, which has increasingly meant that we have tried to show what might be the resultant and combined effect of relationships that, in their isolated form, we had described and explained earlier.

In the present chapter we shall carry all of these tendencies still further. We shall begin by looking at some empirical findings on the relationships between conformity and status. Earlier we considered each of these phenomena separately. Now we bring them together. Our argument will attempt to show how a status system, once it has been established, may influence the degree to which persons in different positions in the system conform to group norms.

Status and Conformity: Experimental Research

For once we turn first for evidence to experimental rather than field research, beginning with an experiment by Kelley and Shapiro (1954). On the same topic, see also Jackson and Saltzstein (1956).

The investigators brought the subjects, who were college freshmen, into the experimental room in groups of five or six at a time. There the members introduced themselves to one another; each told the others something about himself; and then the investigators had each one answer a simple sociometric test in which he was to say, on the basis of this brief acquaintanceship, how acceptable as a co-worker he found each of the other members. After this, the investigators put each member into an alcove by himself and asked him not to communicate with the others. While he was there, they handed him a slip of paper purporting to show how he had scored on the sociometric test: whether his fellow members had chosen him as an acceptable co-worker or not. As soon as he had read the slip, the investigators hastily withdrew it, as if they had handed it out inadvertently, never meant to do so at all, and only now realized their mistake. Naturally this little act had the effect of stamping their scores all the more indelibly upon the subjects' minds. Some of the subjects were thus persuaded that they were highly acceptable to the others, and some that they were not in the least acceptable. A further questionnaire asked each member to say whether he wished to continue as a member of the same group. Not surprisingly, members in the high-acceptance condition were much more apt than the others to wish to continue.

The investigators then told each member that he was to carry out a certain task, that his score on his ability to do so would be pooled with those of the other members of his group, and that the group with the highest average score would get a prize of fifteen dollars. The task was this: he was shown a series of ten pairs of white cardboard squares, the two squares in each pair being labeled *A* and *B*. He was to say which square contained the greater number of dots; the investigators told him that the same square was the correct answer every time, but did not tell him which one it was, *A* or *B*. Unknown to the subject, the squares in the first pair contained an equal number of dots, but thereafter with each presentation square *A* lost a few dots and *B* gained a few, so that it became more and more clear to an unprejudiced observer that *B* contained the greater number. After every presentation, each member gave his choice of square and indicated his confidence in it. At that time he was allowed to write notes to his fellow members. These were collected but not delivered. Instead the investigators delivered to each subject a set of notes, actually the same for every member, but purporting to come from other members. All of the notes suggested that the correct answer in every case was square *A* and not square *B*. That is, each member received increasingly unambiguous visual evidence that one answer was correct, while being informed by his fellow members that the other one was. He also believed that a correct answer would help his group win a prize. Would he conform to the apparent influence of other members even though his conformity might be detrimental to achievement of the group?

From each member's choice of square in each presentation, and from the degree of confidence he expressed in that choice, the investigators calculated his score in conformity, a measure of the degree to which he had given in to the influence of other members; and then they correlated these scores with members' acceptance or nonacceptance by the others and their willingness or unwillingness to continue in the group.

The most interesting findings were the following. Members that set a low value on membership in the group, most of whom also believed that they were not acceptable to the other members, tended—as we might expect from the argument presented in Chapter 5 on conformity—to conform little. Yet members that set a high value on membership did not simply behave in the opposite way and conform much. On the average, they were somewhat more apt to conform than the others, but individually they varied in their conformity far more than did the nonconformers in their nonconformity: some conformed much and some little, as if a behavioral wedge had driven them apart, to one extreme or to the other.

It seems to have been from a desire to explore further the bearing of this last, ambiguous finding that Kelley, this time in company with Dittes, embarked on a second study (Dittes and Kelley, 1956). Since the procedure of the new experiment was in many ways the same as that of the last, we shall only report the ways in which it differed. Several groups met separately to discuss the question which of two gangs of juvenile delinquents should be judged more worthy of help. The discussion was based on two sets of fictitious court records, so doctored that the members of a group were almost sure to reach the decision that one of the gangs was worthier than the other, but only after they had talked the matter over for some time. In their instructions, the investigators emphasized that a group's decision ought to be unanimous, like a jury's, and when the group did reach unanimity, each member was to register the fact by rating the gangs both in public and private on a number of different scales.

The investigators interrupted each discussion three times in order to ask each member to rate the others on the desirability of their remaining in the group. At the end of the discussion they announced the average score the group as a whole had received on these tests, and then let each member look in private at what purported to be his own score in relation to the average. In fact, of course, the scores were fictitious and were designed to produce a finer discrimination among degrees of acceptability than had been achieved in the earlier experiment. Of the six members of each group, one found his score to be above the average (the "high" condition), two found theirs to be about average ("average"), two found theirs to be slightly below the average ("low"), and one found his to be far below ("very low"). The investigators also discussed his score with each member and allowed the highs and the averages to

322   *Status, Conformity, and Innovation*

believe that their ratings were pretty stable and unlikely to change in the future, while they persuaded the lows and very lows that their ratings were liable to change and become even worse. Besides status itself, the investigators thus tried to manipulate the degree to which status was perceived as established. The higher a subject's status, the more stable his status, they suggested.

After each subject understood his apparent standing in the group, the members renewed their discussion of the gangs; but this time the investigators provided the members with new evidence designed to suggest that the group's original and unanimous decision was incorrect, and that the other gang was probably the worthier of the two. The experimental question then became the following: Under what conditions of perceived acceptance by the others were members more or less likely, in the face of the new evidence, to abide by the group's original decision? The investigators used three different measures of conformity: the degree to which a member expressed agreement with the group's decision in a private rating of the gangs, the degree to which he did so in his public rating, and the degree to which in discussion he tended to discount or explain away the new information. The investigators also noted how long it took each member to make his new ratings, their assumption being that a man who took little time was probably sticking automatically to the group's original decision. They also measured how large a part each member took in the discussion following the release of the new information.

The investigators then asked each group to work on another problem, the members this time judging, in a succession of pairs of squares, which square contained the larger number of dots. Since this procedure was much like that of the previous experiment we shall not describe it further. When work on both problems had come to an end, each member answered a final questionnaire, reporting how highly he valued his membership in the group, how free he felt to express opinions contrary to the group's judgment, and how secure he felt in his social standing—especially how strongly he believed that the group would in the future reject him even more than it had already.

And now for the results. As we might have foretold, the order of the four classes in acceptance was their order in evaluation of their membership in the group: the more fully a member felt he was accepted by the others, the more highly he valued his membership; but the differences in this respect between the very lows and the lows, and between the lows and the averages, were much more significant statistically than the differences between the averages and the highs. In other respects, the averages and the highs behaved quite differently from one another. The previous experiment had managed, in effect, to lump the two together in the high-acceptance condition, and got from them much conformity as well as much of its opposite. The present experiment separated them, and in so doing managed also to separate conformers from noncomformers. By almost every measure, the present highs conformed less to, and expressed more freedom to differ from, the group judgment than did any other class, whereas the averages, in sharp contrast, turned out to be the greatest conformers of all. The averages also turned in their new ratings sooner than did any other class and participated most in the discussion of the new information, largely by discounting it and explaining it away. The investigators suggest that the averages found it rewarding to belong to the group and felt considerable acceptance by the others, but thought they might win even more acceptance in the future. They suggest that the conformity of the averages reflected their aspirations to still higher social standing.

Turning now to the lows, we find that, as in the earlier experiment, they tended somewhat toward nonconformity but, unlike the earlier one, not as strongly as did the highs. With the very lows, the same general tendency presented a slightly different twist. We shall remember that there was only one of them in each group: he was both low and alone in his status. More apt than members of any other status to feel that they were about to be rejected altogether, setting at the same time a low value on membership and expressing little conformity in their private judgments, the very lows nevertheless expressed in public more conformity than did any other status, took less part in discussion, and felt less freedom to disagree. As the investigators say: "In the extreme case . . . where acceptance is so low that actual rejection is presumably an imminent possibility, anxiety about rejection is especially high, and the result seems to be a pattern of guarded public behavior."

Upper Status and Originality: Experimental Research

We now have experimental evidence that it is not just members of low status, but members of high status as well, who are prone at times to nonconformity in a group. But before we ask whether both lows and highs are nonconformers for the same reasons, let us look at one more piece of research, this time carried out on natural groups rather than on artificially formed, experimental ones (Bartos, 1958).

The subjects of the research were 231 active members of six teen-age Y.M.C.A. clubs in a small Midwestern town. At the first meeting of the year each club elected eight officers, four of whom were to serve for the first term of the school year and four for the second; and after his election the president of the club appointed several other officers to help him with the work.

The clubs may appear somewhat over-officered, but that only helped the investigator to divide their membership into four classes differing in status. From high status to low they were: (1) the presidents, or leaders, (2) the remaining elective officers, whom the investigator called elected lieutenants, (3) the appointed officers, or appointed lieutenants, and (4) the members holding no office, or followers, this last class being obviously the largest. Whereas the preceding studies were forced to create differences in status by experimental manipulation, here the investigator had them handed to him naturally by the election and appointment system. But note that, if any comparison at all is valid, the "lows" and "very lows" in the last study correspond to only a small section of the followers in the present one, and that most of the followers must have been equivalent to the "averages."

The investigator had each subject look at a series of twelve pairs of cards and asked him "to match one of the three lines appearing on each of the right-hand cards with the one line appearing on each of the left-hand cards." Since the line on the left was always just the same length as one of the lines on the right, the job of matching should have been simple. But naturally the investigator did not mean to let his subjects off as easily as all that. While a subject was making his choice of lines, he heard offstage the voices of six persons, which he was led to believe were the voices of members of his club, urging that one of the lines in the right-hand card was the proper match for the line on the left-hand one; and in seven instances out of the series of twelve the voices unanimously urged the choice of the wrong line. The investigator in fact played the voices from a tape recorded in advance of the experiment.

After putting each subject through the experimental condition, the investigator had him do the same matching job all over again with what seemed to be a fresh set of cards but was actually the same old one, and this time without the chorus of voices. As a good experimenter, he wanted to make sure that the subjects would not make the same mistakes when not under the apparent influence of their fellow members as they had when they were under it. Not surprisingly they made many more mistakes in the first condition than they did in the control condition, and they made them by doing what the voices told them to do. Accordingly, the investigator concluded that the number of mistakes a subject made by giving in to the influence brought to bear on him was a valid measure of his conformity.

The investigator had the subjects take two further tests. The first, called the independence-of-judgment scale, consisted of a series of fifteen statements with each of which the subject was to say whether he agreed or disagreed. For instance, one of the statements was: "It is easy for me to take orders and do as I am told." Not unnaturally, agreement with statements like this was held to be evidence of a propensity to conform. The experiment itself was modeled on an earlier one by Asch (1953), and answers to such statements had in fact discriminated between those of Asch's subjects that conformed and those that did not. Finally, in the second test the subject looked through a series of drawings, both freehand drawings of strange asymmetrical figures and ruled drawings of symmetrical and geometrical shapes, and decided which ones he found most pleasing aesthetically. These drawings the investigator had borrowed from another piece of earlier research, which had seemed to show that the number of "complex" cards a man chose was a valid measure of his "originality."

The problem now was to relate the statuses of the members to their differences in the various measures of conformity and originality. On the line test the leaders of the clubs were far less likely to be conformers than were the other members. Most likely to be conformers were the elected lieutenants in the next highest status, but there was no great difference in conformity between them and the people in the two lowest statuses: the appointed lieutenants and the followers. Much the same thing was true of the independence-of-judgment test: the leaders were far less likely to be conformers than were the others; this time the followers were most likely to be conformers but not much more so than the elected and appointed lieutenants. In the readiness of the members of highest status to resist influence from the rest of the group, these results are in accord with those of the Kelley experiments. But there is little hint, such as appeared in the final Dittes-Kelley study, that the members lowest in status, the followers, were also prone to nonconformity. We must remember that the followers in the present study made up more than half of the whole membership and so included many people equivalent to the "averages" of Dittes and Kelley. The "averages" were, of course, strong conformers.

As for the results of the originality test, the leaders were the most original, followed by the elected lieutenants, with the other two classes— the appointed lieutenants and the followers—at the bottom of the list and about equally unoriginal. But we lay much less weight on these findings than we do on the results of the line-matching test, where the subjects were actually under the influence of the apparently unanimous but incorrect judgments of other members of their groups. This test, it seems to us, comes closest to simulating the conditions of actual social behavior.

Though the last three studies we have examined—those of Kelley-Shapiro, Dittes-Kelley, and Bartos—do not reach identical results, they tend in the same general direction. The members holding middle status in a group, whether they actually do so or only believe that they do, seem most disposed to give in to influence coming apparently from a large number of other members or to cleave to an opinion that other members have once accepted. Less prone to conformity are members holding either upper or lower status. We suspect that this latter finding would have emerged from the research even more clearly if, in the

Kelley-Shapiro study, the membership had been divided into three statuses instead of two and if, in the Bartos study, the lower status had not embraced more than half the whole membership.

Be that as it may, let us tentatively accept the main tendencies revealed in these researchers and ask how they are to be explained. For this purpose we shall assume that there are three main types of status in any group: upper, middle, and lower. We need not assume that in most groups the boundary lines between them can be drawn by any rule other than an arbitrary one, but we do believe that a three-fold division in itself is not arbitrary but corresponds to significant differences in the strategic positions of the statuses. Thus lower-status persons have many others above them but few or none below; upper-status persons have many others below them but few or none above, and middle-status persons have others both above and below them. We shall now take up each of these statuses in this order, adduce further evidence about the behavior of persons occupying them, and ask whether or not, given the differences in their strategic positions, the same general kind of explanation will account for the behavior of all three. It may be, for instance, that what looks like nonconformity in upper-status persons may really be quite a different phenomenon from nonconformity in lower-status ones.

Nonconformity in the Lower Status

Let us begin by considering a field study of a low-status nonconformer. In his study of sixteen agents in a federal law enforcement agency, which we have already cited and which we shall describe at length in the next chapter, Blau (1955) pays special attention to the behavior of one unpopular agent, unpopular because he violated norms held dear by the other members of the group. He reported to the supervisor of the department the fact that the management of one of the firms he investigated had offered him a bribe, and he adopted a threatening stance toward management in general. The other agents interpreted his reporting the bribe as an attempt to curry favor with the supervisor, and they had other reasons for disapproving of it. The firms they investigated, they felt, were under so great a temptation to offer bribes that it was unfair to tell on them if they succumbed. The offer of a bribe also gave an agent an unofficial hold over a firm, a hold he would lose if bribes were ever reported. In the opinion of the others, this agent also talked too much, completed more work than they thought proper, and refused to help them out when they came to him with technical problems.

For these reasons this agent received little esteem; indeed he was ostracized: so far as possible the others cut off interaction with him.

But to ostracize a man is to remove him from social control: if he holds out against that pressure there is nothing more the group can do to bring him back into line, short of physical violence. The group has lost its leverage on his behavior. The next time he has a choice whether or not to do something they wish him to do, he is the less apt to do it, the less there remains for them to take away from him in the way of esteem and interaction. He has nothing to lose by not conforming and perhaps even something to gain by it if it vexes them: "He does it only to annoy, because he knows it teases."

The investigator says of him (Blau, 1955: 155):

> To be sure, his deviant behavior contributed to his continued isolation, but this position also encouraged lack of conformity. . . . His overproductivity had made him an isolate and, once in this position, he became the only member of the agency who ignored a very important unofficial norm. The individual who had adapted himself to an isolated position could more readily violate the norms of the group.

His previous actions had won him low esteem from others, and his low esteem in turn made it likely that his further actions would also be unacceptable to the group, confirming him in his low esteem. Social behavior is full of such vicious spirals, as it is of favorable ones. Once, moreover, he had built up a record of bad behavior, as the others viewed it, no single action he took in conformity to group norms could have done much to raise his esteem. Indeed the others might not grant him an opportunity to conform or perceive him as conforming even if he were doing so in fact. In his very person he would present a stimulus in the presence of which the actions of others directed at him had been punished, and therefore they would be slow to perform similar actions again. At best it would take him a long time to live down his past, which meant that on any immediate occasion he had little to gain by conformity as well as little to lose by its opposite. This sense of being trapped by their pasts makes some people anxious to start fresh in new groups. "They know me," they say, "too well in there. Nothing I do is ever right."

This is, of course, the classic case of the nonconformer over whom group efforts at control have failed. It describes the conditions that make persons of low status particularly apt to be nonconformers. Let us review the conditions in more general terms. It may well have been their nonconformity that won them their low status in the first place, but at the moment we are interested in the reverse process, in low status as cause and nonconformity as effect. Once for any reason they have acquired low status—or, which amounts to the same thing, an experimenter has presented them with stimuli indicating that their status is low—their propensity for not conforming to the norms of the group increases. As usual, they are faced with alternative actions leading to alternative rewards. One of the alternative actions is conformity to the norms of the group, the reward of which is the approval of others. The other is action that gets them a different kind of reward. This may be, as in some of the experiments we have described, the self-respect that comes from successfully standing by one's own opinions. It may be the increased piecework wages that are gained by violating an informal ceiling on production. It may be the very real delight that sometimes attends irresponsible behavior: drinking, fornication, violence, and so on. The probability that they will take one of the two actions rather than the other depends on its net reward, reward less cost, the cost being the forgone reward of the alternative. For persons of low status, the cost of the nonconforming alternative is comparatively low, since they have no more status to forgo. Accordingly even if the rewards of nonconformity are not very great, the probability that they will not conform increases, for its costs are lower still.

There is a further aspect of the process. If a person already ranks low on some of the other dimensions of status, his nonconformity makes his status congruent in rank on a further dimension. And in becoming more congruent his status becomes more difficult to change. Just as persons of high status sometimes come by the process of *noblesse oblige* to behave even "better" than they might otherwise have done, so by an analogous process persons of low status sometimes come to behave even "worse," depending on what counts as "worse" in the groups they belong to.

This leads us to the next step in our argument. Whether or not a person will perform an action depends not only on the value of the reward it might conceivably get him but also on his perception of the probable success of the action in actually getting that reward. His perception of its success depends in turn, at one remove or another, on his actual past experience of success. In the case of the low-status nonconformer, we have talked as if what determined his behavior were the low value of the reward he might get by conformity, but it may be only the low probability of success in getting it. Even if a person sets a high value on the social approval that is theoretically the reward of conformity, he may still not conform, if conformity in his case is unlikely in fact to fetch him the approval. It is the less likely to fetch him approval, the more fully established is his low status, either by his previous actions or by the stimuli he presents, which activate what we shall now call prejudice. The reasons why a person of low and established status is particularly likely not to conform to the norms of his group are, first, that at least he has little to lose by nonconformity, and second, that, even if he should conform, the chances are low that by so doing he would in fact succeed in raising his status.

Let us turn briefly to analogous questions in the society at large. There is a tendency in many societies for the rates of various kinds of criminal activities—or, if you like, those defined as criminal by the middle and upper classes—to be highest in the lower class, that is, among the poor. The incidence of certain other kinds of behavior may also be higher, such as an unwillingness to save money, even when saving is possible. These tendencies are specially well marked when many members of the lower class are set apart from the rest of society in other ways than their poverty, as the blacks in the United States are set apart now or various other ethnic groups were set apart in the past.

These differences cannot be wholly explained by such an obvious argument as that poor people will naturally be more tempted to rob than will the rich. Some social scientists have tried to explain them by arguing that there is a special "culture of poverty" or even that the poor hold essentially different values from those of the rest of society. If a phrase like "the culture of poverty" refers simply to the fact that the poor, on the average, inculcate in their children ways of behaving that they have found will work to their advantage within their environment, then no doubt there is a culture of poverty. Aside from that, the explanation amounts to arguing that the poor are different because the poor are different, which must remind us of the famous interchange between F. Scott Fitzgerald and Ernest Hemingway:—"The rich are different from us." "Yes, they have more money." It is the business of social science not just to describe how cultures are different but to explain why they are different. Before we fall back on "the culture of poverty" as an explanation, let us first try making the assumption that the values of the poor are exactly the same as those of the rest of us, and then apply to their situation the argument we have just used to explain the behavior of persons of low status in small groups. Even if the poor set a high value on social advancement, that value will not suffice to elicit from them whatever is defined as "good" behavior, if "good" behavior in their experience has not in fact been successful in getting them social advancement—and it is especially likely not to have done so if the poor are set apart from the rest of society for other reasons than their poverty itself. Under these conditions they will perform alternative kinds of action, which in the nature of the case may well be defined as "bad." These actions may not get them rewards of very high value, but at least they are successful in getting them, such as they are. The poor will be especially likely to behave "badly" if the costs of doing so are not great. Already at the bottom of society, "bad" behavior cannot sink them further than they have sunk already. They will, in a wry way, relax and enjoy themselves.

Vying for Acceptance

It follows from the same argument that, if a person is of low status but not yet of established low status, his behavior may not bear out the generalization that low status is apt to be associated with nonconformity.

If a man has not given up, or been made to give up, if he still sees a chance of being accepted by his companions, if he is still vying for membership in his group, he is more apt than not to be a conformer. Indeed he is apt, if anything, to be an overconformer. Conformity has not yet failed to win for him its expected reward. We shall remember the experiment by the Sherifs which we described in Chapter 8. They divided the boys in a summer camp into two rival groups. As hostility between the two groups increased, the low-status members of each group became more vociferous than the rest in taunting the other group, as if they hoped thereby to demonstrate that they were full-fledged members of their own (Sherif and Sherif, 1953: 284).

People are the more ready to go on vying for membership, the more fully they accept their original assignments to low status as being in accord with the rule of distributive justice. Whether they accept it depends on what we have called their investments. A person whose investments might justify a higher status than the other members are ready to accord him will add resentment against them to whatever other reasons he may have for failing to conform to their norms, and this may speed up the vicious spiral that will separate him from the group. But a person who recognizes that his investments are low to begin with, because he is a newcomer to the group or a youngster or something else of the sort, has no reason for resentment; and since his investments can only improve with time, he may hope that, if he is patient and does what the others ask of him, he will sooner or later be admitted to full membership. Such a man will not begin his career in a group by being a nonconformer, though he may become one in the course of time and failure.

In a study of the machining and assembly department of the Industrial Controls Corporation, the investigators found two small subgroups, whose members were of equally low status but who reacted differently to the norms of the group as a whole (Zaleznik, Christensen, and Roethlisberger, 1958: 375–380). One subgroup consisted of workers, low in pay and skill, whose backgrounds were apt to include one or more of the following characteristics; they were Protestant and of middle-class or white-collar origin. As such they were different from, and in their own eyes better than, the urban, lower-class Irish Catholics that made up half of the membership of the department and dominated it socially. By working as hard as they could, the members of this subgroup violated the output norm praised and perpetuated by the dominant cliques, and so reinforced their low status. No doubt the moral value set on hard work, which Weber (1930) called the Protestant Ethic and which they had inherited along with their background, helped them to behave as they did, but so did their pleasure in showing up the workers of higher status, whose willingness to rank them low they resented. They were typical nonconformers who were not vying for membership and of whom their group had lost control.

The other subgroup consisted of workers whose backgrounds resembled those of the members of the dominant cliques, except that they were not Irish but Italians or members of other nationalities ranking lower than the Irish in ethnic status. The dominant members of the department tended to joke at their expense, the jokes emphasizing the ethnic element: for instance, they might call them "Guineas." But the joking was not enough to prevent their vying for full-fledged membership in the group. They took the jokes in good part; they hung around on the outskirts of the games the "regulars" played; they were ready to accept menial jobs as coffee-carriers; and they started various low-valued activities, such as temporary betting pools, which high-status workers were ready to take part in but not to organize. They were, moreover, ultra-conformers: they abided by the output norm and "articulated all the subtleties of the sentiments involved in restriction of output." It was as if they felt that their investments entitled them to no higher status than the others were willing to grant them to start with, but that if only they stuck to the rules, time was bound to be on their side. They were low-status conformers of whom, because they were still vying for membership, their group could still keep control. We may well ask how long a group can keep people vying for a rise in status without doing something to satisfy them.

Conformity and Nonconformity in the Upper Status

Let us turn now to members who hold high status in a group. For them the question of conformity presents even more ambiguities than it does for members of low status. And let me begin by speaking personally in order to acknowledge a mistake. In my book, *The Human Group* (Homans, 1950: 180–181), I put forward the proposition that a member of high status would conform to a high degree to all the norms of his group. What I had in mind was a man like Taylor in the Bank Wiring Room of the Western Electric Company, a piece of research reviewed in that book. Besides being held in high esteem for other reasons, Taylor also conformed, indeed conformed more closely than any other member, to the highly valued output norms of that industrial group. I still hold that a member of high status will conform to the more highly valued norms of his group. His conformity in this respect may only be one aspect of the behavior that wins him high status: his capacity to provide the others with rare and valued rewards. He may, indeed, as a leader have done more than any other member to get the norms accepted, and may even himself set a higher value on conforming to them than do any of the others. But I no longer believe that a member of high status conforms fully to *all* the norms of his group. Instead, his high status may itself allow him some freedom in lesser matters.

The margin of freedom from group control enjoyed by a man of high and established status has been well described by Everett Hughes (1946: 517):

> Here is an apparent paradox: Admittance to the group may be secured only by adherence to the established definitions of the group, while unquestioned membership carries the privilege of some deviant behavior. This is, of course, not a paradox at all; for it is characteristic of social groups to demand of the newcomer a strict conformity which will show that he accepts the authority of the group; then, as the individual approaches the center of a group and becomes an established member, they allow him a little more leeway.

The newcomers Hughes refers to here are of course those that are still vying for membership in the group.

Hollander has carried out a number of experimental studies bearing on the relative freedom of the member of high status. Let us consider only one (Hollander, 1964: 194–204). The investigator formed twelve groups to solve by discussion a series of fifteen intellectual problems. There were five members of each group, one of whom was a secret confederate of the experimenter's. Each group adopted a set of procedural rules, like rules of order, for conducting the discussions, and then went on to deal with the substance of the problems. The investigator arranged that his confederate in each group should have knowledge not possessed by other members, which would enable him to propose an excellent solution to each problem, and measured his changing influence on the group by the number of times within each block of discussions the members adopted his solutions. At specified points in the series of discussions, each confederate deliberately violated the rules of order the members had agreed upon; but the investigator instructed some of his confederates to violate them early in the series, others to violate them in the middle, and still others to violate them toward the end.

Not surprisingly, the influence of the confederates tended to increase as the discussions went on and as the members accumulated experience of the value of the solutions they proposed. But within this overall trend, the earlier a confederate violated the rules of order, the less his influence was apt to increase. Finally, an especially high degree of influence on the part of a confederate was associated with a combination of his conforming to the rules toward the beginning of the discussions but not conforming toward the end. That is, a confederate who started out both by conforming to the rules and by progressively providing the group with excellent solutions to its problems acquired a high degree of status and of influence over the members, which he did not lose when he came to violate the rules toward the end of the series of discussions. Hollander argues that a person who acquires high status and leadership in a group by performing more acts that reward the rest than do other members is allowed by them what he calls *idiosyncrasy credit*: he is allowed by them some freedom to act differently from the rest without losing status as a result. It is obvious how much this experimental finding resembles the conclusion Hughes reached from field research.

Let us now try to explain the nonconformity of high-status persons in a somewhat more general and abstract manner. Suppose that the members of a group are performing two kinds of action. First, they are either conforming or not conforming to the norms of the group, and second, they are performing other actions that are more or less rewarding to the rest of the members. A member who is to win high status in the end will begin by conforming to the norms. Otherwise, for reasons given earlier, he may not even get the opportunity to perform for the rest the rare and valuable actions that may lead him into his upward path. The others will not approach him; they will not even recognize that he can do anything worthwhile. But if he does conform, he may get his chance.

Once his chance has come and he has seized it, once he has shown what he can do and gained high status thereby, the situation changes. He may not find any alternative actions more rewarding than conformity, but if he does, the other members are now less well able than they were in the beginning to impose on him high costs for not conforming, and therefore he becomes somewhat more likely not to conform. They now value what he has to offer them, and they may lose it by punishing him too severely and driving him out of the group. As a person of high status, moreover, there may be other groups ready to take him in. These conclusions follow directly from the theory of balance, of the effect of one type of exchange upon another, which we discussed in Chapter 3. Thus the members of a group forfeit some degree of control over a person of established high status, just as they forfeit it over a person of established low status, though for different reasons. They have too much to lose if they take action in the former case; the nonconformer has too little to lose in the latter one.

In any event, who is to take the initiative in bringing a high-status member to book if he does violate a norm? Who will bell the cat? The question is difficult to answer, especially since the leader of a revolt puts himself by that very fact above his erstwhile peers in the middle level of status, and they may not be ready to swallow his presumption. None of this implies that successful revolts against the elite never occur in groups either small or large. What it does imply is that revolts have much to overcome, and that a person in winning a position of high status has also won means of maintaining himself in it over and above those that got him the status in the first place.

So far we have tried to explain why members of high status, if they had any interest in not conforming to some of the lesser norms of a group, might be especially well able to get away with it. Now let us consider a different kind of nonconformity, which perhaps ought not to be called nonconformity at all. Suppose that it is not a question of conforming to already established norms but rather of deciding what to do in some new situation. Suppose, for instance, that one is asked to reach some judgment about new and ambiguous information. This was the sort of question that faced the subjects in the experiments we opened the chapter by describing. What does a member of established high status do then, compared to one of lower status? What, in particular, is the likelihood that he will go along with the opinion of the rest of the group, when it is not altogether certain that the opinion is correct.

There are reasons, again, why a member of high status might be less likely to conform in this new sense of the word than one of middle or low status. A member of high status gets his position by performing actions different from, and "better" than, those of the others. Simply to concur in group opinion hardly rates as a different and better action than theirs. A member of high status is apt also to be a leader; yet simply to go along with the group is to be a follower. Accordingly, to conform in this sense is out of keeping with, incongruent with, high status in other respects, and if persisted in too long, will, according to an argument we have developed several times already, throw doubt in the minds of the beholders upon a member's right to the status itself. No doubt a man of high status will not be different just for the sake of being different. If the facts are unambiguous, if they are susceptible of only one interpretation, if it is obvious which is the correct decision to make, no doubt he will concur. But such action in itself will do nothing for him; and if the right answer is not obvious, he will have more reason than those immediately below him to take an independent stand, to try something new. If he does so and he turns out to be justified, that action is most assuredly in keeping with his high status in other respects and serves to reinforce it. Once more he has delivered for the benefit of the others an especially rare and valuable reward. Even if he turns out to be wrong, that fact will do him less immediate harm than it will to a person of middle status. Compared to the latter he has more status to lose before he goes broke. It is as if he had more capital and thus more freedom to maneuver. In short, a member of high status is somewhat more apt than others to become a nonconformer in the sense of an innovator.

Roles

In this chapter and in earlier ones we have analyzed the process of development by which a person, because he has acquired high status through one set of activities, comes to perform other activities different from those of persons of lower status. By the rule of status congruence, which in his case takes the form of *noblesse oblige*, his other activities tend to become "better" than theirs on whatever dimensions the members of his group use for assessing status. He tends to take command of the joint efforts of the members. They tend to thrust upon him the job of doing justice between them in case of dispute. When the question arises what is the correct opinion on some new issue or what ought to be done in new circumstances, he is apt to be more independent than the other members, more of an innovator.

We say he "tends" to undertake these other activities. What we mean of course is a little more than this. To the extent that he does not undertake them, he presents stimuli that throw his higher status in doubt as far as other members of his group and indeed outside spectators are concerned; and since status is itself a reward to many persons, many persons of high status will in fact undertake them. Not all will and certainly not all at all times. We must never forget that high status also entails costs. Trying to behave "better" than others is often very costly. It may mean giving up gross material advantages; it always means hard work. Many leaders have dreamed of escaping from their responsibilities, and many, after experiencing them, have in fact chosen to escape. Yet some tendency remains for persons of high status to undertake these other activities; and to say that, if they do not, they put their status in jeopardy is the same thing as saying that not only other members but also they themselves believe they ought to undertake them.

But to say that a person who occupies a certain position in a group—in the present case, high status—is expected both by himself and by others to behave in certain ways is in turn to say, by an old tradition of sociology and anthropology, that he has a particular *role* to play in his group. Many social scientists spend their time describing the roles that persons holding particular statuses have acquired in particular societies, especially the role associated with a given position as it meshes with the roles associated with other positions. Thus social scientists may describe the role of a father toward, or over against, his children or the role of a doctor toward his patient. (Actually they are more apt to use the elegant French term *vis-à-vis* rather than the common English terms, though the latter say just as much.)

Some sociologists have gone further and asserted that *role* either is or ought to be the fundamental concept of our science. But here we must disagree. A role falls into the class of things called *norms* or *rules:* statements of how persons are expected to behave and therefore, in the eyes of many, ought to behave in particular circumstances. Since under the very best of conditions many people do not behave as they ought to behave, and since many more depart systematically from their roles in times of social change—indeed that is one meaning of social change—a social scientist who begins with roles and never tries to go behind them is condemned to a static description of social behavior and of ideal rather than actual behavior at that. He abandons any possibility of explaining it, certainly of explaining social change. Yet even the temporarily static features of social behavior were all reached originally through a process of social change.

A book like this one, which is concerned with the fundamentals of social behavior, must not allow such a charge to be laid against it. It is especially concerned with showing how social structures—relatively stable relationships between persons—might arise out of the choices individuals make between alternative courses of action, in the context of the choices made by other individuals. A role is certainly part of a relatively stable, though never absolutely stable, structure. Accordingly a role cannot be something we begin with; at best it is something we might end with. It is something we have to explain, not something we can use in explanation. It is an *explicandum*, not an *explicans*. It is our job, not to take the content of a particular role as given, but to explain why the role has that content and not some other one. More generally, it is our job to explain why roles of any kind might emerge out of the interactions of men. In explaining how a person of high status tends to develop a special role in a group we have tried for one particular but important case to do both jobs.

Conformity in the Middle Status

We turn finally to the third of the, to some extent, arbitrary strata into which we have divided a group. The evidence, such as it is, suggests that persons of middle status are more apt to conform to group norms and concur in a real or fictitious consensus in opinion than persons of either high or established low status. In explaining why both the upper and the lower status show a relatively high incidence of nonconformity, we have perhaps done all we need to do to explain why the middle status shows a relatively low incidence. But we do not merely mean to imply that, if the other two statuses are nonconformist, the middle status must naturally be conformist, that is to say, conformist in comparison with them. Let us also look at the more positive reasons why a member of middle status might be especially apt to become a conformer. Remember that the middle status of a group is made up of persons who have not much in the way of scarce and highly valued rewards to offer the others, but who at least offer rewards of some sort and not punishments. They carry out the run-of-the-mill work of the group, and they provide conformity itself, which is a reward though not a scarce one.

Whereas the well-established member of low status has little to lose by nonconformity, the member of middle status does have something to lose by it. So far as his not conforming hurts the other members, they may withdraw from him the outward signs of his status in approval and "social" interaction, and there are still some of these things left to withdraw. They are especially likely to do so, since he may have little but his conformity to reward them with, and when that is gone there is nothing left. Moreover, to bring him, unlike the member of high status, to heel, they do not need to withdraw much: a short fall will bring him to the bottom. He has something to lose and what he has to lose is his all. Accordingly, if a member is of middle status he has by that fact some reason for conforming to the norms of his group. Should, indeed, the behavior of the lower status become more than usually "bad," persons of middle status, particularly those placed toward its lower edge, may tend by reaction to become more than usually conformist. They may deliberately differentiate their behavior from that of the lower status and so obviate any danger that observers inside or outside the group might mistake them for their inferiors.

If, moreover, a person of middle status should violate a norm or disagree openly with a received opinion, and should somehow turn out to be correct in doing so, this result may not do him all that amount of social good, whatever it may do for his self-respect. The act itself and its vexing quality of being correct tend to set him above his equals, the other members of middle status, and they may not be ready to concede his superiority, especially if he has done nothing else to distinguish himself, to reward them in some rare and valuable way. It is as if they said: "Who is he to be correct?", like the man in the old Jewish story inquiring about another who affects superiority by conspicuously deprecating his supposed achievements: "What's he ever done that he should be so modest about it?" It is our equals that hold us back. If the rewards of nonconformity are uncertain, a person of middle status at least manages by conforming to minimize his risks of punishment. If he goes along with the group, he will have avoided the very real costs incurred in thinking and acting for himself. Again, this does not mean that no persons of middle status ever rise to the top. It only means that they have something to overcome.

Status and Conformity in Society at Large

Let us end this chapter by looking briefly at large-scale phenomena that bear some resemblance to the ones we have just been examining on a small scale. We ought never assume that the informal group is a microcosm of society at large, that what holds good of the one must also hold good of the other. It would be difficult, for instance, to make out that upper-class people in society at large, like upper-status ones in small groups, are especially likely to be innovators. And yet, though the resemblances may be superficial, some characteristics of some systems of social class at some times seem to resemble what we have noticed about status in small groups—particularly the tendency for members high and low in status to resemble one another in their nonconformity and to differ from members of middle status. In the recent past of the South of this country (see Dollard, 1937: 75–97), and in England in the sixteenth century, there are hints that both upper and lower classes were less re-strained in the fields of gambling, drink, and fornication, more ready to indulge in the simple sensuous pleasures of life than were the climbers, the strainers, the insecure of the middle classes.

The landed aristocrat, already at the top, has little to gain from a rigid compliance with the minor moral standards of society. Since his social position is secure, whatever his economic position may be, he finds other rewards—including an indulgence in his eccentricities and in the pleasures of the flesh—relatively more rewarding than further striving for status. And the poor farm laborer, who has little to gain by respect-ability and nothing to lose by its opposite, is similarly attached to the simple sensuous pleasures—riot and debauchery—which have the further charm of not costing much money. Respectable people treat him like an animal, and his natural response is indeed animalistic, which comfort-ably confirms the respectable in the moral judgment they have passed on him. Yet they have their moments of envying him his license, his irresponsibility, above all, his freedom from striving. He can afford to relax and be a natural man. In a wry way, he is making the best of what is, for him, a bad society. But the people in the middle, particularly if they see some chance of rising in the world, which in the cases we have in mind the poor do not, must seek, by close adherence to a rigid moral-ity, to differentiate themselves from what they call the rabble and estab-lish their claims to social recognition. These middle-class people are more apt to be puritanical than either upper- or lower-class ones. Yet in saying this we are at once reminded how dangerous it is to generalize from the small group to society at large. For in the England of the six-teenth century, middle-class people, though they certainly were con-formists in morality, were far from being conformists in other respects. Indeed we owe the very word *nonconformist* to the fact that their ene-mies called them by that name. Puritanical in the general sense in man-ners, they were also Puritans in the special sense in religion: they were religious reformers, not conformers. And when the crisis came in the seventeenth century, when King and Commons faced one another in arms in the Civil War, middle-class people were especially likely to sup-port Parliament, while the other two classes—not all but many of their members—tended to identify themselves with one another and with the king (see Baxter, 1931: 34).

Summary

In the present chapter we have examined the relationship between a person's status and his conformity to the norms of a group to which he belongs. If we consider a group as being roughly divided into three layers of status, upper, middle, and lower, each in a different strategic position from the others, then the evidence suggests that members of both upper and lower status are more prone to nonconformity than those of middle status. Yet nonconformity in the lower status may not mean quite the same thing as nonconformity in the upper, nor occur for quite the same reasons.

For a member of lower status, the costs of his failing to comply with the norms of his group are relatively low, because he has no more status to lose by it, since he is already at the bottom. Accordingly, if nonconformity offers some positive reward, as it often does, he is apt to become a nonconformer, especially if his previous behavior has established him firmly in his status, so that he cannot easily expect to raise it even by behaving "better." But if he is of low status simply because he is new to the group and has not yet had an opportunity of proving himself, he is more apt to become an over- than an underconformer.

A member of upper status is apt to conform to norms strongly held in his group. His is apt, indeed, to have done most to get such norms established, and to conform closely to them afterwards. Such are among the rare and valued services that win him his status. But in lesser matters he is allowed, and takes, more freedom. Who is in a position to stop him? And when the group faces some new problem, the solution to which is not at all obvious, he is much less apt just to go along with the crowd than is a member of middle status. There is nothing especially rare and valued about behavior of that sort, and it will do him no good. Only if he reaches an independent and correct decision will his behavior be in keeping with his status and help maintain it. Yet action of this sort partakes more of the character of independence, innovation, and leadership than it does of nonconformity in the usual sense of the violation of established norms.

As for a member of middle status, he, unlike a member of low status, has something to lose by nonconformity. He may have something to gain by innovation and leadership but he risks something too. Actions of this sort tend to raise him above his former equals. They may not be ready to accept his superiority and may punish him for his presumption. Accordingly, members of middle status are more likely than not to conform in both senses of the word.

15 A Summary Group

IN MY BOOK, *The Human Group* (1950), I EXAMINED FIELD studies of five different groups and tried to show that some of the same propositions held good in all of them. My primary emphasis was on the groups; my secondary, on the propositions. In this book we have come close to reversing the process. We have taken up a wide range of propositions about social behavior and found evidence from both field and experimental research to support them. The emphasis has necessarily fallen on the isolated proposition: we have not done much, though we have done more in later chapters than we did in earlier ones, to show how a number of the phenomena combine to produce the distinctive structures of particular groups. In the current chapter, by way of a summary of what has gone before, we shall try to do just this: we shall take one excellent field study of a single group—a study that had not appeared at the time *The Human Group* was published—and show how a number of the phenomena we have described earlier made their joint appearance in the behavior of its members. The group in question is one of the two analyzed by Peter Blau in his book, *The Dynamics of Bureaucracy* (1955).* We have spoken about it several times already; in fact it suggested the situation we used as our model for the interaction of those two hardworked characters, Person and Other. In using it as a summary group we shall have to repeat some of the things we said about it in other connections; for whatever may be the needs that a summary meets, it certainly meets them at the cost of repetition.

We must not mistake our sample group for a typical group: there is no such thing. The fact that we have used a single set of general propositions certainly does not imply that there is only one kind of group. For in explaining actual social behavior we must apply the general propositions to particular given conditions, and a small change in the givens may make a big difference in the structure of relationships that the propositions would lead us to expect. Far from being typical, the present

* See footnote on p. 275.

340

group was rather simply organized, as groups go. We should not look on it as "the" eternal group but as a highly individual instance, which by very reason of its simplicity sets off to advantage many of the phenomena we wish to summarize.

A Federal Agency: Consultation among Colleagues

The group consisted of a supervisor, sixteen agents, and one clerk, who formed in 1949 a department in a local branch of a federal agency that had its headquarters in Washington, D.C. In order to protect the anonymity of the group, the investigator does not tell us what the precise mission of the agency was. Broadly it was concerned with the enforcement of a certain set of federal laws. Since we are not interested in formal organization, and since the supervisor was hardly a member of the group, we shall not have much to say about him; nor was the clerk a member. Our business is with the sixteen agents.

The members of the department were fairly well experienced in their work: only one had been with the agency for less than five years. Two held the civil-service grade 9, which was the highest represented among the agents; two were in grade 7; and the rest, the great majority, were in the middle with grade 8. But regardless of their different grades, all did much the same kind of work. Only three were women, and only one was a black. On the average, an agent spent about 40 percent of his time in the home office, where he had a desk of his own along with the other agents. But because their duties took them often into the field, not all the agents were together in the office at any one time.

An agent's main duty was investigation. On assignment by the supervisor, he went to the office of a business firm, obtained from it a wide variety of information, then came back to the agency where, from the information he had collected, he wrote a report stating whether or not and in what way the firm had violated federal law. In order to determine whether a violation had occurred, an agent had to know how a large and complex body of legal rulings applied to the circumstances of a particular case. And since his report might become the basis for legal action against the firm, he had to be sure of his facts, his argument, and the clarity of his presentation.

The quality of the reports an agent turned in to the supervisor determined more than did anything else the kind of efficiency-rating the latter gave him, and this in turn affected his chances for promotion to a higher grade in the civil service. Thus an agent had to do a job difficult in itself, and his success in doing it made a difference to his future. Moreover, unlike the members of many industrial groups, the agents believed strongly in the value of the work the agency was doing, and so were doubly motivated to do it well.

Yet in spite of his long experience, an agent was often in doubt which legal rules might be applicable to the case under consideration and what decision he ought to reach about it. An agent was left free to make his own decision, the only formal rule being that if he had any doubt or question, he was to bring it to the supervisor without consulting any of his colleagues. But like many formal rules, this one was disregarded. Not unnaturally the agents believed that to take a question to the supervisor was to confess one's incompetence and so to prejudice one's rating for efficiency; accordingly they did go to their colleagues for help and advice, and the supervisor seems to have winked at the practice.

Although the agents all had much experience, they still recognized that some of their number were better than others at solving the problems that came up in writing reports. The first research procedure the investigator carried out was to ask every agent to put all the others in order of their competence as he saw it. The individual rankings agreed highly with one another, and they also agreed with the supervisor's ranking of the competence of the different agents.

The investigator next tried to relate the perceived competence of the different agents to the number of times other agents went to them for help and advice. He spent many hours simply observing behavior in the department and during this period kept a record of every contact between agents, however brief it might have been, such as a word spoken in passing. He discovered that an agent, while he was in the office, had an average of five contacts per hour with colleagues. Some of these were casual and social conversations, but many were discussions of technical problems. The investigator decided that the longer contacts were probably those of the latter kind and therefore in studying the distribution of technical consultations he included only contacts that lasted more than three minutes. The investigator also asked every agent to name the other agents whom he consulted when he ran into difficulties with his work.

The results showed a rather marked pattern. As we should expect, the more competent an agent was, the more contacts he was apt to receive, and the higher was the esteem in which he was held. But the correlation was not perfect. Two of the agents whom their colleagues believed to be competent seem to have discouraged people that came to them for help and thus to have choked off further advances. As the investigator says (Blau, 1955: 119): "The two experts who were considered uncooperative by their colleagues were generally disliked and received only few contacts. To become accepted, an expert had to share the advantages of his superior skill with his co-workers."

It is worth noting that, in a later study of an agency concerned with social work (Blau, 1960), the same investigator found no relation between esteem and contacts received. The reason was that in this agency, unlike the federal agency, the workers set a negative value on expert knowledge of procedures. Accordingly an expert was less apt to be approached for technical advice and less apt to get esteem in return than he was in the federal agency.

With the two exceptions, the workers in the federal agency were ready to help one another if they could. A few of them, and these among the most competent of all, were consulted by a large number of others, but did not themselves go regularly for advice to any one agent. Thus four agents had no regular partners, but all four were highly competent. Three of them were also very popular as consultants. "These three were by no means isolated from the exchange of advice. On the contrary, they participated so widely in it that they did not spend much time with any single co-worker" (p. 108). The fourth agent had only recently been assigned to the department and had not yet been brought into much use as a consultant. The rest of the agents, on the other hand, were apt to take regular partners. Each one of them, though occasionally consulting the few highly competent men, was apt to link himself especially closely with one or two others whose competence was more nearly equal to his own. On any occasion when he needed help, he felt free to consult his partner, as long as he was ready to allow the latter the same kind of access in return.

Rewards and Costs of Consultation

Now let us see what the investigator has to say (p. 108) about the social economics of consultation:

> A consultation can be considered an exchange of values; both participants gain something, and both have to pay a price. The questioning agent is enabled to perform better than he could otherwise have done, without exposing his difficulties to the supervisor. By asking for advice, he implicitly pays his respect to the superior proficiency of his colleague. This acknowledgement of inferiority is the cost of receiving assistance. The consultant gains prestige, in return for which he is willing to devote some time to the consultation and permit it to disrupt his own work. The following remark of an agent illustrates this: "I like giving advice. It's flattering, I suppose, if you feel that the others come to you for advice."

The expert who was willing to give advice got various advantages incidental to his rise in status. From the consultation he drew renewed confidence in his own capacity to solve technical problems. He might, indeed, pick up ideas useful to him in doing his own work without paying the price of an admission of inferiority. Each of the three most popular consultants, whom many others asked for help, could, moreover, when he needed help in return, scatter his requests among these many and did not need to concentrate them on any single agent, which would have made more conspicuous the fact that it was help he was asking for. As the investigator puts it (p. 108): "Besides, to refrain from asking any particular individual too many questions helped to maintain his reputation as an expert. Consequently, three of the most popular consultants had no regular partners."

The cost that an expert incurred in return for his increased esteem is obvious: he had to take time from his own work. "All agents liked being consulted, but the value of any one of very many consultations became deflated for experts, and the price they paid in frequent interruptions became inflated. . . . Being approached for help was too valuable an experience to be refused, but popular consultants were not inclined to encourage further questions" (p. 108).

The investigator is quite explicit that asking for help as well as giving it incurred an agent costs (pp. 108–109): "Asking a colleague for guidance was less threatening than asking the supervisor, but the repeated admission of his inability to solve his own problems also undermined the self-confidence of an agent and his standing in the group. The cost of advice became prohibitive, if the consultant, after the questioner had subordinated himself by asking for help, was in the least discouraging—by postponing a discussion or by revealing his impatience during one."

The cost in inferiority of asking a colleague for help was rendered greater in this group than it would have been in some others by the fact that, formally, the agents were not greatly unequal: all held the same job title; all did the same kind of work, and most of them held the same grade in the civil service. A man who is already another's inferior has much less to lose in asking a service of him than one who begins as his equal.

That asking for help did indeed incur a man costs is shown by the practice some agents adopted of elaborately pretending that help was not really what they were looking for. Such an agent would bring his problem to a colleague as if it were a case presenting special points of interest well worthy of dispassionate analysis between two discriminating judges. As one of the agents said, "Casey asks me sometimes, too, but he does it with a lot of finesse. He will just seem to ask what my opinion is, not as if he were worried about the question" (p. 112). And the investigator adds the comment (p. 113): "Such manipulative attempts to obtain advice without reciprocating by acknowledging the need for the other's help were resented. . . . If his advice was needed, the agent demanded that the respect due him be paid by *asking* for his assistance. An official whose deliberate disguise of a consultation was discovered created resentment without averting loss of esteem." In short, this maneuver broke the rules of fair exchange: it attempted to get help without conceding superiority in return. We have encountered behavior of the same sort in the machine shop described in Chapter 9 on status.

As we have seen, three of the most competent agents did not enter into partnerships, did not regularly exchange help and advice with particular other agents. Two highly competent agents did take regular partners, but, on the whole, partnerships were confined to people of middle and low competence. The investigator implies that it was precisely the cost a man incurred in asking the most competent agents for advice that led most of the agents to seek out partners among people more nearly of their own rank, with whom they could exchange help without losing status; for the essence of partnership was that, if one man asked his partner for help on one occasion, the partner might ask the same favor back on the next. Speaking of the fact that an agent who tried to consult one of his more competent colleagues might meet with a refusal, the investigator says (p. 109):

> To avoid such rejections, agents usually consulted a colleague with whom they were friendly, even if he was not an expert. . . . The establishment of partnerships of mutual consultation virtually eliminated the danger of rejections as well as the status threat implicit in asking for help, since the roles of questioner and consultant were intermittently reversed. These partnerships also enabled agents to reserve their consultations with an expert whom they did not know too well for their most complicated problems.

That is, the advice a man got from his partner might not be of the highest value, but it was purchased at low cost since a partner was apt to be his equal. And thus he was enabled to save his really difficult problems for the most competent agents, whose advice, since it did come high in confessed inferiority, he did not wish to ask often.

It should be clear how these findings illustrate the arguments we put forward earlier in this book. Social behavior is an exchange of more or less valuable rewards. The expert agents provided for the others a service that these others found valuable and rare. In return, the experts received much interaction and were able to command from the rest a high degree of esteem, thus establishing a social ranking in the group. But in getting these rewards both parties to the exchange incurred costs —the experts in time taken away from their own work, the others in implicit admissions of inferiority. The costs, moreover, increased and the rewards declined with the number of exchanges, thus tending for the time being to cut off further exchange. The experts began to rebuff new requests, and the rest began to hesitate before approaching the experts. Indeed the rest began to look for sources of help they could exploit at lower cost. In the nature of the case, these sources could only be agents who were more nearly of their own rank than were the experts. With such people they could both give and take advice without incurring loss in status.

Finally, most agents met the conditions of distributive justice. For instance, the experts who were ready to give help got much esteem but incurred heavy costs in time taken away from their own work: their costs were in line with their rewards. Therefore, the other agents not only respected but liked them. To win esteem it was not enough to *be* expert: a man had to devote his expert knowledge to the service of others. Thus a couple of agents, known to be competent, who repelled others approaching them with requests for help, were much disliked and left much alone. In failing to enter into exchange at all they had deprived others of services that the others had come to expect of persons with so much to give.

"Social" Interaction

The investigator next turned to the relation between the competence of the agents and their more purely "social" behavior. Of the latter he made two different kinds of observations. In his period of watching the group he had kept a record of all the contacts (interactions) an agent received from others, but in mapping out the pattern of consultations he had included only the relatively long contacts—three minutes or more—on the ground that long contacts were more likely than short ones to have to do with the official business of the agency. Now, in mapping out "social" behavior—passing the time of day, gossiping, telling jokes—he included all the contacts an agent received, long or short, and called this a measure of *contacts received*. The investigator also asked each agent to keep a record every day of the colleagues he lunched with. "If a luncheon engagement is defined as eating with one colleague once, the total number of engagements reported (which often included several colleagues on the same day, and the same colleague on repeated days), divided by the number of days on which the respondent went out to lunch from the office, defines the value of this index" (p. 237)—which the investigator called a measure of an agent's *informal relations*.

He then proceeded to study the interrelations of the three variables: competence, contacts received, and informal relations. For this purpose, he divided the rank order of the agents on each variable into two parts, but the division did not necessarily come at the midpoint of the distribution. Thus he rated seven agents as high in competence and eight as low, but rated six as high in contacts received and nine as low. (One agent transferred out of the department in the course of the study, reducing the total number of agents considered for the present purpose to fifteen.)

Agents high in competence were statistically likely to be high also in contacts received. Not all were: the two highly competent agents who were unwilling to give the others the benefit of their expertise and who were accordingly disliked received few social contacts; but the tendency was in this direction. By the same token, the less competent agents tended statistically to get few contacts.

Perhaps this finding tells us little more than we knew already. An expert who was willing to share his knowledge with others was much sought after by the others for consultation, and we know that many of the contacts an expert received were of this sort. But not all were: some were more purely "social." Once a man has won esteem by providing others with rare and valuable services, another reason for their seeking him out comes into play: he is now able to offer a new kind of service. In Chapter 13 on stratification we explained why a man tends to seek out his equals for interaction on "social" occasions. But once this is recognized to be a common occurrence, then for Person to interact with Other and be seen doing so is to provide the outward and visible sign that he is Other's equal, and this, paradoxically, creates a new reason for his interacting with his social superiors. For if Other is a man of high status, then Person by being seen in his company has offered prima-facie evidence that he is of high status too. Accordingly, some members of a group, those not unduly burdened with self-respect, seek out interaction with a member of high status for reasons other than getting the service that first won him the status. But how will a member of high status receive their advances? If he is in any doubt about his status, social contacts with his inferiors will tend to bring him down to their level, and he is apt to rebuff them; but if his status is so firmly established that he need not worry about it, his willingness to allow them social access to him provides them with a new and valuable service and enhances the esteem in which they hold him.

"Contacts received" was measured by the number of interactions a man received in the office, and this might include "business" contacts as well as "social" ones. The best index of purely "social" contacts was "informal relations," which was measured by luncheons. The investigator found that, statistically speaking, agents of high competence were apt to have few informal relations and agents of low competence to have many. Some of the competent agents did not use their knowledge to help others; therefore they did not enjoy high status, and the others were not much interested in lunching with them. Some enjoyed a status both high and secure, and could afford to wait until others approached them. And some may not have been quite sure of their high status, which may have led them to rebuff the advances of their inferiors. All of these effects tended to reduce the informal relations of the more competent agents. But the less competent agents, who on the average were less secure in their status than the more competent ones, tended actively to seek others out for luncheon dates. They sought out the agents of high status if they could engage them, but if they could not, they found lunching with somebody better than lunching alone. No doubt man is a gregarious animal and enjoys lunching with his fellows regardless of what it does to his status. Our only point is that differences in status provide additional reasons for (or against) making social contacts. By lunching with any one of his fellows an agent of low status could at least make good the assumption that he was the other's equal, that he was at least an accepted member of the group. At any rate, the less competent agents "lunched in larger groups than experts and made greater efforts to arrange their work so that they would have to eat alone as rarely as possible" (p. 120). By eating in large groups they necessarily piled up a high score in informal relations, since each person present at the table added to the score.

Though the competent agents tended to have fewer informal relations than the less competent, lunching more often alone or with fewer companions, the relationship was statistical and did not hold good of all of them. One agent of whom it did not hold good was the one who, in the office, was most encouraging to people who came and asked him for help. He was better liked than any other agent, and became, as we shall soon see, the informal leader of the group. In short, his status was both high and secure. "His great willingness to assist others," the investigator comments (p. 236), "was his price for maintaining this position." But this was not the only service he did for them; he was also willing to provide them with the secondary reward of lunching with him. "He was particularly hospitable to colleagues who consulted him, and he deliberately fostered informal relations with them. 'If anyone asks me for lunch,' he told the observer, 'I never say, "I have a date with another fellow; I can't." I always say, "Of course, come along." ' In contrast to most experts, this agent had very extensive informal relations" (p. 122–123).

The investigator finally turned to the third of the possible relations between the three variables, the relation between informal relations and contacts received, and he found that agents who took part in many informal relations (luncheons) were statistically likely to receive many contacts. Now this may seem curious. For if x varies as y, and x also varies as z, we might expect y to vary as z; but in this study it did not. Contacts received (x) varied as competence (y), and contacts received (x) varied as informal relations (z); but we saw earlier that informal relations (z) did not vary directly as competence (y) but rather inversely: the greater the competence of an agent, the fewer his informal relations were likely to be.

This apparent departure from common sense was made possible by the statistical method used and by the fact that the correlations, while often significant, were never perfect. Enough of the competent had few informal relations, and enough of the incompetent had many, to produce the inverse relationship between competence and informal relations, but not all men in either category behaved as the greater part did. And the same was true of the direct relation between competence and contacts received. Accordingly it was possible for the few competent agents who both enjoyed extensive informal relations and received many contacts to combine statistically with the few less competent ones who also did both things and so create a direct relationship between informal relations and contacts received.

But to show that the reported results are possible does not add very much. It is much more interesting to reconstruct from the investigator's data what the actual pattern of social engagements among the agents must have been. We shall not reproduce here the tedious reasoning that leads to the reconstruction but only its conclusions. The less competent agents must have lunched with one another often and in large groups, without the more competent agents being present—indeed the investigator implies as much. The competent agents must also have lunched with one another often without the less competent agents being present—but in small groups. This suggests that they may have rebuffed some of the social advances made to them by the less competent agents, or that the latter may have waited in vain for invitations. And finally some of the less competent managed to get some of the more competent to lunch with them fairly often, in large groups. In fact the investigator tells us that the informal leader was one of the competent men who thus allowed his social inferiors to lunch with him. Equals, then, tended in general to lunch with equals, but some inferiors made successful approaches to their superiors in status.

We have here further evidence of the complex interplay of two tendencies we have encountered again and again in this book: a tendency for a person to interact with his superiors in status and a tendency for him to interact with his equals. A man establishes superior status by providing superior services for others. By the same token, accepting the superior services costs a man something, since he thereby acknowledges his inferiority. Sooner or later he will turn to others who can offer him services that no doubt reward him less but that also cost him less in inferiority. In the nature of the case, these others can only be his equals. As the partnerships in the federal agency suggest, he will turn to his equals for services at work that he can return in kind; but he is particularly apt to turn to them in the "social" field of activity, just because it is *not* the field in which his superiors win their high esteem—and he his low. A secondary development then builds on this primary one. The rest of mankind can "see" the equations of elementary social behavior just as clearly in their way as we social scientists can, and once the relationship between social interaction and equality of status is established, it provides new rewards for interaction. By interacting with his fellows a person can then provide evidence for himself and for them that he is at least their equal. Still better, if he can get his superior to interact with him he may do something to raise his apparent status.

Esteem and Authority

As we have just seen, and as earlier chapters have taught us, persons of high status tend to receive much interaction. Indeed to maneuver a man into coming to you is to establish the presumption that you are his superior. But persons of high status also give much interaction, especially in the sense of originating activity. They tell a relatively large number of others what they ought to do, and the others often do it. The higher the esteem in which a man is held, the higher his authority—this is a proposition for which the federal agency provided much evidence.

Let us consider particularly the agent whom the investigator believed to be the top informal leader in the department. (The supervisor was of course the formal leader.) He was highly competent at his job and recognized as being so by both the supervisor and the other agents. Of the more competent agents, he was the one most receptive and least discouraging to requests for help from others. That is, he was the most willing to incur the cost of taking time off from his own work. And he was highly popular. Note here the congruence of his status, his willingness to follow the rules of distributive justice, his acceptance of *noblesse oblige*. He received high awards in esteem from the other members of the group, but in so doing he incurred, as they saw it, high costs too.

He rewarded the others not only in the business side of their lives but in the social one too. He was always ready to accept an invitation to lunch with his social inferiors, and in this he was unlike most of the other competent agents. But the very liberality with which he distributed his favors prevented his becoming identified with any one of the cliques whose members met regularly for lunch. He was in touch with everybody and not exclusively in touch with any single person or subgroup. We have seen this combination of aloofness and closeness in the leaders of other groups we have looked at, and we have encountered evidence, in Fiedler's reseach reported in Chapter 12 on leadership, that such behavior may make leadership more effective in attaining group goals.

As we saw in Chapter 12, the more competent agents tended to take the lead in any undertaking in which several members of the group were engaged. They made most suggestions, and their suggestions were most often followed, whether the question was where to go for lunch or what to do about a project on which a number of agents were working together. And of all the competent agents, the one held in highest esteem was the one who also held highest authority. When a committee was appointed to draft a change in one of the regulations, he dominated the discussion, and his opinion was the one finally adopted. Above all, like some of the popular girls in the New York State Training School at

Hudson, he stood up for the other agents against the supervisor. In this connection the investigator says of him (p. 123):

> This agent became the informal leader of the group, whose suggestions the others often followed and who acted as their spokesman. For example, in a departmental meeting the supervisor criticized certain deficiencies in the performance of most agents, clearly exempting experts from his criticism. Nevertheless, this official spoke up on behalf of the group and explained that agents could not be blamed for these deficiencies, since a legal regulation that restricted their operations was responsible for them. Generally, the high regard in which this agent was held made his advice and opinion influential among colleagues, and even among superiors.

A person to whom many others come singly for valuable services, in this case advice on how to do their work, and who in rendering the services incurs costs visibly proportional to the esteem they have given him, earns the right to tell them jointly what to do in new conditions that may affect the welfare of many of them, himself among the rest. By serving he becomes a leader. We must always remember that the services he provides need not be ones that you or I should find rewarding or even approve of. Leaders get to be where they are by doing some of the strangest things, and the rest of us are always asking ourselves, "What's he got that I haven't got?" The answer is that what he has got does actually reward some other men, whether or not it ought to do so; and that what he has got is rare in the actual circumstances, whether or not it would be rare in others.

Nor should we lay too much stress on the difference between the followers coming to him singly for advice and his telling them jointly what to do. In both cases, whether he gives them advice they take or orders they obey, the important point is that he controls their behavior; and the fact that a new occasion may call for his advising them jointly is a nonessential detail. His past behavior has won him the capability of doing so, should the occasion present itself, but it may not. The advice he has given them singly they have in the past rewarded with approval, and so he is more likely to give advice again on a new occasion. He has, as we say, acquired confidence in his ability to give them advice. Nor is it just that he has more confidence but that the others have less: persons whose status is lower than his own are persons whose advice has less often won approval in the past, and who are therefore less apt to have the gall to speak up now: what wise ideas they may have do them no good if they lack the confidence to come out with them.

The relation between past behavior and present that holds good for the leader holds good also for the followers. Having taken his advice singly and found it rewarding, they are more ready to take it jointly—to obey him when he tells them what to do for their welfare and his own.

In doing so, he puts his social capital at hazard, since if they obey and fail to find the outcome rewarding, he has done injury to his own status and to their future willingness to obey. But he has much capital to risk, and if they do find that the outcome is to their satisfaction, he has replaced his capital and more. Finally, though the leader may lay himself open to the social advances of his followers, he cannot allow himself to get too close to any one of them or any single clique; for frequent "social" interaction implies equality, and equality between persons tends to be incongruent with the fact that one of their number gives orders to the rest. But the best guarantee that he shall not be too close to anyone lies in the very profusion with which he scatters his favors abroad.

Nonconformity and Isolation

A member of a group acquires high esteem by providing rare and valuable services for the other members. But these are obviously not the only services a member can perform: he can also perform services that, without being rare, nevertheless have their value. Prominent among them is conformity to the norms of the group—a norm being a statement of what behavior ought to be, to which at least some members find it valuable that their own actual behavior and that of others should conform. Since a norm envisages that a relatively large number of members will behave similarly in some respect, conformity cannot be a rare service: any fool can conform if he will only take the trouble; and therefore if all a man did was conform, he would never win much esteem, though he would always win some. But it does not follow that if conformity will not get a man much esteem, nonconformity will not lose him much—if he has any to lose. For his failure to conform, when the other members see no just reason why he should not, deprives them unfairly of a valuable service, and so earns him their positive hostility.

Among themselves the agents had, over time, worked out several unofficial norms. They felt that no agent, as a maximum, should complete more than the eight cases a month that the supervisor expected of every agent as a minimum. And they felt that no agent should take a report home from the office in order to work on it in the evening. Agents that showed any sign of doing these things the others kidded until they stopped. Violation of these norms injured the members of the group, and conformity rewarded them, because an agent who finished more than eight cases a month or worked on cases at home might get an advantage over the others in the race for promotion; and if everyone had started to violate the norms, they would all have found themselves, through competition, working harder than they ever had before—not that the supervisor was at all displeased with the quantity and quality of their present work: the agents were devoted civil servants. In practice, these norms of output conspired to preserve existing differences in competence, since they prevented slower agents from catching up with their superiors by working longer.

The agents laid an even more severe taboo against reporting to the supervisor that firms had offered them bribes, though by the official rules of the agency they were bound to report such offers. It was not that the agents actually accepted bribes and wished to prevent a colleague who was squeamish about such matters from spoiling their game. Far from it: when they suspected that an officer of a firm was working up to offering a bribe, they did their best to cut him off before he could commit himself openly. In the agents' view, it was inevitable that businessmen, given the pressures they worked under, should think of bribery; therefore it ought not to be held against them, and an agent reporting them and so making them subject to legal action was a "squealer." The agents also had a more practical interest in the norm against reporting bribes. If possible an agent was expected to induce the firm he was investigating to obey the law voluntarily and not under the compulsion of legal action expensive to both parties. An offer of a bribe, however tactfully it was made, put into an agent's hand a lever by which he might without legal action get the firm to comply with the law. But it was a lever that became worse than useless once the proffered bribe was officially reported. Indeed, the report might make the company all the more ready to fight the whole issue out with the government in the courts. Accordingly, agents discouraged all tendencies in their colleagues to "get tough with" and "crack down on" companies, except as a last resort. Should the agency get the reputation of behaving in this way, their work would become much more difficult: all firms would meet every agent with automatic hostility, and the chances of persuading them instead of compelling them into compliance would be gone forever. For these reasons most agents felt they had a direct personal interest in seeing that all their colleagues conformed to this norm.

With these norms in mind, let us look at one of the isolates in the department. When we call him an isolate, we mean that he received few social contacts and often lunched alone. Although he appears to have been considered fairly competent, he not only was not ready to use his competence for the benefit of others but spent his time instead turning out more work than the others considered proper. Already held in low esteem for behavior of this sort, he proceeded also to take a "get tough" attitude toward the firms he investigated; indeed such behavior was generally more characteristic of the less popular agents than of the more popular ones. And he was the only agent who violated the strongest taboo of all by reporting to the supervisor that a bribe had been offered him. The investigator tells us little or nothing about the social background of any of the agents, including this one, and so we cannot tell what features of his past history may have predisposed him to behave as he did. He himself admitted that he had made a mistake: though he had violated the norm, he was ready to concede that it was a good one in principle.

For his action the group had for a time deliberately ostracized him. Cutting off interaction with a member and thus depriving him of any social reward whatever is the most severe punishment a group can inflict on him; in fact he ceases to be a member. But once a man has stood that, he can, so to speak, stand anything; and his group has lost control of him, for it has left him with nothing more to lose. Certainly the department had pretty well lost control of this agent. Though he reported no more bribes, he did much as he pleased in other ways. The agents, for instance, felt that he wasted their time by talking a great deal too much in meetings of the department, where the agents of higher esteem usually took the largest part in discussion. But in spite of the laughter his remarks provoked, he kept at it and would not be cowed. In a better cause he might have been a hero. The investigator believes that this agent provided only the most conspicuous example of a general tendency: that agents of established low status conformed least closely to the norms of the group, while those of middle status—particularly those, like relative newcomers, whose position was least well established—were the greatest conformers of all.

Social behavior, in a group as elsewhere, is a continuous process in which members influence other members, and the success of influence in the past changes the probability of its success in the future. One result of the process of influence is that the members of a group become differentiated in a more or less stable way—stable so long as external circumstances do not change much. As some members, for instance, succeed in providing, under the influence of requests from others, more valuable services for these others than the latter can provide for themselves, the members become differentiated in status. This fairly stable differentiation in some pattern other than a random one is what we mean by the structure or organization of the group. But the structure is never so stable that it does not itself sow the seeds for further change, and we have been studying a particular example of this. The process of influence that has landed a man at the foot of the ladder of status may render any future influence, so far as it comes from other members, still less likely to succeed with him. Suppose that he would ordinarily lose esteem by doing something other than what they wish, but he happens as a result of his past behavior to be left without any esteem to lose. If there is any other way in which he finds nonconformity rewarding—and it may be rewarding just because it vexes *them*—the fact that its costs have been reduced to zero raises the odds in favor of his taking such action.

A group controls its members by providing rewards for them which it can then threaten to withdraw. If the group has to make good the threat too often, it may wind up with nothing left to withdraw. Its control is always precarious so long as the members have any alternative to accepting the control, such as the alternative offered by another group they can make their escape to. We have been speaking of the member of low status who has hit the bottom. But very high status may have something of the same effect as very low. A person who has so much status to lose that he will not mind if he loses a little of it can afford to try something new and take the risk that it may not turn out to be acceptable to the membership. In his way, he too is exempt from the control of the group. There are deviates and deviates; some from the point of view of members are bad deviates, some are good ones. But both are innovators; and if one looked only at the innovations they propose, it would sometimes be difficult to tell which was which.

In this book we try to describe and explain what happens in human behavior without taking any moral stand about it—unless laughter is a moral stand. Or rather we take only one stand out of the many open to us. We have nothing to say in favor of conformity or against it. All we have done is point out that a man who does not conform takes certain risks. But a man is born to take risks. Morally we cannot object to him unless he wants his nonconformity made easy, unless he wants to kick the group in the teeth and have it love him too. For then he is being unfair to the rest of us by asking that an exception to the human condition be made in his favor.

16 The Institutional and the Subinstitutional

ACCORDING TO MY LIGHTS, A LAST CHAPTER SHOULD RESEMBLE a primitive orgy after harvest. The work may have come to an end, but the worker cannot let go all at once. He is still full of energy that will fester if it cannot find an outlet. Accordingly he is allowed a time of license, when he may say all sorts of things he would think twice before saying in more sober moments, when he is no longer bound by logic and evidence but free to speculate about what he has done.

I propose to take my orgy out in putting a frame around this book. In this last chapter I shall return to a question I raised in the first, when I tried to set up some sort of definition of elementary social behavior. It consists of an exchange of actions between at least two persons, where the action of each rewards or punishes the action of the other; the exchange takes place directly between the two rather than through some intermediary; and the actions in question are real actions and not just norms specifying what behavior ought to be. (But remember that a person's statement of a norm, as distinguished from the content of the norm itself, is as much an action as any other.) Granted that they grade into one another by degrees, and that nothing more than an arbitrary line can be drawn between the two, what are the relations between the elementary and the more complex forms of social behavior, between the informal and the formal, between the subinstitutional and the institutional?

The Group as a Microcosm

We gain our fullest understanding of the elementary features of social behavior by observing the interactions between members of small, informal groups. In their private speculations, some sociologists were once inclined to think of the small group as a microcosm of society at large: they felt that the same phenomena appeared in the former as did in

356

the latter but on a vastly reduced scale—a scale that, incidentally, made detailed investigation possible. No doubt there are striking resemblances between the two. We have seen how members roughly equal in status within a small group are apt to associate with one another on "social" occasions more often with either their inferiors or superiors. Their behavior has obvious points of similarity with the more salient features of class and stratification systems—where, for instance, members of families equal in status as recognized in the larger society are especially apt to visit, go to parties with, and marry one another. The resemblances are not fortuitous: some of the same processes are at work in both cases. But this is not to say that one is a microcosm of the other, that the one is simply the other writ small. The two are not wholly similar, if only because in an informal group a man wins status through his direct exchanges with the other members, while he wins status in the larger society by wealth, inheritance, occupation, office, legal authority—in every case by his position in some institutional or organizational scheme, often one with a long history behind it.

Yet I must be careful to say just what I mean. A person often raises his status in an organization, just as he does in a small group, by providing others with rewards of relatively high value. But in the small group he usually does so through direct exchanges with the others. In the organization, on the other hand, he raises his status—for instance, he gets promoted—if his bosses consider that he has done a good job. His activity rewards the bosses only because it contributes to reaching the goals of the organization, and the organization in turn rewards them for securing such contributions. (Remember that "the organization" is itself shorthand for the persistent, concerted activities of a number of persons.) In the organization, in short, the chains of action and reward are longer and linked in more complicated ways.

To take another example, when a number of followers get help from a leader, to whom they yield some authority to control their behavior, his position may look much like that of an appointed supervisor whose designated subordinates report to him and to whom he in turn gives orders. Perhaps in the distant past, when formal organizations were first deliberately designed, the span of control—the number of men put under the command of a single officer—may have been modeled on what is apt to spring up spontaneously in a small group. But of course the situations are not identical. The fact that higher authority has appointed the formal leader, that he is responsible to it, and that the punishments he inflicts are made possible by its support, makes all the difference, as anyone who has been both an informal and a formal leader knows. In the formal situation, moreover, both leaders and followers get some of their rewards not from exchange with one another, but from the exchange of work for pay with the organization of which they are a part. Both parties, though certainly dependent on one another, are less dependent than they are in the small, informal group. It is true that a formal leader may be more successful in his own job if he has something of the informal leader about him too, but though the two roles overlap, they are not quite the same.

If the informal group, like elementary social behavior in general, is not a true microcosm of society at large, the reason again is not that the fundamental processes of behavior—the ways in which the performance of an activity is governed by its stimuli and its payoffs—are different in the two cases: far from being different, they are indentical. The reason lies rather in the fact that, in the institutions of society at large, the way the fundamental processes are combined are more complex.

The Small Group in History

The question then is how the more complicated chains get established. As far as social organization is concerned, mankind has spent almost all of its history in social units no larger than small groups, that is, in bands of hunters and gatherers. The genetic characteristics themselves that, in interaction with the processes of learning, determine the nature of man's social behavior—as distinguished from that of other mammals—must have been acquired in the course of his life in such groups. Indeed at the level of the informal group mankind continues to betray its essential social unity. The social processes that I have tried to describe and explain in this book, processes often revealed in studies of industrial work-groups or street-corner gangs in American society, seem in their fundamental features, underlying the obvious differences in environment and technology, to resemble those occurring in small groups of hunters and gatherers. Sociologists often make a distinction between societies and small groups. But for many millennia the only human societies *were* small groups, displaying the features of elementary social behavior, such as the emergence of leadership, that we find in small groups today.

Again I must be careful. The behavior found in small groups within modern societies resembles but is not identical with that found in the small groups that were the earliest human societies. In particular, the former do not often maintain their social identity from one generation to another as the latter often do. I have had nothing to say in this book about the special forms of human activity with their special rewards, such as the begetting, bearing and rearing of children, that may perpetuate the identity of a society and, if the physical and social environment does not change too drastically, its norms as well. I wished to concentrate on the features of social behavior that all small groups have in common, and adopting that policy meant leaving out of consideration a special kind of small group, the family, and with it the processes of marriage and education in the broadest sense of the word that, in providing continuity between the generations, allow some groups to become societies.

From Group to Society

If all human societies were once small groups, it follows, though we cannot know all the details, that all the great nation-states, which make up the bulk of societies today, and which contain many small groups within them, grew out of small groups by various processes of social development or evolution. Indeed it is impossible—and it is one of the fallacies of the so-called functional school of sociology to believe that it *is* possible—to explain the characteristics of any modern society without making some reference to its past history as well as to its present circumstances. This does not mean that we must always go back to origins, of which in any event we have no record. And the fact that some societies, under the influence of strong converging forces that override the diversity of their origins, tend to become at some times more similar, so as to provide something like a common starting-point, makes the work of explanation easier. But we cannot avoid some reference to past history. It is, for example, impossible to explain some of the features of American society today, which differ from those of other societies, without referring to political developments in English society in the Middle Ages, the social ancestor of our own society, and to later historical developments that differentiated our political society in turn from that of England. The maxim to bear in mind is: As the twig is bent so is the tree.

The question here, though, is not that of the particular features of development leading to the institutions of particular modern societies but that of the general features that might lead from a society as a small group to a society as a complex organization. Let me illustrate. The leadership of many bands of hunters and gatherers is not hereditary. If the conditions described by Lévi-Strauss (1955) for the Nambikwara are at all characteristic, the leader, as in informal groups today, is simply the member who is willing to do the work and obedience to whose orders leads to the greatest rewards for the other members. I suspect that the first step on the road toward a modern society is that by which the leader is succeeded, not just by some other man who happens to possess these qualities, but specifically by some kinsman of the last leader. The point is not that succession to authority becomes hereditary, but rather that it is determined by some rule or norm. Yet that is not quite the point either. Many small groups develop norms. What is important is not the existence of a norm but what kind of a norm it is. For the first time the group possesses an organization persisting over time in the sense that at least one office, the chieftainship, is recognized as existing apart from the individuals who temporarily occupy it. I can imagine the stimulus-conditions that might lead the members of a group, accustomed to obeying a particular leader, to obey after his death some member of his family, say a son, in his place. But I doubt that these conditions would be enough to maintain him in the chieftainship, if he had to rely on the chance that he possessed the personal qualities of his father. By virtue of his inheritance he would have to possess other resources that he could use to reward his followers. These other resources might include some form of capital under his control, such as hoards of food, perishable only slowly, which the members of the usual hunting-gathering band do not possess. No norm maintains itself, but these resources might allow the successor to take the first steps toward obtaining conformity to the norm or, if you like, to the institution of chieftainship.

At the origin of even the most modern industrial society lies a social unit not much more complicated than this. I myself have always been much interested in the social history of England. Let me, accordingly, look back at the earliest description of the society that, in my view, should count more than any other—more than Greece, Rome, or Israel—as the institutional ancestor of English society and, through English society, of our own. Look back at Tacitus' (1932) description of the tiny Germanic tribal kingdoms of the first century A.D. Of course the society is already highly institutionalized, governed to a high degree according to rules inherited from the past, perhaps from a remote past. But the rules outline an organization that is closer to what naturally and spontaneously appears in any small group than anything we have known in more modern times. Consider the kingship itself. It is already in theory something a man inherits and does not acquire by his own actions. True, if he turns out to be incompetent, his high birth is unlikely to save him. Even so, the rule still holds, and another member of the royal lineage, rather than some mere adventurer, will usually take his place. But the relation between the king and his "companions" (*gesiths, comites*), who eat and drink in his hall in peace and follow him in war, and whom he rewards with food, with jewelry, and finally with rights over land, much more resembles the relation between the leader of a group and his followers than do most political systems that we have known in our society since that time. At the same time, I must not oversimplify the picture. I have been speaking of only one social class. The "companions," who alone possess the relatively very expensive arms and armor of the period, are themselves supported by a dependent peasantry. Yet the relation between a "companion" and his villagers in turn resembles that between a chief and his followers. (See Bloch, 1940, pp. 369–379.) At the back, historically, of any of the great modern societies we shall find some such society as this—institutionalized indeed, but institutionalized in a pattern that betrays its kinship with the primeval small group.

Now suppose such a society has created a capital of some sort. Men need capital before they can get any technical invention adopted, but I have organizational inventions particularly in mind here. By capital I mean anything that allows them to postpone actions leading to some immediate reward in order to undertake others whose rewards, though potentially greater, are both uncertain and deferred. The capital may take the form of unusually well-disciplined soldiers. It may take the form of a surplus of food or money, and here we must always remember the potential for accumulating capital made possible by the neolithic revolution that invented agriculture, pastoralism, and the smelting of metals. Most important of all, it may take the form of a moral code, especially a code supporting trust and confidence between men: a well-founded belief that they will not always let you down in favor of their private, short-term gain.

Without some capital, no institutional elaboration can get off the ground. But given the capital, the society—really some man or group of men within the society, perhaps always ultimately a single man—is apt to invest it by trying out some set of activities that departs from the original or primeval institutional pattern. The new pattern envisages an intermeshing of the behavior of a larger number of persons in a more complicated or roundabout manner than has hitherto been the custom. Having, for instance, conquered new territory with the help of his companions, the king may try to maintain permanent control over it, and to do so he will have to rely, since he now has more people under his rule, not just on his own ties with his companions but on his companions' ties with companions under them. That is, he may have to encourage or acquiesce in the development of some sort of feudal system, and in so doing he will have to spell out, to make a matter of explicit norms, the behavior toward one another of the people now made interdependent. He will have to do so for the same reason that makes a modern firm, when it has grown beyond a certain size, begin to spell out its organizational chart. Even small groups develop norms, but as a society develops out of a small group, and more and more people become members, it must rely more and more on formal rules, formally enforced, to control their behavior—which does not in the least mean that the old, informal controls disappear. But the question always remains whether the new arrangement will pay off before the capital runs out. Probably most such attempts by most human societies have failed.

Instead of handling his own finances and keeping the treasury, as did the Anglo-Saxon kings, in a chest under the royal bed, the king may appoint a full-time treasurer. Instead of dispensing his own justice, as did Saint Louis, king of France, sitting under a tree, he may appoint full-time judges. And both the treasurer and the judges sooner or later acquire subordinate staffs. That is, specialized organizations are born. These institutions may ultimately increase the efficiency of his administration, attract to his rule, by the prospects of speedy justice, men who might otherwise have been drawn to mere local sources of power and authority, and maintain the precarious peace on which his ability to levy increasing taxes finally depends. They may even begin to set him free from his exclusive, and therefore dangerous, dependence on the loyalty of his companions. They may provide him with arms to use if necessary against the companions themselves. But these rewards take time to come in; and while he waits for them, he must invest the capital to pay the treasurer and the judges enough to make up, and more than make up, for the time they take from their private affairs. He must arrange that the rewards they get from doing their duty are greater than those they would get from appropriating the king's funds to their own use or selling the king's justice for money in their own pockets. But to do these things the king must have the capital; he must, for instance, be able to spare enough land from other uses so that his officers can be paid out of the rent, and this means that he must have effective control over his domains. In all these undertakings the king, whom I have chosen as my exemplar, though of course he is not alone in stimulating the growth of institutions, is a risk-taker just as surely as is any venture-capitalist today: the institution of royal judges, for instance, may not pay off. Indeed the risks the king takes are greater, for they may include his life.

Once the king has succeeded in maintaining peace and persuading common men that mere anarchy presents no regular threat to their enterprises, other organizational changes may occur. Markets may flourish. Through markets men may enter a wider web of economic exchanges and in the long run begin to specialize efficiently in one kind of production or trade. Remember, though, that markets are seldom self-regulating, and to make the market attractive to many buyers and sellers, there must be some procedure for settling commercial disputes quickly and preventing speculators from trying to corner the market by buying up goods on the way to market before they reach it—the crimes our ancestors called forestalling and regrating. Regulating the market demands some degree of political control over the marketplace and its environs, a control that in Europe the emerging corporations of the boroughs and cities usually provided. Their markets could be the richest source of their prosperity.

To take another example, a man who with the members of his family once made woolen cloth by performing every operation from the original carding and spinning to the final retail sale may undertake to specialize on one operation, let us say the weaving itself. In so doing he may achieve economies of scale by applying a narrower skill to a larger volume of work, but he can gain these advantages only if general demand is high, which may mean a larger and more concentrated population, and only if he is sure of his suppliers (the spinners) and of his outlets (the finishers) who must now become specialists too. Unless the whole chain of transactions can be maintained, so that the consumer gets his cloth in the end, every single specialization collapses. The volume of business may finally become great enough to furnish a payoff for a person whose specialization is the financing and coordination of the other specialists—in the medieval cloth trade they called him a draper or clothier—and then we are at the threshold of modern industrial organization. We are also at the point where increased taxes on cloth may help pay the king off for maintaining the peace.

The Pattern of Social Behavior in the Emerging Society

Of course I cannot go into all the details, which in any event differ somewhat from one emerging society to another. Nor does the point of my argument depend upon the details. All of these innovations, whether at the top of society or at the bottom, possess the following characteristics. They require some form of social capital before men can attempt them at all, for their payoffs at best are not immediate but deferred. The capital must increasingly take the form of generalized rewards like money or status, generalized in the sense that leaders can distribute them so as to induce people to perform some mix of a wide variety of activities. But note that even the ability of a society to provide rewards of this sort depends on its having previously accumulated some little social capital. Money is of no use to men unless they are confident that it can be converted into goods and services, and someone who is worrying about where his next meal is coming from is unlikely to find status particularly rewarding.

The political units, in the most general sense of the word "political," to which people belong tend to increase in area and in density of population. Indeed the former may lead to the latter: the increased area within which the king maintains his peace may allow an increase in population. What we usually call the division of labor also increases: individuals and families become more specialized in their activities. They may thus act more efficiently, but they also become more limited and more dependent on others. Finally, not just specialized individuals but specialized organizations begin to appear. Within themselves these organizations may develop some of the characteristics of the primordial small group, but the activities they exchange with outsiders, with their clienteles, are limited in kind.

It has always been recognized that an increasing division of labor goes along with changes in the interactions between people. A person may be able to interact with a larger number of others, as in a market; he may become at one time or another the client of more organizations. Nor is it just the number of persons who are able to interact with one another that increases: their interactions link them together in more complicated networks. The increasing division of labor is apt to demand a longer chain of transactions before some final result is achieved; and the chain becomes, so to speak, more roundabout: if a person is to walk from one place to another he just starts straight out, but if he is to ride on a subway, someone must have built, for instance, a steel mill first. Finally, the proportion of open networks in which people take part may increase at the expense of closed ones. Closed networks, we shall remember, are those of the type, characteristic of the small group, which link A to B, B to C, and C back to A.

But if the number of other persons a man interacts with increases, and the networks in which he takes part become more complex, the kinds of rewards he exchanges with any particular other person may become more limited. In this sense, their relationship becomes more impersonal, whereas in the characteristic small group members come to exchange a number of different kinds of reward. Thus after the Industrial Revolution people were apt to complain that the relationship between master and man had been impoverished, reduced to the cash nexus: so much money for so many pieces of work. I think the process had begun long before that. Speaking for myself I do not believe that an individual is necessarily the loser if the proportion of his more impersonal ties increases, provided that he preserves a few personal ones. Contrary to what seem to be the tastes of those who start communes today, I think that being locked into the intense personal relations of a single small group would be intolerably boring. Herman Melville found himself trapped in the little valley of Typee. It was a tropical paradise, but he got out of it as soon as he could. Even New England was better than that.

In this course of development, the proportion of others with whom a man's relationships are impersonal increases in another sense of that word. The larger is the number of persons in contact with one another, the more complex are the networks in which they take part, but the more limited is the scope of any particular tie. As the values of all these variables change together, the less is it possible to leave the mutual adjustments of all these persons to the chances, to the rough-and-tumble, of interpersonal contact. When persons enter into many exchanges with one another in a small group, the different kinds of exchange exert, as we have seen, some mutual control over one another. In the new conditions, control becomes more external and formal. Persons must to a greater degree go by the rule, work by the book, which does not mean that rules do not get broken or become dead letters any less in the new kind of society than they do in all human groupings. It only means that the broken rules are apt to be replaced by new rules, rather than by informal controls. Although all recurrent behavior tends in time to get described and consecrated in explicit norms, now the process is hastened. These formal rules and their formal sanctions are what we refer to when we say that behavior in society at large is somehow more institutionalized than it is in the primordial small group. Indeed one of the institutional inventions in whose absence the others cannot advance very far may be an organization that specializes in formulating and sanctioning norms, that is, a legal system.

The Precariousness of Civilization

Except for a few recent economic historians who specialize in the study of economic development, scholars seldom, it seems to me, examine in detail the processes of institutional growth. Above all, they do not explain them. They tell us, for instance, that Henry II was the first king of England to send royal judges regularly on circuit throughout the country. They never ask what capital—social or economic—enabled him to undertake the innovation, what risks it ran, or what returns replaced the capital and allowed the institution to persist. True, the requisite information is often lacking; but only answers to questions like these would explain the most important developments in social history. After all, there are other entrepreneurs than economic ones; nor are the economic ones always the most important. Given some capital, every society tries institutional innovations. If they manage to pay off—and a great deal of capital may be spent before they do—they persist. They may replace or even increase the capital, and allow the society to go on to make another innovation. But there must be a payoff; it is never automatic and always problematical, and it may not continue. External circumstances may change; other parts of the social organization may fail and bring the institution down in their ruin; and the institution itself may exhaust the sources of its own reward—as when an exploitative agriculture works out the soil available to it. In general, to explain the disintegration of institutions, we must examine each link in the networks of exchange that once sustained them, and ask why in one or more of the links men could not or did not take the actions that others had at one time expected of them. Naturally it is easier to advocate such a study than to carry it out.

All history is there to remind us how precarious is the process of civilization. The decline of the Roman Empire, the first large-scale experiment in Western civilization, is there to remind us of it. But even the recovery of the West from the Roman collapse has been far from uninterrupted. Feudalism in northwestern Europe was in trouble from the beginning; indeed it could never have corresponded in the least to what its doctrine said it ought to be, had it not been supported by sources outside itself: by national loyalties transcending the feudal tie and by a kingship that only just managed to remain something more than the top rung in the feudal ladder. The great wave of economic and institutional development from the eleventh through the thirteenth century was followed by the relative stagnation of the fourteenth, as if the very success of medieval institutions in exploiting new sources of reward had used up for the time being the available supply. And in the sixteenth century English industry made tentative approaches to factory organization, which could not be maintained in the face of a market collapse and which were not revived until the eighteenth, when power-driven machinery at last provided factory organization with a payoff that no other form of industrial production could match. The same refrain repeats itself over and over: institutions do not keep going just because they are enshrined in formal rules—through formal rules are essential to institutions—and it seems extraordinary that anyone should ever talk as if they did. They keep going because they have payoffs, ultimately payoffs for individuals. Nor is society a perpetual-motion machine, supplying its own fuel. It cannot keep itself going by planting in the young a desire for those goods and only those goods that it happens to be in shape to provide. It must provide some goods that men find rewarding not simply because they are sharers in a particular culture but because they are men.

The Persistence of Elementary Social Behavior

As the institutions of society depart further and further from the elementary forms of social behavior, the latter do not quietly wither away. Far from it, they persist obviously and everywhere, ready to take their revenge. They may persist most luxuriantly in places where institutional arrangements have broken down and left gaps. I have argued that street gangs display an elaboration of informal pattern not unworthy to rank with that of a primitive hunting band. If street gangs included girls and the members married them the resemblance would be even closer. And further the institutional breakdown goes, as in natural disasters, revolution, or defeat in war, the more fully do the characteristics of elementary social behavior reassert themselves.

But I am not much interested in the elementary social behavior that lies outside the institutional system, as the street gang does. Much more important is the behavior that lies within the system. It sprouts in the "grapevine"; it is as well developed in the personal loyalties that surround some executives and political leaders as it is in a group of workers who will not let the exuberant production of one of their number show up the deficiences of the rest. It appears in the invention of, and concern for, outward and visible signs of rank and status never warranted by the formal organization alone. Sometimes the activities exchanged in elementary social behavior derive their value from the rules of the institution. Thus the help people exchanged for esteem in the federal agency I have described so often would have had no value, had the persons concerned not been employed to do a certain kind of job. But though the institution gave value to the help, the process of exchange itself remained just as elementary, just as subinstitutional, as anything seen in a street gang. Elementary social behavior does not grow just in the gaps between institutions; it clings to institutions as to a trellis. It grows everywhere—if only because the norms that define institutions and the orders given in instituted organizations can never prescribe human behavior to the last detail, even if they were obeyed to the letter, which they are not. Indeed, the elementary features of social behavior help explain how and why they are disobeyed.

Yet we ought not to look upon the subinstitutional as necessarily a kind of friction holding the institutional back, to be gotten rid of only to the advantage of the latter. On the contrary, the motives characteristic of elementary social behavior often mobilize solid support behind institutional aims. An obvious example is the way in which the soldiers' determination not to let their comrades down contributes more than anything else to the fighting power of an infantry outfit. Institutions are often maintained by other rewards than the one each is primarily designed to achieve. Infantry combat is meant to defeat the enemy; this is undoubtedly a reward, though often one long in coming; but effective combat may also be rewarded, and more immediately, by the approval of your fellow soldiers whom you have covered as they have you. And sometimes elementary social behavior manages to support an institution in the institution's spite. The help exchanged in the federal agency may well have made the work of the agency more effective than it would have been otherwise—but it was exchanged only by disregarding an official rule against helping.

The Conflict between the Institutional and the Subinstitutional

Elementary social behavior, then, is not driven out by institutionalization but survives alongside it, acquiring from it new reasons for existence. Sometimes it contributes to the support of the institution. But sometimes, as we also know, the two work against one another.

Since the relatively bad situations are the ones we are most interested in, for the reason that we might try to do something about them, I shall spend the rest of my time considering what happens when the two are at odds.

Consider then a working group in an American office or factory—a group like those we have studied so often in this book. Exchange—it has been our main theme—is the basis, acknowledged or unacknowledged, of much human behavior, and each member of the group has obviously entered into exchange with the company in question. But the exchange as institutionalized, as subject to explicit rules, is a limited exchange: each member has agreed, in return for receiving a money wage, to contribute his labor as directed by representatives of the company. To be sure, he has received many rewards for his labor besides money: a pleasant place to work, a job that gives him standing in the community, and sometimes interesting work to do. But the most fully institutionalized aspect of the exchange is that of labor for money: the company is not legally bound, as part of its bargain, to provide the other things. Industrialization has specialized exchanges. As it has advanced, it has ceased to give formal recognition to many sorts of things that entered into the exchange between superior and subordinate at a time when society had moved less far away from elementary social behavior. No transaction engages as much of the individual as it used to.

What happens, we may ask, to the behavior that has been simplified and rationalized away, that goes unrecognized institutionally? Has it really disappeared, or has it only been swept under the carpet? As the worker gets down to his job in his department, he encounters many activities on the part of his fellow workers that reward or punish him, and he learns activities that reward or punish his fellow workers. Though their nature may derive from arrangements made by the firm, they are treated as institutionally irrelevant to the exchange of labor for money. Thus the ledger clerks in the Eastern Utilities Company found that their job was more skilled and more responsible than that of the cash posters, but it earned the same pay and was allowed less autonomy. By the standards of elementary social behavior, justice had not been done them, and their status was threatened. But none of this was institutionally relevant to the bargain struck between them and the company.

I do not mean in the least to imply that the management of the Eastern Utilities Company was unconcerned with justice. Just as much as the union did, it believed in "a fair day's work for a fair day's wage," though the two might have disagreed about the exact value either variable in the equation ought to take. But the notion of fair exchange, so far as it was institutionalized, took little into account besides work and money, and treated as beyond its scope many of the aspects of justice that elementary social behavior in fact insists upon. This may easily be seen in the replies the supervisors made when the ledger clerks complained. In effect they pointed out that the clerks had made a bargain to do, in return for a fair wage, what they were told to do in the way of work. So long as the management stuck to its part of the bargain, what call did the clerks have to ask for more than theirs? Institutionalization makes more complex the chains of transactions between men, but does so at the price of simplifying any one link. Elementary social behavior may compensate for the simplification, as it does at times in military units, but it may also make the simplification uncomfortable, as it did here. The ledger clerks expected the company to maintain justice in general and not justice within the particular terms of their bargain. Incorrigibly, and against one of the strongest trends of human history, they expected the management to behave like men and not just like actors playing an institutionalized role. Thank God they did; but at points like this elementary social behavior begins to break in on institutionalization and, instead of supporting it, does it damage. This is of course only one illustration of the way the two can fall at odds.

Let us recognize that workers like the ledger clerks might not have felt so much threatened by loss of status nor so much rewarded by success in maintaining it, if they had not already secured plenty of rewards of a different kind. There is a hierarchy of values, and not until the lower ones have been satisfied will the higher ones begin to attract: it is a rich man who can afford to worry about his status. Only in a few places like the United States are wages so high that workers can begin to interest themselves in the finer points of distributive justice; and this has consequences for both management and organized labor. Business has on the whole been so successful in providing money that other values have risen in relative importance; its old assumption, child of past penury, that money would be enough to enlist the full energy of labor no longer works quite as well as it did, and business can hardly make it work at all without continually creating new and desirable products to be bought with money. As for organized labor, the more successful it is in getting the general level of wages raised, the more likely it is to undermine its own unity; for then workers can begin to interest themselves not just in the absolute amount of wages but in wage differentials, and wage differentials are obviously apt to set one group of workers against another. A working class is perhaps most unified when its members have gained enough above mere subsistence so that the bosses cannot buy them off one by one—they can wait out a strike together—but not so far above that wage differentials rise in value relative to the general level of wages. The reformers of the nineteenth century, by the way, must have founded their demand for universal suffrage on the assumption, which was true then, that the poorest class was also the largest: if all these people got the vote, they would be able to get their other deserts. But now that the curve of income distribution has changed in shape, and so many families have moved up that the middle-income levels have become the most populous, we Americans may be able, if we wish, to oppress the poor by perfectly democratic methods: the poor have got the vote but they no longer have the votes. What I am suggesting here is that the very success of the specialized exchange of money for wages is one of the conditions that allows subinstitutional behavior to break in on the institutional. We are at last, through perhaps only for the time being, rich enough to indulge our full humanity.

But let me return to the office. The ledger clerks complained to their supervisor of the injustice of their position over against the cash posters, expecting him, in turn, to take the matter up with the officer above him in the managerial pyramid. When he did little or nothing, they added his behavior to their complaints: "He does not stand up for us." They were expecting from him the sort of action that would indeed have been natural in an informal leader: in return for the loyalty they would have given him, an informal leader would certainly have represented their interests against any outside party. Once more the assumptions of subinstitutional were coming up against those of institutional behavior: just as the ledger clerks had demanded a less specialized justice from the company, so now they asked for less specialized leadership. They were asking again for a man or woman and not a supervisor. But how could their supervisor stand up for them? He too was trapped by the institutional rules. He might report to higher authority that the ledger clerks were disaffected, but he had no further power to do anything about it. Institutionally speaking, he too was paid to do as he was told. To do anything effective for the ledger clerks he might have had to use with higher authority his own informal ties rather than his formal ones.

At this point the story of the ledger clerks ends. Although they were thinking of going to the union and asking it to take the matter up, they had not in fact done so. They were dissatisfied, but not really very angry. Nor is their case particularly striking in itself; I use it only to illustrate what I believe to be a large class of cases. Suppose that the office had not been unionized and that many groups were nursing grievances—not only grievances about the absolute amount of wages, that is, about a matter the institutional bargain did take cognizance of, but also grievances, like the ledger clerk's, about matters it did not. Certainly the members of these groups would approach their supervisors first; when they found that the supervisors could not effectively stand up for them, they would cast about for something else to do. Many of the groups would have developed informal leadership, and if they felt their complaints at all deeply, the leaders, as a condition of keeping their positions, would have had to try to bring the complaints home to management. The first thing you know they would have gotten together and organized a strike; and if their followers had enough of what I have called social capital, material and nonmaterial, to keep the strike up, they would have forced the company to accept a union—collective bargaining, grievance procedure, and all. Some such event has often been the origin of unionization in a plant.

Note what has happened: subinstitutional has come into conflict with institutional behavior. The result is not a collapse of the old institution and a return to more elementary forms of behavior, but the founding of a new institution, the union, of a particular sort—an institution designed, among other things, to maintain subinstitutional values. The union attempts to force the company to take a less specialized view of justice—for the grievance procedure in some degree does this—and tries to recapture for the workers some control over their social environment by giving them more effective representation than either their supervisors or their informal leaders could have provided. Of course the new institution, once formed, may in time run into the same trouble with elementary social behavior as the old did earlier.

I suspect that many of our institutions have had the same kind of origin. Indeed in another book (Homans, 1950, 464–466) I made this claim for the complex of institutions we call democracy. In informal groups it is difficult for government *not* to be carried on with the consent of the governed. Democracy aims at re-establishing this elementary value in a much more complicated institutional setting. It is an institution designed to make good some of the human deficiencies of other institutions.

The invention of new institutions is not the only way of coping with the conflict between subinstitutional and institutional behavior. The conflict may be resolved, and resolved for long periods of time, by "good administration"—the sort of thing the ledger clerks would have enjoyed if their supervisor had managed to bring their complaints home to his own boss, and he, in turn, had begun to consider what adjustments he might make. Good administration is intelligent behavior within a more or less unchanging institutional framework, and it can compensate for many defects in the latter. If it were not so, we should not see so many autocracies and tyrannies so successful for so long—and successful even apart from their use of terror in governing their subjects.

But the problem need not be solved at all, temporarily or permanently. The society may tear itself asunder in conflict without ever creating a new institution that will stick. Still more often the problem may simply persist without issuing in overt conflict but without resolution either. New forms of behavior that might have proved rewarding enough to establish themselves are not invented; or no one commands the social capital to risk in trying them out. The result is a society of people to some extent apathetic, or institutions to some extent frozen in an unnatural equilibrium—unnatural in the sense that out of the elements lying around here and there something better might conceivably have been made.

Something of this sort seems to some of us to have happened to American industry even when it has been unionized. (See Zaleznik, Christensen, and Roethlisberger, 1958, 394–411.) The original institutional compact of money for obedience to orders has not encouraged management to try to turn the worker into a slave of a machine—as the humanists would have it—but to turn him into the machine itself, into something, that is, which has the admirable property that if you will only feed it the right materials and power it will do just what you want it to do, no more no less. If you will only feed the worker money, you should get out of him exactly what you want. When you do not get it, and since elementary social behavior is always breaking in you never do, you never conclude that your theory is inadequate but only that you have not applied it rigorously enough. You redesign the controls on the machine so that now—you hope—it simply cannot get off the track. For this purpose the assembly line, where manpower is machine-paced, is the best thing yet devised. But it is so unnatural that you must feed your human machines still more money in order to induce them to work on it at all. And the more money they get, the more valuable relatively they find the elementary social behavior you have done your best to eliminate. The worker is left so apathetic, so many activities in his repertory have gone unrewarded, that management seems justified in believing him incapable of independent responsibility and therefore in treating him only as a machine fueled up with money and made to run on a track. And so the wheel comes full circle.

What industry often lacks is what we have seen to be characteristic of strong and lively institutions: not one. motive only but a wide variety of motives held by the men whose activities the institution coordinates are enlisted in support of its aims and not left to work against them or at best at cross-purposes. Industry might consider joining the forces it has so far shown itself unable to lick. As usual, this is easier said than done, especially as industry under its present design does accomplish, after a fashion, what it sets out to do.

Of course you are at liberty to take a moral stand and approve the present situation, though for reasons opposite to the ones an industrialist might bring up. You may argue that workers ought not support the purposes of management, which cannot fail to be utterly at odds with their own. They ought to stick to the original narrow bargain and make it work for their material interests. They ought to get as much money, for doing as little work, as they can. They will not behave quite the way you think they ought to, but the price a man pays for holding high moral standards is seldom seeing them realized. And at least your moral stand will allow you to disregard the immediate problem: for all practical purposes you will be just as conservative as the most hard-boiled businessman. But the general problem you will have a harder time disregarding. Sooner or later, in this society or another, you will find an institution whose purposes you approve of, and then you will have to consider how the many and varied motives of many men can be brought to support it.

The trouble with civilized men is that they cannot live with the institutions they have themselves invented. In rewarding some kinds of behavior better than savage society could ever have done, the new institutions look as if they would drive other behavior underground. But it does not stay there long. Sometimes the very success of the institutions allows an opening for behavior that men could little afford to indulge in while they were still on the make. If a poor society must be human because it has nothing else, and a rich society can be human because it has everything else, we moderns are *nouveaux riches* trying to acquire aristocratic tastes. Sometimes the great rebellions and revolutions, cracking the institutional crust, bring out elementary social behavior hot and straight from the fissures. They always appeal, for instance, to the simplest principles of distributive justice. When Adam delved and Eve span, who was then the gentleman? To call them simple is not, of course, to call them bad: the question of value comes later. For the institutions the rebels invent in the endeavor to realize and enforce justice on earth are just as apt to sacrifice something human as the institutions that preceded them: they come out corrupted by the very anger that gave them birth. And then men wonder whether the struggle was worth its cost if it leaves them still facing their old problem: how to reconcile their social institutions with their social nature. Yet men have invented one peculiar institution that may just conceivably help them get out of their rat race. To call it science is almost as embarrassing as calling your wife Mrs. Smith: the name is too formal for the bedroom. If men are ever to feel at home in the world of their making, they will come to understand better what it is their institutions are to be reconciled with—and "better" means in just those ways science has committed itself to. This is the only reason for studying the familiar chaos that is elementary social behavior—except, of course, the sheer pleasure of the thing.

REFERENCES

Adams, J. Stacy, and Romney, A. K., 1959. "A Functional Analysis of Authority," *Psychological Review*, 66:234–251.

Adams, J. Stacy, 1965. "Inequity in Social Exchange," in Leonard Berkowitz, ed., *Advances in Experimental Social Psychology*, Vol. 2. New York: Academic Press, 267–299.

Adams, Stuart N., 1953. "Status Congruency as a Variable in Small Group Performance," *Social Forces*, 32:16–22.

Aristotle, 1967. *Politics*, H. Rackham, trans. Cambridge, Mass.: Harvard University Press (Loeb Classical Library).

———, 1968. *The Nicomachean Ethics*, H. Rackham, trans. Cambridge, Mass.: Harvard University Press (Loeb Classical Library).

Asch, Solomon E., 1952. *Social Psychology*. New York: Prentice-Hall.

Back, Kurt, 1950. "The Exertion of Influence through Social Communication," in L. Festinger, K. Back, S. Schachter, H. H. Kelley, and J. Thibaut, *Theory and Experiment in Social Communication*. Ann Arbor, Mich.: Institute for Social Research, University of Michigan, 21–36.

Bales, Robert Freed, 1950. *Interaction Process Analysis*. Cambridge, Mass.: Addison-Wesley Press.

———, 1953. "The Equilibrium Problem in Small Groups," in T. Parsons, R. F. Bales, and E. A. Shils, *Working Papers in the Theory of Action*. Glencoe, Ill.: The Free Press, 111–161.

———, 1956. "Task Status and Likeability as a Function of Talking and Listening in Decision-Making Groups," in Leonard D. White, ed., *The State of the Social Sciences*. Chicago: University of Chicago Press, 148–161.

Bandura, Albert, and Walters, Richard H., 1963. *Social Learning and Personality Development*. New York: Holt, Rinehart and Winston.

Bandura, Albert, 1969. *Principles of Behavior Modification*. New York: Holt, Rinehart and Winston.

Barnard, Chester I., 1938. *The Functions of the Executive*. Cambridge, Mass.: Harvard University Press.

———, 1948. *Organization and Management*. Cambridge, Mass.: Harvard University Press.

Bartos, Otomar J., 1958. "Leadership, Conformity, and Originality." Unpublished paper presented at annual meeting of the American Sociological Association.

Baxter, Richard, 1931. *The Autobiography of Richard Baxter.* J. M. Lloyd Thomas, ed. New York: E. P. Dutton (Everyman's Library).

Bernard, Claude, 1952. *Introduction à l'étude de la médecine expérimentale.* Paris: Flammarion.

Blalock, Hubert M., Jr., 1969. *Theory Construction.* Englewood Cliffs, N.J.: Prentice-Hall.

Blau, Peter M., 1955. *The Dynamics of Bureaucracy.* Chicago: University of Chicago Press (Revised edition, 1963.)

———, 1960. "Social Integration, Social Rank, and Processes of Interaction," *Human Organization,* 18:152–157.

———, 1964. *Exchange and Power in Social Life.* New York: John Wiley and Sons.

Bloch, Marc, 1940. *La société féodale,* Vol. II: *La formation des liens de dépendance.* Paris: Editions Albin Michel.

Bott, Elizabeth, 1957. *Family and Social Network.* London: Tavistock Publications.

Bovard, E. W., Jr., 1951. "The Experimental Production of Interpersonal Affect," *Journal of Abnormal and Social Psychology,* 46:521–528.

Braithwaite, Richard Bevan, 1953. *Scientific Explanation.* Cambridge: Cambridge University Press.

Bronfenbrenner, Urie, 1944. "A Constant Frame of Reference for Sociometric Research: Part II, Experiment and Inference," *Sociometry,* 7:46–75.

Brown, Roger, 1965. *Social Psychology.* New York: The Free Press.

Browne, C. G., and Cohn, Thomas S., eds., 1958. *The Study of Leadership.* Danville, Ill.: Interstate Printers and Publishers.

Cartwright, Darwin, and Harary, Frank, 1956. "Structural Balance: A Generalization of Heider's Theory," *Psychological Review,* 63:277–293.

Chapple, Eliot D., 1940. "Measuring Human Relations: An Introduction to the Study of the Interaction of Individuals," *Genetic Psychology Monographs,* 22:3–147.

———, 1953. "The Standard Experimental (Stress) Interview as Used in Interaction Chronograph Investigations," *Human Organization,* 12:23–32.

Clark, J. V., 1958. "A Preliminary Investigation of Some Unconscious Assumptions Affecting Labor Efficiency in Eight Supermarkets." D.B.A. Thesis, Harvard Graduate School of Business Administration, unpublished.

Dalton, Melville, 1948. "The Industrial Rate-Buster: A Characterization," *Applied Anthropology,* 7:5–18.

Davis, James A., 1959. "A Formal Interpretation of the Theory of Relative Deprivation," *Sociometry,* 22:280–296.

———, 1963. "Structural Balance, Mechanical Solidarity, and Interpersonal Relations," *American Journal of Sociology,* 68:444–462.

Deutsch, Morton, 1952. "The Effects of Cooperation and Competition upon Group Process," in Darwin Cartwright and Alvin Zander, eds., *Group Dynamics: Research and Theory.* Evanston, Ill.: Row, Peterson, 319–353.

Dittes, J. E., and Kelley, H. H., 1956. "Effects of Different Conditions of Acceptance on Conformity to Group Norms," *Journal of Abnormal and Social Psychology,* 53:100–107.

Dollard, John, 1937. *Caste and Class in a Southern Town*. New Haven, Conn.: Yale University Press.

Durkheim, Émile, 1927. *Les règles de la méthode sociologique*. Paris: Librairie Félix Alcan.

Emerson, Ralph Waldo, 1903. *Essays: Second Series* (*The Complete Works of Ralph Waldo Emerson*, Centenary Edition, Vol. III). Boston: Houghton Mifflin.

Emerson, Richard, 1962. "Power-Dependence Relations," *American Sociological Review*, 22:31–41.

Ferster, C. B., and Skinner, B. F., 1957. *Schedules of Reinforcement*. New York: Appleton-Century-Crofts.

Festinger, Leon; Schachter, Stanley; and Back, Kurt, 1950. *Social Pressures in Informal Groups*. New York: Harper.

———; Back, Kurt; Schachter, Stanley; Kelley, Harold H.; and Thibaut, John, 1950. *Theory and Experiment in Social Communication*. Ann Arbor, Mich.: Institute for Social Research, University of Michigan.

———, and Thibaut, John W., 1951. "Interpersonal Communication in Small Groups," *Journal of Abnormal and Social Psychology*, 46:92–99.

———; Gerard, H. B.; Hymovich, B.; Kelley, H. H.; and Raven, B., 1952. "The Influence Process in the Presence of Extreme Deviates," *Human Relations*, 5:327–346.

———, 1957. *A Theory of Cognitive Dissonance*. Evanston, Ill.: Row, Peterson.

Fiedler, Fred E., 1958. *Leader Attitudes and Group Effectiveness*. Urbana, Ill.: University of Illinois Press.

Fortes, Meyer, 1949. *The Web of Kinship among the Tallensi*. London: Oxford University Press for the International African Institute.

French, John R. P., Jr., and Snyder, Richard, 1959. "Leadership and Interpersonal Power," in D. Cartwright, ed., *Studies in Social Power*. Ann Arbor, Mich.: Institute for Social Research, University of Michigan, 118–149.

Gerard, H. B., 1954. "The Anchorage of Opinions in Face-to-Face Groups," *Human Relations*, 7:313–325.

Goffman, Erving, 1959. *The Presentation of the Self in Everyday Life*. Garden City, N.Y.: Doubleday Anchor Books.

Gouldner, Alvin W., 1960. "The Norm of Reciprocity," *American Sociological Review*, 25:161–178.

Harsanyi, John C., 1966. "A General Theory of Rational Behavior in Game Situations," *Econometrica*, 34:613–634.

Heider, Fritz, 1958. *The Psychology of Interpersonal Relations*. New York: John Wiley and Sons.

Hempel, Carl G., 1965. *Aspects of Scientific Explanation*. New York: The Free Press.

Herrnstein, Richard J., 1971. "Quantitative Hedonism," *Journal of Psychiatric Research*, 8:399–412.

Herzberg, Frederick, 1956. *Work and the Nature of Man*. Cleveland: World Publishing Co.

Hollander, E. P., 1964. *Leaders, Groups, and Influence.* New York: Oxford University Press.

Holmes, Oliver Wendell, Jr., 1953. *The Holmes-Laski Letters,* Mark DeWolfe Howe, ed. Cambridge, Mass.: Harvard University Press.

———, 1964. *The Holmes-Einstein Letters,* J. B. Peabody, ed. New York: St. Martin's Press.

Homans, George Caspar, 1950. *The Human Group.* New York: Harcourt Brace Jovanovich.

———, 1953. "Status among Clerical Workers," *Human Organization,* 12:5–10.

———, 1954. "The Cash Posters: A Study of a Group of Working Girls," *American Sociological Review,* 19:724–733.

———, and Schneider, David M., 1955. *Marriage, Authority, and Final Causes.* Glencoe, Ill.: The Free Press.

———, 1958. "Social Behavior as Exchange," *American Journal of Sociology,* 63:597–606.

———, 1961. *Social Behavior: Its Elementary Forms* (Original ed.) New York: Harcourt Brace Jovanovich.

———, 1964. "A Theory of Social Interaction," *Transactions of the Fifth World Congress of Sociology,* 4:113–131.

———, 1967. *The Nature of Social Science.* New York: Harcourt Brace Jovanovich.

Hughes, Everett C., 1945. "Dilemmas and Contradictions of Status," *American Journal of Sociology,* 50:353–359.

———, 1946. "The Knitting of Racial Groups in Industry," *American Sociological Review,* 11:512–519.

Jackson, J. M., and Saltzstein, H. D., 1956. *Group Membership and Conformity Processes.* Ann Arbor, Mich.: Institute for Social Research, University of Michigan.

Jennings, Helen Hall, 1950. *Leadership and Isolation* (Second ed.). New York: Longmans, Green.

Jouvenel, Bertrand de, 1957. *Sovereignty: An Inquiry into the Political Good,* J. F. Huntington, trans. Chicago: University of Chicago Press.

———, 1963. *The Pure Theory of Politics.* New Haven: Yale University Press.

Kelley, Harold H., and Shapiro, M. M., 1954. "An Experiment on Conformity to Group Norms Where Conformity Is Detrimental to Group Achievement," *American Sociological Review,* 19:667–677.

Lemann, T. B., and Solomon, Richard L., 1952. "Group Characteristics as Revealed in Sociometric Patterns and Personality Ratings," *Sociometry,* 15:7–90.

Lenski, Gerhard E., 1966. *Power and Privilege.* New York: McGraw-Hill.

Lévi-Strauss, Claude, 1955. *Tristes Tropiques.* Paris: Librairie Plon.

Lippitt, Ronald, 1948. "A Program of Experimentation on Group Functioning and Group Productivity," in W. Dennis, R. Lippitt, *et al., Current Trends in Social Psychology.* Pittsburgh: University of Pittsburgh Press, 14–49.

———; Polansky, N.; Redl, F.; and Rosen, S., 1952. "The Dynamics of Power," *Human Relations,* 5: 37–64.

Malinowski, Bronislaw, 1959. *Crime and Custom in Savage Society*. Paterson, N.J.: Littlefield, Adams.

Marak, George E., Jr., 1964. "The Evolution of Leadership Structure," *Sociometry*, 27:174–182.

Maslow, Abraham H., 1954. *Motivation and Personality*. New York: Harper & Row.

Mauss, Marcel, 1954. *The Gift*, Ian Cunniston, trans. Glencoe, Ill.: The Free Press.

Merton, Robert K., and Kitt, Alice S., 1950. "Contributions to the Theory of Reference Group Behavior," in R. K. Merton and P. Lazarsfeld, eds. *Continuities in Social Research: Studies in the Scope and Method of "The American Soldier."* Glencoe, Ill.: The Free Press, 40–105.

Miller, Neal E., and Dollard, John, 1941. *Social Learning and Imitation*. New Haven: Yale University Press.

Montaigne, Michel de, 1958. *The Complete Essays of Montaigne*, Donald M. Frame, trans. Stanford, Cal.: Stanford University Press.

Moreno, J. L., 1934. *Who Shall Survive?* Washington, D.C.: Nervous and Mental Disease Publishing Co.

Morse, Nancy C., 1953. *Satisfactions in the White-Collar Job*. Ann Arbor, Mich.: Institute for Social Research, University of Michigan.

Nagel, Ernest, 1961. *The Structure of Science*. New York: Harcourt Brace Jovanovich.

Newcomb, Theodore M., 1956. "The Prediction of Interpersonal Attraction," *American Psychologist*, 11:575–586.

———, 1961. *The Acquaintance Process*. New York: Holt, Rinehart and Winston.

Norfleet, B., 1948. "Interpersonal Relations and Group Productivity," *Journal of Social Issues*, 4:66–69.

Ofshe, Lynne, and Ofshe, Richard, 1970. *Utility and Choice in Social Interaction*. Englewood Cliffs, N.J.: Prentice-Hall.

Olson, Mancur, Jr., 1965. *The Logic of Collective Action*. Cambridge, Mass.: Harvard University Press.

Parsons, Talcott, 1963a. "On the Concept of Influence," *Public Opinion Quarterly*, 27:37–62.

———, 1963b. "On the Concept of Political Power," *Proceedings of the American Philosophical Society*, 107:232–262.

Patchen, Martin, 1961. *The Choice of Wage Comparisons*. Englewood Cliffs, N.J.: Prentice-Hall.

Potashin, R., 1946. "A Sociometric Study of Children's Friendships," *Sociometry*, 9:48–70.

Purcell, Theodore V., 1953. *The Worker Speaks His Mind on Company and Union*. Cambridge, Mass.: Harvard University Press.

Riley, M. W.; Cohn, R.; Toby, J.; and Riley, J. W., Jr., 1954. "Interpersonal Relations in Small Groups," *American Sociological Review*, 19:715–724.

———, and Cohn, R., 1958. "Control Networks in Informal Groups," *Sociometry*, 21:30–49.

Roethlisberger, F. J., and Dickson, William J., 1939. *Management and the Worker*. Cambridge, Mass.: Harvard University Press.

————, 1941. *Management and Morale.* Cambridge, Mass.: Harvard University Press.

Schachter, Stanley, 1951. "Deviation, Rejection, and Communication," *Journal of Abnormal and Social Psychology,* 46:190–207.
————; Ellertson, N.; McBride, D.; and Gregory, D., 1951. "An Experimental Study of Cohesiveness and Productivity," *Human Relations,* 4:229–238.
Schelling, Thomas C., 1960. *The Strategy of Conflict.* Cambridge, Mass.: Harvard University Press.
Schoeck, Helmut, 1969. *Envy: A Theory of Social Behavior.* New York: Harcourt Brace Jovanovich.
Scott, John Finley, 1971. *Internalization of Norms.* Englewood Cliffs, N.J.: Prentice-Hall.
Seashore, Stanley E., 1954. *Group Cohesiveness in the Industrial Work Group.* Ann Arbor, Mich.: Institute for Social Research, University of Michigan.
Sherif, Muzafer, and Sherif, Carolyn W., 1953. *Groups in Harmony and Tension.* New York: Harper.
Simon, Herbert A., 1957. *Models for Man.* New York: John Wiley and Sons.
Skinner, B. F., 1938. *The Behavior of Organisms.* New York: Appleton-Century-Crofts.
————, 1953. *Science and Human Behavior.* New York: Macmillan.
Staats, Arthur W., and Staats, Carolyn K., 1963. *Complex Human Behavior.* New York: Holt, Rinehart and Winston.
Stouffer, Samuel A.; Suchman, Edward A.; DeVinney, Leland C.; Star, Shirley A.; and Williams, Robin M., Jr., 1949. *The American Soldier: Adjustment During Army Life. (Studies in Social Psychology in World War II,* Vol. I.) Princeton, N.J.: Princeton University Press.

Tacitus, P. Cornelius, 1932. *Germania,* Maurice Hutton, ed. New York: G. P. Putnam's Sons (Loeb Classical Library).
Tagiuri, Renato, 1952. "Relational Analysis: An Extension of Sociometric Method with Emphasis upon Social Perception," *Sociometry,* 15:91–104.
Theodorson, G. A., 1957. "Leadership and Popularity Roles in Small Groups," *American Sociological Review,* 22:58–67.
Thibaut, John W., 1950. "An Experimental Study of the Cohesiveness of Under-privileged Groups," *Human Relations,* 3:251–278.
————, and Kelley, Harold H., 1959. *The Social Psychology of Groups.* New York: John Wiley and Sons.

Von Neumann, John, and Morgenstern, Oskar, 1944. *Theory of Games and Economic Behavior.* Princeton, N.J.: Princeton University Press.

Walker, Edward L., and Heyns, Roger W., 1962. *An Anatomy for Conformity.* Englewood Cliffs, N.J.: Prentice-Hall.
Waller, W. W., and Hill, R., 1951. *The Family: A Dynamic Interpretation.* New York: Dryden Press.
Weber, Max, 1930. *The Protestant Ethic and the Spirit of Capitalism,* Talcott Parsons, trans. New York: Scribners.
————, 1947. *The Theory of Social and Economic Organization,* Talcott Parsons,

ed.; A. M. Henderson and Talcott Parsons, trans. New York: Oxford University Press.

Whyte, William Foote, 1943. *Street Corner Society*. Chicago: University of Chicago Press.

————, 1948. *Human Relations in the Restaurant Industry*. New York: McGraw-Hill.

Zaleznik, Abraham, 1956. *Worker Satisfaction and Development*. Boston: Graduate School of Business Administration, Harvard University.

————; Christensen, C. R.; and Roethlisberger, F. J., 1958. *The Motivation, Productivity, and Satisfaction of Workers*. Boston: Graduate School of Business Administration, Harvard University.

Zander, Alvin; Cohen, Arthur R.; and Stotland, Ezra, 1959. "Power and the Relations among Professions," in Darwin Cartwright, ed. *Studies in Social Power*. Ann Arbor, Mich.: Institute for Social Research, University of Michigan, 15–34.

INDEX

(Page numbers in italics refer to tables and figures.)

Acceptance, vying for, 329–331
Acquaintance process, 139–143
Acquired value, 27
Activities, defined, 21
Acts, defined, 20
Adams, J. S., 265, 267, 269, 374
Adams, S. N., 208, 374
Aggregate matrix for eighteen sessions of six-man groups (table), *185*
Aggression, 38–39
Aggression-approval proposition, 37–40, 58, 61, 64, 103; 176
Alternate statuses, links between, 315–316
Alternative actions, *21–22*
Alternative reward, 124
Ambivalence toward authority, 290–293
Anger, 38
Apparent distribution of opinion (table), *128*
Approval, 117–118, 159; and interaction, 175–178
Aristotle, 9, 37, 248, 249, 250, 374
Asch, S., 324–325, 374
Authoritarianism, 296
Authority, 89–90; ambivalence toward, 290–293; defined, 70, 77, 276–277; and esteem, 350–352; and power, 91–93
Average-chosen, 162
Avoidance, 80

Back, K., 118, 292, 374; *see also* Festinger, L., 376
Balance, defined, 59–60; process of, 139
Balance, theory, 69, 140; defined, 60, 64
Bales, R. F., 11, 185, 186, 187, 188, 189, 190–191, 286–289, 304, 305, *306*, 307, 374
Bales' matrix, *287–288*
Ball, J., 251
Bandura, A., 12, 24, 25, 91, 194, 374
Bank Wiring Observation Room Study, 180, 207–210, 261–262, 274, 291, 331

Bare causality, 78; defined, 77
Bargaining, 87–89; economic, 87
Barnard, C., 77, 269, 274, 295, 374
Bartos, O. J., 323, 325–326, 375
Bases of power, defined, 74–75
Behavior, bureaucratic, 4–5; conscious, 49; emotional, 38–39; measurement of, 18–20; operant, 38; social, 1, 77; unconscious, 49
Behavior control, 85–87, *86* (table); revised, *86* (table)
Bernard, Claude, 175, 375
Blalock, H., 153, 375
Blau, P. M., 20, 53, 78, 274–275, 326, 327, 340, 342, 375
Bloch, M., 360–361, 375
Bott, E., 4, 375
Boundary conditions, 175
Bovard, E. W., Jr., 177, 180, 375
Braithwaite, R. B., 8, 37, 375
Bronfenbrenner, U., 161, 375
Browne, C. G., 270, 375
Brown, Roger, 7, 313, 375
Bureaucratic behavior, 4–5

Cartwright, D., 142, 375
Causal chain, 152
Central members, 258
Chapple, E. D., 19, 375
Civilization, precariousness of, 365–366
Clark, J. V., 202, 215, 375
Clique, 210; defined, 172
Closed network, defined, 4
Clusters, defined, 142
Coercive power, 78–82, *79*
Cognition, 24
Cognitive dissonance, 129, 254; defined, 122, 123; reduction of, 62
Cohesiveness, 149, 292; and conformity, 147–152, 153–157; defined, 181; group, 154–157

Cohn, R., 290; *see also* Riley, M. W., 379
Cohn, T. S., 270; *see also* Browne, C. G., 375
Collective goods, 98–100
Command, channels of, 275–276; and liking, 282–285, 285–290, *287*
Communication, channels of, 275–276; measurement of, 126
Comparison group, defined, 252
Competition, 111–112, 133–137
Competitive treatment, 134
Compliance, 117–118
The condition of least interest (table), *71*
Conformers, 100–102, 129, 148
Conform, pressure to, 102–105
Conformity, and cohesiveness, 147–152, 153–157; in middle status, 336–337; and noncomformity, in upper status, 331–334; process of, 2, 4; and status, 319–323, 337–338
Congruence, and job assignment, 209–211; liking, and effectiveness, 208–209; medium, 209; similarity, and productivity, 202–208; status, 201–202, 208
Conscious behavior, 49
Consensus on status, 196–199
Consultation, social economics of, 343–346
Contempt, and familiarity, 293–297
Contingent, defined, 8
Control, defined, 85
Convergent forces, 41–42
Cooperation, 10–11, 133–137
Cooperative treatment, 133
Core members, 193
Corrected interaction matrix (table), *184*
Corrective justice, 248–249
Cost, 119–124, *121*; of consultation, 343–346; defined, 31; dimensions, 245
Court standards, 148
Covering–law view, 9, 10
Criminal tendencies, 328–329
Culture, of poverty, 329
Curvilinear, defined, 209

Dalton, M., 106, 375
Davis, J., 142, 233, 375
Decision-making, participation in, 276–277
Deductive system, 9
Deference, 222
Democracy, 250, 296
Deprivation-satiation proposition, 29–30, 71
Deutsch, M., 133, 375
Developmental psychology, 42
Deviate, 106, 107, 112–113, 128–129, 131, 148
Dickson, W. J., 80, 209, 262; *see also* Roethlisberger, F. J., 379
Differentiation, group, 108–110

Discrimination, 23
Dissatisfiers, 227
Dissimilar exchange, 65
Distributive injustice, 255
Distributive justice, 211, 225, 241–268, 255; example of, 242–248; rule of, 248–252
Dittes, J. E., 321, 325, 375
Dollard, J., 37, 337, 376; *see also* Miller, N., 378
Durkheim, E., 12, 376
The Dynamics of Bureaucracy (Blau, P.), 275, 340, 375

Eastern Utilities Company project, 180, 242–248, 286, 368–371
Economics, classical, 67–68, 69
Elementary social behavior, 2–3
Emerson, Richard, 73, 376
Emotional behavior, 38–39
Equality and escape, 302–304; maintenance of, 217–221; and similarity, 299–302; and superiority (table), *306*
Equalization of power (table), *72, 75–76*
Equals, defined, 303
Escape and equality, 302–304
Escapees, defined, 106
Esteem, 160, 189; and authority, 350–352; defined, 108, 109; distribution of, 156–164; and status, 198
Exchange of advice for approval (table), *54*
Exchange, process of, 215–217
Exchange theory, defined, 56
Expectation, defined, 37
Explanation, defined, 8, 9–10, 152–153
Explicandum, 153, 336; defined, 8, 9
Experimental research, defined, 115–116
External system, 175
Extinction, defined, 17

Familiarity, 293–297
Fate control (table), *84*
Fate control revised (table), *84*
Favors, 221–222
Federal agency, example of, 341–343
Ferster, C. B., 17, 376
Festinger, L., 62, 105, 122, 125, 254, 292, 376
Festinger group, 117, 118, 119, 127, 143, 149, 376
Fiedler, F., 295–296, 305, 376
Field research, defined, 116
Fitzgerald, F. Scott, 329
Foch, Marshal, 33
Force functions, 35–36
Forces, convergent, 41–42
Fortes, Meyer, 285, 376
Freeloaders, defined, 102
French, J., 271, 376
Frequency, of interaction, 175–176

Friendship, and conformity, 147–152; and proximity, 144–145, *146*

Frustration, 38

Frustration-aggression hypothesis, 37–38, 263

Generalization, 23

Generalized rewards, 29

Generalized value, 27–28

General propositions, 11–13, 15–50

Geographical location and sociometric choice (table), *146*

Geographical proximity, 144

Gerard, H. B., 119, 120, 377

Gift-giving, primitive, 218–219, 220

Godwinsson, Harold, 46

Goethe, 15

Goffman, E., 211, 376

Gouldner, A., 217, 376

Group, attraction, 120–123, *121*; centered, 178; cohesiveness of, 117, 154–157; comparison, 252; defined, 94, 94–96; differentiation of, 108–110; heterogeneous, 127; homogeneous, 127; in history, 358–359; informal, 4–5; as a microcosm, 356–358; norms, 98–100, 148; power of, 105–106; reference, 252; and society, 359–363; subcommittees of, 131

Halo-effect, defined, 164

Harary, F., 142; *see also* Cartwright, D., 375

Harsanyi, J., 43, 377

Harvard Graduate School of Business Administration, 202

Hatred, defined, 179

Heider, F., 60, 377

Hemingway, E., 329

Hempel, C., 8, 377

Herrnstein, R., 21, 22, 377; his equation, 45

Herzberg, F., 227, 376

Heterogeneity, 126

Heterogeneous groups, 127

Heyns, R., 108; *see also* Walker, E., 380

High-attraction group, 120–123, *121*

High-cohesive groups, 117

High-status teams, 258–262

Historicity, of propositions, 41–43

Holdout, 106–108, 129; defined, 106

Hollander, E. P., 288, 332–333, 377

Holmes, Oliver Wendell, 7, 377

Homans, G. C., 6, 7, 8, 19, 40, 51, 56, 64, 67, 153, 175, 179, 180, 209, 242, 274, 286, 317, 371, 377

Homogeneity, 126

Homogeneous groups, 127

Hooke's Law, 35

Horizontal divisions, 112–113

Hostility, 260–262

Hudson State Training School, 168–171, 172–173

Hughes, E., 200, 332–333, 377

Human Group, The (Homans), 6, 8, 13, 40, 264, 340, 377

Idiosyncrasy credit, 332–333

Imitation, 24–25; defined, 24

Impersonal relationship, 65

Incongruence, 201, 203, 223

Indian giving, 217–218

Individual work, 110–111

Industrial Controls Corporation study, 330–331

Informal group, 4–5

Initiation, defined, 187

Injustice, beneficiaries of, 264–268, *266*; and intergroup hostility, 257–262; and power, 262–264; of rewards, 242

Innate values, defined, 27

Institute of Social Research (University of Michigan) study, 253–257, *256*

Institutional, and subinstitutional, 367–373

Interaction, and approval, 175–178; defined, 56; among equals, 188–191, *190*; and liking, 64; matrix of, 176, 182–187, *183, 184, 185*; social, 346–349

Intergroup hostility, 260–262

Interpersonal relationships, matrices of, 167–171, *169*

Intrinsic reward, 26

Involvement, of members, 134–135

Investments, 246

Irrationality, 48

Isolation, and nonconformity, 352–355

Jackson, J. M., 319, 377

Jennings, H., 157, 160, 169, 172, 183, 300, 302, 303, 377

Job assignment, and congruence, 209–211

Jouvenel, B. de, 248, 269, 377

Justice, conditions of, 265–*266*; corrective, 248–249; distributive, *see* Distributive justice; maintenance of, 280–282

Kelley, H., 31, 51, 73, 319, 321, 325, 378; *see also* Dittes, J. E., 375, Thibaut, J., 380

Kin relationships, 66

Kitt, A., 252; *see also* Merton, R., 378

Law of effect, 16; *see also* Success proposition

Law of gravitation (Newton's), 34–35

Leader-centered groups, 177–178

Leadership, 269–296; qualities of, 269–271; and risk-taking, 282; and status, 271–275

Learning theory, propositions of, 42–43

Least interest, principle of, 73–74

Lemann, T. B., 172, 377
Level of operation, 234
Lévi-Strauss, Claude, 5, 359, 377
Liking, 159, 176, 178–179, 187, 303–304, 305; and command, 282–285, 285–290; and interaction, 64
Lippitt, R., 377
Low-attraction group, 120–123, *121*
Low-cohesive groups, 117
Lower class, solidarity of, 171–174, *172*
Lower status, and nonconformity, 326–329
Low-status teams, 258–262

Macht, defined, 78
Malinowski, B., 6, 76, 104, 378
Marak, G., 275, 378
Marx, Karl, 251
Masochist, defined, 48
Massachusetts Institute of Technology, 133, 143
Material values, 67
Matrilineal societies, 286
Matrix, of interaction, 182–187, *183, 184, 185*
Mauss, Marcel, 217, 218, 219
Mayo, Elton, 209
Measurement, of behavior, 18–20
Melville, Herman, 364
Members, categories of, 101–102; central, 258; defined, 4; of group, 94–95; peripheral, 258
Merton, R. K., 252, 378
Middle status, conformity in, 336–337
Miller, N., 37, 378
Mode, 131
Model interaction matrix (table), *183*
Model learning, defined, 25
Model sociometric matrix (table), *169*
Montaigne, Michel de, 222, 378
Moreno, J. L., 157, 378
Morgenstern, O., 48; *see also* Von Neumann, J., 380
Morse, N., 227, 228–229, 229–231, 232, 233, 234, 236, 378
Multiple exchanges, effect of, 59–63

Nagel, E., 8, 378
Nambikwara, 5
Network, closed, 4; open, 3–4
Newcomb, T. M., 139, 140, 142, 179, 378
Newton, Sir Isaac, 34; law of gravitation, 34–35; *Principia*, 11
New York State Training School for Girls at Hudson, New York, 157, 299–302
Nichomachean Ethics (Aristotle), 248
Noblesse oblige, 215–217, 267, 328, 334; defined, 216
Nonconformers, 100–102
Nonconformist, 338

Nonconformity, and isolation, 352–355; and lower status, 326–329
Noncontingent, defined, 8
Norm, 96, 97, 335; defined, 2; group, 98–100; of reciprocity, 217, 218
Norton Street Gang, 180, 281

Obedience to orders, 277–280
Ofshe, L. and R., 43, 378
Oligarchy, 250
Olson, M., 102, 104, 378
Open network, defined, 3–4
Operant behavior, 38
Operants, defined, 16
Orders, obedience to, 277–280
Originality, and upper status, 323–326
Origination, defined, 188
Over-chosen, 162, 164

Parameters, defined, 175
Parsons, T., 90, 92, 378
Patchen, M., 253, 254, 256, 257, 378
Patrilineal societies, 285–286
Payoff matrix, 51–53, *52*, 54, 70, *71, 72, 79, 84, 85, 86*
Percentage of subjects changing toward paid participant (table), *121*
Percentage of subjects changing toward someone in the group (table), *121*
Perception, 24
Peripheral members, 258
Personal relationship, 66
Persuasion, 90–91
Politics (Aristotle), 250, 374
Pope, Alexander, 263
Positive value, 16
Potashin, R., 176, 177, 378
Potlatch, 218, 220
Poverty, culture of, 329
Power, 85; and authority, 91–93; bases of, 74–75, 81; coercive, 77, 78–82, *79*; defined, 70, 76–78, 92 (Parsons), 277; distribution of, 156–164; equalization of, 75–76; general definition of, 83; group, 105–106; and injustice, 262–264; interpersonal, *71*; and status, 193–196
Primitive societies, 285–286
Principia (Newton), 11
Productivity, and satisfaction, 235–239, *238*; of workers, 154
Profit, 119–124, *121*; defined, 31–32, 122
Proportionality, constant of (*k*), *21*
Propositions, defined, 9; general, 11–13, 15–50; success, 15–18
Protestant Ethic, 106–107, 330
Proximity, 144–145, *146*
Psychology, behavioral, 11–12; developmental, 42
Punishment, effect of, 26–27
Purcell, T., 231, 378

Rank, defined, 7; *see also* Status
Rationality, 47–48
Rationality proposition, 43–47, *44, 45*
Receipt-initiation ratio (Bales), 289
Reference group, defined, 252
Reinforcement, defined, 21
Reinforcing stimulus, 23
Reinstated action, 17
Rejection, *161,* 162
Relationship, impersonal, 65; kin, 66; personal, 66
Relative advantage, 252
Relative deprivation, 252; defined, 241–242
Relative earnings, occupation, and satisfaction (table), *256*
Research Branch, Information and Education Division (U.S. Army) study, 232
Research, experimental, 115–116; field, 116
Respect, 187
Reward, 16–18; alternative sources of, 124–127; of consultation, 343–346; dimensions of, 245; generalized, 29; injustice of, 242; irregular, 18; and satisfaction, 226; scarcity of, 70–73, *71, 72;* withholding of, 26
Riley, M. W., *et al.,* 188, 290, 304, 378
Rival, defined, 179
Roethlisberger, F. J., 180, 209, 213, 262, 378–379
Roles, 334–336
Romney, A. K., 269; *see also* Adams, S., 374
Rules, 335
Rule of distributive justice (Aristotle), 37
Rule of distributive justice, 248–252, *249*
Rules of Sociological Method (Durkheim), 12, 376

Saltzstein, H. D., 319; *see also* Jackson, J. H., 377
Satiation, defined, 226–227
Satisfaction, 225–240; determinants of, 227–229; and level of aspiration, 233–235; and productivity, 235–239, *238;* proposition, *236, 237;* quantity (Q), *236, 237;* and reward, 226; in the white-collar job (Morse), 227, 228–229, 229–231, 378
Satisfiers, 227
Schachter, S., 117, 120, 131, 176, 292, 379; *see also* Festinger, L., 376
Schelling, T., 82, 379
Schneider, D., 286; *see also* Homans, G., 377
Schoeck, H., 257, 379
Scientific Explanation (Braithwaite), 37, 375
Seashore, S., 153, 379

Secondary actions, 88
Section, defined, 153
Self-concept, 91
Seniority, 246
Sentiment, defined, 40; matrix, *172–173*
Sentiment matrix: solidarity in the lower class (table), *172*
Sequential effects, defined, 57
Shapiro, M., 319, 325; *see also* Kelley, H., 378
Sherif, M. and C., 257, 330, 379
Similar exchange, 65
Similarity, 127–130, *128,* 157; and equality, 299–302
Simon, H., 77, 379
Skeptical conformers, defined, 103
Skinner, B. F., 11, 16, 17, 379; *see also* Ferster, C. B., 376
Slider, 131
Small groups, 3–6; defined, 4; research, 3
Snyder, R., 27; *see also* French, J., 376
Social behavior, defined, 1, 77; elementary forms of, 2–3, 366–367; patterns of, 363–365
Social classes, 308–*310*
Social climbing, 310–313
Social contact range, 183
Social-contact test, 159
Social ease, 207
Social exchange, 53–57, *54*
Social interaction, 346–349; initiation of, 313–315; rewards of, 103
Social Psychology (Brown), 7, 313, 375
Social Psychology of Groups, The (Thibaut and Kelley), 57, 83–84, 85, 380
Social scientist, 1
Social stratification, 307–*310, 309*
Socio-emotional field, defined, 305, 307
Sociometric test, 131, 158, *161,* 178
Solidarity, lower-class, 171–174, *172*
Solomon, R., 173; *see also* Lemann, T. B., 377
Staats, A. and C., 27, 379
Status, 7, 160, 165, 189, 193–224; back effects of, 215–217, 217–221; and conformity, 319–323; and conformity in society, 337–338; congruence, 164, 200–202, 208; consensus on, 196–199; defined, 182; dimensions, 199–200; and disposition to communicate (table), *190;* and esteem, 198, and exchange, 215–217; group, 157; and leadership, 271–275; lower, 326–329; and power, 193–196; symbols, 211–214, defined, 212; system, 3; upper, 323–326; *see also* Rank
Stimulus, reinforcing, 23
Stimulus proposition, 22–24; defined, 22
Stouffer, S., *et al.,* 232, 379
Stratification, 299–318, 307–*310, 309*

Street Corner Society (Whyte), 264
Symbolic logic, 214
Subgroups, 127
Subjective value, 193
Success proposition, 15–18, 275; defined, 16
Superiority and equality, 304–307
Surplus value, 251

Tacitus, P. C., 360, 379
Tagiuri, R., 159, 380
Tautology, and value proposition, 33–37
Theodorson, G. A., 292, 379
Theoretical concepts, 36–37
Theory, defined, 10–11
Theory of Games (Von Neumann and Morgenstern), 48, 49, 50, 379
Thibaut, J., 31, 51, 73, 125, 257–258, 379; *see also* Festinger, L., 376
Toy society, 168, 172, 183–184
True believers, defined, 101

Unconscious behavior, 49
Under-chosen, 162
Uniformity, pressure towards, 126
Unintended conflict of interest (table), 52
University of Michigan, 139

Upper status, and originality, 323–326

Value, 217; acquired, 27; defined, 25; generalized, 27–28; innate, 27; material, 67; proposition, 25–28, 31–32, 33–37, *34, 35*, 73–74, 108; subjective, 217
Verbal action, frequency of, 19
Vertical division, 112–113
Vicarious reward, 24–25
Von Neumann, J., 48, 379

Walker, E., 108, 379
Walters, R., 25; *see also* Bandura, A., 374
Weber, Max, 78, 83, 106–107, 330, 379
Western Electric Company (Hawthorne Plant), 209–210
Westgate Building (M.I.T.), 143–144, 147–152
Westgate West Building (M.I.T.), *143–147, 146*, 150–151
Whyte, W., 180, 216, 222, 264, 380
William the Conqueror, 46

Your Money or Your Life (table), *79*

Zander, A., *et al.*, 315, 380
Zaleznik, A., 219, 330, 372, 380